The Java 2 Developer Cram Sheet

ASSIGNMENT REQUIREMENTS

1. A graphical user interface (GUI) demonstrating good Human/Computer Interface (HCI) principles of design.

2. A network connection, using Remote Method Invocation (RMI) or sockets, to connect to an information server.

3. A network server that connects to the database; the assignment download includes the database class skeleton code.

4. A database server created by extending the functionality of the skeleton code for the database class. The assignment download includes limited documentation for this code.

5. A database that does not use Java Database Connectivity (JDBC). Rather, it is a simple file reader/writer and the data file supplied by Sun in the assignment download.

6. List some of the major choices you make for your project's design and implementation, including the following:

   - List some of the main advantages and disadvantages of each of your choices.
   - Justify your choices by comparing your design and implementation objectives and including their advantages and disadvantages. Also, you should identify design patterns used in your project's design.

ASSIGNMENT DELIVERABLES

7. Full source and object code, including new classes, modified versions of supplied classes, and copies of supplied classes that were not modified. The source files and class files should be in an appropriate directory structure along with the class files.

8. The database file, which is the same one supplied with the assignment download.

9. The HTML/javadoc documentation for all classes, whether supplied, modified, or new. Make sure you comment your code thoroughly to make the documentation easy to generate.

10. The user documentation for the database server and the GUI client. This documentation can be packaged with your project or, the more common method, available online as a Web page (be sure to supply the correct URL).

11. A README.TXT file that tells the evaluator how to use your application. This file must be in your project's root directory.

12. A design choices document explaining how you tackled the assignment's two major issues. You need to convince the evaluator that you know what you are doing, not that your approach is the best one. The two major design choices are whether you choose RMI or socket communication and whether you choose to modify or extend the supplied classes.

13. All your project elements must be packaged into a single JAR file for submission. Nesting JAR files inside the main JAR is permitted.

README DOCUMENT SECTIONS

The README.TXT document should tell the evaluator how to start your solution. It should also mention any configuration settings necessary to run your application. I added a Quick Start section to make it easy for the evaluator to simply start my application. You can adapt the following example for your Readme document.

Quick Start

14. The Quick Start section should show how to start your application with brief commands, as shown in these examples:

   - For local mode:

     ```
     java
     myPpackage.client.SuperBowlClient -
     dbpath myDatabase.bin
     ```

DEPRECATED METHODS

30. Deprecated methods should not be used in your new code, but Sun did sneak a few into the assignment intentionally to see what you would do about them. They aren't hard to fix, and every time you compile the classes they are in, you see the deprecated message. Some candidates modify these methods, and some override them. Both approaches have met with success. I chose to override them, the method most experts prefer.

GENERAL CONSIDERATIONS

31. Go through this Cram Sheet again before you upload your JAR file, and make sure it includes all the required items. Many candidates put a lot of effort into the certification project, yet forget to include, say, the README.TXT file. Sometimes they put it in the wrong place, so the evaluator has trouble finding it, which leaves a bad impression.

THREADS

32. If you use sockets, you will most likely use the `static` methods, including `wait` and `notify`, in the `Thread` class. If you use RMI, you will probably need to synchronize only a few methods.

33. Java provides the `synchronized` keyword for preventing multiple threads from modifying the same object simultaneously. Many of the methods in the supplied classes are already synchronized, but you will need to synchronize a few more in your new code.

34. You can coordinate threads with the `wait`-`notify` mechanism, which is especially important in your locking mechanism.

ERROR HANDLING

35. The `Exception` and `Error` classes descend from `java.lang.Throwable`. An important component of your score is based on how well you handle errors. Be sure to declare methods so that they throw an exception when appropriate.

36. Be sure to use `try`-`catch`-`finally` when necessary. Don't just declare exceptions in the method declaration. Catch all exceptions thrown in a `try` clause.

37. Provide users with status messages. Make sure that a user input error doesn't crash your application. Instead, it should prompt a gentle message, such as "Pardon, you probably typed an incorrect letter in your seat request. Please try again."

- For remote mode:
  JVM #1 (server)

```
java
myPackage.server.DatabaseRMIServer
-host localhost -port 1234 -dbpath
myDatabase.bin
```

  JVM #2 (client)

```
java
myPackage.client.SuperBowlClient -
host localhost -port 1234
```

Introduction

15. Your introduction should explain the general approach to your solution and mention the RMI or sockets decision you made.

JDK Version and Platform

16. Tell the evaluator what version and platform you used.

17. Explain that objects are eligible for garbage collection only when they have no reference that lets an active thread reach them.

Execution Instructions

18. *Local mode*—Explain how to start your application in local mode.

19. *Remote mode*—Explain how to start your client and server in remote mode.

Location of Key Files

20. *Database file*—State where the binary database file included in the assignment download has been placed in your package structure.

21. *Design choices document*—You must state where this document is in your package structure.

22. *File listing*—You must list the directories and major files in your JAR archive and supply a short description for each.

23. *User help page*—You must describe where the user help file is and how the user is expected to view it. If it is online, give the URL. If it is in the JAR file, explain how the user can find it (such as clicking the Help menu item).

DESIGN CHOICES DOCUMENT

24. Your design choices document can be in ASCII or Microsoft Word format. Make sure you include the following components to get a high score on this portion of the exam:

   - *Summary*—Provide an abstract of your design approach and major decisions.
   - *Modifying versus extending the supplied classes*—Describe which method you used, making sure to explain your reasoning and the advantages of your decision.

   - *Locking mechanism*—Explain how you implemented a locking mechanism and why your method is the most effective one.
   - *RMI versus sockets communication*—Describe how you supplied networking to your application, and explain your reasoning and the advantages of your decision.
   - *Search function*—How did you implement the required search functionality? Describe the algorithm you used.
   - *Coding standards and readability*—Mention how you followed coding standards.
   - *Documentation*—The README.TXT file explains where the user help page is, but you should also describe your solution's documentation in the design choices document.
   - *Exception handling and error testing*—Explain how you handled exceptions and errors.
   - *Design patterns*—List all the design patterns you used, and describe how they work in your solution.
   - *Issues*—Do not mention any problems that might crop up in your certification project, even though it sounds like helpful information to include.

GUI DESIGN

25. Make sure your GUI has a JTable component.

26. Be sure to follow the recommended Java look and feel. This certification is not the time to get fancy and inventive.

27. Use only Swing components. Do not use Abstract Windowing Toolkit (AWT) components. Sun allows developers to use an IDE such as Forte for the GUI design, as long as the code you submit doesn't include any vendor- or IDE-specific code. The evaluator should be able to compile your application.

DATABASE SERVICE DESIGN

28. Sun supplies the skeleton pieces, which you must use to build your database. Although many candidates modify the base classes Sun provides, I did not. Consider subclassing them and isolating changes and added functionality (such as searching) in the subclasses.

NETWORKING

29. Unlike the database classes, Sun provides nothing to get you started on the assignment's networking portion. I recommend using RMI because of its maturity and ease of implementation. (For example, multithread issues are easier to handle with RMI.)

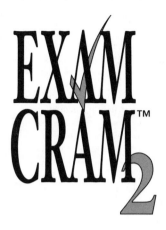

Java 2
Developer

Alain Trottier

CERTIFICATION

Java 2 Developer Exam Cram 2 (Exam CX-310-252A and CX-310-027))

Copyright © 2004 by Que Publishing

International Standard Book Number: 0-7897-2992-X

Library of Congress Catalog Card Number: 2003100805

Printed in the United States of America

First Printing: September 2003

06   05   04   03   4   3   2   1

Que Publishing offers excellent discounts on this book when ordered in quantity for bulk purchases or special sales. For more information, please contact:

U.S. Corporate and Government Sales
1-800-382-3419
corpsales@pearsontechgroup.com

For sales outside of the U.S., please contact:

International Sales
1-317-581-3793
international@pearsontechgroup.com

Trademarks

All terms mentioned in this book that are known to be trademarks or service marks have been appropriately capitalized. Que Publishing cannot attest to the accuracy of this information. Use of a term in this book should not be regarded as affecting the validity of any trademark or service mark.

Warning and Disclaimer

Every effort has been made to make this book as complete and as accurate as possible, but no warranty or fitness is implied. The information provided is on an "as is" basis. The author and the publisher shall have neither liability nor responsibility to any person or entity with respect to any loss or damages arising from the information contained in this book or from the use of the CD or programs accompanying it.

Publisher
Paul Boger

Executive Editor
Jeff Riley

Acquisitions Editor
Carol Ackerman

Development Editor
Michael Watson

Managing Editor
Charlotte Clapp

Project Editor
Elizabeth Finney

Copy Editor
Lisa M. Lord

Indexer
Ken Johnson

Proofreader
Juli Cook

Technical Editors
Steve Heckler
Andy Yang

Team Coordinator
Pamalee Nelson

Multimedia Developer
Dan Scherf

Interior Designer
Gary Adair

Cover Designer
Anne Jones

CERTIFICATION

Que Certification • 201 West 103rd Street • Indianapolis, Indiana 46290

A Note from Series Editor Ed Tittel

You know better than to trust your certification preparation to just anybody. That's why you, and more than two million others, have purchased an Exam Cram book. As Series Editor for the new and improved Exam Cram 2 series, I have worked with the staff at Que Certification to ensure you won't be disappointed. That's why we've taken the world's best-selling certification product—a finalist for "Best Study Guide" in a CertCities reader poll in 2002—and made it even better.

As a "Favorite Study Guide Author" finalist in a 2002 poll of CertCities readers, I know the value of good books. You'll be impressed with Que Certification's stringent review process, which ensures the books are high-quality, relevant, and technically accurate. Rest assured that at least a dozen industry experts—including the panel of certification experts at CramSession—have reviewed this material, helping us deliver an excellent solution to your exam preparation needs.

Best Study Guides

We've also added a preview edition of PrepLogic's powerful, full-featured test engine, which is trusted by certification students throughout the world.

As a 20-year-plus veteran of the computing industry and the original creator and editor of the Exam Cram series, I've brought my IT experience to bear on these books. During my tenure at Novell from 1989 to 1994, I worked with and around its excellent education and certification department. This experience helped push my writing and teaching activities heavily in the certification direction. Since then, I've worked on more than 70 certification-related books, and I write about certification topics for numerous Web sites and for *Certification* magazine.

In 1996, while studying for various MCP exams, I became frustrated with the huge, unwieldy study guides that were the only preparation tools available. As an experienced IT professional and former instructor, I wanted "nothing but the facts" necessary to prepare for the exams. From this impetus, Exam Cram emerged in 1997. It quickly became the best-selling computer book series since "...*For Dummies*," and the best-selling certification book series ever. By maintaining an intense focus on subject matter, tracking errata and updates quickly, and following the certification market closely, Exam Cram was able to establish the dominant position in cert prep books.

You will not be disappointed in your decision to purchase this book. If you are, please contact me at etittel@jump.net. All suggestions, ideas, input, or constructive criticism are welcome!

Ed Tittel

This book is dedicated to my wife, Patricia, the love of my life, and to my son, Devyn, whose stories are better written than mine.

About the Author

Alain Trottier observes the dot-com warfare of Southern California as a board member for Strategic Business Resources, Inc., an adjunct professor at Vanguard University, technical advisor to Que, and the associate director of Internet Services at Verizon Wireless, the largest U.S. wireless voice and data network, where he is responsible for software engineering standards, architecture, strategy, and implementation. Verizon Wireless is doing very well, partly because of the complex infrastructure and software built and maintained by the strong development team he is privileged to work with. His team services millions of customers online. He has authored *Java Core Language* (Paraglyph Press), *Sun Certification Training Guide (310-080): J2EE Web Component Developer* (Que Publishing), and *Sun Certification Exam Cram: J2EE Web Component Developer* (Que Publishing). When he isn't responding to pagers, cell phones, or email, he likes to spend time with his wife and son, and doesn't mind losing at chess, karate, and racquetball. Please email him (type "SCJD" in the subject line) from the book's Web site at http://www.inforobo.com/java/scjd.

About the Technical Editors

Steve Heckler is president of Accelebrate (http://www.accelebrate.com), an Atlanta-based IT training and application development firm specializing in Java, .NET, ColdFusion, Flash, and related technologies. An avid Java developer and trainer, Steve's experience with Java dates all the way back to the first release of the 1.0 SDK.

Before founding Accelebrate, Steve served nearly seven years as vice president and president of a leading U.S. East Coast IT training firm. He holds bachelor's and master's degrees from Stanford University.

Andrew Yang is a senior Java architect with the Sun Software Services (formerly known as Sun Java Center). He has more than 15 years of experience in computer technology and software development. In recent years, he has focused on designing and implementing scalable enterprise applications using object-oriented methodologies, J2EE technologies, and design patterns. He has led the design and development of several enterprise applications currently in production. He received his Ph.D. from Pennsylvania State University in 1991 and is a senior member of the Institute of Electrical and Electronics Engineers (IEEE). He has given presentations in various technical conferences, published articles in technical journals, contributed book chapters, and has been awarded two U.S. patents. He is also actively involved in local Java user group activities.

Acknowledgments

. . . .

I would like to thank Jeff Riley (executive editor), Carol Ackerman (acquisitions editor), and Margot Maley (my agent), who made this book possible. Thank you, Michael Watson (development editor), for your valuable guidance and encouragement. It was a terrific experience working with Que's team; their contributions added much to the book. I admit having fun talking about and even sparring over the details. Every book purchase is a nod to Que's preeminent team.

We Want to Hear from You!

As the reader of this book, *you* are our most important critic and commentator. We value your opinion and want to know what we're doing right, what we could do better, what areas you'd like to see us publish in, and any other words of wisdom you're willing to pass our way.

As an executive editor for Que, I welcome your comments. You can email or write me directly to let me know what you did or didn't like about this book—as well as what we can do to make our books better.

Please note that I cannot help you with technical problems related to the *topic* of this book. We do have a User Services group, however, where I will forward specific technical questions related to the book.

When you write, please be sure to include this book's title and author as well as your name, email address, and phone number. I will carefully review your comments and share them with the author and editors who worked on the book.

Email: feedback@quepublishing.com

Mail: Jeff Riley
            Que Publishing
            201 West 103rd Street
            Indianapolis, IN 46290 USA

For more information about this book or another Que title, visit our Web site at http://www.quepublishing.com. Type the ISBN (excluding hyphens) or the title of a book in the Search field to find the page you're looking for.

Contents at a Glance

Table of Contents

. . . .

Introduction

Welcome to *Java 2 Developer Exam Cram 2*! This book will help you complete the Sun Certified Java Developer (SCJD) assignment (310-252A) and then take—and pass—the (310-027) essay exam. This introduction explains Sun's certification programs in general and how the Exam Cram 2 series can help you prepare for this exam and other certification exams from Sun. Before beginning the Sun Certified Developer for Java 2 Platform program, you must be a Sun Certified Programmer for the Java Platform (any edition). To get the SCJD, you must complete these two steps:

➤ *Sun Certified Developer for Java 2 Platform, Programming Assignment (CX-310-252A; $250)*—The assignment tests the candidate's ability to analyze requirements and then build an "extended" application.

➤ *Sun Certified Developer for Java 2 Platform, Essay Exam (CX-310-027; $150)*—The developer then takes an essay exam to answer questions about issues and trade-offs involved in completing the assignment.

Purpose of This Certification

The purpose of this certification is to see whether you can do a full object-oriented analysis and design cycle. The assignment has many subtle aspects that are easy to overlook, including gathering requirements accurately from the instructions, making a decision about extending versus modifying, and implementing design patterns correctly.

Do you understand object-oriented development? This certification assignment forces programmers to step up from coder to object-oriented analysis and design, which should be done with Unified Modeling Language (UML) if possible (although Sun doesn't require using UML). This book uses UML to describe software components. I hope you are in the practice of doing the same because UML has become the lingua franca of software design artifacts. UML enables you to draw a picture of an application that everyone can understand. For example, it's easier to see a design pattern in your project if you depict it with UML before writing the code. You don't need special software; just paper will do for this assignment. Of course, creating UML diagrams is easier if you have Visio or the market-best MagicDraw UML.

The assignment requires applying a few, perhaps three to six, design patterns, those "best practice" superheroes of reusability. These patterns dictate the best way to define your objects and their relationships. Patterns are more than just another requirement; their proper use facilitates your overall development effort. So I'm advocating a pattern-based, OOP project using UML as a sure-fire way to get a great score. This same advice is good for development in general.

How This Book Helps You Get Certified

Exam Cram 2 books help you understand and appreciate the subjects and materials you need to know to pass Sun certification exams. Each Exam Cram 2 book focuses strictly on exam preparation and review. Exam Cram 2 books are not intended to teach you everything you need to know about a technology. Instead, they cover the topics you are likely to encounter on the certification exam. The books are built around the vendor's objectives and the author's experience with the exams.

How This Exam Cram Differs from the Others

This Exam Cram 2 book is different from other Exam Cram 2 books because the certification it prepares you for is a combination of an assignment and essay exam instead of an objective exam. This book's structure is different from other Exam Cram 2 books to better guide you through this certification.

Most of the Exam Cram 2 books also focus on a particular certification exam, but this book focuses on a development project, the main requirement to become a Sun Certified Java Developer. This certification assesses your ability to provide a complete software development life cycle solution for the Java 2 Standard Edition (J2SE) platform.

On this certification exam, Sun is testing you for all phases of the software development life cycle, including analysis, design, development, testing, and implementation of a client/server project. The project includes enhancements to an existing skeleton application as well as new development. The main challenge is to develop strong analytical skills so that you can read the requirements, and design and code to those requirements, no more or less. Sun gives you the requirements, but you design, build, test, and, finally, deploy (that is, submit your project) your application.

Preparing for the Assignment

I recommend beginning your exam preparation by reading the messages at the JavaRanch certification forum (http://www.javaranch.com). I've read more than a thousand of these messages, and the forum helped me narrow the assignment requirements to the core pieces of the puzzle. I learned about a few requirements that weren't in the instructions, but were buried in code comments (javadoc) of the base classes supplied as part of the assignment. Many of the same questions are asked repeatedly on the forum, so you will certainly spot trends. Reading about others' struggles and what they did to overcome them is helpful. Occasionally, you read a posted question, see a response that sounds good and then *wham*, a moderator shoots the response full of holes for reasons that become clear after you think about it. The moderators, by and large, do a good job of answering so many questions. Sometimes they clash and debate each other on the best way to approach a task. Like a heavyweight boxing match, these exchanges are the best.

As another step in your preparation, take the self-assessment included in this book. This tool helps you evaluate your own knowledge and experience base in terms of the requirements for the Sun Certified Developer for Java 2 Platform. Notice that no J2ME or J2EE is required for this certification. This fact alone reduces the scope of the possible assignment requirements dramatically.

I strongly encourage you to install and configure the software and tools that you'll be tested on. That means downloading and installing the latest Software Development Kit (SDK) for J2SE. Some folk use an Integrated Development Environment (IDE), and some don't. Some of you might be interested in tools, so I'll tell you how I recommend you proceed: Skip the fancy IDEs. They are wonderful, admittedly. However, for this assignment, you'll learn more without an IDE. In fact, several posts I read at JavaRanch were complaints about IDE troubles. The IDE either added vendor libraries (which causes an automatic failure on the exam; you'll see this dreaded warning throughout the book) or built the code in a way that made it hard for the evaluator to verify compliance with the assignment requirements. A great IDE is like a friend, but going spartan has its advantages.

After analyzing the requirements, I usually sketch the architecture on paper or use a simple drawing tool, such as Microsoft Excel. Then I write the UML (please see `http://www.objectsbydesign.com/tools/umltools_byCompany.html` for an extensive list of products). Many UML tools are available, including ArgoUML (a good open source tool found at `http://argouml.tigris.org`), my favorite UML freeware. Sometimes I use Microsoft Visio, which has a helpful graphical user interface (GUI) for constructing diagrams with just a click to generate code, but it doesn't generate UML diagrams from code. Whatever you choose, use one to architect the assignment solution.

Then generate the code from within the IDE to lay a clean foundation. Experiment with one if you don't yet have a favorite. Make sure the tool you choose converts UML to Java class definitions, fields, and method signatures. I recommend a good tool for more than the UML-to-code shortcut. The main reason is the clean path of requirements → analysis → architecture → UML → skeleton code. The better tools offer UML-to-code functionality and the other way around (round-trip). This capability enables you to adjust the UML and regenerate code, or adjust the code and regenerate the UML. Round and round you go, until it is right. This method saves a lot of time and lays a solid foundation, something your assignment evaluator is sure to notice.

Finally, use a code editor to build the application from the skeleton code. Any code editor is permitted, as long as the code you submit doesn't have vendor- or editor-specific libraries or references. The evaluator must be able to compile your source code. Several editors are available, but make sure you select one with the features you need. For example, Dreamweaver's features are geared toward Web site building, so it isn't the right tool for this assignment. Also, it isn't as strong for Java usage as JBuilder or WebSphere Application Developer (formerly VisualAge), but is much better than a plain text editor. Actually, I used inexpensive UltraEdit (`http://www.UltraEdit.com`) for the certification, but any code editor with a Java library (one that highlights keywords) will do. Hands-on experience is king, so crank out the application manually, and you'll have more fun.

The Sun Java Technology Professional Program

How do you code an MVC pattern? What is refactoring? How do you meet all the requirements without changing the base code Sun provides? Which is worse—an application that has been overengineered with too many patterns, and one that works but isn't reuseable because the developer never heard of patterns? The Java community has adopted patterns faster than other language communities have. Having Java leaders champion something as theoretically sound as patterns is a healthy trend.

One of the results of Java's popularity is the high demand for skilled Java programmers and developers. However, because of Java's brief existence, experienced Java programmers are hard to find. Few in the field have more than five years of experience in developing Java applications. This is a problem for both employers and programmers. Employers cannot rely on the traditional number of years of experience in selecting senior-level Java programmers and software engineers, and star Java programmers have a hard time differentiating themselves from entry-level Java programmers.

Sun's Java certifications help both employers and programmers figure out who knows their stuff and who just says they do. Employers can identify skilled Java programmers by their certification level. Programmers and software engineers can attest to their knowledge of Java by citing their certification credentials.

The Java certification program consists of four certification exams:

> *Programmer exam*—The Programmer exam tests the candidate's knowledge of the Java language and basic application programming interface (API) packages. The exam consists of 59 multiple-choice questions.

> *Developer exam*—The Developer exam tests the candidate's ability to complete an extended programming assignment and answer questions about issues and trade-offs involved in completing the assignment. Programmer certification is a prerequisite to Developer certification. This book prepares you for the Developer exam.

> *Web Component Developer exam*—The Web Component Developer exam tests the candidate's knowledge of developing Java Web applications using Java servlets and JavaServer Pages (JSP). The exam consists of 60 multiple-choice questions. Programmer certification is a prerequisite to Web Component Developer certification.

> *Architect exam*—The Architect exam tests a candidate's familiarity with the technologies used to build Java-based enterprise applications and the candidate's ability to resolve issues in Java application design. This exam focuses on much higher-level software- and system-engineering skills than the other exams. It consists of a 48-question multiple-choice exam, an architecture and design project, and a four-question essay exam.

The Java Community Process is the group that decides which features go into the next version of Java, but has nothing to do with the Java certification exam. This group holds the responsibility for developing Java technology. It is an open, inclusive organization of active members and nonmember public input. If you point your browser to `http://www.jcp.org/introduction/overview/index.en.jsp`, you can pitch in or just watch.

About This Book

Each topical Exam Cram chapter follows a regular structure and includes graphical cues about important or useful information. Here's the structure of a typical chapter:

➤ *Opening hotlists*—Each chapter begins with a list of the terms, tools, and techniques that you must learn and understand before you can be completely comfortable with that chapter's subject matter. The hotlists are followed by one or two introductory paragraphs to set the stage for the rest of the chapter.

➤ *Topical coverage*—After the opening hotlists, each chapter covers a series of at least four topics related to the chapter's title. Throughout these sections, I highlight topics or concepts likely to appear on a test by using a special Exam Alert layout, like this:

This is what an Exam Alert looks like. Normally an Exam Alert stresses concepts, terms, software, or activities that are likely to relate to one or more certification test questions. For that reason, any information offset in an Exam Alert format is worthy of considerable attention on your part. Indeed, most of the information on the Cram Sheet appears as Exam Alerts within the chapters.

Pay close attention to material flagged as an Exam Alert; although all the information in this book pertains to what you need to know to pass the exam, I highlight certain items that are especially important. Because this book's material is very condensed, I recommend using this book along with other resources to achieve the maximum benefit.

In addition to the Exam Alerts, I have provided Tips, Notes, and Cautions that help build a better foundation for J2SE knowledge. Although the information might not be on the exam, it is certainly related and will help you become a better developer.

This is how Tips are formatted. Keep your eyes open for these elements, and you'll become a J2SE developer guru in no time!

➤ *Details and resources*—Every chapter ends with a "Need to Know More?" section, which provides direct pointers to Sun and third-party resources offering more details on the chapter's subject.

Chapter 19, "The Essay Exam," includes a sample written test that gives you a good review of the essay exam. This part of the certification is actually easier than the objective exam you take for the Sun Certified Java Programmer exam, if you develop the solution as the book suggests.

I've included a few appendixes that should provide all the information you need for the nuts and bolts of UML, the code style that Sun likes, and documentation standards that will help you document your project, which tends to improve the quality of your work. You'll also find a glossary that defines terms and an index you can use to track down where terms appear in the book.

Finally, the tear-out Cram Sheet at the front of this book is a condensed collection of facts, figures, and tips that you should study before writing any code. Also, look at the Cram Sheet one last time just before taking the essay exam. Unlike the SCJP exam that tests fine details, the SCJD is looking for a general understanding of concepts. The Cram Sheet helps you see the difference.

Getting Started

To use this book, you need a computer and an operating system that support the Java 2 platform. Many operating systems, including Windows, Linux, and Solaris, support the Java 2 platform. Ports of the Java 2 platform to many other operating systems are in the works. The examples used in this book were developed using J2SE 1.4 running on Windows 2000 Professional. However, the code samples will run on any Java Virtual Machine (JVM) that is implemented according to specifications on the Java 2 platform. Although the wording of the certification instructions is vague, I recommend using J2SE 1.4 (see http://java.sun.com for more on this edition).

How to Use This Book

Start with Chapter 1, "Certification Steps and Submission Grading," to make sure you get the right assignment downloaded and to get a bird's-eye view of what you need to do. Then proceed through each chapter of the book in order, working through all code examples. Passing the Programmer exam is a prerequisite to taking the Developer exam, so that level of familiarity is assumed. However, I hate reading books that assume too much. I want to tell the author, "Hey, I'm not stupid! I'm just new to this particular topic." I don't want you to get that feeling, either, so I provide enough details to avoid assuming too much.

Given all the book's elements and its specialized focus, I've tried to create a tool that will help you get great marks on the SCJD assignment and prepare for—and pass—the essay exam. Please share your feedback with me through Que Publishing.

The Book's Web Site

To help you with your certification studies, a Java certification Web site has been put together to supplement the information presented in this book. The Web site provides a forum for feedback on the certification exams and contains any corrections for errors discovered after the book's printing. The URL for this Web site is http://www.inforobo.com/java/scjd/. If you have any questions, comments, or suggestions concerning the book, its Web site, or the certification exams, please direct them to atrottier@hotmail.com.

Self-Assessment

. . . .

Of the more than two million Java programmers, the majority started by downloading the Java Software Development Kit (J2SE 1.4 SDK) and teaching themselves how to program in Java. This method sounds like a humble beginning, but has proved to be a valid way to start learning a new language.

To verify programmers' Java skills, Sun (who wants developers to properly represent Sun) and employers have driven the certification industry. The Sun Certified Java Developer (SCJD) is another significant step in proving your Java ability. Unlike the Sun Certified Java Programmer (SCJP) and the Sun Certified Web Component Developer (SCWCD) certifications, the SCJD requires that you develop an application that meets an assignment's list of requirements. Frankly, this certification is hard to pass. Even though I was careful, I found a bug in my client after submitting my project, so I suspect the evaluator did, too. Still, the extra care contributed to my score of 94%.

For the SCJD certification, you can't cram overnight and then take an easy multiple-choice exam. It takes two to four months to develop a solution and then take an essay exam. There just isn't a shortcut, such as a mock exam, to ease the pain. However, this book is packed with hints, examples, and plans to make your experience positive instead of dreadful.

Before you pay Sun $400 (currently, it costs $250 for the assignment and $150 for the essay exam) to attempt the solution, make sure you are ready. You need to be familiar with J2SE 1.4 and must have passed the programmer certification. This certification is not dependent on the Web component developer or the architect certifications.

Are You Ready?

The SCJD certification is designed for developers who are well versed in J2SE 1.4. Of course, Sun expects you to know the basic structure and syntax of the Java programming language. Beyond that, Sun wants to test your ability to design and build a moderately challenging application that could be the basis for a production-level program.

You need to be aware of several aspects of the assignment. Although you can still pass without doing the activities mentioned in the following list, you'll do better if you use Unified Modeling Language (UML), plan a software development process, use object-oriented analysis and design, and meet the assignment requirements in the downloaded instructions. Generally, candidates who have passed this certification have used industry-standard practices, including object-oriented technology and software development methodologies: requirements gathering and analysis, system architecture and design, implementation, testing, and deployment.

The following activities are the most helpful in trying to to achieve this certification:

➤ Analyze the project requirements to define the problem domain and the requirement list.

➤ Design an application architecture that meets the assignment requirements within the stated constraints (for example, must use Swing and JTable components).

➤ Describe your solution clearly and accurately, including the key application features and the development methodologies and techniques you used.

The Ideal Developer Certification Candidate

The following list describes some of the ideal candidate's characteristics. If you already have many of them, you are ready to tackle the certification project. You will learn the characteristics you don't have as you work through the assignment. If you have only a few of these characteristics, however, you should consider studying and practicing more before tackling the SCJD certification. The certification tests your ability by expecting you to be capable of the following:

➤ Design Java programs using the tools in Sun's SDK version 1.4.

➤ Have a thorough understanding of programming in Java.

➤ Have experience in the systems development process.

➤ Explain the object-oriented software development process.

➤ Be able to model the software development process.

➤ Be proficient with a development methodology, such as the waterfall methodology, Extreme Programming, or Rational Unified Process (RUP).

➤ Use the `wait`, `notify`, and `notifyAll` methods in the appropriate places to avoid thread blocking.

➤ Understand how the Java Virtual Machine (JVM) starts and runs stand-alone and networked applications.

➤ Design strong error handling, including throwing and catching exceptions.

➤ Analyze the downloaded instructions to determine the assignment's functional requirements.

➤ Use Java's conditional and loop constructs and flow-control `break` and `continue` statements.

➤ Understand how to declare a class as an interface and then implement that interface in a concrete class.

➤ Understand how to use anonymous classes for Swing events.

➤ Be familiar with phases and documentation involved in requirements gathering, requirements analysis, architecture, design, implementation, testing, and deployment.

➤ Take advantage of the benefits of encapsulation and inheritance in Java's object-oriented design.

➤ Effectively use overloading and overriding methods in inheritance relationships.

➤ Handle multiple threads in your code with the `synchronized` keyword to avoid data corruption in a network-capable application.

➤ Understand how to implement Java I/O and graphical user interfaces (GUIs) that follow Human/Computer Interaction (HCI) principles.

➤ Properly package and document your solution to make it clear to the evaluator that you met all requirements.

➤ Use design patterns, such as Model-View-Controller and Adapter.

➤ Document code in a way that takes advantage of javadoc, which is required.

Assessing Your Readiness

Are you ready to take this certification? It is harder than Sun's other certifications, so you need to make sure you're prepared to download the assignment and start working on it. The following lists help you assess whether you have the skills required to build a successful solution to the assignment. Read through the lists and judge whether you are competent in most of these skills.

Programming Background

1. Do you have significant experience with Java? [Yes or No]

   Little or no Java experience: Although Java is easy to learn, you shouldn't attempt this certification without experience in hands-on coding. This certification is for intermediate to advanced programmers, not beginners.

   Yes: You need to plan your project and schedule milestones if you expect a high score.

2. Do you have experience designing and building network-capable programs? [Yes or No]

   Yes: Skip to the next section, "Expected Skills Needed for the Assignment."

   Little or no experience: This certification is not the right place to start learning network-capable programming because these tasks are difficult for beginners, and completing the assignment could take too long. Other books for learning Java development are available at http://www.quepublishing.com.

Expected Skills Needed for the Assignment

3. Your design requires multiple classes and inheritance.

4. Although you might not write a fancy System Requirements Specification (SRS) based on the requirements in the instructions, you should survey an SRS to understand the concerns of designing an application of this complexity.

5. Identify and describe the essential elements in Unified Modeling Language (UML) diagrams based on the SRS to ensure an architecturally sound design.

6. Distinguish between architecture and design.

7. Design a graphical user interface (GUI) application that includes a client and a server.

8. Define your solution's architecture workflow.

9. Use a distributed object-oriented architecture for your solution model.

10. Design and extend a rudimentary database system based on the skeleton code downloaded from Sun.

11. Define your solution's attributes, object relationships, methods, and constructors.

12. Use appropriate design patterns, such as Observer-Observable, Model-View-Controller, Data Access Object, and Business Delegate, in your application modeling.

13. Design a distributed, multitier application using Remote Method Invocation (RMI) or sockets, using GUI design principles and adding functionality so that your application can interact with a networked database server.

14. Design, implement, and test your program using design patterns and RMI or sockets.

15. You must build a multithreaded database server that can handle multiple simultaneous users by synchronizing key sections of code.

16. Apply the principles of good GUI design, using Swing containers, components, and layout managers to form an object-oriented GUI.

I Think I'm Ready, So What's Next?

Before you put up the money and schedule the test, read this book to gain a realistic view of what the exam requires. Try to build some of the examples in the following chapters. Take the sample essay exam in Chapter 19. Regrettably, none of the mock Java exams you'll find at various places on the Web, even the high-quality mock exams at `http://www.jchq.net` and `http://www.javaranch.com`, are helpful for this certification. There are numerous mock exams for the SCJP and SCWCD, but not for this one. However, don't let that scare you. After you have reviewed the information in this self-assessment and feel comfortable with about 70% of the topics mentioned, you are ready to download the assignment and start designing.

Certification Steps and Submission Grading

. . . .

Terms you'll need to understand:

✓ Waterfall
✓ Rational Unified Process (RUP)

Techniques you'll need to master:

✓ Planning your software development project
✓ Following the certification instructions carefully, especially understanding the requirements

This chapter describes certification issues and requirements and explains the steps you need to take to get a great score for your solution. Keep in mind that many simple things can cause an automatic failure on the exam, such as placing the database file in the wrong directory or omitting the README.TXT file.

This certification exam tests your ability to extract a set of requirements from project instructions, code a solid application, and document your work. Nothing in it is complicated. It is simply a matter of being careful about details and, perhaps, researching a topic you haven't handled before. For example, not many candidates have experience with Remote Method Invocation (RMI) before taking this exam.

Introduction

In this chapter, you review the certification steps and how Sun grades your submission. Unlike the other objective exams, the Sun Certified Java Developer (SCJD) exam is a software development project. As such, you are more likely to do well if you approach it as you would a real project at work or final course project at school. That means you need a plan, and this chapter helps you write one. Take a long morning to think your development plan through, and you'll be glad you did. The design of your solution can take days, but first, plan your project. This step is easy, and it helps keep you on schedule. I realize most people wing it and don't write a plan. That is fine for them, but the idea behind the SCJD certification is to demonstrate your competence at completing a software development project. This chapter reviews the most important aspects of managing a development project. Each exam aspect introduced in this chapter is covered in more detail later in the book, so consider the following material a quick map to completion.

Your SCJD plan should be simple; you aren't building a Mars probe data management system. However, the main elements of a software project plan are required for projects of any size, including your small certification project. This plan includes the minimum documentation a small software project should produce. Avoid the temptation to build it ad hoc.

Having a sound software development methodology divides professionals from the amateurs. Just recently, I was brought on to a seven-figure software project as the technical head. Even before I saw the code, red flags were waving before my eyes. From a project-management perspective, a lot was missing from my short list of "must-haves or failure is guaranteed." As I was bearing down on particular missing items, the development team I inherited started objecting and pointing the "he doesn't know what he is doing" finger at me. They had been on the project for a year, so I lost all credibility. After all, there were quite a few of them, and I stood alone as the incompetent newcomer.

The client was oblivious to fundamental cracks in the project and elated with all the pretty screenshots and pages of marketing geek-speak paraded by the original development team. The client even broadcast a press kit announcing the soon-to-be software marvel as the key piece of its national initiative.

This project further convinced me of how necessary the requirements documents, design specifications, and testing plans can be. Because this project was missing these key elements, it became one giant, expensive piece of junk.

When I finally studied the code, it scared me. No, not because it was bad, but because it looked great. The style was clean. The modules had descriptive names. The coders seemed to have a good sense of programming. I couldn't understand how this much talent could go so far without requirements and designs. Long story short: There were so many problems that I couldn't keep up with user complaints, and the client killed the project a year later. A postmortem revealed that a poor design left a lot of good code sitting on a bad foundation. It could not be fixed because the problem was too deep, so they would have to start over.

This anecdote illustrates how proper project management provides essential guidance. In particular, use proper methodology for the certification assignment to help you produce a reliable and cost-effective (in terms of time) product. Also, good methodology can help you with bug tracking, code control, and documentation. Whatever way you go, make sure your approach is consistent with industry best practices for the software development life cycle.

 Do not write code for this project (or at work) unless you have a requirements document, even if it is brief and in rough form. If the project owner can't give you that, you are wasting your time. This advice includes prototype work. The implication of not having requirements is that management has not committed to the project, so what you code might never see a production server. If you don't write a small requirements document for this certification project, that means you didn't carefully read the instructions and are likely to make mistakes; you could possibly miss a key requirement and face an automatic failure on the exam.

Software Project Management

By "best practices," I mean the software-engineering methodology based on the principles and standards advocated by industry leaders, such as the Institute of Electrical and Electronics Engineers (IEEE). Following best practices enables you to earn the best marks on your certification project.

Large projects have reviews, inspections, and audits, but they aren't necessary in a formal sense for this project. However, as with large projects, you do need to manage the artifacts, including configuration, software, data, and technical documentation.

The software-engineering methodology prescribed for this certification project includes all aspects of the software life cycle. You start with project planning, and then move to producing code, conducting testing, writing the documentation, and, finally, submitting the project. Only the maintenance phase of the life cycle is missing from this project.

These are the main steps for achieving the best score:

1. Download the assignment

2. Concept development

3. Planning and scheduling

4. Requirements definition

5. Functional design

6. Detail design

7. Programming

8. Software integration and testing

9. Installation and acceptance

10. Documentation

11. Packaging and submission

12. Software maintenance

Other development methodologies are available. One is the Rational Unified Process (RUP), which has challenged the waterfall methodology IEEE espouses. You can find more about this excellent approach to software projects at http://www.rational.com/products/rup/. RUP supports a classic waterfall development process. However, unlike a strict waterfall activity arrow, RUP allows for iterations and for backward flow in the waterfall methodology. Another is Extreme Programming (http://www.extremeprogramming.org), in which the iterations are very short and efficient compared to the waterfall methodology. Component Based Software Engineering (CBSE) or Commercial Off-the-Shelf (COTS; see http://www.sei.cmu.edu/cbs/) takes advantage of preexisting components better than the other methodologies do. Please note that such third-party components cannot be submitted with your exam. However, some open source solutions can act as guides to certain parts of your solution. Jakarta has several projects that you can download and view the code, which may provide hints at how to solve some portions of your assignment. Finally, there is Open Source of Linux fame; however, this approach is inappropriate for the assignment; Open Source needs developers to coordinate efforts, but the certification assignment forbids such coordination.

Download the Assignment

As it plainly states on Sun's certification page, "Prior to beginning the Sun Certified Developer for Java 2 Platform program, you must be a Sun Certified Programmer for the Java Platform (any edition)." Certification consists of two parts. The first part is the Programming Assignment (CX-310-252A). The second part is the Essay Exam (CX-310-027).

Use the following steps to download the Programming Assignment part of the certification exam:

1. *Purchase your assignment*—First, you purchase the Sun Certified Developer for Java 2 Platform assignment ($250) by calling 800-422-8020. If you reside outside the United States or Canada, you must contact your local Sun office. Sorry, the vendor of the world's most advanced software language has yet to offer this purchase online. After you pay for the assignment, you set up an account on the CertManager Web site, and then log on and download it, as explained next.

2. *Log in to CertManager*—Log into Sun's CertManager database (http://www.certmanager.net/sun/) and select Sun Certified Developer from the menu. This choice takes you to a page with the option to select the version of the assignment you want to download. The next page contains instructions on how to download the assignment. You are allowed to select an assignment once, as the button immediately changes from Download to Upload. If you make a mistake, exit CertManager and start again. Assignment instructions are given in the download's files. If you get stuck at this point, your only option is to email CertManager.

   To use the CertManager Web site, you need to log in using the Prometric Student ID (for example, your SSN) given at the time of your first exam. You create your password the first time you log in. If this is the first time you have used this Web site, you must register a new student account (http://suned.sun.com/US/catalog/register.html). After you have a user account, you can do the following at the CertManager Web site:

➤ You can update your contact information, including your email address, phone number, and postal address.

➤ You can view your certification history. For every exam you've taken, CertManager shows you the test name, date taken, pass/fail status, and score.

➤ This site is the only way to download and upload the Sun Certified Java Developer assignment. You get the assignment here, develop your solution, and then upload it to the same URL.

➤ You can view your progress on any certification. CertManager lists all of them and places a colored box next to each one. If the box is empty, you haven't started it. If it is green, the assignment is in progress (for example, between assignment download and the assessor's grading it). If it is blue, the assignment is complete.

➤ In the event something goes wrong (for example, you upload the assignment, but it doesn't show up), you can submit an online help request to Sun's customer service. Actually, Sun posts only an email address (`correspondence@prometric.com`).

➤ If you lose your username and/or password, you can get another one from the CertManager site. Likewise, you change them at the site.

3. *Download the assignment*—Click the Test History button at the left of the page, which displays your test history, as mentioned previously. Click the Assignment button on this page to get the assignment page, where you choose the Sun Certified Developer Assignment for Java 2 option and then click the Download Assignment button. Later, return to the assignment page to submit your solution by clicking the Upload Assignment button. Sun's Web site is clunky, and this process could be improved. It is easy to make the mistake of trying to download an assignment before you have purchased the exam. It won't work, but the Web site doesn't tell you what is wrong. If anything goes awry, please see your contact for each country at `http://suned.sun.com/USA/certification/`. If you have already purchased the exam but can't download the assignment, you should send the payment confirmation you received to Sun by using the comment box at the bottom of the screen.

Concept Development

Concept development is the very front-end process of software development. In this case, it begins with Sun's instructions, which specify the need for a new software system based on a few base classes included in the assignment download. However, Sun goes only so far: It supplies skeleton classes and a few requirements. From these pieces, you have to conceptualize and assemble the complete solution. Then you figure out the best way to perform the work.

Planning and Scheduling

If you don't have a good plan, completing the assignment takes longer and you risk failing the exam. This section offers a plan that will get you to the end smoothly. The schedule is intended to give you guidance in identifying and preparing your project submission. This way, you eliminate the chance of failure caused by a boneheaded mistake, such as forgetting to include user documentation, the README.TXT file, or a particular requirement. By following this schedule, you can achieve the assignment objectives faster and better, and still get some sleep.

The 100-hour schedule in Table 1.1 offers a general list of tasks you should complete. I've read the forum posts from a supposed guru who did it in two weeks in his spare time. Perhaps he had recently completed a similar project, or maybe this genius is that much smarter than everyone else. I wouldn't hire this cowboy, however. Please use the industry's best practices and include all the steps. Although you shouldn't skip steps, you can trim some time here and there. If you follow this plan, you'll do great on the certification project and further polish and demonstrate your software project management skills.

Table 1.1	Assignment Schedule		
Task	Activity	Hours	Date
1	Download the assignment	2	
2	Concept development	5	
3	Planning and scheduling	3	
4	Requirements definition	5	
5	Functional and detail design	10	
6	Programming	45	
7	Software integration and testing	10	
8	Installation and acceptance	5	
9	Documentation	10	
10	Packaging and submission	3	
11	Software maintenance	2	

These tasks are done top to bottom, as listed in Table 1.1. However, don't follow the list blindly. For example, documentation (step 9) should be done throughout the project; don't wait until the very end. Also, steps 5 to 7 are done repeatedly.

The time estimates help you gauge your efforts, but your approach to completing the assignment directly affects the number of hours needed for each step. Some candidates don't spend much time planning and designing. If you are highly experienced, you might complete the assignment in under a month. Some candidates take the time to thoroughly understand the assignment and take several months to craft their solutions. Just be aware that developers tend to underestimate how long it takes to accomplish a task. Doesn't the download take only 5 minutes? No, it doesn't. The first time you try to log in to the CertManager site, you have to get a password. After you finally download the assignment, you still have to unpack the download JAR and place files in a proper directory tree. Take your time because if you make a mistake, you might have to beg a favor from Sun to upload again.

Requirements Definition

The requirements definition step involves writing the Software Requirements Specifications (SRS), which should precisely describe each essential requirement of the software and the external interfaces. Consult the ANSI/IEEE Standard 830-1998 (`http://standards.ieee.org/reading/ ieee/std_public/description/se`), "Recommended Practice for Software Requirements Specifications," as a model, and tailor it to your needs. Somebody went to a lot of trouble to think through this standard. You can tweak it, of course, but the model is a good base for writing your requirements definition. Whatever you come up with, your specification should include all the details you, or someone else, needs to create the design.

The SRS establishes the contract between you and the Sun evaluator on what the software product is supposed to do. Break this contract, and it is an automatic failure. The instructions in the download sketch out the requirements in not-so-obvious ways. Your challenge is to read through it carefully and make sure you pull all the requirements from the instructions *and* the source code comments. That's right: A few requirements are buried in the javadoc comments. For example, for some candidates, a requirement hidden in the supplied base class code specifies that only the owner of a database lock should be allowed to unlock the database. This requirement is certainly not obvious, so many people overlook it and lose points on the certification project.

The following is a loose adaptation of the IEEE standard 830-1993, "Recommended Practice for Software Requirements Specifications" (IEEE provides 830-1993 at `http://standards.ieee.org/reading/ieee/std_public/ description/se/`, but not 830-1998):

1.	Introduction	3.2	Usability
1.1	Purpose	3.3	Interfaces
1.2	Scope	3.3.1	User interfaces
1.3	Definitions, acronyms, and abbreviations	3.3.2	Hardware interfaces
		3.3.3	Software interfaces
1.4	References	3.3.4	Communications interfaces
1.5	Overview	3.4	Reliability
2.	Overall description	3.5	Security
2.1	Product perspective	3.6	Maintainability
2.2	Product functions	3.7	Performance
2.3	User characteristics	3.8	Portability
2.4	Constraints	3.9	Performance
2.5	Assumptions and dependencies	3.10	Design constraints
3.	Specific requirements	3.11	User documentation and help system
3.1	Functionality	4.	Supporting information

The order of items in section 3, Specific requirements, is flexible. The standard suggests many ways to organize this core section of the SRS. The preceding example is just my own. You can arrange it how you want; just make sure you include all the items.

For the assignment, you need only a sentence or two for the main items. This step forces you to think through the project requirements. For example, for portability you might state: "The solution must work on Unix." Remember, the evaluator may test your project submission on Unix, Solaris, or Windows. If you are developing on another OS (I'm using Windows 2000), this one requirement should prompt you to test your solution on Unix before submitting the project. Testing is especially important for this assignment, as part of the solution must read/write to a file. File handling is a little different among OS file systems. In particular, the file path separator is different (\ in Windows, and / in Unix), so the best approach is to use forward (/) slashes for all paths, and Java will automatically handle translation to Windows path format if the program is running on Windows. If the evaluator cannot open the database file supplied in your uploaded assignment, it means an automatic failure on the exam. Don't let the lowly slash doom you!

Functional Design

The functional design step is optional. Most software development shops do this step as part of the detail design, not as a separate document. If you want to perform this step, it is time to develop your functional design document, which defines the system's functions in user terminology, not geek speak.

For the certification project, the functional design should define only a dozen functions because the assignment is no larger than that. It narrows the scope of work to just these functions, which later become the foundation for the detail design. The functional design is written from the user's perspective. You can write a draft functional design document by following the instructions in the assignment download files (see Chapter 6, "Application Analysis and Design," for more detail on this topic). For example, the traditional assignment for this certification is a reservation system. (This is no secret; just read the thousands of posts on the subject.) One of the functions you need to build enables the user to reserve seats, so this part of the functional design might be stated as "The user will be able to indicate the number of seats needed for the reservation."

Detail Design

The instructions that came with your assignment download describe the system you are to build. In this document are items best described as functional requirements. From these requirements, you can write a short detail design document. The idea is that applicability is not restricted by the software's size, complexity, or criticalness. Follow the IEEE standard 1016-1993 (http://standards.ieee.org/reading/ieee/std_public/description/se/), "Guide to Software Design Descriptions," which has the following outline:

1.   Overview

1.1.   Purpose

1.2   Scope

2.   References

3.   Definitions

4.   Description of IEEE standard 1016-1993

5.   Design description organization

5.1   Design views

5.2   Recommended design views

5.3   Design description media

6.   Considerations

6.1   Selecting representative design methods

6.2   Representative design method descriptions

6.3   Design document sections

6.4   Method-oriented design documents

7.   Design methods

7.1 Function-oriented design methods	7.4 Object-oriented design methods
7.2 Data-oriented design methods	7.5 Formal language-oriented design methods
7.3 Real-time control-oriented design methods	8. Bibliography

This document is a detailed description of the classes and methods of each software component. It is very concise and is used by programmers to guide them in building the actual code.

Programming

Write code using a style that is acceptable to Sun. This step takes the most time, but if you did your design properly, it is easier than the tasks you've already done in the preceding steps. Most of the book expands on this step, so I'm mentioning it only in passing here.

Testing

Submitting your solution without proper testing isn't smart. Many people have done this and had to pay another $250 to take the exam again, all because of a simple mistake that could have been caught with proper testing. Follow the ANSI/IEEE standard 1008-1987, "Standard for Software Unit Testing" (http://standards.ieee.org/reading/ieee/std_public/description/se/), which has the following outline:

1. Scope and references	3.3 Refine the general plan
1.1 Inside the scope	3.4 Design the set of tests
1.2 Outside the scope	3.5 Implement the refined plan and design
1.3 References	
2. Definitions	3.6 Carry out the test procedures
3. Unit testing activities	3.7 Check for termination
3.1 Plan the general approach, resources, and schedule	3.8 Evaluate the test effort and unit
3.2 Determine features to be tested	

This document describes a testing process that includes phases, activities, and tasks. It also sets a minimum number of tasks for every activity.

While the assignment is not large, the above document can provide assurance that the each unit in your submission is properly tested. Even if you don't complete a full document, it is helpful to at least use part of it.

Installation and Acceptance

You should definitely test your application on Unix. Your evaluator might be using Solaris, Sun's flavor of Unix. One of the concerns with portability is the database and user documentation location. The path separator differs among the various platforms; for example, Windows uses \ and Unix uses /. It would be a shame to lose points because the evaluator couldn't pull up the user documentation. Develop the application on your platform, but before you submit it, run it on Unix once to make sure all is fine.

Documentation

You must submit ample documentation with your certification project. The documentation includes javadoc, a README.TXT file, user help, and a design choices document, which explains why you designed the project that way.

The README.TXT file goes in the root or installation directory. Don't place it anywhere else.

Javadoc Comments

If you are new to javadoc, it is the Sun Microsystems tool (http://java.sun.com/j2se/javadoc) for generating application programming interface (API) documentation in HTML format from document comments in source code.

Writing javadoc comments can become an entire project in itself, and you need to do a fair job at writing comments because Sun does review them. The javadoc comments are enclosed in the multiline comment. The text must be written in HTML; must precede a class, field, constructor, or method declaration; and must be structured as a description followed by block tags, such as @param, @return, and @see.

This documentation is part of your grade, so don't be shy about commenting your code. Every class and method should be commented in such a way that javadoc can grab it.

While you don't have to use the full complement of javadoc tags, you do have to comment to some extent every class and method.

README.TXT File

 It is an automatic failure if you do not specify how to start your application from the command line.

You must create a single text file (plain ASCII format; word processor formats are unacceptable) called README.TXT. Place it in the root or installation directory of your project submission. This file describes to the evaluator the following information in exactly the order listed in your instructions. This is the structure I used for my README.TXT file (see Chapter 5, "Documentation & Javadoc Comments"):

➤ The exact Java Development Kit (SDK) version you used, including the platform you worked on. You can get this information by using the `java -version` command.

   In my case, this command returned the following:

```
java version "1.4.1"
Java(TM) 2 Runtime Environment, Standard Edition (build 1.4.1-b21)
Java HotSpot(TM) Client VM (build 1.4.1-b21, mixed mode)
```

➤ Explain how to run the program. You must provide exact command-line instructions. If any environmental setup is required, do not just say what needs to be done; include instructions on how to perform the setup. For example, do not say something like "Add server.jar to your classpath." You should document exactly how to add the JAR file to the classpath. *Note:* Your program must run correctly, no matter what directory it is installed in.

➤ The location of your database file (for example, db.db).

➤ The location of your design choices document (for more detail, see Chapter 5, "Documentation and Javadoc Comments").

➤ The names of the files you have submitted, a note specifying their location in the directory structure, and a general description of each one's purpose.

User Help

Although it is true most developers wouldn't be caught dead writing a user manual, you have to do it for the exam. The evaluator only glances at the written user help, and it should be just a short page. The challenge is to write for users who don't care about the code. They just want to know how to operate the application quickly, without hassle.

Therefore, you must include an online user manual in HTML format. Don't consider it the least important deliverable. The user manual is so easy to do that you might think of this portion of the exam as low-hanging fruit. I recommend you include the following:

➤ *Interface text*—Describe the labels on interface elements, such as menu items, fields, and buttons.

➤ *Application messages*—Explain any popup, status, or error messages.

➤ *Tutorial*—Include a small tutorial explaining the steps needed to use the application.

Design Choices Document

You must also provide a file that documents your major design choices and the reasons for those choices. Include your choices of RMI versus serialized objects and modifying versus extending the Data class. This document can include some of the following optional sections:

➤ Assumptions about your design, such as expecting the database file to be accessed by one client in local mode

➤ How you handled deprecated methods

➤ How you implemented specific methods (for example, must expand the search capability)

➤ Database-locking mechanism

➤ Client/server architecture

➤ GUI information, such as how you implemented the table model for JTable (a required component)

➤ Your approach to error and exception handling

➤ How your application manages threads

Packaging and Submission

Your project submission has to be uploaded as one JAR file. Anything else, including TAR or ZIP files, results in automatic failure. Your project must address the following questions. How do you arrange all the files within a single JAR? You can nest JAR files inside the main JAR. How is the evaluator supposed to run the application? For that matter, how is the evaluator supposed to get his hands on the README.TXT file that explains how the evaluator is supposed to get his hands on the README.TXT file?

The instructions in the assignment download will tell you this, but here it is again as a reminder: When you submit your assignment, you should provide the following parts:

➤ Full source and object code, including new classes, modified versions of supplied classes, and copies of supplied classes that were not modified. These classes should be in an appropriate directory structure along with the class files. You can use JAR files to contain groups of elements in your project submission, as you deem appropriate—for example, to support the running of your programs.

➤ The original database file db.db. You should make a backup copy of all files that you downloaded, but especially this one.

➤ You must provide HTML/javadoc documentation for all classes, whether supplied, modified, or new. You don't have to touch the comments on classes you downloaded unless you modified them.

➤ You must provide user documentation for the database server and the GUI client. Sun does allow you to place the user documentation online. If you do that, you must supply the URL in the README.TXT file.

➤ You must include a single text file called README.TXT.

I've read that some people have created an elaborate directory structure, but don't do that, or you'll be asking for trouble. In fact, if you have more than five directories, you will likely irritate your evaluator. The directory structure can be as simple as this:

➤ suncertify.server

➤ suncertify.database

➤ suncertify.client

Don't complicate it. You shouldn't have more than four directories, and three or even two will do. You take the chance of making a mistake if you use too many directories.

Software Maintenance

On a production project, the software maintenance step is where you provide support, work on bugs, and start working on the next version. After you submit a certification project, what are you supposed to do with your code and files? Hang on to them for a while, or at least wait until you get confirmation that you passed. If you fail (which is not the end of the world), you can reexamine the score breakdown and fix the low-scoring section. Remember that you have to pay again to resubmit your fixed certification project.

If you have failed the exam and want to resubmit your project for another attempt, you need to call Sun to purchase a resubmission option for your exam. The cost is generally one half the original amount.

Submission Grading

Sun has been using essentially the same assignment, with minor variations, for a couple of years. Sun grades your project according to very specific criteria. It seems to use the same grading (the Sun term is "marking") criteria for all application submissions. The grading is done in two phases. First, the evaluator runs the code, ensuring that it functions correctly through the specified operations. This phase is critical to earn the certification; if the evaluator runs into trouble or gets an error, you flunk. Next, the evaluator assesses whether you provided the assignment's essential requirements, as explained in the instructions. Next, the evaluator investigates the design and implementation of your assignment. Sun says the grading process is closely controlled to ensure consistency and fairness, but how would any of us know if the evaluators goofed? From what I've seen, however, they do a good job.

After you upload your assignment, check the CertManager site to see whether Sun received it. If so, you can buy a voucher and take the essay exam. The instructions say, "This exam tests your understanding of your submission and asks you to justify a number of design choices embodied in that submission." Because of the way Sun handles this certification, the questions are generic. The evaluator checks to see whether you did your own work, essentially. You don't actually get points for the essay exam directly, but clear answers that are consistent with your code raise your grade. Mainly, Sun wants to see that you repeated what you wrote in the design choices document included in your project submission. For example, a question on the essay exam might be "Why did you choose RMI over sockets?"

Remember, 124 out of 155 points is a passing score.

The following grading criteria are used to evaluate your project submission:

➤ General considerations (one third), including ease of use, code readability, and clean design.

➤ Documentation (one sixth), including user documentation, javadoc source documentation, and code comments.

➤ A user interface (one sixth) that uses good/accepted Human/Computer Interaction (HCI) principles.

➤ Server design (one third), including database locking, error handling, and a database search algorithm.

Need to Know More?

 http://standards.ieee.org/catalog/olis/se.html—IEEE's list of currently available software engineering standards. You have to subscribe to get the standards, and you need a PDF client (Adobe Acrobat 3.0 or above) to view them.

 http://cio.doe.gov/ITReform/sqse/sem_toc.htm—This outstanding example of standards applied to software engineering is provided by the U.S. Department of Energy, Office of the Chief Information Officer.

 http://standards.ieee.org/reading/ieee/std_public/description/se— You can view the major software engineering standards in outline form, at no cost, on this page. The actual standards do have a fee, so this page is a great reference.

Preparing Your Environment with J2SE 1.4

. . . .

Terms you'll need to understand:

✓ Java 2 Standard Edition (J2SE)
✓ Deprecated

Techniques you'll need to master:

✓ Compiling Java source code files and then running the resulting application from the command line
✓ Identifying differences between the Java editions
✓ Recognizing J2SE 1.4 key features
✓ Knowing how to specify the command line needed to run your application

In this chapter, you review the basics of the Java editions and the differences between them and learn how to install J2SE. The Sun Certified Java Developer (SCJD) certification uses J2SE, not J2EE or J2ME. Most likely, you will use J2SE 1.4 to code your certification project, but you can use 1.3. Your documentation must state which version you use, but any production version is valid when you submit your project. Although many developers already know how to use J2SE, not everyone has actually installed it. Perhaps they work at a company that set it up for them, or maybe they use a fancy Integrated Development Environment (IDE) that hides the command line and has automatically installed Java previously.

The project you upload must include instructions to the evaluator on how to run your application from the command line. If you have not compiled and run Java programs from the command line, perhaps you have used an IDE until this point in your Java career. Therefore, please be careful to test the steps in your instructions so that you can avoid a costly mistake in your project's instructions. It is an automatic failure if the evaluator can't start your otherwise perfect application.

I recommend using a plain editor and command line instead of a commercial IDE for this assignment. Use a good programming text editor (for example, TextPad or UltraEdit) with the Sun Microsystems Software Development Kit (SDK), previously known as the Java Development Kit (JDK). Some people still use the term JDK, but Sun now calls it the SDK.

If you normally use an IDE, jump to the command line for this assignment. That is how the evaluator is going to use your application, so it is best to get used to this mode. This way, you can supply correct instructions in your project upload on how to run your application, and ensure that the application runs properly from your command line.

Java Editions and Versions

Programming in Java does not start with writing source code. First, you have to choose an edition. Sun has three editions for each platform or version (currently, Java is on platform or version 2). Sun has three editions for the current platform:

> ➤ *J2ME*—Java 2 Micro Edition is targeted for the consumer and embedded market. The application programming interface (API) specifications are based on J2SE, but modified to meet the unique requirements of each product. J2ME makes it possible to write Java applications for cell phones, SmartCards, pagers, and other consumer devices.

➤ *J2SE*—Java 2 Standard Edition is for the server and desktop. This edition is the one you will use for the assignment.

➤ *J2EE*—Java 2 Enterprise Edition is for very large programs running on servers that typically manage heavy traffic and complicated transactions. These programs are the backbone of many online services, such as banking, e-commerce, and Business to Business (B2B) trading systems. You need this edition for Web applications that use JavaServer Pages (JSP) and servlets. *Note:* You must install J2SE before installing J2EE.

Regardless of the edition, Java programs are always defined in source code files, which always have a file type of java. Also, the core Java language works the same for all editions. The keywords work the same on all editions, all platforms, and all versions. So what is different between editions? The libraries are what make editions. I'll rarely mention J2ME and J2EE again. Instead, I'll concentrate on the J2SE libraries that are required for this certification.

Java Software Development Kit

SDK is the name for the set of Java software development tools, consisting of the API classes, a Java compiler, and the Java Virtual Machine (JVM) interpreter, regardless of which version you use. Sun gives away the SDK for each edition, which has everything you need to compile and test programs. All the code in this book was developed with the J2SE SDK.

The SDK is a development environment for building programs using the Java programming language and includes everything you need to develop and test programs. The tools in the SDK are designed to be used from the command line. Although these tools do not provide a graphical user interface (GUI), the character interface is the way the evaluator is going to look at your project.

The J2SE 1.4 SDK is composed of core classes, tools categorized as basic (the compiler and runtime engine), Remote Method Invocation (RMI), internationalization, security, Java Interface Definition Language (IDL) and Remote Method Invocation over Internet Inter-ORB Protocol (RMI-IIOP), and the Java plug-in. For the assignment, you need the basic and RMI tools. All these tools are compiled to a specific OS (Windows, Unix, and Solaris), but most of them have equivalent functionality regardless of operating environment.

Each development tool comes in a Microsoft Windows version (Windows), a Linux version, and a Solaris version. You won't see any difference in features between the Windows and Solaris versions. However, there are differences in configuration and usage to accommodate each operating system's special requirements, such as directory separators. To see the individual tool documentation, go to `http://java.sun.com/j2se/1.4.1/docs/tooldocs/tools.html` and click the link next to the corresponding tool for your OS. The following SDK tools and parts are the ones you are most likely to use for the assignment:

➤ *javac*—This is the compiler.

➤ *java*—This is the launcher for Java applications.

➤ *javadoc*—This is the API documentation generator.

➤ *jar*—This is the archive tool to create Java Archive (JAR) files.

➤ *rmic*—This tool generate stubs and skeletons for remote objects.

➤ *rmiregistry*—This is the remote object registry service.

➤ *policytool*—This is the GUI tool for managing policy files.

➤ *Runtime environment*—This is an implementation of the Java 2 runtime environment found in the jre subdirectory, for use by the SDK.

➤ *Source code*—These are the actual source files (src.zip) for all classes that make up the J2SE API (for example, source files for the java.* and javax.* packages). The source code is a wonderful educational resource. I've learned as much from browsing the source code as I have from any book. Notice that these files do not include platform-specific implementation code and cannot be used to rebuild the class libraries. To extract these files, use any common zip utility.

 One of the tasks you must complete is replacing a few deprecated methods in the classes supplied in the assignment download. A deprecated method is one that Sun will not support in future releases. You can find these methods by compiling with the deprecation flag: **javac -deprecation YourClass.java**. It displays a description of each use or override of a deprecated member or class.

Installation Instructions

Sun offers three versions of the SDK—Windows, Solaris, and Linux—and each version has different installation instructions. The following sections contain condensed installation instructions for each version and supply a link for the more detailed instructions. Please visit the link, as this information changes.

After it's installed, the Java 2 SDK has the following directory structure for Windows:

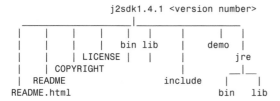

```
              j2sdk1.4.1 <version number>
    _____|_____
   |   |   |   |   |   |   |      |   |
   |   |   |   |  bin lib  |    demo  |
   |   |   | LICENSE |  |      |      jre
   |   | COPYRIGHT         |         _|_
   | README           include  |    |
README.html                    bin   lib
```

The directory structure for Solaris and Linux looks like this:

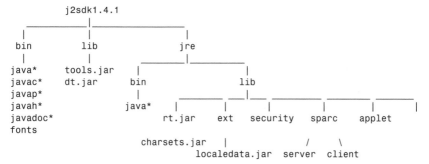

```
        j2sdk1.4.1
   _____|_____
  |         |            |
 bin       lib          jre
  |         |        _____|_____
java*     tools.jar  |            |
javac*    dt.jar     bin          lib
javap*     |    _____ __|__ _____ _____ _____ _____
javah*   java* |      |     |      |      |      |     |
javadoc*      rt.jar  ext  security  sparc       applet
fonts
        charsets.jar  |        /    \
            localedata.jar  server  client
```

Windows Installation Instructions

The following are the quick steps for installing the SDK on a Windows machine. For the full explanation, please refer to http://java.sun.com/j2se/ 1.4.1/install-windows.html.

1. Check the download file size to ensure that you have downloaded the full, uncorrupted file. The download page on the Web site displays the byte size, so compare what you get to the displayed size. After the download is completed, check the file size. For example, I downloaded the Java 2 SDK, Standard Edition 1.4.1_01. The j2sdk-1_4_1_01-windows-i586.exe file is displayed on Sun's site as having a file size of 37,731,236 bytes. However, my file manager reports it is 36,847,000 bytes, but the actual properties list it as 37,731,236 bytes.

2. Uninstall any previous installation of the Java 2 SDK, per Sun's recommendation.

3. Run the Java 2 SDK installer (the j2sdk-1_4_1_01-windows-i586-i.exe file). The installer prompts you with the instructions.

4. Delete the file you downloaded.

Solaris Installation Instructions

You can install the self-extracting binary, but you won't see all the packages and source code. I recommend you install the full package structure. The following are the quick steps for installing the SDK on a Solaris machine. For the full explanation, please refer to `http://java.sun.com/j2se/1.4.1/install-solaris.html`.

1. Check the download file size to ensure that you have downloaded the full, uncorrupted file. The download page on the Web site displays the byte size, so compare what you get to the displayed size.

2. With execute permission, extract the contents of the compressed TAR file:

   ```
   SPARC: zcat j2sdk-1_4_1_0-solaris-sparc.tar.Z | tar -xf -
   x86: zcat j2sdk-1_4_1_0-solaris-i586.tar.Z | tar -xf -
   ```

3. Log in as root by running su and entering the superuser password.

4. Uninstall any previous version of the Java 2 SDK.

5. To install the Java 2 SDK 1.4.1 into the /usr/j2se directory, run the following command:

   ```
   pkgadd -d . SUNWj3rt SUNWj3dev SUNWj3man SUNWj3dmo
   ```

6. Delete the TAR files and extracted directories.

Linux Installation Instructions

The following are the quick steps for installing the SDK on a Linux machine. There are two ways to go: the self-extracting binary file or the rpm command. For the full explanation, please refer to `http://java.sun.com/j2se/1.4.1/install-linux.html`.

Linux Self-Extracting Binary

This is how you install J2SE for the Linux OS:

1. Download the self-extracting binary file named j2sdk-1_4_1_03-linux-i586.bin. As mentioned for the other platforms, please check the download file size to ensure that you have downloaded the full, uncorrupted file.

2. Copy the binary file you just downloaded to the install directory.

3. Run the file you downloaded with the following commands from its directory:

```
chmod a+x j2sdk-1_4_1_03-linux-i586.bin
./j2sdk-1_4_1_03-linux-i586.bin
```

4. Delete the binary file you downloaded.

Linux RPM Installation

This is how you install J2SE for the Linux OS using the `rpm` command:

1. Download the self-extracting binary file named j2sdk-1_4_1_03-linux-i586-rpm.bin. Again, check the download file size to ensure that you have downloaded the full, uncorrupted file.

2. Run the file you downloaded with the following commands from its directory:

```
chmod a+x j2sdk-1_4_1_03-linux-i586-rpm.bin
./j2sdk-1_4_1_03-linux-i586-rpm.bin
```

3. Switch to the root user with the `su` command.

4. Run the `rpm` command, like so:

```
rpm -iv j2sdk-1_4_1_03-linux-i586.rpm
```

Need to Know More?

`http://java.sun.com/j2se/`—This document gives you an overview of J2SE 1.4. Start here if you aren't sure where to go.

`http://java.sun.com/j2se/1.4.1/docs/index.html`—This document gives you an overview of the entire Java 2 SDK, Standard Edition.

`http://java.sun.com/j2se/1.4.1/docs/tooldocs/windows/jdkfiles.html`—This document gives you an overview of the Java 2 SDK, Standard Edition directories and the files they contain for Windows.

`http://java.sun.com/j2se/1.4.1/docs/tooldocs/solaris/jdkfiles.html`—This document gives you an overview of the Java 2 SDK, Standard Edition, directories and the files they contain for Solaris.

`http://java.sun.com/j2se/1.4.1/docs/tooldocs/linux/jdkfiles.html`—This document gives you an overview of the Java 2 SDK, Standard Edition directories and the files they contain for Linux.

`http://java.sun.com/j2se/1.4.1/docs/tooldocs/tools-changes.html`—This document describes some of the changes made to the tools in version 1.4 of the Java 2 SDK, Standard Edition.

`http://java.sun.com/j2se/1.4.1/docs/tooldocs/tools.html`—This document gives you an overview of the Java 2 SDK tools.

`http://java.sun.com/docs`—This document provides access to white papers, the Java tutorial, and other documents.

`http://java.sun.com/j2se/1.4.1/README.html`—This README document is the first page to read if you are new to the SDK because it tells you the essentials, such as what it is, where to submit bug reports, and the like.

`http://java.sun.com/j2se/1.4.1/changes.html`—This document summarizes some of the significant changes introduced in the J2SE 1.4.1 platform.

3

Objectives and Deliverables

Terms you'll need to understand:

✓ Assignment requirements
✓ Graphical user interface (GUI)
✓ Javadoc

Techniques you'll need to master:

✓ Making software design decisions by analyzing requirements
✓ Providing a complete application as one JAR file, following the detailed instructions provided

In this chapter, you review the objectives and deliverables for the Sun Certified Java Developer (SCJD) certification. Because this certification has an assignment (the Sun Certified Enterprise Java Architect exam also has an assignment), it differs from most certification exams. In fact, the moderately difficult assignment, which can take months to complete, separates it from most industry certifications, which are usually proctored exams.

Objectives

The following are the main objectives for this certification:

➤ Write an application program with Java. The application requires the following:

   ➤ A graphical user interface (GUI) demonstrating good Human/Computer Interaction (HCI) principles of design.

   ➤ A network connection, using RMI or sockets, to connect to an information server.

   ➤ A network server that connects to the database; its skeleton is included in the download.

   ➤ A database created by extending the functionality of the skeleton code, which comes with limited documentation.

➤ In the DESIGN_CHOICES.TXT document and essay exam, you are asked to list some of the major choices you made for your design and implementation.

➤ In the DESIGN_CHOICES.TXT document and essay exam, you are asked to list some of the main advantages and disadvantages of each of your choices.

➤ In the DESIGN_CHOICES.TXT document and essay exam, you are asked to justify your choices by comparing your design and implementation objectives, including the advantages and disadvantages of each.

 The database does not use Java Database Connectivity (JDBC). Rather, it is a simple file reader/writer supplied by Sun. Also, Sun supplies the data file, called database.bin. Sun wants you to create a database from these two elements.

The challenge is to convince the Sun evaluator that you understand how to build a client/server application that meets a given set of requirements.

Along the way, this certification helps you understand and model a business need. I hope, however, that this book provides a solid guide to identifying and refining Sun's instructions and requirements. Although these requirements are written with or without formal language for requirements, they are good enough to see what you can do.

A better way to certify developers is to define a project by using standard documentation. For example, the SCJD certification's quality and utility would be improved if Sun used a three-part process. First, Sun would provide a project charter with a few owner interviews, the software objectives, and the overall purpose. Using this information, you would write a formal Software Requirements Specification (SRS; IEEE standard 830-1993, "Recommended Practice for Software Requirements Specifications") for that project. You would then exchange your SRS for Sun's by uploading your SRS and downloading Sun's SRS. Second, you would write a design document meeting those requirements, following the IEEE standard 1016.1-1993, "Guide to Software Design Descriptions." Third, you would exchange your design document for Sun's (which is what your design document is graded against) and write code to that document. This process is better and closer to reality. More important, it removes the ambiguity every candidate finds in the current instructions bundled in the assignment package.

Some would argue that my suggested certification process would be too difficult to standardize. Perhaps the reverse is true: Because the current assignment instructions are in nonstandard form, using industry-standard documentation and the software development life cycle would improve consistency and quality, representing a more reliable measure of a developer's skill.

GUI Design

One of the key ingredients for earning top marks is to design a clean interface for the user. As the human interface designer, you need to choose the interface components and lay them out proportionally. Java makes the nuts-and-bolts aspect of this exercise straightforward. Chapters 13, "The GUI," 14, "The Swing Components and Event Handling," and 15, "The JTable Component," discuss this topic at length. For now, please be aware that although there are many ways to build the screens for your assignment, Sun will surely appreciate your project following its recommended design guidelines.

The Java look and feel provides a distinctive platform-independent appearance and standard behavior, which is why one of the requirements specifies that you use Swing components, not Abstract Windowing Toolkit (AWT) components. Using the single look and feel that Swing provides helps ensure that what you see is what the evaluator will see. Sun wants to know whether you can take advantage of built-in Swing components. For example, you must use the JTable component. It is a helpful grid component, and feeding data into it is easy. However, the event model takes a little getting used to.

Database

The heart of the project is the database. Sun provides the skeleton pieces, which you must use to build your database. It is not as big a task as it sounds. The base classes Sun provides are already good enough. You just have to decide how much to modify the main piece (Data.java) and what you need to add in any additional classes. One common mistake is to overengineer the solution. My database met all the requirements and seemed to be a clean design, yet I added only two classes and didn't modify any Sun-supplied code. I've read many forum posts from developers who were looking for help on their code, but had clearly gone too far. What they were doing was unnecessary, or worse, obscured the real functionality they should have built.

One major ingredient of the database design is the locking mechanism. Chapter 7, "Databases and Atomicity," discusses the details of a good lock manager, the better way to go for this project. One hidden requirement is that only the client who locks a row can unlock it. This means there has to be a way to track clients within the locking mechanism. I've seen some clever ways to tackle it and some truly bizarre approaches that would surely lose points. A tricky part is what to do if the client locks a record and then dies. One elegant way to handle that situation is to let the system worry about it rather than invent some polling or timed checker design. This method is also explained in Chapter 7.

Networking

The assignment demands two modes of operation. The client that presents the information must be able to get it from a local database file or a remote one. The local mode is simple to implement, but the remote mode is harder. You have to design the network piece with RMI or sockets. Most people use RMI because it came later than sockets and is built on top of them. The early version of RMI was crude, but the current version, although it still needs another revision, is a better choice for this assignment than naked sockets. The big problem with sockets is thread management; you have to manually handle threads. RMI takes care of threads automatically, so the code is simpler. Some want to argue the merits of one over the other, but why not do that after passing the certification exam? I don't think sockets are worth the effort for this project. However, you might love them, so I talk about them in Chapters 11, "Networking with NIO," and 12, "RMI." Unlike the database classes, Sun provides nothing to get you started on the networking portion of the assignment.

Database Transparency

You can write a lot of fancy code so that the client handles the local database interaction one way and the network database another way. Here's a hint, however: If you design your solution the best way, there is no local– or network mode–specific code in the client. That is one of the challenges: Can you design the architecture in such a way that the database location is transparent to the client? The solution to this challenge is elegant, but not obvious. The trick is to use one interface, but have the signatures present the exact same types to the client when the database methods are called, regardless of whether the database was created by the factory from a local file or on the other side of the network through RMI. Also, the assignment forces you to build a database connection factory that generates a local or remote database connection based on command-line parameters. This factory is a marvelous example of the power behind design patterns. This design pattern is demonstrated in Chapter 9, "Interfaces," where you see a clear reason for having interfaces.

Design Choices

Some people can code fast and furiously. However, they are taking chances and might overlook important details, so what they end up doing is quickly building something that will fail even faster. There are many ways to design the GUI and the network pieces, but you need to make sure you are using a reasonable approach and are able to justify why you chose it.

One of the documents you must include in your certification project is the DESIGN_CHOICES.TXT file. In it, you list some of the major design choices you made and explain your choices by describing their main advantages and disadvantages. Also, you need to compare the design and implementation objectives with the advantages and disadvantages of your choices.

Deliverables

When Sun mentions deliverables, it is referring to the actual files you must submit with your project, described in the following list:

➤ Full source and object code, including new classes, modified versions of supplied classes, and copies of supplied classes that were not modified. The source files and class files should be in an appropriate directory structure along with the class files. You can use JAR files to contain groups of elements of your project as you deem appropriate—for example, elements needed to support the running of your programs.

➤ The database.bin database file, which is the same one supplied with the assignment download.

➤ Full documentation, including the following:

➤ You must provide HTML/javadoc documentation for all classes, whether supplied, modified, or new. Make sure you comment your code thoroughly, and then this documentation is easy to generate.

➤ You must provide user documentation for the database server and the GUI client. Most people provide the GUI documentation as a Web page. It can be packaged with your project or available online (be sure to provide the correct URL).

➤ You must provide a README.TXT file that tells the evaluator how to use your application. This file must be in the root directory of your project.

➤ You must provide a document called DESIGN_CHOICES.TXT that explains how you tackled the assignment's two major issues. You need to convince the evaluator that you know what you are doing, not that your approach is the best one. The two major design choices are whether you chose RMI or Serialized objects, and whether you chose to modify or extending the supplied Data class.

➤ All your project elements must be packaged into a single JAR file for submission. Nesting JAR files inside the main JAR is permitted.

 The README.TXT file must be in plain ASCII format. I recommend providing the DESIGN_CHOICES.TXT file in ASCII format also, although the evaluator will accept it in Microsoft Word format.

 Your entire project must be uploaded as one JAR file. Don't try any other method of packaging your project, or the evaluator might fail you for not following this simple instruction. Evaluators aren't amused if they receive projects requiring them to unzip, untar, unlock, decrypt, or unravel your submitted ball of files.

Source Code Files

The biggest part of your grade is the source code. The first thing the evaluator does is read the README.TXT file to figure out how to test the application to make sure it works. If it doesn't work or those instructions cause a mistake, you automatically fail the assignment. The evaluator then reads your DESIGN_CHOICES.TXT document to learn how you designed the application and reads through your code.

Your project submission has to include all the class files so that the application runs, but it must also include all the source files used in your application's final build. This includes the Sun-supplied files (if you modified a class file, include the modified version) and the ones you added. Although the evaluator won't actually build your application from the source code, he should be able to. If you modified one of Sun's supplied files, don't include both the original and the modified file; just include the modified one.

The directory structure is another source of confusion. I've seen mostly simple and reasonable structures, but also some unnecessarily complicated ones. My project submission had only four directories (suncerity.client, suncerity.server, suncerity.db, and javadoc), but your directory structure is determined by how you package the classes. Don't be ingenious; just be practical. If you need more than four directories, it could raise a red flag for the evaluator. It might indicate that you can't organize your classes and perhaps your solution is overengineered. There is no magic number of directories, but if you have more than four, I recommend rethinking the structure so that it is more compact.

The database.bin Database File

Sun supplies a binary database file named database.bin that you must return with the rest of your project submission. You can place this file anywhere you like, as long as the application can find it. I recommend placing it in the root directory to make the file access code simpler. If you put the database.bin file somewhere else, just make sure the pathing parameters to the file access code are right: Use / for Unix and let the software take care of translating to a backslash on Windows. My application determined the delimiter at runtime, so the delimiter character didn't matter in my case. Whatever your approach, just be sure you don't make the mistake of writing code that can find the file in one place on your system, but can't find the same file on the evaluator's machine because you packaged it differently.

Documentation

Four documentation pieces should be in the JAR file: the README.TXT file, the DESIGN_CHOICES.TXT document, the full javadoc set, and a user help Web page. In your javadoc documentation, be sure to use the special comment tags—starting with /** and ending with */—in your source code so that the javadoc program can process the code to produce HTML-formatted documentation. Creating javadoc comments is part of the assignment, so make sure you use regular javadoc conventions.

Javadoc

Depending on your design, the number of files javadoc generates vary. In my case, I had 100 javadoc files. If your application is clean, you should have about 10 source files. Certainly, you can add lots of functionality, resulting in 20 source files and several hundred javadoc files. However, you will lose points with this approach. Instead, strive to design an elegant and clean application that meets the requirements. Be warned: Adding functionality that doesn't satisfy a specific requirement is inviting trouble. Doing so raises questions about your ability to follow simple instructions, and the extra functionality could introduce errors that cost you points.

User Help

Another document you need to supply is the user help file, which should be a Web page. You can include it in the JAR file or simply hard-code the URL in the client to the Web page hosted somewhere else on the Internet; there are merits to both methods. The local file is faster and just as easy to include as it is to include the README.TXT file. The online reference method means there is one fewer file to include in the JAR file. You can assume that the evaluator has access to the Internet.

The user help document should be a Web page. It can be included in your project submission or hosted on a Web site, in which case the client should be able to view it from a menu.

Neglecting to provide user help costs points that are so easy to earn. Also, don't rely on users viewing help with their favorite browsers. You should provide a window (for example, a JTextPane in a JScrollPane) for it.

README and DESIGN_CHOICES

As mentioned in Chapter 1, "Certification Steps and Submission Grading," you must create a README.TXT file and a DESIGN_CHOICES.TXT document. Chapter 5, "Documentation and Javadoc Comments," provides a thorough explanation and an example of both files.

Deprecated Classes and Other Items

In the transition from Java 1 to the current SDK 1.4, the libraries have changed. In some cases, the signatures remained the same, but in other cases, they have changed. These revisions to the standard library resulted in some classes, variables, and methods becoming outdated. Sun keeps these outdated items in the library to support older programs, but refers to them as *deprecated*. Deprecated methods should not be used in new code, but Sun did sneak a few into the assignment intentionally to see what you would do about them. They aren't hard to fix, and every time you compile the classes they are in, you see the deprecated message. Also, the javadoc API documentation provides a convenient listing of deprecated items and marks them in the class documentation.

You can modify these deprecated methods or override them in a subclass. I chose the latter approach and justified it in the DESIGN_CHOICES.TXT document by arguing that the legacy code would still work in previous uses, and the new subclass isolates the changes for better maintenance going forward. Either approach is fine, but you have to justify your choice.

Need to Know More?

 http://suned.sun.com/US/certification/java/java_devj2se.html—This page lists the SCJD certification objectives.

 http://java.sun.com/products/jlf/ed1/dg/higtoc.nf .htm—The official Java look and feel design document.

 http://java.sun.com/docs/—This site is where you can download the Java API documentation in javadoc-generated form as an example of what your javadoc documentation should look like.

Code Clarity

Terms you'll need to understand:

✓ Code clarity
✓ Whitespace
✓ Javadoc

Techniques you'll need to master:

✓ Writing code that is easy to read and maintain
✓ Identifying sections of code that require comments to explain
  the code's purpose

In this chapter, you review the principles and practices that make code easy to read; this topic is referred to as *code clarity*. One aspect of being a strong developer is writing clean code. The compiler ignores whitespace, so it is happy to process code that has proper syntax but might be so ugly few people would care to read or work with it.

The justification for spending extra time on the project's readability comes from the assignment instructions, which highlight having a clear design that should be readily understood by junior programmers. Sun prefers a simple design to a complex one, even if the complex one is a little more efficient. Also, using custom algorithms when standard solutions are well known will be penalized. The code itself should be as clear as possible. Although "obvious" comments should be avoided, be sure that complex code has descriptive comments. For more information on this topic, please see Appendix C, "Code Conventions."

General Principles

The primary reason developers should write clean code is so that it can be read and understood easily. If the code is readable, the next person working on the code, including the original author at a later date, will be more efficient. This principle is similar to a well thought-out plan improving the result in all endeavors. When the code is clean, it acts as a mini-plan, illustrating the logic to an algorithm. If you can't simply read down the page without getting lost, the code is considered "dirty." In rare cases, dirty and clumsy code might work, but poorly styled code is most often a sign of poorly designed code, the bane of a developer shop.

Whatever style and convention you choose, just be consistent. Don't change from class to class.

Good style itself doesn't actually affect application performance directly. You can strip code of extra whitespace, and it will recompile fine and run at the same speed as before. In fact, it will compile faster (but not run faster). However, while having a standard filing system makes dealing with paperwork more efficient, using a standard style makes it easier to work with your code. Therefore, you should strive to use a standard style for your application code.

The following short checklist helps ensure that your project submission looks clean and professional:

➤ Use one statement per line.

➤ Align related program parts.

➤ Be consistent with indenting and braces.

➤ Use enough vertical and horizontal whitespace.

➤ Don't use the tab character; use spaces instead.

➤ Comment empty body sections to avoid confusion.

➤ Use braces even when an `if`, `for`, or `while` loop has just one statement.

➤ Comments should have the same indenting as code.

➤ Comments should be spell checked.

➤ Eliminate obvious comments.

➤ Use one class per file (inner classes are okay).

➤ Use one exit from loops and methods.

➤ Don't repeat code; use a method instead.

➤ Avoid OS-dependent code, such as path delimiters and absolute paths (use relative paths).

➤ Don't use identifiers longer than 20 characters.

➤ Spell out the words in names; do not use abbreviations.

➤ Use names different enough from one another to avoid confusion.

➤ Don't differ names by letter case alone.

➤ Use meaningful names, except for loop increments, for which single-letter names such as `i` or `j` are acceptable.

➤ The names of all instance methods and fields start with a lowercase letter, and subsequent words within the method or field name are capitalized.

➤ Capitalize class names.

➤ Package names must be all lowercase letters.

➤ Boolean method names should begin with `is`.

➤ Use nouns when naming classes and variables.

➤ Use verb phrases for methods.

➤ Restrict the visibility of variables and other identifiers.

➤ Use constants (final) instead of variables whenever possible.

➤ Use meaningful default values.

➤ Use getxxx() and setxxx() methods for getting/setting field values.

Use the same style you'll find in the classes Sun supplies with the assignment download.

Naming Conventions

More than anything else, names give meaning to code. I recommend telling a little story with your code. The nouns are the variable names, and the verbs are the method names. The following example uses a fictitious situation, but it illustrates the point:

English:

```
Jack and Jill went up the hill,
To fetch a pail of water;
```

Java:

```java
public class JackJillStory
{
    String maleActor = "Jack ";
    String femaleActor = "Jill ";
    String pailContents = "empty ";
    String location = "hill ";
    String direction = "went up ";
    String story = "";

    public static void main(String[] args)
    {
        JackJillStory jackNjill = new JackJillStory();
        jackNjill.fillPail("water");
        jackNjill.story = jackNjill.getStory();
        jackNjill.tellStory(jackNjill.story);
    }

    void tellStory(String story)
    {
            System.out.println(story);
    }

    String getStory()
    {
            String tale = maleActor
                    + femaleActor
                    + direction
                    + location
```

```
                    + "to fetch a pail of "
                    + getPail();

        return tale;
    }

    void fillPail(String contents)
    {
        pailContents = contents;
    }

    String getPail()
    {
        return pailContents;
    }
}
```

This example clearly demonstrates how good use of names tells a story. In real life, other people should be able to read your code like a story, even if it is obscure poetry.

Table 4.1 offers good examples of how to follow standard Java naming conventions for the main items in Java that need a name, including the package, classes, methods, method parameters, and fields. These names are from the J2SE 1.4 Software Development Kit (SDK) source code.

Table 4.1 Good Examples of Identifier Names		
Code Item	Example	Purpose
Package	**java.util.logging**	These classes and interfaces compose Java's core logging facilities.
Class	**Level**	The **Level** class defines a set of standard logging levels that can be used to control logging output. There are logging **Level** objects that are ordered and specified by ordered integers. Enabling logging at a given level also enables logging at all higher levels.
Method	**getLocalizedName()**	Return the localized string name of the **Level** object (mentioned previously) for the current default locale.
Method parameter	**Level(String name, int value, String resourceBundle Name)**	A constructor that creates a named **Level** object with a given integer value and a given localization resource name.
Field	**SEVERE**	This message level indicates a serious failure.

The following example is adapted from the Level class in the J2SE 1.4 SDK
and demonstrates how to use good names and comments throughout. It is
the same class that provided the preceding name examples. Most of the
source code in the SDK is done professionally, as shown in the following
example. I removed much of the code for space reasons, but you can see how
clear this class is and how well it is commented. Although the following code
is incomplete and will not compile, I recommend running javadoc against it
and looking at the resulting documents.

```
/*
 * @(#)Warning.java     1.10 3/21/2003
 *
 * Copyright blah blah
 */


package mypackage;
import java.util.ResourceBundle;

/**
 * The Warning class defines a set of warning levels that
 * can be used to for event monitoring.
 * <p>
 * Normal usage is:Warning.SEVERE.
 *
 *
 * @version 1.10, 02/25/02
 * @since 1.4
 */
public class Warning implements java.io.Serializable
{
    private static java.util.ArrayList known = new java.util.ArrayList();
    private static String defaultBundle = "sun.util.logging.resources.
➥logging";

    /**
     * SEVERE is a warning level indicating a serious failure.
     * <p>
     * In general, SEVERE messages should describe events that are
     * of considerable importance and that will prevent normal
     * program execution. They should be reasonably intelligible
     * to end users and to system administrators.
     * This Warning is initialized to <CODE>1000</CODE>.
     */
    public static final Warning SEVERE = new Warning("SEVERE",1000,
➥defaultBundle);

    /**
     * Create a named Warning with a given integer value and a
     * given localization resource name.
     * <p>
     * @param name the name of the Warning, for example "SEVERE".
     * @param value an integer value for the Warning.
     * @param resourceBundleName name of a resource bundle to use in
     *    localizing the given name (can be null).
     */
    protected Warning(String name, int value, String resourceBundleName) {
        this.name = name;
        this.value = value;
        this.resourceBundleName = resourceBundleName;
```

```
        synchronized (Warning.class)
        {
            known.add(this);
        }
    }

    /**
     * Return the localized string name of the Warning for
     * the current default locale.
     * <p>
     * If no localization information is available, the
     * non-localized name is returned.
     *
     * @return localized name
     */
    public String getLocalizedName()
    {
        try
        {
            ResourceBundle rb =
➡ResourceBundle.getBundle(resourceBundleName);
            return rb.getString(name);
        } catch (Exception ex)
        {
            return name;
        }
    }

    /**
     * Generate a hashcode.
     * @return a hashcode based on the Warning value
     */
    public int hashCode()
    {
        return this.value;
    }
}
```

 Unfortunately, many candidates get overzealous and comment everything. You will lose points if you do this, however.

Code Conventions

Programming in Java consists of writing source code, but the conventions used vary widely. For the most part, Sun has done a better job of educating its developer community about the guts of Java and even which code style to use than most vendors have in the past. For example, Microsoft has always had a strong developer community because it has treated them well. Visual Basic created a buzz when it first came out. However, Microsoft wasn't clear about code style in those days and still could do better. Sun can't compete with Windows developer tool GUIs, but it is much better about supplying code convention instructions.

The following example shows the two most common brace conventions. Most of the code in the SDK, Sun's documentation, and the Web site follow the second convention. I prefer the first one, so that is how you will find code in this book.

```
1]   if (x < y)        Good: Easy to match braces.
     {                 Bad: Dilutes lines of code measurement.
         x = y;            Number of lines is a scarce
         y = 0;            resource on the monitor.
     }

2]   if (x < y){       Good: No wasted lines.

         x = y;        Bad: Hard to match braces.
         y = 0;
     }
```

Statements

Statements are the equivalent of sentences. It is hard to make a mistake with them, but I've seen it done. Be consistent with the style you choose.

Simple Statements

The following are examples of simple statements:

```
/**
 * Constant for the maximum height of flight possible.
 */
public static final int MAXIMUM_FLIGHT_HEIGHT = 50000;

char ch = seq.charAt(i);
```

Compound Statements

Statements that combine more than one method call or more than one assignment or condition test are compound statements. The following is an example:

```
int c = ASCII.toLower(seq.charAt(i+j));
```

return Statements

The two most important ideas to keep in mind when you write your return statements are to avoid using more than one in each method and to avoid making assignments in the return statement. Some developers think you should minimize expressions and simply pass a variable that was assigned before the return statement. The following example shows a complex return statement:

```
return ((ch-lower)|(upper-ch)) < 0
       && next.match(matcher, i+1, seq);
```

if, if-else, and if else-if else Statements (Conditional)

The if statement can vary from simple to very complex, with nested if and loop statements inside it. Sometimes the nesting is several levels deep, so using good indents, braces, and comments is important. You might want to comment at the closing brace if it ends especially complicated code. The following are a few snippets from java.util.regex.Pattern to demonstrate how Sun uses common Java statements and blocks including for, while, and try in the J2SE 1.4 SDK:

```
if (not)
{
    return new NotSingle(ch);
}else
{
    return new Single(ch);
}

if (!matchLimited || matchList.size() < limit - 1) {
    String match = input.subSequence(index, m.start()).toString();
    matchList.add(match);
    index = m.end();
} else if (matchList.size() == limit - 1) { // last one
    String match = input.subSequence(index,
                             input.length()).toString();
    matchList.add(match);
    index = m.end();
}

if (matchRoot instanceof Slice) {
    root = BnM.optimize(matchRoot);
    if (root == matchRoot) {
        root = new Start(matchRoot);
    }
} else if (matchRoot instanceof Begin
    || matchRoot instanceof First) {
    root = matchRoot;
} else {
    root = new Start(matchRoot);
}
```

for Statements

The following two examples of the for statement are easy to read:

```
NEXT:      for (i = patternLength; i > 0; i--)
           {
               // j is the beginning index of suffix being considered
               for (j = patternLength - 1; j >= i; j--)
               {
                   // Testing for good suffix
                   if (src[j] == src[j-i])
                   {
                       // src[j..len] is a good suffix
                       optoSft[j-1] = i;
                   } else
                   {
```

```
                    // No match. The array has already been
                    // filled up with correct values before.
                    continue NEXT;
                }
            }
        }

for (int index=0; index<groupSize; index++)
{
    char c1 = seq.charAt(i+index);
    char c2 = seq.charAt(j+index);
    if (c1 != c2)
    {
        c1 = Character.toUpperCase(c1);
        c2 = Character.toUpperCase(c2);
        if (c1 != c2)
        {
            c1 = Character.toLowerCase(c1);
            c2 = Character.toLowerCase(c2);
            if (c1 != c2)
            {
                return false;
            }
        }
    }
}

//another example of a quick for loop
for (int j = 0; j < len; j++)
{
    if (buf[j] != seq.charAt(i+j))
    {
        return false;
    }
}
```

while Statements

The following examples show easy-to-read while statements:

```
while(read() != '}')
{
    //do something
}

while(Character.getType(c) == Character.NON_SPACING_MARK)
{
    i++;
    if (i >= patternLength)
    {
        break;
    }
    c = normalizedPattern.charAt(i);
    sequenceBuffer.append(c);
}
```

do-while Statements

The following is an example of how you should format your do-while statements:

```
do
{
    Object current = iterator.next();
    if (current.equals(target))
    {
      break;
    } else
    {
      tests++;
    }
} while (iterator.hasNext());
```

switch Statements

The following two switch statements illustrate proper style:

```
switch(ch)
{
    case '0':
    case '1':
    case '2':
    case '3':
    case '4':
    case '5':
    case '6':
    case '7':
    case '8':
    case '9':
        int newRefNum = (refNum * 10) + (ch - '0');
        // Add another number if it doesn't make a group
        // that doesn't exist
        if (groupCount - 1 < newRefNum)
        {
            done = true;
            break;
        }
        refNum = newRefNum;
        read();
        break;
    default:
        done = true;
        break;
}

int ch = peek();
for (;;)
{
    switch (ch)
    {
            case 'i':
            flags &= ~CASE_INSENSITIVE;
```

```
        break;
    case 'm':
        flags &= ~MULTILINE;
        break;
    case 's':
        flags &= ~DOTALL;
        break;
    case 'd':
        flags &= ~UNIX_LINES;
        break;
    case 'u':
        flags &= ~UNICODE_CASE;
        break;
    case 'c':
        flags &= ~CANON_EQ;
        break;
    case 'x':
        flags &= ~COMMENTS;
        break;
    default:
        return;
    }
    ch = next();
}
```

try-catch-finally Statements

The following is a try-catch-finally construct that is easy to read:

```
try
{
        statements;
} catch (ExceptionOneClass e)
{
        statements;
} catch (ExceptionTwoClass e)
{
        statements;
} finally
{
        statements;
}
```

Code Structure

The following sections describe aspects of code structure and style that are often overlooked. It doesn't take much effort to follow a consistent and easy-to-understand organization, so I recommend the following ideas for your consideration.

Package Organization

This section explains how to package your classes for submitting your project. You should have only two, three, or at most four directories. More than that, and the evaluator will think you complicated your design needlessly. For example, you could use the following three packages:

```
suncertify.client
suncertify.dbatabase
suncertify.server
```

File Organization

Your filenames should clearly indicate the purpose of files in your project. For example, I added the following three classes to my project. The names alone are enough to explain what they do:

```
suncertify.db.Database
suncertify.db.DatabaseFactory
suncertify.db.LockManager
```

Be sure to group classes together by functionality.

Code Comments

Make sure you comment your code where it isn't clear what is happening. Don't go too far with this, however, and add trivial comments. If the reader needs more than 20 seconds to understand a piece of code, explain it in a succinct comment. Throughout your project, use a mix of inline, trailing, end-of-line, and javadoc comments. The point total for comments in the grading portion of the instructions understates how much poorly commented code can affect your overall grade.

Javadoc

Chapter 5, "Documentation and Javadoc Comments," explains how to use comments in your project so that you get high marks for the documentation portion of your grade.

You must be careful to read the javadoc comments in Sun's supplied code for requirements and hints. At least one requirement is buried in there (hint: tracking the client ID for locking and unlocking database records).

Need to Know More?

 Vermeulen, Ambler et al. *The Elements of Java Style*. Boston, MA: Cambridge University Press, 2000 (ISBN 0-521-77768-2).

 http://java.sun.com/docs/codeconv/html/CodeConvTOC.doc.html—This document contains Sun's Style Guide.

 http://www.cs.cornell.edu/Courses/cs211/2001fa/handouts/javastyle. html—This document contains Cornell's Style Guide.

 http://www.javaranch.com/style.jsp—At this site, you can view the JavaRanch Java Programming Style Guide.

Documentation and Javadoc Comments

. . . .

Terms you'll need to understand:

✓ Design choices
✓ Javadoc

Techniques you'll need to master:

✓ Writing javadoc comments in Java source code files
✓ Making key design decisions and justifying them
✓ Writing a README.TXT file to be included in your project

In this chapter, you review the documentation required for a successful project submission. Documentation is often the last thing a developer thinks about; however, documentation, or a lack of it, affects a product's useability, acceptance, and effectiveness. Good documentation increases user understanding and, in this case, your grade.

There is no reason to lose points on this portion of the assignment. The documentation is part of development. Many developer shops don't think of it that way, but the best ones integrate documentation development with software development. For your project, you need to inform the evaluator of how you designed your solution and demonstrate that you know how to document code properly. There are two parts to this requirement. The first part is the javadoc comments that go in your source code. The second part requires three documents: the README.TXT file, the DESIGN_DECISIONS.TXT document, and user help.

Javadoc Comments

Javadoc is the Sun Microsystems tool (http://java.sun.com/j2se/javadoc) for generating application programming interface (API) documentation in HTML format from document comments in source code. In the code, you use special comment characters—starting with /** and ending with */—to indicate that the javadoc tool should process the comment to produce HTML-formatted documentation.

Writing javadoc comments can become an entire project in itself, and you need to be thorough because Sun does review code comments. There are several approaches to javadoc commenting. You do not have to worry about it, however. Just be sure to add comments that are enclosed in the multiline comment for every major declaration. The text is written in HTML and must precede a class, field, constructor, or method declaration. These comments are structured as a description followed by special javadoc tags, such as @param, @return, and @see.

Javadoc comments are part of your grade, so don't be shy about commenting your code. Every class and method should be commented in such a way that the javadoc tool can grab it. To see how to do this please refer to Sun's guidelines on writing javadoc comments in code at http://java.sun.com/j2se/javadoc/writingdoccomments/index.html. For detailed reference material on Javadoc tags please refer to http://java.sun.com/j2se/javadoc/index.html#javadocdocuments. The following is an example of how to comment a method that results in proper javadoc documentation:

```
/**
 * Returns a Blob object that represents a customer.
 * The id argument must specify a single customer. The last_name
 * argument is a description that will be displayed later.
 * <p>
 * This method will either return a Blob or a null if the
 * Blob doesn't exist.
 *
 * @param  id        the customer unique identifier
 *         last_name the customer's last name
 * @return       the customer Blob
 * @see          Blob
 */
public Blob getBlob(int id, String last_name)
{
    try
    {
        Blob blob = getCustomer(id);
        if(blob != null)
        {
            blob.setLastName(last_name);
            return blob;
        }
    } catch (NoBlobException e)
    {
        return null;
    }
}
```

You can also check your comments with a tool at Sun called DocCheck. It will give you a report describing style and tag errors in your source code. The home page is http://java.sun.com/j2se/javadoc/doccheck/index.html.

The README.TXT File

You must create a single text file (in plain ASCII format; word processor formats are unacceptable) called README.TXT and place it in the root directory of your project. Make sure you include the following information:

➤ The exact SDK version you used, including the platform you worked on. You can get this information by using the java -version command.

➤ Explain how to run the programs. You must provide exact command-line instructions. If any environmental setup is required, be sure to include instructions on how to perform the setup. For example, do not say something like "Add server.jar to your classpath." You should document exactly how to add the JAR file to the classpath. Also, perhaps you will require scripts to set up the environment and run the application. If you do use scripts, be sure your instructions tell the evaluator how to run the application using these scripts. Note that your program must run correctly, no matter what directory it is installed in.

➤ The location of your database file (for example, database.bin). It should be in the install directory, not a subdirectory.

➤ The location of your design choices document.

➤ The names of the files you have submitted, a note specifying their location in the directory structure, and a short description of each one's purpose.

Each project's README.TXT file will differ. However, they should all follow the order given in the preceding list. Some people put too much information in this file. One common mistake is to confuse this file with the design choices document. Don't explain how or why you did things here. Also, don't bother explaining any problems you had with configuration issues.

Make sure the README.TXT file is in the root directory, not in a subdirectory. This is such a simple instruction that if you don't follow it, the evaluator will get a bad impression from the start.

The following example shows the complete contents of a README.TXT file. Can someone quickly run your application by reading the first few lines? This file should be especially concise and the sections arranged in the correct order.

README FILE

SUPER BOWL README FILE

Candidate: Firstname Lastname

Date: March 10, 2004

TABLE OF CONTENTS

1. Quick Start

2. Introduction

3. SDK Version and Platform

4. Execution Instructions

5. Location of Data File

6. Design Choices Document

7. File Listing

8. User Documentation Web Page

1. Quick Start

1.1 Local Mode:
```
java myPackage.client.SuperBowlClient -dbpath database.bin
```

1.2 Remote Mode:
JVM #1:
```
java myPackage.server.DatabaseRMIServer -host localhost
➥-port 1234 -dbpath database.bin
```

JVM #2:
```
java myPackage.client.SuperBowlClient -host localhost -port 1234
```

2. Introduction

Thank you for your efforts toward grading this submission. This submission used the Java 2 SDK development environment for building the Super Bowl Reservation application, and components were written in the Java programming language (Java 2 SDK, Standard Edition Version 1.4.1) to be deployed on the Java platform.

The RMI portion of this submission allows the user to access the database remotely. RMI was chosen for its maturity over plain sockets, as is evidenced by the fact that RMI is built on sockets. The RMI parts do not provide a graphical user interface.

3. SDK Version and Platform

The SDK version used for this project was 1.4. The following is detailed information on the exact Java version:
```
java version "1.4.1"
```
```
Java(TM) 2 Runtime Environment, Standard Edition (build 1.4.1-b21)
```
```
Java HotSpot(TM) Client VM (build 1.4.1-b21, mixed mode)
```

This project was developed and tested using Windows 2000. The following details the exact operating system information:

```
Microsoft Windows 2000

5.00.2195

Service Pack 2
```

This project was developed and tested on a Dell laptop. The following details the exact hardware information:

```
Dell Inspiron 8000 Laptop

Pentium III 900MHz

15 inch UXGA screen

256MB SDRAM

32MB DDR 4xAGP NVIDIA GeForce 2 Go

20GB HD
```

4. Execution Instructions

There are two ways to run the Super Bowl Reservation application: in stand-alone mode and in networked mode. In either mode, please change the current working directory to the install directory before executing commands. After successfully starting the client, you should see a GUI with buttons on the left and a table in the middle.

4.1 Standalone Mode

In standalone mode, you need to start only one JVM to run the client application.

4.1.1 Start the Server in Local Mode

The server is not used in local mode.

4.1.2 Start the Client in Local Mode

Change the directory to the install directory and run the following command:

```
java myPackage.client.SuperBowlClient -dbpath database.bin
```

or

```
java myPackage.client.SuperBowlClient -dbpath $ROOT\database.bin
```

Where:

```
$ROOT=install directory
```

```
The path separator is "\" for Windows, but "/" for Unix.
```

4.2 Network Mode

In network mode, you need to start the server in one JVM and the client in another JVM.

4.2.1 Start the Server with No Parameters

To start the server without parameters, run the following command:

```
java myPackage.server.DatabaseRMIServer
```

If you start the server without parameters, the following conditions are assumed:

```
HOST=localhost
```

```
PORT=1099
```

```
DBPATH=$ROOT\database.bin
```

```
$ROOT=install directory
```

4.2.2 Start the Server with Parameters

You can start the server with parameters. The parameter pairs can be in any order, but all three pairs are required, like so:

```
-host {HOST} -port {PORT} -dbpath {DBPATH}
```

For example:

```
java myPackage.server.DatabaseRMIServer -host localhost
➥-port 1234 -dbpath database.bin
```

After successfully starting the server, you should see a confirmation message.

4.2.3 Start the Client with Parameters

After the server has been started, you can start the client in network mode. This requires two parameter pairs. The pairs can be in any order, but both pairs are required. Notice that the parameter pairs used to start the client must match exactly the parameter pairs used to start the server, like so:

```
-host {HOST} -port {PORT}
```

For example:

```
java myPackage.client.SuperBowlClient -host localhost -port 1234
```

5. Location of Data File

The data file, database.bin, used for this assignment is located under the install directory. You can specify the location of the database.bin file, assuming it is in the installed location, with the following statement:

```
-dbpath database.bin
```

Or you can provide the entire path, like so (using "\" for Windows, or "/" for Unix):

```
-dbpath $ROOT\database.bin
```

6. Design Choices Document

The design choices document is located in the install directory under the name DESIGN_DECISIONS.TXT.

7. File Listing

The following list outlines the contents of the Super Bowl Reservation application directory, as well as the purpose of each directory or file:

```
Install_Directory
    README.TXT                 This document
    DESIGN_DECISIONS.TXT       The major design decisions
    database.bin               The database file
    instructions.html          The instructions
    userHelp.html              Help file for the GUI
    + myPackage                Contains all the object class files
      +- client                All the client class files
         SuperBowlClient        The application GUI
      +- server                All the server (RMI) class files
         DatabaseRemote         Database decorator for remote operation
         DatabaseRemoteServer   Registers object for remote mode
      +- database              All the database related classes
         Database               Provides database services
         DatabaseException      General exception object for application
         DatabaseFactory        Generates local or remote database
         DatabaseInterface      Methods for local-remote modes
         LockManager            Insert Row Locking
    + source                   Contains all the Java source files
```

```
+- client              All the client source files
+- server              All the server (RMI) source files
+- database            All the database source files
+ javadoc              Directory for documentation
+- index.html          javadoc start
```

8. User Documentation Web Pages

The user documentation can be viewed from the client menu under HELP or directly at Install_Directory/userHelp.html.

Design Choices Document

You must also provide a file documenting your major design choices and the reasons for those choices. Most candidates write this file in ASCII format. However, you can submit a Microsoft Word file with UML diagrams, which the evaluator will appreciate. The two most important topics you must include are whether you chose Remote Method Invocation (RMI) versus serialized objects over TCP socket connections and whether you modified or subclassed the supplied Data class. Chapter 1, "Certification Steps and Submission Grading," discussed additional topics you could include, although none of them are required. I recommend carefully reading the section of your instructions that explains how the assignment is graded. The point items listed in that section are the key factors evaluators will be looking for. Why not make it easy for them to give you full credit by explaining what you did?

The following example of a design choices document gives you a good idea of what to write in yours and what style to use as you explain your thinking. To maintain Sun's confidentiality requirement, you need to adapt the DESIGN_DECISIONS.TXT file shown here, as you will have to do with all examples in this book. I follow this philosophy throughout the book, but it gets tricky when I show you code in later chapters. We should be able to share a lot of information as we help each other. Isn't that what Sun and third-party SCJP mock exams do—give away details about the exams? It is a horse race. If Sun doesn't keep changing the exams, the mock exam folks get so close to the real exam that the certification's value diminishes. Conversely, if we aren't told what is on the exam, too few developers take and pass the exam, and the certification's value never increases.

Most of the items discussed in your design decisions document apply to a variety of applications. The evaluator wants to know whether you understand why you designed your solution the way you did.

Super Bowl Reservation System
Table of Contents

1. Design Decisions

1.1 Design Decisions Summary

➤ Chose RMI over serialized objects instead of sockets.

➤ Extended the supplied class instead of modifying it.

➤ Didn't modify method signatures in supplied classes; rather, I overrode them in a subclass.

➤ Subclassed the supplied class to Database, whose name is better for its responsibilities.

➤ Implemented on-the-fly local database switching.

➤ Relied on RMI distributed garbage collection for releasing stale locks.

➤ Used Factory, MVC, and Adapter patterns.

➤ Implemented single DatabaseInterface for both local and remote database operations.

➤ Implemented separate LockManager class.

➤ Provided online help.

The following is an architecture snapshot of the Super Bowl Reservation system:

➤ *Supplied classes*—Unchanged from the original download.

➤ *DatabaseInterface*—Defines all public methods used in the Database class.

➤ *DatabaseRemote*—This is the same as Database, except it uses a LockManager for multiuser operation.

1.2 Modifying Versus Extending the Data Class

I created a new subclass of Data called Database. I extended the Data class to maintain legacy compatibility with the Data class, to cleanly separate the new functionality and the changes from the original Data class, and to use a new name that seems more descriptive of the class responsibilities. The Database class, which is a subclass of Data, is responsible for being a more complete database, providing access to a single local database file, and comprising reading, writing, and searching facilities. Two methods in Data use deprecated code, which might be required for legacy applications, but are overridden in the Database subclass.

1.3 Separate LockManager Class

I implemented a separate LockManager class that allows Insert Row Locking (IRL) so that if two clients attempt to perform the sequence lock-read/modify/write-unlock concurrently, both modification attempts will be handled correctly. The LockManager class provides consistent and concurrent access to data in a multiuser environment (RMI). Because IRL is necessary only in remote mode, not in local mode, it makes better sense to implement it as a separate LockManager class. Locks prevent simultaneous updates of the same row of data. With a separate lock manager, only one user at a time can update a row of data. So while one user is reserving a seat for a given game, another user can't do the same thing. Without a good lock manager, users could overwrite each other's seat reservations, giving the impression that someone can sell the same seat to more than one person.

The row is locked by a given client ID. The adapter for Database (DatabaseRemote) has a one-to-one relationship with a single client, so the client ID is the reference to DatabaseRemote. In the LockManager class, the client ID is referred to with a WeakReference. That way, should another client try to lock a record previously locked by a client who has died, the LockManager removes the lock because the garbage collector will have nullified that reference. The responsibility for record locking is kept in the LockManager, and the responsibility for references to dead objects stays with the JVM, a clean separation of responsibilities.

DatabaseRemote is a wrapper around Database that implements the same interface (DatabaseInterface), but changes Database's local, single-user semantics into networked, multiuser semantics by implementing locking with the help of a LockManager class.

1.4 RMI Versus Sockets Communication

In the remote connection mode, I use a proxy pattern to design the socket connection. The DatabaseRemote_Stub class is the proxy for the client side. I chose RMI over sockets communication for the following reasons:

➤ Thread safety is built into RMI, whereas in sockets, multithreading issues need to be addressed.

➤ Sockets need a communication protocol that has to be custom defined, but RMI has RMP built in.

➤ RMI presents a simpler programming model over sockets.

➤ RMI supports dynamic class loading.

➤ RMI gives more scope for scalability. New objects can easily be introduced without requiring changes to the communication protocol.

➤ The socket technology is the foundation on which RMI is built, but RMI is more mature and using it is much simpler.

➤ RMI is a better standard, so it would be easy for other developers to understand the design for future development.

➤ Because remote objects appear local, method calls are completely type-safe.

➤ The Registry acts as a central lookup for finding various remote objects.

1.5 DatabaseRemote Implements All Public Methods of the Data Class

I chose to use one interface, DatabaseInterface, for both the local Database class and the remote DatabaseRemote class. This design is cleaner and reduces the chance of errors.

1.6 Search Function

The search method is abstracted so that it can return a DataInfo object containing all rows that have at least one value matching one criteria value. The column names and values are dynamic, so this method processes any number of criteria for any table, not just the one that came in the download. This is the algorithm used:

1. Parse the criteria string with StringTokenizer.

2. Get a new row of data from database.

3. Find the column that matches the criteria field name.

4. Test for a match between row value and search value.

5. If the values match, save the row of data and start at step 2 again for the next row.

6. If there's no match for the current criteria, go to the next criteria and start at step 3.

7. When the criteria are exhausted, start at step 2 again for the next row.

The search method uses java.util.StringTokenizer to parse the search criteria. This class breaks Strings into chunks at the delimiters. The requirements made the search criteria String simple, so I stayed with the StringTokenizer. I would have chosen the regular expression route if the input search String had been more complicated.

1.7 Single Interface for Both Remote and Local Network Modes

Because both Database and the DatabaseRemote adapter implement the same interface, DatabaseInterface, the client doesn't know whether the database is local or remote. The client has no local or remote specific code; it is all coded to the DatabaseInterface type, which defines one set of public methods for Database, the base class.

1.8. User Interface Designed for Ease of Use

The user interface is designed for ease of use following good Human/Computer Interaction (HCI) principles. For example, the user simply clicks on Games to select one for reservation. Also, the search feature is easy, with drop-down combo boxes to select stadium seats to search. It accomplishes this with Swing components, especially the JTable. It also uses menu bars, buttons, and tool tips set in a JSplitPane for a user-friendly window look and feel. There are other helpful features, such as table sorting. The user can sort the entire table by clicking on any column heading. The main interface uses the BorderLayout, with the status bar and connection bar in the south part. The left side of the main JSplitPane is another JSplitPane, which includes a reservation area in the upper part and a search panel in the lower part. The right side of the main JSplitPane is the main data output section of the user interface, which is the JTable. The BorderLayout is the main layout manager because it makes it easy to position components proportionately and it handles window resizes.

1.9 Coding Standards and Readability

Industry coding standards were followed to enhance code readability and reuse. I used conventional coding style, except that opening braces fall under the first letter of the declaration (also known as "West Coast style"). I packaged classes so that similar classes went into the same package. I used three packages: myPackage.database, myPackage.client, and myPackage.server.

1.10 Clarity and Maintainability

The application was designed for clarity and maintainability. For example, comments are thorough, but obvious code is not commented. Another example is the search method, designed so that it can be used on any table without code modification. Last, the command-line parser makes it very clear what the parameters are, so the user is less likely to get confused or make a mistake.

1.11 Documentation

The application is submitted with full documentation. The user can access a helpful Web page via the GUI. Because standard formatting conventions are used, the user can learn how to best use the application to reserve Super Bowl seats. For the evaluator, all source code has been documented thoroughly, and javadoc was used to generate a complete set of source documentation.

1.12 Exception Handling and Error Testing

The application has strong exception handling. For example, if a client locks a record in remote mode and then crashes, the application accurately releases the lock when the next lock is attempted on the same record. Also, the client is designed to reduce the possibility of user errors. For example, the user cannot type the Super Bowl number; he just clicks the Super Bowl row in the table instead. The user clicks the Super Bowl origin or destination to search for Super Bowls, so he cannot mistype it. Last, the user can type only the number of seats he wants. If the number is higher than the number of seats available, or the seats available equals zero, or the user doesn't type a number (accidentally types a letter, for example), the application kindly displays a message to the user describing the error, but no harm is done.

For most exceptions, the application cascades them up into a user-friendly message. In the remote connection mode, all exceptions happen in the server-side cascade, all the way to the ClientWindow object, so that the end user is shown the correct response or error message about the operation.

2. Design Patterns Used

The following are the design patterns used in the solution along with a specific explanation of how they were implemented.

2.1 Client Tier

2.1.1 Model-View-Controller Pattern

The following describes how the MVC pattern was used in this application:

➤ *Model*—SuperBowlTableModel, which extends AbstractTableModel.

➤ *View*—Swing GUI, including menus, buttons, combo boxes, and a JTable.

➤ *Controller*—Event methods and JTable-triggered code.

The JTable is set up to allow only row selection. Cell editing is forbidden to avoid confusion. Tool tips and a status bar keep the user informed.

2.1.2 Business Delegate Pattern

I used a Business Delegate pattern to reduce coupling between the presentation-tier client and the business service (remote database). This pattern hides the underlying implementation details of the business service, such as lookups, reads, and writes of data to the database. The Business Delegate acts as a client-side business abstraction; it provides an abstraction for, and therefore hides, the implementation of the business services.

2.1.3 Value Objects Pattern

The Value Objects pattern is used in this application to transfer data between business objects and clients across tiers. The actual value object is an object representing a row, or rows, of data from the database.

2.1.4 Connection Factory Pattern

The Factory pattern uses one class object (the factory) that returns references to objects of another class. This way, the factory class encapsulates management of the resource connection objects, allowing caching, object recycling, and other types of optimizations. Additionally, the Factory pattern separates the container's implementation from the Enterprise JavaBean (EJB) code, allowing the maximum degree of extensibility and scalability. These are the two parts of a factory pattern:

➤ *Factory*—DatabaseFactory

➤ *Object*—Database

2.2 Server Tier

2.2.1 Data Access Objects Pattern

I used a Data Access Object (DAO) pattern to abstract and encapsulate all access to the data source. The DAO manages the connection with the data source to obtain and store data. The DAO (Database) implements the access mechanism required to work with the data source. The data source is a persistent store (database.bin). The business component that relies on the DAO uses the simpler interface exposed by the DAO for its clients. The DAO completely hides the data source implementation details from its clients. Because the interface exposed by the DAO to clients does not change when the underlying data source implementation changes, this pattern allows the DAO to adapt to different storage schemes without affecting its clients or business components. Essentially, the DAO acts as an adapter between the component and the data source. When using the DAO, keep in mind the following patterns and which objects they represent:

➤ *Business Object*—GUI

➤ *Data Access Object*—Database

➤ *Value Object*—The classes representing database data

➤ *Data Source*—database.bin

2.2.2 Decorator Pattern

The Decorator pattern was used for the DatabaseRemote class, which decorates Database. The intent is to attach a responsibility to an object at runtime. Decorator is a flexible alternative to extending a class. Sometimes you want to add a responsibility to an object A, not its whole class. In this project, DatabaseRemote wraps Database and adds the responsibility of Insert Row Locking via a LockManager. The decorator (DatabaseRemote) implements Database's interface (DatabaseInterface). Database's clients can then interact with DatabaseRemote instead of Database.

User Help

The user help file is the easiest part of the documentation component. Some developers have used plain text and passed, but do a little more that that. Remember, this part of your project is for the users, so don't get technical. Just tell them what to click and in what order they should do so. Figure 5.1 illustrates user help for the project.

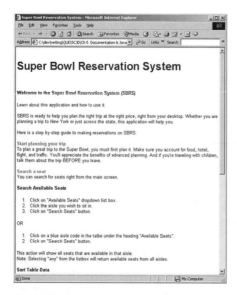

Figure 5.1   An example of user help.

The example in Listing 5.1 of user help code looks clean, is brief, and meets the requirements. Don't get fancy with too many images, although a screen-shot or two is fine.

Listing 5.1   A Sample Help File

```
<!--********************************************************************
XHTML tags that contain a trailing slash (e.g., <br />) are not
understood by the version of the JTextPane class used in the book
because it relies on the class javax.swing.text.html.HTMLEditorKit
which provides only HTML 3.2 support.
*********************************************************************-->
<!DOCTYPE HTML PUBLIC "-//W3C//DTD HTML 4.01 Transitional//EN">
<html>
<head>
<title>Super Bowl Reservation System</title>
<style type="text/css">
 body {
  background-color: #ffffff;
 }
span.c1 {color: #CC6600; font-family: Arial}
</style>
</head>
<body topmargin="0" leftmargin="0">
<table border="0"
       cellpadding="0"
       cellspacing="0"
       width="604">
<tr valign="top">
<td width="16">
<p> </p>
</td>
<td width="100%">

<h1>Super Bowl User Help</h1>
<strong>Welcome to the Super Bowl Reservation System
(SBRS)</strong>
<p>Learn about this application and how to use it.<br>
<br>
SBRS is ready to help you plan the right trip at the right
price, right from your desktop. If you are planning a
trip to the Super Bowl, this application will help
you.<br>
<br>
Here is a step-by-step guide to making reservations on
SBRS:<br>
<br>
<span class="c1"><strong>Start planning your
trip</strong></span><br>
To plan a great trip to the Super Bowl, you must first plan it.
Make sure you account for food, hotel, flight, and
traffic. You'll appreciate the benefits of advance
planning. And if you're traveling with children, talk to them
about the trip BEFORE you leave.<br>
<br>
<span class="c1"><strong>Search a seat</strong></span>
<br>
```

(continued)

Listing 5.1   A Sample Help File *(continued)*

```
You can search for seats right from the main screen.
<br><br>
<strong>Search Available Seats</strong></p>

<ol>
<li>
In the &quot;Search Seats&quot; area, select a Level in which you wish
to sit (or &quot;any&quot; to match all levels).</li>

<li>Select the Aisle in which you wish to sit (or &quot;any&quot; to
match all aisles).</li>

<li>
Click  the &quot;Search Seats&quot; button.
</li>
</ol>

<p>OR</p>

<ol>
<li>
In the table in the bottom half of the screen, you can click on
any Level or Aisle value to update the Level and Aisle values shown
in the Search Seats area.
</li>

<li>
Click  the &quot;Search Seats&quot; button.
</li>
</ol>

<p>Either set of steps will show all seats that match your criteria.</p>
<p><span class="c1"><strong>Reserve a seat</strong></span></p>
<ol>
<li>
If you don't immediately see the seat you want, please follow the
above instructions to search for seats that interest
you.
</li>

<li>
Click on a seat in the table. You can click anywhere in the row
corresponding to that seat.
</li>

<li>
This action will enter the seat number under the
&quot;Reserve Seats&quot; section in the upper left.
</li>

<li>
Now type in the number of seats you want to reserve.
Note that the maximum number of seats available is
displayed in parentheses to the immediate right of
&quot;How Many Seats.&quot;
</li>
```

(continued)

Listing 5.1   A Sample Help File *(continued)*

```
<li>
Click on the &quot;Reserve Seat&quot; button.
</li>

<li>
The number of seats you reserve will be deducted from
the &quot;Available&quot; column.
</li>
</ol>
<span class="c1"><strong>We're here if you need us</strong>
</span>
<br>
When you have questions, call us for the information
   you need.<br>  <br>
   Our customer support representatives are ready to assist
   you 24 hours a day, 7 days a week. Fill out our
    support and feedback form and we'll respond within 4
   hours, guaranteed. If you need immediate assistance, call
   us at (800) 555-6666 or (111) 555-0000.<br>  <br>
   <strong>Candidate</strong><br>
   <em>Alain Trottier</em><br>
   <em>Sun Certified Java Developer</em></td>
</tr>
</table>
</body>
</html>
```

Javadoc Code Comments

Javadoc documentation has been mentioned in previous chapters, but in this chapter, you see the five main uses of javadoc: file, class, method, field, and statement headers. Table 5.1 offers a quick review of the special tags that Javadoc pulls from the source comments and where you are likely to use these tags.

Table 5.1   Javadoc Tags

Tag	File	Package	Class	Method	Field
@author	X	X	X		
{@docRoot}	X	X	X	X	X
@deprecated		X	X	X	X
@exception				X	
{@inheritDoc}				X	
{@link}	X	X	X	X	X
{@linkplain}	X	X	X	X	X
@param				X	

(continued)

Table 5.1	Javadoc Tags *(continued)*				
Tag	File	Package	Class	Method	Field
@return				X	
@see	X	X	X	X	X
@serial		X	X		X
@serialData				X	
@serialField					X
@since	X	X	X	X	X
@throws				X	
{@value}					X
@version	X	X	X		
Custom					

The following list defines the tags shown in Table 5.1:

➤ @author—Adds an "Author-authorName" entry to the generated documents.

➤ {@docRoot}—Represents the relative path to the generated document's (destination) root directory from any generated page. Notice that this feature inserted an extra slash in J2SE 1.4.0 but has been fixed in 1.4.1.

➤ @deprecated—Adds a comment indicating that this API should no longer be used (even though it might continue to work).

➤ @exception—The @exception tag is a synonym for @throws.

➤ {@inheritDoc}—Inherits documentation from the nearest superclass into the current doc comment (broken in J2SE 1.4.0, but fixed in 1.4.1).

➤ {@link}—Inserts an inline link with a visible text label that points to the documentation for the specified package, class, or member name of a referenced class.

➤ {@linkplain}—Identical to {@link}, except the link's label is displayed in plain text instead of code font.

➤ @param—Adds a parameter to the "Parameters" section.

➤ @return—Adds a "Returns" section with the description text. This text should describe the return type and permissible range of values.

➤ @see—Adds a "See Also" heading with a link or text entry that points to the reference. A doc comment can contain any number of @see tags, which are all grouped under the same heading.

➤ `@serial`—Used in the doc comment for a default serializable field. An optional field description should explain the meaning of the field.

➤ `@serialData`—The data description documents the types and order of data in the serialized form.

➤ `@serialField`—Documents an `ObjectStreamField` component of a serializable class's `serialPersistentFields` member.

➤ `@throws`—Adds a "Throws" subheading to the generated documentation (same as `@exception`).

➤ `{@value}`—When used in a static field comment, it displays the value of the constant.

➤ `@version`—Adds a "Version" subheading with the specified version text to the generated docs.

 Be sure you add a javadoc comment header to every file, class, and method in your project's source code. You don't have to touch the supplied files unless you choose to modify instead of extend them.

The following are examples from the SDK source javadoc documentation. The majority of the javadoc comments go into what some call "block headers." The first one goes at the top of the file and describes the file. The rest are placed immediately preceding the declarations for the class, method, and field.

File Header

Each source file should begin with a multiline comment that mentions its purpose, author, and date. The following is an example of a package header javadoc comment:

j

Class Header

The following is an example of a class header javadoc comment from the SDK `WeakReference` class source:

```
/**
 * Weak reference objects, which do not prevent their
 * referents from being made finalizable, finalized, and
 * then reclaimed.  Weak references are most
 * often used to implement canonicalizing mappings.
 *
 * <p> Suppose that the garbage collector determines at a
```

```
* certain point in time that an object is
* <a href="package-summary.html#reachability">weakly
* reachable</a>.  At that time it will automatically clear
* all weak references to that object and all weak
* references to any other weakly reachable objects
* from which that object is reachable through a chain of
* strong and soft references.  At the same time, it will
* declare all the formerly weakly reachable objects to
* be finalizable.  At the same time or at some later time,
* it will enqueue those newly cleared weak references that
* are registered with reference queues.
*
* @author    some author
* @version   some date
* @since     1.2
*/
public class WeakReference extends Reference {
```

Method Header

The following is an example of a method header javadoc comment from the
SDK Pattern class source:

```
/**
* Compiles the given regular expression into a pattern
* with the given flags.  </p>
*
* @param  regex
*          The expression to be compiled
*
* @param  flags
*          Match flags, a bit mask that may include
*          {@link #CASE_INSENSITIVE},
*          {@link #MULTILINE}, {@link #DOTALL},
*          {@link #UNICODE_CASE}, and {@link #CANON_EQ}
*
* @throws  IllegalArgumentException
*          If bit values other than those corresponding
*          to the defined match flags are set in
*          <tt>flags</tt>
*
* @throws  PatternSyntaxException
*           If the expression's syntax is invalid
*/
public static Pattern compile(String regex, int flags){
    return new Pattern(regex, flags);
}
```

Field Header

The following is an example of a field header javadoc comment from the
SDK Pattern class source:

```
/**
* Enables case-insensitive matching.
*
* <p> By default, case-insensitive matching assumes
* that only characters in the US-ASCII charset are
```

```
 * being matched.  Unicode-aware case-insensitive
 * matching can be enabled by specifying the {@link
 * #UNICODE_CASE} flag with this flag.
 *
 * <p> Case-insensitive matching can also be enabled
 * via the embedded flag expression <tt>(?i)</tt>.
 *
 * <p> Specifying this flag could impose a slight
 * performance penalty.  </p>
 */
public static final int CASE_INSENSITIVE = 0x02;
```

Need to Know More?

 http://java.sun.com/j2se/javadoc/writingdoccomments/index.html— This page explains how to write doc comments for the javadoc tool.

 http://java.sun.com/j2se/javadoc/index.html—This is the definitive javadoc home page. If you want to know something about javadoc, start here.

 http://java.sun.com/j2se/javadoc/faq/index.html—This page is where you can find the javadoc FAQ.

 http://java.sun.com/j2se/1.4/docs/tooldocs/javadoc/doclet/index. html—You can find the javadoc doclet home page here. Doclets are used to modify how javadoc behaves.

Application Analysis and Design

. . . .

Terms you'll need to understand:

✓ Systems analysis methods
✓ Project management
✓ Requirements discovery
✓ Project management
✓ Use case analysis

Techniques you'll need to master:

✓ Learning the techniques for discovering and analyzing requirements
✓ Writing a Software Requirements Specifications document and its sibling, a Software Design Descriptions document
✓ Exercising effective project management techniques
✓ Understanding the tools and techniques of systems analysis
✓ Understanding the systems development life cycle
✓ Knowing how to document systems development techniques and methodologies
✓ Conducting use case analysis and writing a Software Requirements Specification according to accepted standards
✓ Using requirements to identify necessary classes and their relationships
✓ Performing simple systems planning, systems analysis, systems design, systems implementation, and systems support
✓ Performing database design and specification

In this chapter, you survey the methods and means of designing, building, and supporting computer systems. In particular, this chapter focuses on analysis and design of the certification assignment and how to meet the requirements in Sun's instructions. The entire process, from requirements analysis to implementation, is explained as it relates to this certification. The process of implementing code or system changes after careful analysis of problems and alternative solutions is also covered.

The assignment is modeled after a real software project. Therefore, you will do best if you manage your work accordingly. Some candidates just write code until their solution works. That might be enough, but you improve your chances for a great score if you design your application following industry best practices. Also, most candidates get the instructions and just start coding. Starting that way might be easier; however, it isn't the best approach. I recommend taking the time to follow the international standards mentioned in this book. They are well-established standards for software development and will improve your score. I especially recommend turning to the International Organization for Standardization (ISO) and Institute of Electrical and Electronics Engineers (IEEE) as the last word on software standards for the foreseeable future.

According to ISO and IEEE studies, the most common weakness of information technology (IT) projects in the software industry is lack of planning. Further, poor documentation is evidence of poor planning, so this chapter also emphasizes documentation, which is part of the assignment. You should complete a brief Software Requirements Specifications (SRS) document and its sibling, the Software Design Descriptions (SDD) document.

This chapter covers material normally not found in other certification books. Unfortunately, some candidates and authors do not think that formal analysis and design are necessary for this certification. This is a mistake. Worse, this attitude finds its way into development shops. I've seen many projects that lack accurate requirements analysis and design specifications. This attitude will catch up to those developers, however. Perhaps a little attention to the development phase in this chapter will demonstrate how big an impact it can have on a software project.

The assignment you download includes skeleton code and instructions that are much like a project charter. This charter isn't complete enough to code the solution, however. Like all projects, your assignment needs to be defined in more detail as the project moves from idea to reality. Professional shops don't just take an idea and start coding. To increase your chances of creating a successful solution, you need to plan the work carefully. This rule applies to the assignment as well as the rest of the software industry.

The instructions do provide a written roadmap defining the key issues and the general project deliverables. Because it is a single-developer project, there is no information about the project team's composition and the relationship of the project to the organization's strategic or operational goals, as you find in a commercial project.

Because computer systems have become so complex, advanced methods are required to figure them out. For example, support managers want an automated problem-tracking system to respond better to customer needs. This basic business need is easy to understand, but actually building something to meet the need is more difficult. As you go deeper into the solution, it becomes more difficult to know exactly what bytes to use and how to organize them for consistent, reliable, and accurate behavior.

This chapter introduces you to systematic analysis and development using contemporary methodology. This chapter just might be the most helpful in this book because it provides the overall assignment approach and context, which comes from experience alone. You can't figure out the approach and context just by sheer thinking; there are too many wrinkles in the real world of IT. Therefore, this chapter explains the nontechnical aspects and sets the stage for the techniques explained in the remainder of the book.

Several activities in this certification overlap many or all development phases during your project. For example, analysis is continual. Likewise, you need to conduct fact-finding, documentation, and project management throughout the assignment.

In an earlier project, I was part of a contractor team advising a client on designing a new system. The client was a B2B buyer-seller exchange. The team discovered that the client needs (that is, problems) involved much more than a new software system. The client had more than 100 software developers and designers. Why did it need a contractor? Because the client's development business unit was in disarray. We went beyond software and actually started redesigning the client's product development processes—going to the root of the client problem by fixing the process first. Only then would the contractor be able to make a lasting contribution. The contractor went on to redesign much of the client's software design, build, and deployment processes. This client would have benefited from better software development project management. This chapter discusses what defines effective software design and the larger information systems design.

Project Management

Programming in Java consists of more than writing source code; it also demands project management. Project management skills are in great demand in the IT community. Of all areas that need improvement in the software industry, project management is number one. The lack of project management or poorly executed project management has been responsible for most IT project failures. Compared to other industries, the IT record for completing projects satisfactorily (on schedule and under budget) is abysmal. The reports vary widely, but stating that 30% of IT projects fail completely and a higher percentage misses the mark are fair estimates. Can you imagine hearing such disappointing news about the automobile manufacturing? Your software development effort for this certification needs to do better than that. Project management is such a large topic that I could easily spend several chapters on it, but I've focused the discussion on reviewing the aspects of project management that apply to systems analysis and design for this certification.

When managing a software project, many activities need to be scheduled and monitored. Although the certification assignment is small enough for one person to complete in a few months, it is still large enough to benefit from project management techniques. This chapter contains some formal documents to help you design a successful solution. For example, use the requirements document to write a short list of actual requirements, such as needing a record-locking mechanism and a search-by-criteria algorithm.

 Approach this certification as a project and manage it that way. If you do, you will avoid costly mistakes that so many candidates have made in the past. For example, a project plan keeps you on schedule. It helps you stay focused and complete the certification on time instead of letting that achievement slip away.

Managing the Software Development Life Cycle

There are various standards for and approaches to managing software projects. Even though there is controversy around the software development life cycle, I recommend starting with the top standards. Arguably, the three most important software engineering standards are ISO 12207, ISO 9000-3, and ISO 15504. For this project, I have focused on ISO 12207 (proposed in 1988 and published in August 1995), the international standard on software life cycle processes. The idea behind this standard was to define the best practices for developing software, and it establishes a common international framework for acquiring, supplying, developing, operating, and maintaining software. ISO 12207 is broad in scope. For the certification, you need only concern yourself with the following list, which contains various aspects of ISO 12207 and explains how these aspects apply to the certification:

➤ *System requirements analysis*—This component defines and documents the requirements the system must meet. In your document, you should include information about functional requirements. For example, the solution services simultaneous users on the network.

➤ *System architectural design*—This component defines and documents systemwide design decisions. In your document, you should describe your system architecture, including Remote Method Invocation (RMI) or sockets communication between the client and the database while your application is in remote mode.

➤ *Software requirements analysis*—This component defines and documents your solution's functional characteristics and conditions for its acceptance. For example, you should mention that the solution has a JTable-based GUI.

➤ *Software detail design*—This component defines and documents details of the classes and methods that form your solution. You should mention that the Model-View-Controller (MVC) pattern is used for the GUI.

➤ *Software coding and testing*—This component defines and documents the coding conventions you use and how you conduct system and unit testing.

➤ *Software integration*—This component defines and documents unit integration and testing, which means integrating the classes into a complete application and testing the resulting software to ensure that it works together as intended. You need to answer the question "Does the database part of your solution work with the GUI part?"

➤ *System integration*—This component defines and documents how your solution will work on the network. You should explain how RMI or sockets allow the client to communicate with the database server.

➤ *Software acceptance test*—This component defines and documents the acceptance criteria. For your certification project, it could be a simple checklist noting that all major behavior is evident in the final solution. You can ask another person to try your solution by giving him or her this checklist.

The general order of development activities is the definition, design, implementation, and test phases. How you combine these steps and how strictly you follow the previous list of documents for your project are up to you. Regardless, documenting a brief plan for your assignment is a smart choice.

The Software Management Project Plan

One way to manage all these activities is with a Software Management Project Plan. This plan is the controlling document for managing a software project, as it defines all processes—technical and managerial—needed to deliver the project requirements. It specifies who is building what and when it is due. It provides the plan for a team, or just yourself, to translate the requirements into specifications and then actual code.

You will benefit from developing and recording plans for conducting the activities required to submit a successful solution. The following outline will help you do so, as it is a loose adaptation of the IEEE standard for Software Project Management Plans (1058):

1.   Scope and References

1.1   Scope: This part defines and documents an overview of the assignment, including goals and objectives, user needs, and the critical functionality. You need to mention that your solution provides an application written with J2SE 1.4 that is a two-tier, client/server architecture, in which the client allows the user to reserve seats and the database stores reservation transactions.

1.2   References: This part defines and documents the references found in the documentation. You can mention Sun materials and your favorite Web sites.

2.   Definitions: This part defines and documents the key terms used in the document. You can include a small glossary defining RMI, threads, and row-level locking, for example.

3.   Software Project Management Plans: This part defines and documents the project in a timeline format.

3.1   Introduction: This part is an overview of the project's purpose and general goals. You can mention the project description defined at the beginning of your instructions in the README.TXT file.

3.2   Project Organization: This part might not be useful in a small project, but it describes how the project is organized, including personnel and their roles.

3.3   Managerial Process: This part might not be useful in a small project, but it describes how the development work is managed.

3.4   Technical Process: This part might not be useful in a small project, but it describes the technical manner in which the build process is conducted (code, checked in source control, tested, deployed).

Systems Analysis

During systems analysis, you figure out what you need in terms of a system. For example, you need two machines to properly test your solution, and you need to know what software goes on these systems. You conduct systems analysis and design methods to develop your solution for this certification. Throughout the certification project, you review and modify the downloaded program. You code, test, debug, and install your new application before submitting it. All these activities are defined first in the project management plan. After you have an overall project management plan, you take the next step, which is analysis.

Before writing code, you need a clear understanding of the assignment requirements and design. As outlined in Chapter 1, "Certification Steps and Submission Grading," start by writing a Software Requirements Specifications (SRS) document. It seems like so much documentation, when it is easier to just start coding, and this document and the others mentioned in this book aren't required. However, my goal is to provide you with the best chance to pass the certification. The SRS document is one that definitely helps achieve that goal.

Requirements

Requirements determine what Sun wants you to build, not how to do it. For example, the statement "The application keeps the user informed about what is going on with a reservation" is broad, but it does nail down a single function—giving users status messages. Obviously, more requirements are needed to design a successful solution, but the point is you now know that the system will have to generate status messages.

Defining the status messages are part of the requirements definition phase. How these messages are generated (such as using exception handling to alert users of incorrect input) is not defined until later, in the Software Design Descriptions document. The requirements specify what the software needs to do precisely, concisely, and unambiguously. This phase is the most crucial, so a mistake here is the most costly. In fact, after poor planning, mistakes in defining requirements are probably the second biggest risk in a software project. A mistake in writing code later is not desirable, but it happens and isn't a big deal. A mistake at the requirements phase, however, is sometimes costly enough to kill a project.

You need the tools and techniques necessary to discover and analyze requirements for your solution. Many candidates submit a solution that is missing a requirement or two, but you can avoid this costly mistake if you learn how to use various fact-finding techniques to gather information about the assignment's instructions and challenges. After you have that information, you can start writing requirements. This step is where errors sneak into the project but don't get discovered until much later. Be careful—this is the project-killer step.

The requirements document provides information about the application's requirements, both functional and nonfunctional, by addressing the following three areas:

➤ *Describes the operational environment*—For example, the application operates in local and remote modes. While in local mode, the client communicates with the database as a local file. While in remote mode, the client communicates with the database remotely via RMI.

➤ *Describes the application's capabilities*—For example, the application is limited to booking seats. Assume that cancellation is not possible after a seat has been reserved.

➤ *Describes the application's functional and nonfunctional requirements*—For example, the application allows a user to choose a seat by clicking on the JTable grid, which displays the seats and related information.

The requirements are the system's constraints. One of the tools designers use to illustrate these constraints is the use case diagram. Figure 6.1 shows you the use case diagram for the hypothetical assignment this book uses. As you can see, the diagram is simple, but still clearly illustrates the core functionality of the Super Bowl Reservation System.

Super Bowl Reservation System

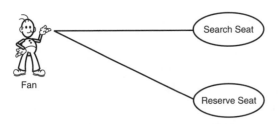

Figure 6.1   The use case diagram for the Super Bowl Reservation System.

Design

Now it's time to look at the Software Design Descriptions (SDD) document, which describes the software structure, components, interfaces, and data used to build the solution. The design's key value is that each requirement in the SRS document is linked directly to one or more design entities in the design. The question of *how* the project will be built is answered in detail in the SDD document. Philosophies differ: Some analysts believe this document should be abstract enough to build with different languages, and some think it should be language or technology specific. The latter approach is more practical. Rarely does a company actually intend to build a product from many different languages, even if it does plan to target several platforms (for example, must work on Unix, Windows, and Macintosh).

 Identify opportunities for reuse and apply design patterns. Sun's evaluators want to see patterns in your design. They will frown on custom solutions that do not take advantage of known design patterns. For example, you must use the MVC pattern in the GUI and probably the Factory pattern for the local/remote connection to the database.

Chapter 1 outlined the IEEE standard 1016.1-1993, "Guide to Software Design Descriptions," but I've revised it for brevity. Remember that these standards are helpful tools, but in this assignment you can pick and choose what is useful to you. The following brief example of a system design document describes a project similar to the certification assignment:

1.   Introduction

1.1   System Objectives

Briefly describe the system, owner, and functions of the system. This system is the Super Bowl Reservation System. It is being built for the Sun Certification Java Developer assignment. It provides seating information for the Super Bowl. The project objective is to extend a skeleton database system into a useable application that provides a convenient way to search for and reserve seats....

1.2   Plan Objectives

Briefly describe the objectives of this design document, especially how this document will transform the requirements into actual design specifications. The purpose of this document is to translate the requirements into actual functional specifications....

1.3   References

Identify your reference and sources of information used to develop this document. IEEE Standard 1016.1-1993, "Guide to Software Design Descriptions," was used to develop this document.

2.   System Architecture

2.1   Hardware

Describe the hardware and its architecture that your solution will support including local/distributed modes. The Super Bowl Reservation System will operate in local mode on hardware that supports the operating system, which in turn supports J2SE 1.4. For example, the hardware can be an Intel- or AMD-based workstation running Windows 2000 or a Sun box running Solaris. In remote mode, this system will support a client running on one machine and the remote database server on another machine, as long as the two can communicate over the network via TCP/IP....

2.2   Data Communications

Provide a detailed description of how the system communicates over the network. This system uses Java's built-in RMI feature. Through RMI, the database server and the client can communicate with each other. RMI uses a stub for a remote object, which acts as a client's local proxy. The client invokes a method on the local stub, which in turns invokes a method call on the remote object....

2.3   Software

Describe all software that is needed to support the system. The system uses the J2SE 1.4 SDK. The software application can be considered as two parts: the Sun-provided code and the new code. The system extended the supplied classes instead of modifying them. This way, it didn't modify lock/unlock signatures on the supplied classes, but overrode them in a subclass. The system used Factory, MVC, and Adapter patterns for better architecture and reuse....

2.4   Architecture Diagram

Illustrate the hardware, software, and communications designs to show the structure of your system. For this section, you might provide a diagram illustrating key portions of the system. For example, perhaps you could use a hardware layout to describe the server machines and their relationships. Often, each server shows the IP address, machine type, OS, name, and the major software application running on it.

3   Data Design

3.1   Data Objects and Resultant Data Structures

For each data object, describe how it will be used to store and process the data. The Field object describes a single field in the database. It has several attributes to create a description, including size, data type, value, name, maximum value, and minimum value....

3.2   File and Database Structures

Describe the logical and/or physical data model for your system. This may include file structures and their locations. You might also describe how data is structured in the selected database management system. The system stores and retrieves its data from a binary file–based database. Within the database, data is stored as a sequence of fields that together form a row. Each row is separated by a carriage return. These rows are stored in a single file that acts as a table....

4.   Modular Design

4.1   Modules

This is where you describe the software modules used to satisfy the system's operational requirements. When a user selects a seat from the GUI, the request is passed to the application's client functional controller. The controller determines whether that seat is available. If not, the system provides a status message saying so. If it is, the seat is reserved by GUI objects communicating with database objects, which work in the background as systemwide application objects.

4.2   Processing Narrative

Describe the process by which each module interacts with other parts of the system, including the input and output structures to each module. Also, describe the system's key algorithms that transform data. The system allows users to search for seats at the Super Bowl. The algorithm that handles this search is called the searchSeat method. This method is abstracted so that it can return a tableRow object containing all rows that have at least one value matching one criteria value. The column names and values are dynamic, so this method processes any number of criteria for any table, not just the one supplied in the assignment download. The algorithm used is....

4.3   Internal Data Structures

Describe the internal data structures of each module. The seat data is stored in the database. To identify a given seat, users must also know the gate, level, aisle, and row it is in. The database has a table that allows each seat to be unique by associating these other key data items....

4.4   Design Language

Specify the programming language for each module. All modules in this system were written with Java, J2SE 1.4.

Document Format

Most of the documentation you must include in your certification project is in ASCII format. The design and requirements documents advocated throughout the book can be in any format you want. These documents are for your benefit; they are not included in the solution you upload to Sun.

The exception is the design choices document. Fortunately for Windows users, Sun allows the design choices document to be supplied in Microsoft Word format. That means you can provide UML diagrams. (You can draw them in Word or paste them in from another application, such as Microsoft Excel.) I didn't, but still received a perfect score for the documentation. However, I lost a few points elsewhere and might not have if I had provided UML diagrams that explained my design. I strongly urge you to use at least a few UML diagrams for your design. Then just add them to the design choices document to make it easier for your evaluator to give you a higher score.

NOTE | Appendix A, "UML Glance Card," reviews the basics of UML. UML is currently at version 1.4 and can be downloaded from the Object Management Group's Web site at **http://www.omg.org**. Be aware that it is a 4MB PDF file.

Last, your certification project will be considered a success when you see a passing score on Sun's CertManager site in your "Test History" section. There are two major criteria to check before that day. First, make sure you have included the required components and performed various use tests. Second, ensure that all files in your single JAR file are accounted for and are in the right place. You must accomplish both tasks for your project to be successful.

Need to Know More?

 Larman, Craig. *Applying UML and Patterns: An Introduction to Object-Oriented Analysis and Design and the Unified Process (2nd Edition).* Indianapolis, IN: Prentice Hall, 2001 (ISBN 0130925691). This book tells you how to use UML and design patterns.

 Coad, Peter and Mark Mayfield. *Java Design: Building Better Apps and Applets.* Indianapolis, IN: Prentice Hall, 1999 (ISBN 0139111816). This book explains object-oriented design.

 Whitten, J.L., L.D. Bentley, and K.C. Dittman. *Systems Analysis and Design Methods, Fifth Edition.* Boston, MA: Irwin/McGraw Hill, 2000 (ISBN 0072315393). This book explains how to conduct good analysis and design. I don't mind the dry format, but some programmers do.

 http://standards.ieee.org/software/—View IEEE software standards.

 http://www.iso.ch/—The home page for the International Organization for Standardization (ISO), a worldwide federation of national standards bodies from more than 140 countries, one from each country. They are considered the world's top standards organization, including for software.

 http://www.computer.org/—The home page for the Institute of Electrical and Electronics Engineers (IEEE) Computer Society. With nearly 100,000 members, the IEEE Computer Society is considered by many to be the world's leading organization of computer professionals. Founded in 1946, it is the largest of IEEE's 36 societies.

Database

Terms you'll need to understand:

✓ Structured Query Language (SQL)
✓ Query
✓ Atomicity
✓ Row-level locking
✓ Adapter pattern
✓ Value Object pattern
✓ Remote Method Invocation (RMI)
✓ Database

Techniques you'll need to master:

✓ Creating a data model and transforming it to a database design
✓ Identifying data in a database that should not be duplicated and should remain unique
✓ Developing and performing queries against a database using Structured Query Language (SQL)
✓ Describing an Adapter design pattern and using it in your assignment
✓ Defining a database search algorithm and implementing it for your assignment
✓ Knowing the difference between a database read lock and a database write lock
✓ Implementing a database design in a Web environment
✓ Providing the correct thread management for a multiuser database server

In this chapter, you review the basics of databases and how you should implement one for your certification project. The assignment you download from Sun includes a skeleton for a database. These base classes are not enough to make a database server, however. You have to modify and extend these classes, and add new classes, to meet the certification requirements.

To meet those requirements, you need to master designing, developing, and administering a database system. Although the database you build for the assignment is not a relational database management system (RDBMS), it is a database. To help you understand the key principles, this chapter offers a brief background in database theory and discusses database design concepts from modeling to implementation. You also see a working example of a database system similar to what you should submit to Sun. The example isn't exactly the same as my solution, but several parts have been abstracted to work in many situations, the assignment being one of them.

Sun expects you to demonstrate a solid understanding of database systems. The sample code in this chapter helps you understand database concepts in a practical, rather than logical, manner. The code example is not a true RDBMS. However, you should be able to adapt the ideas it demonstrates for your solution. For a more complete treatment of relational database topics, please refer to the textbooks in "Need to Know More?" at the end of this chapter; these books make use of case studies and supply numerous examples and problem sets for practicing database concepts.

Some candidates think that the search statement coming from the client should be Structured Query Language (SQL) so that the solution is able to upgrade to using a relational database. If you take that route, the "SQL" section of this chapter will be helpful.

This chapter's sample database system consists of an application that approximates the certification assignment, but is not identical to it to comply with Sun's confidentiality requirement for its certification exams. The project code can assist you in designing and building your own solution. The listings in this chapter do not compile by themselves. They don't compile even if you combine all five listings. To compile the code, you'd need other classes, such as `SuperBowlException.java` and `DatabaseInterface.java`. However, the entire project is provided on this book's CD, and the code listings in this chapter will compile from their proper directories found in the supplied code files.

Locking Mechanism

Most RDBMSs, especially commercial ones, provide a built-in locking mechanism. However, this section explains creating your own generic database-locking mechanism that prevents two clients from trying to change the same record simultaneously. The programmatic locking discussed here is required only for the rudimentary database used in the certification assignment.

A locking mechanism is needed for a database because you need to remove the possibility of two users simultaneously trying to update the same record—also called *colliding*. Collisions can corrupt database records, so you need to add the capability of allowing database records to be locked while changes are pending. One client locking a record prevents other clients from locking or modifying the same record. Although the approach presented here is not the transaction control found in a true DBMS, it does meet the fundamental requirement of preventing updates by more than one user at the same time. Adding record locking helps control simultaneous access to the same records. Choosing the right locking method for your application is important. If you're not sure how you want to support record locking, you can use the locking manager class documented later in this section.

For my solution, I implemented a separate LockManager class that allows Insert Row Locking (IRL), so that if two clients attempt to perform the "lock, read/modify/write, unlock" sequence concurrently, both modification attempts are handled sequentially. The LockManager class provides consistent and concurrent access to data in a multiuser environment (such as with RMI). Because IRL is necessary only in remote mode, not in local mode, implementing it as a separate LockManager class makes more sense. Locks prevent simultaneous updates of the same row of data. With a separate lock manager, only one user at a time can update a row of data. So while one user is reserving a seat for the Super Bowl, another user can't do the same thing. Without a good lock manager, users could overwrite each other's seat reservations, giving the impression that a seat could be sold to more than one person.

A row is locked by a given client, so the lock is associated with that client (for example, track the client with a clientId). You can define this ID many ways. For example, you can use a static counter variable giving each new client a new and unique ID. Probably the easiest way to get an ID is to pass a unique reference to the client.

In the LockManager class shown in this section, the clientId variable is referred to with a WeakReference. Objects that have weak references are those that are weakly reachable, meaning that an object is garbage-collected if it doesn't have any strong references (that is, has only weak references) and the weak reference is set to NULL. For these objects, the garbage collector automatically clears all weak references to them. Then these objects are no longer referenced and can be garbage-collected when they are removed from memory. Therefore, when a lock is related to a weakly referred client, if the client dies, the lock does also, although the timing is not guaranteed. That way, should another client try to lock a record previously locked by a client who has died, the `LockManager` class removes the lock because the garbage collector has nullified that reference. The responsibility for record locking is kept in `LockManager`; the responsibility for references to dead objects stays with the Java Virtual Machine (JVM), a clean separation of responsibilities.

Listing 7.1 shows an example of a locking mechanism.

Listing 7.1   An Example of a Locking Mechanism

```
package superbowl.database;

import java.util.HashMap;
import java.util.Iterator;
import java.util.Map;
import java.lang.ref.WeakReference;

/**
 * This class provides the basic Insert Row Locking (IRL),
 * so that if two clients attempt to perform the sequence
 * "lock, read/modify/write, unlock" concurrently, both
 * modification attempts are handled sequentially. The LockManager
 * provides consistent and concurrent access to data in a multiuser
 * environment for a (e.g., RMI) database service.
 *
 * @author      Alain Trottier
 * @version 1.0   10-Feb-2003
 */
public class LockManager
{
    private final Map lockedRecords = new HashMap();
    public final int DATABASE_LOCK = -1;
    private WeakReference clientId, oldClientId;

    /**
     * Locks a given record by using the record number as key and connection
     * object passed to it as value. A record number of -1 locks the entire
     * database. Checks if another client locks a given record by calling
     * isLockedByAnotherClient(record, client). It waits until the lock
     * is removed. If another client locked this record but has died,
     * the lock is released because the clientId is a WeakReference, which
     * is garbage collected when the reference disappears. This way, there
     * is no need for a fancy timeout or polling mechanism.
     *
     * @param recNum ID of the record for which a lock is requested.
     * @param client client that wants to perform the locking.
     */
    synchronized public void lock(int recNum, Object client)
                        throws InterruptedException
    {

        Integer record = new Integer(recNum);
        Integer lockDB = new Integer(DATABASE_LOCK);
        //if client dies without cleanup,
```

(continued)

Listing 7.1 An Example of a Locking Mechanism (continued)

```
        //you want to automatically ignore its locks
        clientId = new WeakReference(client);

        try
        {
                if ( recNum == DATABASE_LOCK )
                {
                    while (lockedRecords.containsKey(lockDB))
                    {
                        // must wait for database lock to release,
                        // regardless of client
                        wait();
                    }
                } else
                {
                    while (lockedRecords.containsKey(record)
                        && !isLockedByAnotherClient(record, clientId))
                    {
                        wait();
                    }
                }

                lockedRecords.put(record, clientId);
        } catch (InterruptedException e)
        {
                throw new InterruptedException ("Interrupted!", e);
        }

}

/**
 * Checks if a given record is locked by another client.
 * If another client locked this record but has died,
 * the lock is released because the clientId is a WeakReference, which
 * is garbage collected when the reference disappears. This way, there
 * is no need for a fancy timeout or polling mechanism.
 *
 * @param record ID of the record for which a lock is requested.
 * @param client client that wants to perform the locking.
 * @return is record locked or not.
 */
synchronized public boolean isLockedByAnotherClient(Integer record,
                                                    Object client)
{
    oldClientId = (WeakReference)lockedRecords.get(record);
    clientId = new WeakReference(client);
    boolean isLocked = false;

    if (oldClientId == null)
    {
            // Value has been garbage-collected: client has died, so
            // remove unreferenced lock.
            lockedRecords.remove(record);
    }else if (oldClientId != clientId)
    {
        // locked by another client
        isLocked = true;
```

(continued)

Listing 7.1   An Example of a Locking Mechanism *(continued)*

```
        }

        return isLocked;
}

/**
 * Unlocks a given record by using the record number
 * as key and the client passed to it as value.
 *
 * @param recNum ID of the record for which a lock is requested.
 * @param client client that wants to perform the locking.
 */
synchronized public void unlock(int recNum, Object client)
{
    Integer record = new Integer(recNum);
    clientId = new WeakReference(client);

    if (lockedRecords.get(record).equals(clientId))
    {
        lockedRecords.remove(record);
        notifyAll();
    }
}

/**
 * Clears all pending locks for a particular client.
 *
 * @param client client that has previously locked records.
 */
synchronized public void clearLocks(Object client)
{
    clientId = new WeakReference(client);
    Iterator iter = lockedRecords.entrySet().iterator();
    for (Iterator i = lockedRecords.values().iterator(); i.hasNext(); )
    {
        if (clientId.equals(i.next()))
        {
            i.remove();
        }
    }
}

/**
 * Clears all pending locks regardless of client.
 */
synchronized public void clearLocks()
{
    lockedRecords.clear();
}
}
```

An especially strong aspect of this lock manager is that it's abstract enough to work on just about any database system you can invent for the assignment. The core principle is mapping the record number as the key and a reference to the client as the value. With that mapping, you can easily check whether someone has a lock on a record by simply searching for the key. If the key is there, then someone has the lock. This part is easy, but what happens if the lock owner disappears? This question has stumped many candidates. Some use a timeout mechanism by periodically checking whether the lock owner is still valid, or some simply remove a lock that has aged past a certain threshold or time limit.

Although there are many ways to handle dead lock owners, my approach was to place the responsibility for tracking when clients die with the JVM. When the client dies, the reference is scheduled for garbage collection by using a WeakReference object. The client requests a lock on a record by passing a reference of itself, as a WeakReference object, along with the record number. If the client dies, this WeakReference object is garbage collected. You can check whether this happened by testing if clientId is null. There are many ways to assign client IDs, but I thought using the WeakReferenced clientId was a valid approach to this portion of the project.

Database Factory

Now that you have a lock manager, you can address the database factory portion of the assignment. A *database factory* is how the system creates a database object based on command-line parameters. A database factory can create a local or remote database. The client doesn't care which database object the database factory creates because the object reference looks the same to the client, as both are of the type DatabaseInterface. When the client starts, it sends a request for a database connection to the database factory. The factory must determine whether the mode of operation is local or remote. For local mode, the database factory returns an object that has opened the local database file. For remote mode, it returns an object that connects, through Remote Method Invocation (RMI), to a remote server, which in turn opens the database file local to it. The client doesn't care where the database is, and none of its code can be mode specific. The factory bears the responsibility for figuring out how to handle mode-specific matters.

The sample code in Listing 7.2 uses a database that is in-memory (for example, a two-dimensional String array for rows of data). For the real solution, you might use a database file, such as database.bin. The pathing parameters in the listing point to this database file. If you choose to implement a file-based solution rather than an in-memory one, I recommend locating the database.bin file in the install directory. You can provide a default path to database.bin in case no parameters are supplied. The database.bin functionality is provided for completeness here, but the code doesn't actually open that file; it is a template to help you with the real certification project.

Listing 7.2, which shows an example of a database factory, uses RMI. For readers who choose socket communication, the code will be different. Please refer to Chapter 11, "Networking with NIO," for detailed information on sockets if you prefer using them instead of RMI.

Listing 7.2   An Example of a Database Factory

```java
package superbowl.database;

import java.util.Vector;
import java.io.IOException;
import java.rmi.RemoteException;
import java.rmi.NotBoundException;
import java.rmi.Naming;
import java.rmi.registry.Registry;
import java.rmi.registry.LocateRegistry;

/**
 * This class provides a choice of network connections. Depending on the
 * number of parameters, one parameter pair of "-dbpath {DBPATH}" returns a
 * local connection. Two parameters of "-host {HOST} -port {PORT}" will
 * return a network connection. If the parameters are invalid, null will be
 * returned.
 *
 * I used Adapter because I'm able to program the client UI solely in terms
 * of Database type. Whether in local or remote mode, the factory returns
 * an object of type DatabaseInterface.
 * @author      Alain Trottier
 * @version 1.0  10-Feb-2003
 */
public class DatabaseFactory
{
    private Database db;
    private String dbpath;
    private String lookupString;
    private static final String PORT        = "1099";
    private static final String HOST        = "localhost";
    private static final String DBPATH      = "database.bin";
    private static final String RMI_SERVICE_NAME = "DatabaseService";
    private static final String UNEXPECTED =
            "DatabaseRMIServer-Unexpected database access problem: ";
    private static final String cmdError = ""
            + "\nYou must provide either the data file location "
            + "or the RMI host and port parameters:\n"
            + "\n -dbpath " + DBPATH
            + "\nWhere path is either database.bin or $ROOT\\database.bin"
            + " (\"\\\\\" for Windows; \"/\" for Unix)"
            + "\nIf you provide network parameters you must use:"
            + "\n-host {HOST} -port {PORT}"
            + "\nFor example: -host " + HOST + " -port " + PORT
            + "\nThe parameter pairs may be in any order, "
            + "but both pairs are required.";

    /**
     * For the real solution, use a database file such as database.bin.
     * The pathing parameters point to this database file. It should be
     * located in the install directory. You can choose to provide
```

(continued)

Listing 7.2   An Example of a Database Factory *(continued)*

```
 * a default path to database.bin in case no parameters are supplied.
 * This method is provided for completeness, but is not supported.
 * @exception IOException Thrown if cannot open connection.
 */
public DatabaseFactory() throws IOException
{
    String currentDirectory = System.getProperty("user.dir");
    String fileSeperator = System.getProperty("file.separator");
    dbpath = currentDirectory + fileSeperator + "database.bin";
}

/**
 * Depending on the supplied parameters, a specific connection will
 * be returned. Invalid parameters will lead to null return.
 * @param cmdArgs String array of connection parameters
 * @return An instance of the database.
 * @exception SuperBowlException Thrown if cannot open connection.
 */
public DatabaseInterface getDatabase(String[] cmdArgs)
                    throws SuperBowlException
{
    int cmdArgsLength = cmdArgs.length;
    String host     = HOST;
    String port     = PORT;
           dbpath   = DBPATH;

    try
    {
        // test if local database is wanted
        if (cmdArgsLength == 0)
        {

            return new Database("database.bin");
        // test if local database is wanted
        } else if (cmdArgsLength == 2
               && cmdArgs[0].equalsIgnoreCase("-dbpath"))
        {
            dbpath = cmdArgs[1];
            return new Database(dbpath);

        // test if remote database is wanted
        } else if (cmdArgsLength == 4)
        {
            // parse RMI server command line
            int i     = 0;
            while (i < cmdArgsLength)
            {
                String arg = cmdArgs[i++];
                if (arg.equalsIgnoreCase("-host"))
                {
                    host = cmdArgs[i++];
                } else if (arg.equalsIgnoreCase("-port"))
                {
                    port = cmdArgs[i++];
                } else
                {
```

(continued)

Listing 7.2   An Example of a Database Factory *(continued)*

```
                        // exit if user mistypes a command parameter
                        System.out.println( cmdError );
                        System.out.println( "rmi://"
                                    + host + ":"
                                    + port + "/"
                                    + RMI_SERVICE_NAME );
                        System.exit( 0 );
                        }
                    }
                    lookupString = "rmi://"
                          + host + ":"
                          + port + "/"
                          + RMI_SERVICE_NAME;
                    return (DatabaseInterface)Naming.lookup(lookupString);
                } else
                {
                    // user provided wrong parameters
                    throw new SuperBowlException(cmdError);
                }
            } catch (RemoteException rex)
            {
                throw new SuperBowlException(lookupString + "\n"
                              + UNEXPECTED + "\n"
                              + rex);
            } catch (NotBoundException nbe)
            {
                throw new SuperBowlException(lookupString + "\n"
                              + UNEXPECTED + "\n" + nbe);
            } catch (IOException ioe)
            {
                throw new SuperBowlException(lookupString + "\n"
                              + UNEXPECTED + "\n" + ioe);
            } catch (Exception e)
            {
                throw new SuperBowlException(lookupString + "\n"
                              + UNEXPECTED + "\n" + e);
            }
        }

    /**
     * A local database connection will be returned.
     *
     * @return An instance of the database.
     * @exception SuperBowlException Thrown if cannot open connection.
     */
    public DatabaseInterface getDatabase()
                throws SuperBowlException
    {
        try
        {
        // assumes "database.bin" is in the install directory
        return new Database(dbpath);

        } catch(IOException ioe)
        {
            throw new SuperBowlException(UNEXPECTED + ioe);
        }
```

(continued)

Listing 7.2 An Example of a Database Factory (continued)

```
    }

    /**
     * A local database connection will be returned.
     * @param dbpath The database file path
     * @return An instance of the database.

     * @exception SuperBowlException - Thrown if cannot open connection.
     */
    public DatabaseInterface getDatabase(String dbpath)
                throws SuperBowlException
    {
        try
        {
        // opens "database.bin" at beginning of file for random access
        return new Database(dbpath);

        } catch(IOException ioe)
        {
            throw new SuperBowlException(UNEXPECTED + ioe);
        }
    }
}
```

You'll notice that this database factory parses command-line parameters. From the parameters, it figures out whether the client is in local or remote mode. Furthermore, because the database connection is passed to the client typed by an interface (DatabaseInterface), the client can remain unaware of whether the database is actually a local or remote object.

The DatabaseInterface Class

Chapter 9, "Interfaces," covers database interfaces in detail. The interface shown in Listing 7.3 is presented in this chapter, however, because it is specifically for the certification project's database.

Listing 7.3 An Example of a Database Interface

```
package superbowl.database;

import java.io.IOException;
import java.rmi.RemoteException;


/**
 * The interface defines the basic database methods. It uses two
 * other support classes: RowData and ColumnData. It provides the
 * public methods for Database (local) and DatabaseRemote (remote).
 * <p>
 * The methods in this interface can be used by an application to obtain
```

(continued)

Listing 7.3   An Example of a Database Interface *(continued)*

```
* information from a database through the Database class.
* @author     Alain Trottier
* @version    1.0, 2/10/03
*/
public interface DatabaseInterface extends java.rmi.Remote
{

    /**
    * Returns a description of the database columns.
    *
    * @return This array of ColumnData objects
    *    defines the database schema.
    * @exception SuperBowlException Thrown if cannot open connection.
    * @exception RemoteException Thrown if RMI fails.
    */
    public String[] getColumnNames()
            throws SuperBowlException, RemoteException;

    /**
    * Returns a two dimensional array of data.
    *
    * @return This array of data objects
    * @exception SuperBowlException Thrown if cannot open connection.
    * @exception RemoteException Thrown if RMI fails.
    */
    public String[][] getData() throws SuperBowlException, RemoteException;

    /**
    * Gets the number of rows stored in the database.
    * @return The total row number
    * @exception SuperBowlException Thrown if cannot open connection.
    * @exception RemoteException Thrown if RMI fails.
    */
    public int getRowCount()
                throws SuperBowlException, RemoteException;

    /**
    * returns a given row based on row number.
    * @param rowNumber - The row number.
    * @return String[] - The row.
    * @exception SuperBowlException Thrown if database file missing
    * @exception RemoteException Thrown if RMI fails.
    */
    public String[] getRow(int rowNumber)
            throws SuperBowlException, RemoteException;

    /**
    * returns a given value based on row and column.
    * @param row The row number.
    * @param column The column number.
    * @return String The row.
    * @exception SuperBowlException Thrown if cannot open connection.
    * @exception RemoteException Thrown if RMI fails.
    */
    public String getValue(int row, int column)
            throws SuperBowlException, RemoteException;
```

(continued)

Listing 7.3   An Example of a Database Interface *(continued)*

```
/**
* Returns an integer based on the row number.
* @return The row number.
* @exception SuperBowlException Thrown if cannot open connection.
* @exception RemoteException Thrown if RMI fails.
*/
public int getRowNumber()
        throws SuperBowlException, RemoteException;



/**
* returns a given row based on row number.
* @param value The actual cell value.
* @param row The row number.
* @param column The column number.
* @exception SuperBowlException Thrown if cannot open connection.
* @exception RemoteException Thrown if RMI fails.
*/
public void setValue(String value, int row, int column)
        throws SuperBowlException, RemoteException;

/**
* Searches the database for the distinct values for a specified field.
* The distinct values are kept in the Set setDistinctValues
* and updated only if a row is added or deleted.
* This method retains the generic nature of the database.
*
* @param fieldIndex The column or field index.
* @return The unique field values.
* @exception SuperBowlException Thrown when database connection fails
* @exception RemoteException Thrown if RMI fails.
*/
public String[] getDistinctValuesForField(int fieldIndex)
                throws SuperBowlException, RemoteException;


/**
* Searches the database for entries with desired
* fields that exactly match the string supplied. If the required
* row cannot be found, this method returns null. For this
* assignment, the key field is the row number field.
*
* @param criteria - The key field value to match for
*                   a successful find.
* @return The matching rows.
* @exception SuperBowlException Thrown when database connection fails
* @exception RemoteException Thrown if RMI fails.
*/
public String[][] searchSeat(String criteria)
        throws SuperBowlException, RemoteException;


/**
* Lock the row of interest.
* @param row The row number to lock.
* @exception IOException If the row position is invalid.
*/
```

(continued)

Listing 7.3 An Example of a Database Interface *(continued)*

```
public void lock(int row) throws IOException, RemoteException;

/**
 * Unlock the requested row. Ignored if the caller does not have
 * a current lock on the requested row.
 * @param row The row number to lock.
 * @exception SuperBowlException Thrown if cannot open connection.
 * @exception RemoteException Thrown if RMI fails.
 */
public void unlock(int row) throws SuperBowlException, RemoteException;

}
```

This interface is critical for getting RMI to work. It allows the client to reference the database by interface type, not concrete class. An important distinction must be understood: RMI refers to the remote object by interface. Therefore, if you want the client not to care whether the database is local or remote, you need an interface like this one.

The Database Class

The Database class could be adapted to be a subclass of Sun's database-equivalent class that you download for the assignment. You have to decide whether to modify or subclass that Sun class. I recommend subclassing to maintain legacy compatibility for the superclass class, to cleanly separate new functionality and changes from the old, and to use a new name that seems more descriptive of the class responsibilities. The Database class is responsible for being a more complete database, providing access to a single local database file and including reading, writing, and searching facilities. Finally, if any methods in the Sun class use deprecated code, you can override them in a subclass. Some candidates choose to modify the class, but I prefer the subclass route. Both routes are equally valid, but you must account for the deprecated code; doing so is part of your score.

Listing 7.4 shows an example of a Database class that acts as the database. It could be modified to be a subclass of Sun's class, if you chose to do that. Whether you modify or subclass Sun's classes, this class does give you a clear idea of what you need to do.

Listing 7.4 An Example of a Database Class

```
package superbowl.database;

import java.io.*;
```

(continued)

Listing 7.4 An Example of a Database Class *(continued)*

```java
import java.util.StringTokenizer ;
import java.util.Vector;
import java.util.Set;
import java.util.TreeSet;

import java.util.ArrayList;
import java.util.Iterator;


/**
 * This class is a new subclass of Data called Database.
 * I extended the Data class to maintain legacy compatibility
 * for the Data class, to cleanly separate the new functionality and
 * changes from the old, and to use a new name that seems more descriptive
 * of the class responsibilities. The Database class, which is a subclass of
 * Data, is responsible for being a more complete database, providing access
 * to a single local database file, and including reading, writing, and
 * searching facilities. Two methods in Data use deprecated code, which
 * might be required for legacy applications, but are overridden in the
 * Database subclass.
 * @author      Alain Trottier
 * @version 1.0  10-Feb-2003
 *
 * @version 1.0  10-Feb-2003
 */
public class Database implements DatabaseInterface
{
    public int recordCount;
    public int rowNumber;
    public static final String UNEXPECTED =
    "Database: Unexpected database access problem";

        String[] columnNames = {"Gate",
                        "Level",
                        "Aisle",
                        "Row",
                        "Seat",
                        "Available"};
        String[][] data =
          {
            {"North", "100",
             "First", "A", "1", "1"},
            {"North", "100",
             "Second", "V", "24", "1"},
            {"North", "100",
             "First", "B", "39", "1"},
            {"South", "150",
             "Second", "C", "18", "1"},
            {"South", "150",
             "Third", "E", "6", "1"},
            {"North", "100",
             "First", "A", "10", "1"},
            {"North", "100",
             "First", "A", "13", "1"},
            {"North", "100",
             "First", "A", "21", "1"},
```

(continued)

Listing 7.4   An Example of a Database Class *(continued)*

```
            {"North", "100",
             "First", "A", "42", "1"},
            {"North", "100",
             "First", "A", "69", "1"},
            {"North", "30",
             "First", "F", "29", "1"},
            {"North", "30",
             "Second", "W", "4", "1"},
            {"North", "30",
             "First", "L", "95", "1"},
            {"South", "50",
             "Second", "P", "108", "1"},
            {"South", "50",
             "Third", "T", "71", "1"},
            {"North", "10",
             "First", "X", "12", "1"},
            {"North", "10",
             "First", "Q", "41", "1"},
            {"North", "10",
             "First", "N", "52", "1"},
            {"North", "10",
             "First", "U", "25", "1"},
            {"North", "10",
             "First", "A", "8", "1"}
        };


/**
 * This constructor fills the database with data.
 * It could open a database file to do so.
 *
 * @param dbname The name of the database file to open.
 * @exception IOException
 */
  public Database(String dbname) throws IOException
  {
      recordCount = data.length;

      // dbFile = new RandomAccessFile(new File(dbname), "rw");
      // process file
  }


/**
 * Searches the database for distinct values for the specified field.
 * The distinct values are kept in the Set setDistinctValues
 * and updated only if a record is added or deleted.
 * This method retains the generic nature of the database.
 *
 * @param fieldIndex The column or field index.
 * @return The unique field values.
 * @exception SuperBowlException Thrown when database can't be accessed
 */
public String[] getDistinctValuesForField(int fieldIndex)
     throws SuperBowlException
{
```

(continued)

Listing 7.4   An Example of a Database Class *(continued)*

```
        Set setDistinctValues = new TreeSet();

        // add column value to set
        setDistinctValues.add( "any" );

        for (int rowCount = 0; rowCount <= recordCount-1; rowCount++)
        {
              // add column value to set
              setDistinctValues.add( data[rowCount][fieldIndex] );
        }

        // Create a String array of unique values
        String[] distinctValues = (String[])setDistinctValues.toArray(
                                  new String[setDistinctValues.size()]);

        return distinctValues;
    }

    /**
     * Returns an integer based on the row number.
     * @return The row number.
     * @exception SuperBowlException Thrown if cannot open connection.
     * @exception RemoteException Thrown if RMI fails.
     */
    public int getRowNumber() throws SuperBowlException
    {
        return rowNumber;
    }

    /**
     * Returns a two dimensional array of data.
     *
     * @return String[][] - This array of data objects
     * @exception SuperBowlException - Thrown if cannot open connection.
     * @exception RemoteException - Thrown if RMI fails.
     */
    public String[][] getData() throws SuperBowlException
    {
        return data;
    }

    /**
     * Searches the database for entries with desired
     * fields that exactly match the string supplied. If the required
     * record cannot be found, this method returns null. For this
     * assignment, the key field is the record number field.
     *
     * @param criteria - The key field value to match for
     *                    a successful find.
     * @return The matching records.
     * @exception SuperBowlException - Thrown when database connection fails
     */
    public synchronized String[][] searchSeat(String criteria)
        throws SuperBowlException
    {
        ArrayList rowData = new ArrayList();
```

(continued)

Listing 7.4   An Example of a Database Class *(continued)*

```java
String[] values = null;
String[][] newData = null;
String WILDCARD = "any";

StringTokenizer stk = new StringTokenizer(criteria,
                                 "\t\n\r\f'\"=;,");

// return null if tokens are odd or 0
if ( stk.countTokens () % 2 != 0 || stk.countTokens () ==0)
{
    return null;
}

// define and assign criteriaString and fieldIndex array
String [] criteriaString = new String[stk.countTokens()];
for( int i = 0; i < criteriaString.length; i++)
{
    criteriaString[i] = stk.nextToken().trim();
}

try
{
    boolean isMatch = false;
    int column;
    String value;

    NextRow:
    for (int rowCount = 0; rowCount <= recordCount-1; rowCount++)
    {
        values = data[rowCount];

        if (values != null)
        {
            isMatch = false;
            for( int criteriaCount = 0;
                    criteriaCount < criteriaString.length;
                    criteriaCount += 2)
            {
                column = getColumn(criteriaString[criteriaCount]);
                value = criteriaString[criteriaCount + 1];
                // if search criteria is "any" or database field
                // value matches criteria value, go to next test.
                if ( !(value.equalsIgnoreCase(WILDCARD)
                        || values[column].equalsIgnoreCase(value)) )
                {
                    //fails one criteria, so skip row
                    continue NextRow;
                }
            }

            // all criteria are met, so add seat number to the set
            rowData.add(new Integer(rowCount));
            rowNumber = rowCount;
        }
    }
```

(continued)

Listing 7.4   An Example of a Database Class *(continued)*

```
            newData = new String[rowData.size()][];
            int rowCount = 0;
            for (Iterator it=rowData.iterator(); it.hasNext(); rowCount++) {
                newData[rowCount] = data[((Integer)it.next()).intValue()] ;
            }

            // return the 2D array; null if no record found
            return newData;
        }   catch (Exception e)
        {
            throw new SuperBowlException(UNEXPECTED + e);
        }
    }

    /**
     * This method finds which column index a given name matches.
     *
     * @param columnName The name of the column.
     * @return The index of the matching column.
     */
    public int getColumn(String columnName)
    {
        int columnCount = columnNames.length;

        //find column position
        for (int index = 0; index < columnCount; index++)
        {
            if ( columnName.trim().equalsIgnoreCase(
                                    columnNames[index].trim()) )
            {
                    return index;
            }
        }

        return -1;
    }

    /**
     * This method returns a description of the database schema as an
     * array of ColumnData objects.
     *
     * @return The array of ColumnData objects that form
     *          the schema to this database.
     */
    public String[] getColumnNames() {
        return columnNames;
    }

    /**
     * Gets the number of records stored in the database.
     */
    public int getRowCount() { return recordCount; }

    /**
     * Gets a requested record from the database based on record number.
     * @param rowNumber The number of the record to read (first record is 1).
```

(continued)

Listing 7.4   An Example of a Database Class *(continued)*

```
    * @return RowData for the record or null if the record has been
    * marked for deletion.
    * @exception SuperBowlException Thrown if database connection fails.
    */
   public synchronized String[] getRow(int rowNumber)
                                   throws SuperBowlException
   {
       try {
           if (rowNumber<1) {
               throw new SuperBowlException(
                           "Record number must be greater than 1");
           }

           String[] records = data[rowNumber];
           if (records == null) {
               return null;
           }

           return records;
       } catch(Exception ex) {
           throw new SuperBowlException(UNEXPECTED);
       }
   }


   /**
    * Writes a new record to the database using the current location of the
    * underlying random access file.
    * @param newData An array of strings in the database-specified order.
    * @return The value at that row and column.
    * @exception SuperBowlException - Thrown when database connection fails
    */
   public synchronized String getValue(int row, int column)
                                   throws SuperBowlException
   {
       return data[row][column];
   }


   /**
    * Writes a new record to the database using the current location of the
    * underlying random access file.
    * @param newData An array of strings in the database-specified order.
    * @exception SuperBowlException Thrown when database connection fails
    */
   public synchronized void setValue(String value, int row, int column)
                                   throws SuperBowlException
   {
       data[row][column] = value;
   }


   /**
    * Lock the requested record. If the argument is -1, lock the whole
    * database. This method blocks until the lock succeeds. No timeouts
    * are defined for this.
    * @param record The record number to lock.
    * @exception IOException If the record position is invalid.
```

(continued)

Listing 7.4   An Example of a Database Class *(continued)*

```
*/
public void lock(int record) throws IOException
{
     //do nothing in local mode
}
 /**
 * Unlock the requested record. Ignored if the caller does not have
 * a current lock on the requested record.
 * @param record The record number to unlock.

 */
public void unlock(int record)
{
     //do nothing in local mode
}
}
```

Notice that the searchSeat() method finds the row with the seat that matches the search criteria. Although there are numerous ways to conduct that search algorithm, this one is abstract enough to work on any table, not just the one in this particular assignment.

The searchSeat() method is abstracted so that it returns a two-dimensional String array containing all rows that have at least one value matching one criteria value. The column names and values are dynamic, so this method processes any number of criteria for any table, not just the one in the assignment download. This is the algorithm used:

1. Parse the criteria string with StringTokenizer.

2. Get a new row of data from the database.

3. Find a column that matches the criteria field name.

4. Test for a match between the row value and search value.

5. If there's a match, save the row of data and go to step 2.

6. If there's no match for current criteria, go to the next criteria and start at step 3.

7. When the criteria are exhausted, go to the next row and start at step 2.

The searchSeat() method uses java.util.StringTokenizer to parse the search criteria. This class breaks Strings into chunks at the delimiters. The requirements specify making the search criteria String simple, so I stayed with StringTokenizer. I would have chosen the regular expression route if the input search String were more complicated. If you decide to use SQL to define the search criteria, you could parse the SQL string in the searchSeat() method. It is more work, but the result is stronger than what I did.

This Database class is the one used for local mode. Listing 7.5 shows the equivalent class on the RMI side. The comments are the same as in Listing 7.4, so they have been removed from this listing. The two listings are similar, but not the same, so examine this one carefully.

Listing 7.5   An Example of a Database Class for RMI

```
package superbowl.server;

import superbowl.database.Database;
import superbowl.database.SuperBowlException;
import superbowl.database.DatabaseInterface;
import superbowl.database.LockManager;

import java.rmi.RemoteException;
import java.rmi.server.UnicastRemoteObject;
import java.io.IOException;

/**
 * This class is the implementation of RMI for the application.
 * It is here that the RMI engine looks to for the stub. In other
 * words the Database methods (local) are wrapped with these
 * remote methods so the calling routine can treat these remote methods
 * as is they are local.
 * @author      Alain Trottier
 * @version     1.0, 2/10/03
 */
public class DatabaseRMIImpl extends UnicastRemoteObject
                        implements DatabaseInterface
{
    private final static LockManager lockManager = new LockManager();
    private static Database database;
    protected static final String UNEXPECTED =
        "DatabaseRMIImpl-Unexpected database access problem: ";


    public DatabaseRMIImpl(String dbname)
        throws SuperBowlException, RemoteException
    {
        super();
        try
        {
            database = new Database(dbname);
        } catch(RemoteException rex)
        {
            throw new SuperBowlException(UNEXPECTED + rex);
        } catch(IOException ex)
        {
            throw new SuperBowlException(UNEXPECTED + ex);
        }
    }

    /**
     * Returns a description of the database columns.
     *
```

(continued)

Listing 7.5   An Example of a Database Class for RM (continued)

```
 * @return This array of ColumnData objects
 *    defines the database schema.
 * @exception SuperBowlException Thrown if cannot open connection.
 * @exception RemoteException Thrown if RMI fails.
 */
public String[] getColumnNames()
          throws SuperBowlException, RemoteException
{
    return database.getColumnNames();
}

/**
 * Returns a two dimensional array of data.
 *
 * @return This array of data objects
 * @exception SuperBowlException Thrown if cannot open connection.
 * @exception RemoteException Thrown if RMI fails.
 */
public String[][] getData() throws SuperBowlException
{
    return database.getData();
}

/**
 * Gets the number of rows stored in the database.
 * @return The total row number
 * @exception SuperBowlException Thrown if cannot open connection.
 * @exception RemoteException Thrown if RMI fails.
 */
public int getRowCount() throws SuperBowlException, RemoteException
{
    return database.getRowCount();
}

/**
 * returns a given row based on row number.
 * @param rowNumber The row number.
 * @return The row.
 * @exception SuperBowlException Thrown if cannot open connection.
 * @exception RemoteException - Thrown if RMI fails.
 */    public synchronized String[] getRow(int rowNumber)
          throws SuperBowlException ,RemoteException
{
    return database.getRow(rowNumber);
}

/**
 * returns a given value based on row and column.
 * @param row The row number.
 * @param column The column number.
 * @return The particular value at row and column.
 * @exception SuperBowlException Thrown if cannot open connection.
 * @exception RemoteException Thrown if RMI fails.
 */
public String getValue(int row, int column)
        throws SuperBowlException, RemoteException
```

(continued)

Listing 7.5   An Example of a Database Class for RM *(continued)*

```
{
    return database.getValue(row, column);
}


/**
 * Returns an integer based on the row number.
 * @return The row number.
 * @exception SuperBowlException Thrown if cannot open connection.
 * @exception RemoteException Thrown if RMI fails.
 */
public int getRowNumber()
        throws SuperBowlException, RemoteException
{
    return database.getRowNumber();
}


/**
 * sets a given value based on row and column numbers.
 * @param value The actual cell value.
 * @param row The row number.
 * @param column The column number.
 * @exception SuperBowlException Thrown if cannot open connection.
 * @exception RemoteException Thrown if RMI fails.
 */
public void setValue(String value, int row, int column)
        throws SuperBowlException, RemoteException
{
    database.setValue(value, row, column);
}


/**
 * Lock the row of interest..
 * @param recno The row number to lock.
 * @exception IOException If the row position is invalid.
 * @exception RemoteException Thrown if RMI fails.
 */
public void lock(int record) throws IOException, RemoteException
{
    try
    {
        lockManager.lock(record, this);
    } catch(InterruptedException iex)
    {
        throw new IOException(UNEXPECTED + iex);
    }
}


/**
 * Unlock the requested row. Ignored if the caller does not have
 * a current lock on the requested row.
 * @param row The row number to unlock.
 * @exception SuperBowlException Thrown if cannot open connection.
 * @exception RemoteException Thrown if RMI fails.
 */
public void unlock(int record)
        throws SuperBowlException, RemoteException
```

(continued)

Listing 7.5   An Example of a Database Class for RM (continued)

```
{
        lockManager.unlock(record, this);
}

/**
 * Searches the database for entries which have desired
 * fields which exactly match the string supplied. If the required
 * row cannot be found, this method returns null. For this
 * assignment, the key field is the row number field.
 *
 * @param criteria The key field value to match upon for
 *              a successful find.
 * @return The matching rows.
 * @exception SuperBowlException Thrown if cannot open connection.
 * @exception RemoteException Thrown if RMI fails.
 */
public String[][] searchSeat(String criteria) throws SuperBowlException
                                             , RemoteException
{
        return database.searchSeat(criteria);
}

/**
 * Searches the database for the distinct values for the specified field.
 * The distinct values are kept in the Set setDistinctValues
 * and updated only if addition/deletion of row.
 * This method retains the generic nature of the database.
 *
 * @param fieldIndex The column or field index.
 * @return The unique field values.
 * @exception SuperBowlException Thrown if cannot open connection.
 * @exception RemoteException Thrown if RMI fails.
 */
public String[] getDistinctValuesForField(int fieldIndex)
            throws SuperBowlException, RemoteException
{
        return database.getDistinctValuesForField(fieldIndex);
}

}
```

This class uses the Decorator pattern. It decorates Database with the intent to attach a responsibility to an object at runtime. Decoration is a flexible alternative to extending a class. Sometimes you want to add a responsibility to object A, not its whole class. In this project, DatabaseRMIImpl wraps Database and adds the responsibility for IRL via a LockManager. The decorator (DatabaseRMIImpl) implements Database's interface (DatabaseInterface), so Database's clients interact with DatabaseRMIImpl as though it were Database. Transparency enables you to decorate the decorated object, adding many responsibilities.

Notice that the lock() and unlock() methods are different from what you saw in Listing 7.4. In fact, these two methods are the main differences between the two classes. Listing 7.5 shows you how this class uses LockManager. Listing 7.4 didn't because that example is used in local mode and you don't need LockManager. Whether operation is in local or remote mode, the client simply calls for a lock. If the class in Listing 7.4 is referenced, the lock() and unlock() methods are passed to the superclass where these methods are empty. If the class in Listing 7.5 is referenced, the lock() and unlock() methods in LockManager are actually called.

SQL

Now that you have reviewed all the basic components of the database, you can review the basics of SQL, which you might use specifically in the searchSeat() method. SQL enables you to access a database. All major database vendors use SQL because it is an American National Standards Institute (ANSI; http://www.ansi.org) standard language. SQL does not appear on the SCJD assignment or essay exam because of the practical matter of distributing an assignment in a way that includes client/server architecture and includes a database without relying on a non-Sun vendor. At this time, it is too difficult for Sun certification people to figure out a test design that would be fair yet allow the developer to use various databases, such as MySQL, Sybase, Oracle, DB2, or SQL Server. If you look at it from Sun's perspective, you can already hear someone complain about failing the assignment because Sun is biased against Microsoft SQL Server. So, in the current version, Sun wrote its own database engine that everyone must use. This part is understandable, but the unwanted side effect is the loss of SQL. Sun's database packaged with the assignment is too rudimentary to use SQL, but you could choose to add SQL processing capability. You don't have to use much SQL; just use a small portion and argue that it's a smart way to manage interaction between the client and database.

Most popular databases today are based on the relational model, defined in 1970 by Dr. E. F. Codd, a researcher for IBM, who wrote the paper "A Relational Model of Data for Large Shared Data Banks." This paper started a chain of events that gave rise to the RDBMS. In 1974 IBM began the System/R project, which produced Structured English Query Language (SEQUEL). Eventually, in 1983 IBM developed a product based on SQL called DB2. Other vendors did likewise and announced SQL-based products, including Oracle and Sybase.

SQL is quite old and could use some polishing. For example, the statement SELECT * FROM employee; would be understood better as get * from employee. One of SQL's weaknesses is the lack of programming logic, such as loops and objects. Although SQL has a few wrinkles, however, it is the standard way to get information from a database. Naturally, vendors vie for a competitive advantage by adding features to SQL, such as increasingly complex ways to query the database. Of course, these added features created confusion for the poor developers trying to build database applications. However, the government became useful for a change and formed a committee to create a standard. ANSI standardized SQL in 1986 (X3.135) and the International Standards Organization (ISO) standardized it in 1987. In 1989, this standard was revised into what has been commonly known as SQL89 or SQL1. The ANSI organization upgraded it in 1992 to SQL92.

The current standard, also supported by the International Electromechanical Commission (IEC), is SQL99 (ANSI/ISO/IEC 9075-2-1999; also called SQL3). The basic SQL language that conforms to earlier standards (ISO/IEC 9075:1989) also conforms to the latest standard. The technical changes between previous standards and the current SQL99 include improved diagnostic capabilities, support for additional data types and character sets, and additional operations, especially object handling.

Using SQL, you can take the following main types of actions:

➤ select statement: single row, multiple rows

➤ insert statement

➤ delete statement

➤ update statement

➤ create, drop, alter table

➤ create temporary table

➤ create, drop schema

➤ create, drop domain

➤ create, drop view

➤ commit, rollback statement

➤ connect, disconnect statement

➤ grant, revoke statement

➤ get diagnostics statement

Be careful with data types. Java (actually all languages) has its own data types, which are not equivalent to SQL data types. They might even have the same name, but not the same purpose. You must map Java-to-SQL data types carefully, making sure the two corresponding data types are handled accurately in your code.

Different databases have different data types, and they often vary in representations for values such as dates and Booleans. Java data types also differ from other languages and databases. To work with a database, you must correctly map between the Java and database-specific data types. Table 7.1 shows the mappings between Java, ANSI-SQL, and a few of the popular databases.

Table 7.1	Data Type Mapping Between Java, ANSI-SQL, and Popular Databases				
Java	ANSI-SQL	MySQL	DB2	MS SQL	Oracle
Boolean	BIT	TINYINT	SMALLINT	BIT	NUMBER
Short	SMALLINT	SMALLINT	SMALLINT	SMALLINT	SMALLINT
Int	INTEGER	INTEGER	INTEGER	INT	INTEGER
Float	REAL	DOUBLE	FLOAT	FLOAT	FLOAT
Double	DOUBLE	DOUBLE	DOUBLE	DOUBLE	DOUBLE
BigInteger	BIGINT	BIGINT	DECIMAL	INT	NUMBER
String	VARCHAR	VARCHAR	VARCHAR	VARCHAR	VARCHAR
Date	TIMESTAMP	DATETIME	DATE	DATETIME	DATE

In Java, if you use Java Database Connectivity (JDBC), you have to map Java data types to only the data types used in JDBC. Why they are different is anyone's guess, but that is the state of affairs. The good news is that driver vendors map data types from JDBC to those used in vendors' databases. So you need to worry about only JDBC, which is the point of this library inspired by the Adapter design pattern.

The following sections demonstrate a few examples of how to use SQL. SQL has been around longer than Java, so it is stable, but the syntax becomes awkward when constructing complicated queries. Some vendors confuse the matter by extending SQL to include their own language constructs. For example, Oracle has made SQL more powerful by adding the capability to write a whole program with PL/SQL, which is a hybrid; however, portability has been lost. The good news is that if you use the basic syntax described in this chapter, your statements will work with most ANSI-compliant versions of SQL. However, if you venture from the basics, alas, portability will suffer.

Table 7.2 lists vendors and their customized languages and shows their proprietary extensions in addition to the functionality in ANSI-SQL.

Table 7.2 Vendor-Specific SQL Implementations	
Vendor	SQL Implementation
JDBC	ANSI-SQL
MySQL	MySQL
DB2	CLI
Microsoft SQL	Transact-SQL
Oracle	PL/SQL

Table 7.2 specifies implementations that vendors offer with their products. ANSI-SQL works in all of them, but each vendor adds extensions or provides additional functionality beyond ANSI-SQL. For example, IBM's DB2 Call Level Interface (CLI) is an API that adds functions to application programs to process SQL statements. CLI adds a lot of functionality to the database beyond ANSI-SQL. Part of the competition among vendors to sell more database licenses is to add more functionality than the competitor does. The side effect is vendor-specific SQL that is not portable.

NOTE | Every vendor implements the basic ANSI-SQL command set, including **SELECT**, **UPDATE**, **INSERT**, and **DELETE** statements. Vendors diverge when you want to do interesting things, such as leverage built-in functions and fancy stored procedures.

The **SELECT** Statement

The primary SQL statement is the SELECT statement. Think of it as a print statement. Although it's also used to assign values to variables, it's more often used to print out values returned from querying a database. The following is the simplified syntax:

```
SELECT column_names
FROM table_references
WHERE filter_criteria;
```

Here is an example of using SELECT:

```
SELECT firstName
FROM customer
Where id=86;
```

In Microsoft SQL Server, say you have the following query on the pubs sample database:

```
SELECT 'Total income is', price * ytd_sales AS Revenue,
'for', title_id AS Book#
FROM titles
ORDER BY Book# ASC;
```

This query generates the following results:

```
                  Revenue                      Book#
...............  .....................  ....  .......
Total income is 81859.0500            for  BU1032
Total income is 46318.2000            for  BU1111
Total income is 55978.7800            for  BU2075
```

Likewise, say you have the following query on the pubs sample database:

```sql
SELECT ytd_sales AS Sales,
    authors.au_fname + ' '+ authors.au_lname AS Author,
    ToAuthor = (ytd_sales * royalty) / 100,
    ToPublisher = ytd_sales - (ytd_sales * royalty) / 100
FROM titles INNER JOIN titleauthor
    ON titles.title_id = titleauthor.title_id INNER JOIN authors
    ON titleauthor.au_id = authors.au_id
ORDER BY Sales DESC, Author ASC;
```

This query generates the following results:

```
Sales      Author                     ToAuthor    ToPublisher
..........  ........................  ..........  ...........
22246      Anne Ringer                5339        16907
22246      Michel DeFrance            5339        16907
18722      Marjorie Green             4493        14229
```

In MySQL, the following query is valid:

```sql
SELECT CONCAT(last_name,', ',first_name) AS full_name
FROM mytable ORDER BY full_name;
```

And so is this one:

```sql
SELECT * FROM table LIMIT 5,10;
```

All vendors provide a tool for accessing their databases. One that is especially powerful, but ugly, is Oracle's SQL*Plus. It understands much more than vanilla SQL, including the keywords ACCEPT (get input from the user), DEFINE or DEF (declare a variable), and DESCRIBE or DESC (list the attributes of tables and other objects). In Oracle's SQL*Plus, the following query is valid:

```sql
SELECT c.course_name, c.period, e.student_name
FROM course c FULL OUTER JOIN enrollment e
ON c.course_name = e.course_name;
```

This query generates the following results:

```
COURSE_NAME       PERIOD STUDENT_NAME
...............  .........  ...............
English II            4 Michael
Spanish I             1 Billy
Spanish I             1 Jeff
```

The **WHERE** Clause

The WHERE clause specifies a search condition that filters the returned results. This keyword is how you sift through table data, as shown in this example:

```
SELECT Name, Phone, Fax
FROM Contacts
WHERE Name LIKE 'Pat%';
```

This query returns all rows with a Name field beginning with Pat, so rows in which the Name field is Patricia, Patrick, and Pater are returned. You can combine many conditions in your filter. You can use the following operators to create filters. Note that they are SQL99 compliant and supported by most, but not all, vendors. (Many vendors support all these and many more proprietary operators and keywords, such as !<.)

 The difference between = and **LIKE** is important. = is used to make an exact match, but **LIKE** allows wildcards, so it's used for approximate matches.

➤ NOT—Negates the Boolean result from the given expression.

➤ AND—Returns the row if both conditions are TRUE.

➤ OR—Returns the row if either condition is TRUE.

➤ =—Tests equality between two expressions.

➤ <>—Tests the condition of two expressions not being equal to each other.

➤ !=—Same as <>.

➤ >—Tests whether the expression on the left is greater than the expression on the right.

➤ <—Tests whether the expression on the right is greater than the expression on the left.

➤ >=—Tests whether the expression on the left is greater than or equal to the expression on the right.

➤ <=—Tests whether the expression on the right is greater than or equal to the expression on the left.

➤ between—Searches for a value between an inclusive range.

➤ LIKE—Searches for a pattern.

The ORDER BY Clause

The ORDER BY clause is used to sort-order results, as in this example:

```
SELECT employeeName, employeeID
FROM employees
ORDER BY employeeID, employeeName DESC;
```

This query returns all rows in the employees table, and the rows will be ordered by employeeID. In this example, the rows returned from the query are sorted by employeeID first; if there is more than one row for a given employeeID, this subset is then sorted by employeeName in descending order (because the DESC keyword is used). You can also sort in ascending order by using the ASC keyword.

The INSERT INTO Statement

The INSERT INTO statement is used to insert new rows into a table, as shown in this example:

```
INSERT INTO customer (firstName, LastName, ID)
VALUES ('Kasienne', 'Lauder', 8350);
```

This query adds values into the table; value1 goes into column1, value2 into column2, and so forth.

The UPDATE Statement

The UPDATE statement is used to modify data in a table, as shown here:

```
UPDATE product
SET price = 24.81
WHERE productID = 7;
```

This query changes the value in the price column to the new value (24.81) for all rows that meet the WHERE condition, which is the productID column value equals the specified value of 7.

The DELETE Statement

The DELETE statement is used to delete rows in a table, as shown in this example:

```
DELETE FROM customer
WHERE customerid = 35;
```

This query removes all rows, and the data in them, that meet the WHERE condition, which is the column (id) equals the specified value (35). If more than one row meets this criteria, all rows are deleted. If the column is a primary key where the keys are unique, a matching record is found, and only one row is removed.

Database Vendors

As mentioned, there are hundreds of database vendors who peddle databases of various strengths and price points. The database you build for Sun will not compete with the following products, but perhaps you can borrow some ideas from them. Also, if you use SQL in your search functionality, replacing the assignment database with one of these database products will be much easier:

➤ *MySQL*—Free, small, and fast because it implements ASCII SQL features and a few extensions. It doesn't have native transaction or replication capabilities. However, InnoDB, a third-party vendor (`http://www.innodb.com/`), now provides an add-on for basic transaction functionality. It's a good product from the open source community, but only if used within its limitations. Data integrity is lacking, so be careful. (For more information, see `http://www.mysql.com`.)

➤ *Postgres*—Free, more extensive than MySQL, and still fast. It includes some transaction control with transaction statements such as `begin trans`, `commit`, and `rollback`. (For more information, see `http://www.postgresql.org`.)

➤ *Other free databases*—There are many other free, open source database products, such as GNU SQL, but they don't have the reputation to match the two preceding products. (For more information, see `http://directory.google.com/Top/Computers/Software/Databases/Open_Source/`.)

➤ *Microsoft SQL Server*—In my opinion, this database has the most developer-friendly administrative tools. Recently, Microsoft has also responded to previous "can't handle big jobs" criticism. This is the best all-around database for medium-sized corporate projects. However, I wouldn't use it for something like a national class reservation system. (For more information, see `http://www.microsoft.com/sql/`.)

➤ *Sybase SQL Server*—The long-lost twin brother of Microsoft SQL Server. You can still see the resemblance. Microsoft catered to developers while Sybase went after bigger corporate clients. Sybase handles larger data sets, but is not as easy to work with as Microsoft SQL Server. (For more information, see `http://www.sybase.com`.)

➤ *IBM DB2*—This product handles huge databases. DB2 is a good choice if you need a large database that isn't complicated and doesn't require a lot of application development. (For more information, see `http://www-3.ibm.com/software/data/db2/`.)

➤ *Oracle*—If you want to build an airline reservation with lots of features (in other words, you need to do a lot of application development) to handle an ocean of data, use Oracle. Oracle has focused on reliability and scalability, but it has a complex interface and is difficult to use. (For more information, see `http://www.oracle.com`.)

➤ *Other database products*—There are several excellent databases that aren't as popular as those listed previously, ranging from desktop to enterprise size. These databases include such products as Btrieve, FileMaker Pro, Visual FoxPro, Informix, InterBase, and SAP DB. (For a list of the more current ones, please see Google's database directory at `http://directory.google.com/Top/Computers/Software/Databases/`.)

Need to Know More?

Whitehorn, Mark and Bill Marklyn. *Inside Relational Databases, Third Edition.* Heidelberg, Germany: Springer Verlag, 2001 (ISBN 1852334010). An easy-to-read book about relational databases. Low theory, but enough to be useful.

Kroenke, David M. *Database Processing: Fundamentals, Design and Implementation, Ninth Edition.* Indianapolis, IN: Prentice Hall, 2003 (ISBN 0131015141). A college text that covers the primary topics well.

`http://www2.bus.orst.edu/faculty/brownc/lectures/db_tutor/`—A helpful tutorial on relational databases.

`http://www.atlasindia.com/sql.htm`—Another tutorial on database concepts; this one focuses on SQL using MySQL.

`http://www.palslib.com/Fundamentals/The_Relational_Model.html`—An excellent list of resources about relational databases.

`http://www.w3schools.com/sql/`—A tutorial on SQL basics that covers the basic aspects of ANSI-SQL, which means it is vendor neutral.

`http://www.microsoft.com/sql/techinfo/productdoc/2000/books.asp`—Download the SQL Server books online, my favorite SQL syntax reference. Even if you hate Microsoft, this tool is helpful.

`http://www.sqlcourse.com/`—A fun introductory SQL tutorial that provides easy-to-understand SQL instructions.

`http://www.devguru.com`—A wonderful syntax resource for many languages, including SQL. Click the `T-SQL Syntax` item in the menu on the left to see the syntax structure and a brief definition of each code element in Transact-SQL's four most important statements.

8

What's New in J2SE 1.4

. . . .

Terms you'll need to understand:

✓ Extensible Markup Language (XML)

✓ **LinkedHashMap**

✓ Regular expressions

✓ Logging

Techniques you'll need to master:

✓ Parsing XML files

✓ Using regular expressions to parse search criteria for searching a database

✓ Adding logging to your project for debugging and informing the user about application status

✓ Using a configuration file for your project

In this chapter, you review the J2SE 1.4 features that are new or significantly enhanced since J2SE 1.3. There are too many features to list here, but this chapter covers those that are most likely to interest you for the assignment and are not covered in another chapter. For example, Remote Method Invocation (RMI) is discussed in Chapter 12, "RMI."

Logging

Many candidates add logging to their application for debugging purposes, so I'll start with this new area of J2SE. The Java logging application programming interfaces (APIs) enable you to produce log reports. You can easily add any information to these reports. Developers often capture status or configuration information to help them eliminate performance bottlenecks and, in particular, bugs.

 You can justify logging in your application because one of the key certification requirements is error handling, one of the original motivations for logging. However, you can also use logging strictly for debugging. If you do, you can either turn it off or remove it before submitting your project. Logging is not specifically required for the certification project, but neither are buttons. If you include logging in your project, you have the option to leave it in your submission (it won't count against you) or to remove it to eliminate the risk of a logging error (for example, can't open a log file).

The approach Sun has taken is to provide a `Logger` class (think of it as a container) for you to log messages. To log a message, you just dump a message into this container. The `Logger` class enables you to assign log levels to a message, such as "severe" or "info." The level indicates a log message's importance, urgency, or priority. If the message you try to log is assigned a level beneath the level that has been set for a `Logger` object, the message is not logged. You can define your own levels by subclassing the `Level` class, but you must use a unique integer-level value internally to maintain the uniqueness of your new object, which is necessary for serialization. The predefined levels enable you to filter log messages. For example, the difference between fine, finer, and finest is whether the `Logger` object filters them out. The levels, in descending priority order, are as follows (if you use these same named constants in code, be sure they are spelled all upper-case):

➤ Severe

➤ Warning

➤ Info

➤ Config

➤ Fine

➤ Finer

➤ Finest

➤ All

➤ Off

Using a handler, you can tell the Logger class where to store error messages, including file and memory messages (standard error). Although you can write your own error handlers, the following handlers are already in Sun's logging package:

➤ *MemoryHandler*—Logs are placed in memory.

➤ *ConsoleHandler*—Logs are sent to System.err.

➤ *StreamHandler*—Logs are sent to an OutputStream.

➤ *SocketHandler*—Logs are sent to a remote TCP port.

➤ *FileHandler*—Logs are sent to a single file or to a set of rotating log files.

Listing 8.1 is a simple program that logs the parameters provided at the command line.

Listing 8.1 An Example of a Logging Routine

```java
import java.util.logging.Logger;
import java.util.logging.FileHandler;
import java.util.logging.XMLFormatter;
import java.io.IOException;

public class MyClass
{
    public static void main(String[] args)
    {
        MyClass myClass = new MyClass();
        myClass.logParameters(args);
    }

    public void logParameters(String[] args)
    {
        Logger myLogger = Logger.getLogger("MyLogger");

        // use XML formatter handler
        try
        {
            FileHandler xmlHandler = new FileHandler("log.xml");
            xmlHandler.setFormatter(new XMLFormatter());
            myLogger.addHandler(xmlHandler);
        } catch (IOException e)
```

(continued)

Listing 8.1   An Example of a Logging Routine *(continued)*

```
            {}

            // Log the parameters
            for( int i = 0; i < args.length; i++)
            {
                myLogger.warning(args[i]);
            }
        }
    }
}
```

If you use the following on the command line

```
java MyClass cold strawberry ice-cream cone
```

Listing 8.1 sends the following to standard output:

```
Mar 13, 2004 9:53:50 PM MyClass logParameters
WARNING: cold
Mar 13, 2004 9:53:51 PM MyClass logParameters
WARNING: strawberry
Mar 13, 2004 9:53:51 PM MyClass logParameters
WARNING: ice-cream
Mar 13, 2004 9:53:51 PM MyClass logParameters
WARNING: cone
```

Simultaneously, Listing 8.1 produces the following Extensible Markup Language (XML) file:

```
<?xml version="1.0" encoding="windows-1252" standalone="no"?>
<log>
<record>
  <date>2004-03-13T21:53:50</date>
  <millis>1047621230891</millis>
  <sequence>0</sequence>
  <logger>MyLogger</logger>
  <level>WARNING</level>
  <class>MyClass</class>
  <method>logParameters</method>
  <thread>10</thread>
  <message>cold</message>
</record>
<record>
  <date>2004-03-13T21:53:51</date>
  <millis>1047621231041</millis>
  <sequence>1</sequence>
  <logger>MyLogger</logger>
  <level>WARNING</level>
  <class>MyClass</class>
  <method>logParameters</method>
  <thread>10</thread>
  <message>strawberry</message>
</record>
<record>
  <date>2004-03-13T21:53:51</date>
  <millis>1047621231041</millis>
  <sequence>2</sequence>
  <logger>MyLogger</logger>
  <level>WARNING</level>
  <class>MyClass</class>
```

```
    <method>logParameters</method>
    <thread>10</thread>
    <message>ice-cream</message>
  </record>
  <record>
    <date>2004-03-13T21:53:51</date>
    <millis>1047621231041</millis>
    <sequence>3</sequence>
    <logger>MyLogger</logger>
    <level>WARNING</level>
    <class>MyClass</class>
    <method>logParameters</method>
    <thread>10</thread>
    <message>cone</message>
  </record>
</log>
```

As you can see, the Logger object automatically provides the date, message sequence (because you instantiated this Logger), level, class, method, thread, and, finally, the actual message. Logging is clean and simple in J2SE 1.4. You can take advantage of logging especially when you work on the Remote Method Invocation (RMI)/sockets and database portions of your project.

Another interesting feature is the filtering mechanism. If the message passes the filter, it is logged and said to be published; otherwise, it is disregarded. You assign a Filter object to a Logger object by calling the setLoggable (requires a Level to be passed to it) method, which determines whether a log should be recorded or discarded. You must write your own isLoggable method, so it can contain any code you desire, as long as that code returns a boolean. For example, the method could filter on the log length or scan for a keyword. The pseudo code to use a filter looks like so:

```
public boolean isLoggable(LogRecord myRecord)
{
    //do something with myRecord to filter it
    // return true to log message or false to ignore it
    return false; //conservative default
}
```

Java XML Functionality

XML provides basic support for processing XML documents. Developers have been parsing XML with Java for years. However, for the first time, the XML libraries are part of the J2SE library, which makes them a standardized set of Java platform APIs.

The XML libraries offer many powerful features, such as navigating with XPath, transforming one XML document to another one with a different schema, and, my favorite, displaying and styling a document with Extensible Stylesheet Language Transformations (XSLT). For this chapter, however, the discussion is confined to using XML for the assignment.

These are the three main packages you are likely to need if you use XML:

➤ *javax.xml.parsers*—Contains classes for processing XML documents through Document Object Model (DOM) or Simple API for XML (SAX).

➤ *javax.xml.transform.dom*—Contains classes for transforming an XML document parsed with DOM using XSL Transformations (XSLT).

➤ *javax.xml.transform.sax*—Contains classes for transforming an XML document parsed with SAX using XSLT.

➤ *javax.xml.transform.stream*—This package contains the StreamResult class (which holds the output of a transformation) and the StreamSource class (which holds the transformation source in the form of a stream of XML Markup).

The difference between DOM and SAX is how the parser converts the XML document. Using DOM, the parser creates an object in memory that represents the entire XML document as an object tree. DOM makes it easy to reference any part of the document; DOM does to XML what RandomAccessFile does to files. This contrasts with SAX, which is an API that facilitates sequential, event-driven access to the document. As the parser marches through the document, the parser calls certain methods in response to certain events (e.g., the end of tag event method). These methods are treated as events that you respond to. The advantage of DOM is random access, but it uses more resources. The advantage of SAX is speed, but it allows sequential access only.

Many candidates initialize their application by processing the parameters the user provides at the command line. This approach is certainly reasonable and the path of least resistance. However, some candidates prefer the more professional approach of initializing an application through a XML configuration file.

To demonstrate J2SE's new XML functionality, Listing 8.2 demonstrates how to grab application settings from a configuration file that is an XML document. It is in this configuration file where the user can store your project's initial settings. These settings are defined when the application is installed and, if applicable, reconfigured later.

Listing 8.2 shows that when your application is started or restarted, the configuration settings are read from this XML document. These are the steps for initializing your application using a configuration file formatted as an XML document:

1. Create a DOM object.

2. Open the configuration file.

3. Parse the XML by walking the tree.

4. Process the configuration parameters.

5. Initialize your application with these parameters.

If you choose to go this route, be sure to include instructions in the README.TXT file about how the evaluator should edit the configuration file. For example, the application must know the path to the database file supplied with the assignment you downloaded. The evaluator must add this path to the configuration file or the application won't work.

Most candidates use command-line options to configure their project's database binary file location, local/remote mode operation, and, for remote mode, the RMI server's address and port. However, the command line is not the only way. You can justify using a configuration file because it makes the application more robust and easier to use.

Listing 8.2   A Sample Configuration File Handler

```
import java.io.File;
import java.io.IOException;
import java.util.ArrayList;
import org.w3c.dom.Document;
import org.w3c.dom.DOMException;
import org.w3c.dom.Node;
import org.w3c.dom.NodeList;
import org.w3c.dom.Text;
import org.w3c.dom.Element;
import org.xml.sax.SAXException;
import javax.xml.parsers.DocumentBuilderFactory;
import javax.xml.parsers.ParserConfigurationException;

public class ConfigureApplication
{
    //the initialization parameters:
    String app_name;
    String app_client_class;
    String app_server_class;
    String app_database_class;
    String welcome_file;
    String design_file;
    String help_file;
    String mode;
    String db_path;
    String root_path;
    String security_role;
    String nodeName;
    String nodeText;
    int lastType = 0;

    public static void main(String[] args)
    {
        //get filename and pass that to parser
```

(continued)

Listing 8.2   A Sample Configuration File Handler *(continued)*

```
        String filename = "configuration.xml";
        if(args.length>0) filename = args[0];
        ConfigureApplication application =
                            new ConfigureApplication();
        application.configure(filename);
    }

    public void configure(String filename)
    {
        try
        {   //get SAX factory
            DocumentBuilderFactory factory =
                    DocumentBuilderFactory.newInstance();
            factory.setIgnoringComments(true);
            //load document
            Document doc = factory.newDocumentBuilder()
                            .parse(new File(filename));
            //parse document, set initialization parameters
            processChild(doc);
            //now configure application with initialization parameters
            configureApplication();

        } catch (SAXException saxe)
        {
            System.out.println(saxe);
        } catch (ParserConfigurationException pce)
        {
            System.out.println(pce);
        } catch (IOException e)
        {
            System.out.println(e);
        }
    }

    //traverse the DOM tree
    private void processChild(Node node)
    {
        int type = node.getNodeType();
        if(type==Node.ELEMENT_NODE)
        {
            lastType = type;
            nodeName = node.getNodeName();
        }
        //extract text
        if(type==Node.TEXT_NODE)
        {
            String text = node.getNodeValue().trim();

            //skip if empty or not succeeding element
            if ( lastType == Node.ELEMENT_NODE
                && text.length() > 0 )
            {   //you have key-value pair, assign to parameter
                loadParameter(nodeName, text);
                lastType = type;
            }
        }
```

(continued)

Listing 8.2   A Sample Configuration File Handler *(continued)*

```
        for(Node child = node.getFirstChild();
            child != null;
            child = child.getNextSibling())
    {
        //we like recursion
        processChild(child);
    }
}

//initialize application
//printing is eye candy only
public void configureApplication()
{
    String name;
    String desc;
    String value;

    System.out.println("name="+app_name);
    System.out.println("client="+app_client_class);
    System.out.println("server="+app_server_class);
    System.out.println("database="+app_database_class);
    System.out.println("welcome="+welcome_file);
    System.out.println("design="+design_file);
    System.out.println("help="+help_file);
    System.out.println("mode="+mode);
    System.out.println("db path="+db_path);
    System.out.println("root path="+root_path);
    System.out.println("security role="+security_role);
}

////match nodeName with parameter name and assign nodeText to it
public void loadParameter(String nodeName, String nodeText)
{
    //switch replacement, see note at bottom
    //find initialization parameter and assign new value
    switch_(nodeName);
    {                   if(
        case_("app-name"))
        {
            app_name = nodeText;
            break_();  //exit switch
        }
                            if(
        case_("app-client-class"))
        {
            app_client_class = nodeText;
            break_();  //exit switch
        }
                            if(
        case_("app-server-class"))
        {
            app_server_class = nodeText;
            break_();  //exit switch
        }
                                if(
        case_("app-database-class"))
        {
```

(continued)

Listing 8.2   A Sample Configuration File Handler *(continued)*

```
            app_database_class = nodeText;
            break_();  //exit switch
        }
                        if(
        case_("welcome-file"))
        {
            welcome_file = nodeText;
            break_();  //exit switch
        }
                    if(
        case_("design-file"))
        {
            design_file = nodeText;
            break_();  //exit switch
        }
                        if(
        case_("help-file"))
        {
            help_file = nodeText;
            break_();  //exit switch
        }
                    if(
        case_("mode"))
        {
            mode = nodeText;
            break_();  //exit switch
        }
                        if(
        case_("db-path"))
        {
            db_path = nodeText;
            break_();  //exit switch
        }
                        if(
        case_("root-path"))
        {
            root_path = nodeText;
            break_();  //exit switch
        }
                            if(
        case_("security-role"))
        {
            security_role = nodeText;
            break_();  //exit switch
        }
                if(
        default_())
        {
            //process default condition
        }
        }
    }

/*********SWITCH REPLACEMENT START*****************/
//The switch is limited to byte, short, char, or int.
//This switch is an improvement that handles objects.
```

(continued)

Listing 8.2　A Sample Configuration File Handler *(continued)*

```java
   Object switch_expression;
   boolean stop = false;
   boolean match = false;
   boolean is_default = false;

   void switch_(Object item)
   {
      switch_expression = item;
   }

   boolean case_(Object item)
   {
      if (stop) return false;
      if (match) return true;

      //can customize behavior with a
      //custom comparator here, perhaps
      //myComparator(item, switch_expression).
      if  (item.equals(switch_expression)) match = true;
      return match;
   }

   //required to reset switch
   boolean default_()
   {
      match = false;
      if (stop)
      {
         stop = false;
         return false;
      }
      stop = false;
      return true;
   }

   void break_()
   {
      stop = true;
   }
/*********SWITCH REPLACEMENT END ****************/
}
```

Using Listing 8.2, you can configure your project with the following configuration file:

```xml
<?xml version="1.0" encoding="ISO-8859-1"?>

<application>
     <app-name>Super Bowl Reservation System</app-name>
     <app-client-class>myPackage.client.Client
         </app-client-class>
     <app-server-class>myPackage.server.RemoteServer
➥</app-server-class>
     <app-database-class>myPackage.database.Database
➥</app-database-class>
     <welcome-file>README.TXT</welcome-file>
```

```
    <design-file>DESIGN_CHOICES.TXT</design-file>
    <help-file>index.jsp</help-file>
    <mode>local</mode>
    <db-path>myDatabase.bin</db-path>
    <root-path>c:\programs\football\</root-path>
    <security-role>regular user</security-role>
</application>
```

The preceding configuration file is one possibility. You can certainly add more settings. For example, you could save the details of the last reservation. Then when the examiner restarts your application, voilà—details of the last reservation are shown. Running the program on the preceding configuration file produces the following output:

```
name=Super Bowl Reservation System
client=myPackage.client.Client
server=myPackage.server.RemoteServer
database=myPackage.database.Database
welcome=README.TXT
design=DESIGN_CHOICES.TXT
help=index.jsp
mode=local
db path=database.bin
root path=c:\programs\football\
security role=regular user
```

Listing 8.1 produced a log in XML format. By changing the filename and the tags to scan for in Listing 8.2, you can show this log to the user. For example, you could add a menu item for the user to select having a session log displayed in a dialog box.

Listing 8.1 creates a file and places it in the application's root directory, the directory from where the application is run. Should you choose to display the log, Listing 8.2 will find it as is. However, if you move the log, make sure Listing 8.2 uses the new path.

Assertions

Assertions basically throw an error when the Boolean expression you provide is false. It is a simple mechanism. You could easily accomplish the same thing with an `if` statement, where you would throw an exception if the expression is false. However, the three primary advantages of an assertion are that they use simple syntax, they document code, and they can be ignored by the compiler with a command-line switch. Notice that you can throw an error with an `if` statement, but you can't tell the compiler to ignore that `if` statement.

An assertion enables you to place test points in your code and is a quick and effective way to detect and correct bugs. For example, if you want to stop your program running at the point a given variable reaches a predetermined value, you could use an assertion. Mind you, assertions are designed for debugging and easy removal from production classes. As mentioned, an advantage of assertions is you can compile your code so that they are ignored. That way, you can develop with them, but deploy classes without them. This is how they are normally used.

You might want to use assertions in your project to help speed development. The RMI portion is especially difficult. In fact, RMI still needs polish, which is what makes this functionality so hard to work with. I spent weeks trying to fix a problem with it. The RMI portion of my project worked well on Windows, but not on Solaris because there is a bug in the RMI library. I finally figured out a workaround so that my client on Windows could finally talk to the server on Solaris. In theory, the same code, except for OS-dependent items such as the file path, should work the same on all Java Virtual Machines (JVMs), regardless of the OS. That is usually true, but Java isn't perfect. Using assertions is a new feature to help ease debugging tasks and make it much easier to test code sections.

There are two ways to write an assertion. The only difference between the two is whether you want to pass a message to the thrown `AssertionError` in case the expression is false. The statement that doesn't pass a message looks like so:

```
assert expression;
```

The statement that does pass a message looks like this:

```
assert expression: message;
```

The following is an example:

```
assert file(filename)!= null: "could not find " + filename;
```

> Do not use assertions to do any work. If you do, that work is not performed when you compile the code using the switch to ignore assertions. Basically, don't use assignments or call methods that perform an operation that affects your application's behavior.

J2SE Collections

The collections received some welcome new features; two new classes are discussed in the following sections.

The LinkedHashMap Class

The most useful new feature is the LinkedHashMap class, which provides an insertion-ordered Map that remembers in which order you added items to it. Normally, a Map keeps its keys in random order because that is how it stores them. However, sometimes (as in first-come, first-serve situations) you need the insertion order. Previously, you had to manually do this. Now the LinkedHashMap class (and the similar LinkedHashSet class) uses an internal doubly linked list to keep the insertion order. Remarkably, it is nearly as fast as HashMap.

For the assignment, you might want to keep track of user actions. It is extra work, but you could add this functionality with little effort and low risk. Perhaps you want users to be able to review the last reservations they made. You can use the seat number as the key and the aisle as the value, for example. Listing 8.3 demonstrates how to use the LinkedHashMap class.

Listing 8.3 Using the LinkedHashMap Class

```java
import java.util.LinkedHashMap;
import java.util.HashMap;
import java.util.Map;
import java.util.Iterator;

public class MyLinkedHashMap
{
    public static void main(String[] args)
    {
        //Map map = new LinkedHashMap();
        Map map = new HashMap();

        map.put("A", "first");
        map.put("B", "second");
        map.put("C", "third");
        map.put("D", "fourth");
        map.put("E", "fifth");
        map.put("F", "sixth");
        map.put("G", "seventh");
        map.put("H", "eighth");
        map.put("I", "ninth");
        map.put("J", "tenth");

        for (Iterator list=map.keySet().iterator(); list.hasNext(); )
        {
            Object key = list.next();
            String value = (String) map.get(key);
            System.out.print(value + ", ");
        }
    }
}
```

You can play around with the key-value pairs in the code. Listing 8.3 on the CD has a few variations of the key-value pairs mentioned here and below to demonstrate what happens when the same key is added to a Map type object repeatedly. Listing 8.3, using a regular HashMap, produces the following random ordered output:

```
ninth, fourth, first, sixth, eighth, tenth, third, second, seventh, fifth,
```

Compare that with the following insertion-order output, which is produced by using LinkedHashMap instead of HashMap:

```
first, second, third, fourth, fifth, sixth, seventh, eighth, ninth, tenth,
```

The LinkedHashMap class kept the insertion order. Instead of adding items to the Map object in the order shown in Listing 8.3, you might use the following:

```
map.put("A", "first");
map.put("B", "second");
map.put("C", "third");
map.put("D", "fourth");
map.put("E", "fifth");
map.put("A", "sixth");
map.put("A", "seventh");
map.put("A", "eighth");
map.put("A", "ninth");
map.put("A", "tenth");
```

You get the following output using LinkedHashMap:

```
tenth, second, third, fourth, fifth,
```

As you can see, the LinkedHashMap class keeps the insertion order of the keys. Even though the last insertion had the "A" key, LinkedHashMap returns the "tenth" value in the first position because that was when the key was added. Of course, the original value was replaced by the last value of that key.

There is one more interesting use for LinkedHashMap. You can make a copy of another Map with it. You could do that before by using a Map constructor; however, the two copies had independent orders. Now, with a LinkedHashMap, you can copy a Map *and* its order, which was difficult to do previously. If you want to take a snapshot of a Map's order (in which map is the Map instance you'd like to copy), you can do this:

```
Map insertionOrderCopy = new LinkedHashMap(map);
```

The IdentityHashMap Class

The IdentityHashMap class differs from the other Map classes in one important aspect. Internally, a Map tests for equality based on the Object.equals()

method. The IdentityHashMap class doesn't use this method, however. Instead, it checks whether two keys are referencing the same object, like so:

```
key1==key2
```

If you revise Listing 8.3 to include the following code (you'll find the source code file with this revision):

```
Map map = new LinkedHashMap();
String a = new String("A");
String b = new String("A");
String c = new String("A");
String d = new String("A");
String e = new String("A");
String f = new String("A");
map.put(a, "first");
map.put(b, "second");
map.put(c, "third");
map.put(d, "fourth");
map.put(e, "fifth");
map.put(f, "sixth");
map.put("G", "seventh");
map.put("H", "eighth");
map.put("I", "ninth");
map.put("J", "tenth");
```

Listing 8.3 generates the following output:

```
sixth, seventh, eighth, ninth, tenth,
```

However, using the same revision but replacing the LinkedHashMap class with an IdentityHashMap class, you get this:

```
seventh, second, tenth, third, fifth, sixth, fourth, eighth, first, ninth,
```

Notice that all insertions were stored, even though the first six had the same letter. Although the Strings a, b, c, d, e, and f contained the same letter "A", each is pointing to a unique Object, so they were all considered unequal in the IndentityHashMap class. Conversely, the LinkedHashMap class considered them duplicates.

Regular Expressions

Often you need to match a character sequence against a pattern. Unix and Perl made this operation straightforward with their ubiquitous regular expression libraries. Sun has added a powerful new package called java.util.regex, enabling the use of regular expressions in J2SE 1.4. Sun uses the same regular expressions that are in Perl, so you can use the same expression syntax, which is a relief.

Numerous tutorials and examples on the Web describe the pattern syntax in detail (see "Need to Know More?" at the end of this chapter for two good references). You might consider using the following idea in your project. For the requirement of searching the database, most candidates use the StringTokenizer class to break the search string into its tokens and then process those tokens. This approach works fine for very small search strings. If you want to improve the strength of your search algorithm, however, turn to Java's new pattern-matching capabilities.

The basic task is to use a regular expression to find matches in a string. With a little tweak, you can create an effective search criteria handler. Listing 8.4 gets you started.

Listing 8.4   Using Regular Expressions

```
import java.util.regex.*;

public final class SearchCriteriaParser
{
    public static void main(String[] argv)
    {
        String splitOnThese = "[,'=\"]";
        String searchCriteria = "section=\"23\", " +
                                "aisle='first'";
        String searchName="", searchValue="";

        //compiling sets up the string pattern in the object
        //against which to compare the target text.
        Pattern p = Pattern.compile(splitOnThese);
        //split breaks the text into substrings based on the
        //above pattern.
        String[] items = p.split(searchCriteria);
        for(int i=0;i<items.length;i++)
        {
            String token = items[i].trim();
            if(token.length()>0)
            {
                if(searchName.length()>0)
                {
                    searchValue = token;
                    processCriteria(searchName,
                                    searchValue);
                    searchName = "";
                } else
                {
                    searchName = token;
                    searchValue = "";
                }
            }
        }
    }

    public static void processCriteria(String searchName,
                                       String searchValue)
    {
        //Perform search on the database,
        //or perhaps save to a list for later searching.
        //Presently, print eye candy
```

(continued)

Listing 8.4 Using Regular Expressions *(continued)*

```
        System.out.println(searchName + "=" + searchValue);
    }
}
//returns:
//section=23
//aisle=first
```

Regular expressions are a powerful addition to the J2SE core library. You might consider using them in place of StringTokenizer to parse the search criteria. One advantage of regular expressions over StringTokenizer is that you can use more complex parsing rules. For example, if you wanted to build an SQL query parser, it would be a little easier with the regular expression package. Also, upgrading your application to handle more complicated searches is easier with regular expressions. Although not everyone is a fan of regular expressions, they are a powerful addition to J2SE and worth consideration for your certification project.

Need to Know More?

 Friedl, Jeffrey. *Mastering Regular Expressions*. Cambridge, MA: O'Reilly & Associates, 2002 (ISBN 0596002890). Hard to find a better book on regular expressions.

 http://java.sun.com/j2se/1.4/docs/relnotes/features.html—A guide to the new features of version 1.4 of the Java 2 SDK.

 http://java.sun.com/j2se/1.4/docs/guide/collections/changes4.html— A summary of the enhancements made to the collections framework in version J2SE 1.4.

 http://www.google.com/url?sa=U&start=6&q=http://developer.java.sun. com/developer/technicalArticles/releases/1.4regex/&e=912—A gentle introduction to regular expressions in Java.

 http://www.google.com/url?sa=U&start=12&q=http://java.sun.com/docs/ books/tutorial/extra/regex/&e=912—A tutorial on regular expressions in J2SE 1.4.

 http://java.sun.com/j2se/1.4/docs/guide/lang/assert.html—A full explanation for using assertions with examples.

 http://developer.java.sun.com/developer/JDCTechTips/2002/tt0409. html—A helpful Tech Tip about using assertions.

Interfaces and Abstract Classes

. . . .

Terms you'll need to understand:

✓ **Interface** class
✓ **Abstract** class
✓ **extends**
✓ **implements**
✓ **final**
✓ Inherit
✓ Composition
✓ **static**

Techniques you'll need to master:

✓ Differentiating the purposes for an interface and abstract class
✓ Identifying Java keywords used to create an interface and abstract class
✓ Understanding how to inherit an interface and an abstract class
✓ Knowing which methods in an interface or abstract class need to be declared explicitly in the subclass
✓ Knowing the difference between overriding and overloading inherited methods and variables
✓ Choosing correctly between an interface and abstract class for a given scenario

In this chapter, you review the basics of Java interfaces and abstract classes because your assignment will likely use interfaces or abstract classes or both. Java borrows much of its inheritance ideas from other languages, such as C++ and Smalltalk. However, there are unique features to Java's inheritance model, which are pointed out in this chapter. Interfaces and abstract classes affect the behavior of their subclasses differently than simply inheriting from concrete superclasses.

Overview of Interfaces

Interfaces and abstract classes achieve two things. First, they establish the definition of a class and provide the list of method signatures that subclasses will use. This list becomes a binding agreement between the superclass and its subclasses. Second, they enable programmers to subdivide their workload and distribute it among different people or groups to increase productivity. For example, suppose you have two teams of developers. One team specializes on the presentation layer, and the other focuses on the database. If the two groups do not know what each other is doing, chaos will ensue. The presentation team needs to know what data the database team will hand them for presentation. Conversely, the database team needs to know what the presentation team wants to be displayed.

On a technical level, each team needs to know some amount of detail about the other's code to test and integrate their code into the whole. Furthermore, the testing team wants to start preparing scenarios to test the work of both teams. The documentation team wants to start writing manuals. The deployment team wants to start writing installation scripts. Beyond the original two development teams, other people rely on the code's structure to do their jobs.

It helps if everyone knows the list of method signatures, often referred to as the *application programming interface* (API). If an interface is defined, both the presentation and database teams can start coding simultaneously. The testing, documentation, and deployment teams can also start, if not complete, contributing to the overall project.

The analogy of building a house applies here. After the architectural drawings are completed, the tasks of plumbing, wiring, roofing, landscaping, foundation work, and so forth can begin. Everyone can start the actual work or at least plan and set up his or her tasks. The key to having many people work on the same objective is to have a common definition of the house details that all teams share. When work overlaps boundaries, you need a common definition so that each team knows how the other teams' work affects its own work. Interfaces and abstract classes function like software architectural drawings, containing the agreed-on definitions of methods and variables that overlap boundaries.

If the entity schema for a person is defined early, the database and presentation people can both code to this schema. For example, if a person is defined as having a first and last name, an address, and a phone, the HTML page can be written to display these customer attributes. At the same time, the database programmer can create a table with that schema and write a class that encapsulates a person's definition. The presentation and database programmers can work simultaneously. Although this aspect of simultaneous programming is not often considered, interfaces and abstract classes add efficiency and a way to manage software projects.

Understanding the difference between abstract classes and interfaces is important. The following sections delve into details on abstract classes and then interfaces, and finally, the two are compared. If you want to see the comparison first, jump to the section "Interfaces Versus Abstract Classes."

Abstract Classes

If you want all subclasses to share a method's signature and behavior, you can just create a concrete superclass with that method signature and implementation. What if you have a second method whose signature will be shared by all subclasses, but the behavior differs among the subclasses? In this case, you declare an abstract class and include the first method as you normally would, but then add the second method declared as abstract. The first method is simply inherited as expected. The second method that is declared abstract must be implemented in each subclass. *Abstract classes* are designed for those classes in which some methods are simply inherited and others are overridden. This is different from an interface, in which all its methods must be implemented in a subclass. In contrast, only the methods declared as abstract in an abstract class need to be implemented in a concrete class. The other methods in an abstract class, those not declared abstract themselves, are simply inherited.

If you know the behavior that all subclasses will share, place it in methods in an abstract class, without declaring these methods as abstract. If you know a method signature that all subclasses will share but the behavior will be unique to each subclass, declare this method in an interface or declare it as abstract without a body in an abstract class.

To declare a class as an abstract class, begin the class declaration with the abstract keyword, like so:

```
abstract class Number
{
    //class methods
}
```

If you take a concrete class and add the abstract keyword to the class declaration, the only change will be that this class can no longer be instantiated as an object. To make use of it, you have to use it as a superclass. To subclass this abstract class, you extend it in a concrete class. To inherit methods from an abstract class, you must extend that abstract class. This makes sense because you inherit the implemented methods in the abstract class, but override the abstract methods in the subclass. Listing 9.1 shows an example of an abstract class (see Listing 9.2 for its subclass that extends it).

Listing 9.1   An Example of an Abstract Class

```
abstract class MyAbstractSuperclass
{
  protected MyAbstractSuperclass()
  {
      System.out.println("MyAbstractClass");
  }

  public void inherited_method()
  {
    System.out.println("inherited_method");
    must_implement_method();
  }

  public abstract void must_implement_method();
}
```

In Listing 9.1, the class is declared as abstract, which tells the compiler that it cannot be instantiated itself. You will get an error if you try. There is nothing special about the constructor. The inherited_method() is a normal method; it is declared and implemented here as it would be in any concrete class. When this class is extended, the subclass inherits the inherited_method() method as expected. So far, this class is the same as any other except for the abstract keyword in the class declaration.

The must_implement_method() method is what sets this class apart from concrete classes. It has no body. It looks like a method declaration in an interface. Actually, that is how the compiler processes the must_implement_method() method; it must be implemented in a concrete subclass. As you can see, an abstract class is a specialized interface because some abstract methods possess inherited behavior when implemented. The remaining methods are declared as abstract, which is necessary to be implemented in a concrete class.

Listing 9.2 is an example of a class that extends the abstract class in Listing 9.1. Notice which class is inherited and which one is implemented to make the class in Listing 9.2 a concrete class.

Listing 9.2   An Example of a Subclass Extending an Abstract Class

```
class MySubclass extends MyAbstractSuperclass
{

  protected MySubclass()
  {
    System.out.println("MySubclass");
  }

  public void must_implement_method()
  {
    System.out.println("must_implement_method");
  }

  public static void main(String args[])
  {
    System.out.println("main");

    MySubclass mySubclass = new MySubclass();
    mySubclass.inherited_method();
    mySubclass.must_implement_method();
  }

}
/* returns:
main
MyAbstractClass
MySubclass
inherited_method
must_implement_method
must_implement_method
*/
```

Remember that not all methods inside an abstract class are overridden in its subclass. The inherited_method() of the abstract class in Listing 9.1 is simply inherited, and the must_implement_method() method is implemented by the concrete class in Listing 9.2.

Behaviors that are common to all subclasses should be implemented as concrete methods within the parent class (which can be abstract). If you are not sure that any method in a group of methods will have behavior common among all subclasses, then place these method signatures in an interface class. Note that this could be covered by abstract methods within an abstract **superclass** instead of via interface methods, and note that the use of an interface is preferred.

Abstract classes are a powerful way to standardize behavior in an application. If you have a behavior that you want to be exactly the same throughout the application (for instance, inherited in concrete subclasses), implement it in an abstract class. Where should you standardize method signatures within an application? Some developers prefer to place them in interfaces, and others place them in abstract classes. I recommend the following guide to help you decide where to place a given method:

➤ *Interface*—Standardize the signature. The behavior will be implementation specific.

➤ *Abstract class*—Standardize the behavior. The behavior will be the same throughout the application, so define it in an abstract class for all subclasses that will inherit it.

When choosing whether to declare a method in an interface or abstract class, you must consider that Java classes support only single inheritance: A class can extend at most only one superclass. It can, however, implement multiple interfaces. If a base class needs to inherit (or implement) multiple API contracts, these contracts should be defined in an interface, not an abstract class.

The ideal structure has a list of methods that you want to standardize in an interface as signatures only—these methods have no body. Implement the interface in an abstract class where you add the behavior to those methods; you can use a few or all of the methods in the implemented interface that you standardize for the application. Last, write a concrete class that is a subclass of the abstract class, making sure to override all methods in the interface that are not implemented in the abstract class.

An abstract method is a method with no implementation. An abstract class provides its subclasses with method declarations for all the methods required to be implemented. A concrete subclass must implement all abstract methods in the abstract superclass. Note that you can have an abstract class inherit from an abstract class.

Interfaces

Sun defines an *interface* as a named collection of method definitions (without implementations). You define a new reference data type with a new interface. The interface name can appear anywhere a data type name can. This allows you to declare a variable's type by that interface name. You can do that with any class that implements that interface.

You rarely change an interface after it's defined. Doing so breaks all classes that implemented the interface. That is why interfaces must be designed carefully, more so than concrete classes. Concrete classes are easy to change, but interfaces are hard to change. If you do change an interface, normally isolating changes in a new interface that extends the original interface is best.

The subclasses of the original interface don't break, but there is still the option to upgrade to the new interface.

One of Java's better known features, the Collection framework, is an excellent example of how an interface is used. The Collection framework uses a base interface, also called `Collection`. Listing 9.3 is an edited version of the interface.

Listing 9.3   A Sample Interface

```
public interface Collection
{
    //number of elements in this collection
    int size();

    //true if this collection contains no elements
    boolean isEmpty();

    //true if this collection contains the specified element.
    boolean contains(Object o);

    //iterator over the elements in this collection
    Iterator iterator();

    //array containing all of the elements in this collection
    Object[] toArray();

    //array containing all of the elements in this collection
    Object[] toArray(Object a[]);

    //adds the element if it isn't there
    boolean add(Object o);

    //removes the element if it is there
    boolean remove(Object o);

    //true if both collections have the same elements
    boolean containsAll(Collection c);

    //adds all of the elements in the specified collection to this
➥collection.
    boolean addAll(Collection c);

    //removes all matching elements
    boolean removeAll(Collection c);

    //retains all matching elements
    boolean retainAll(Collection c);

    //removes all elements
    void clear();

    //compares the specified object with this collection
    boolean equals(Object o);

    //returns the hash code value for this collection.
    int hashCode();
}
```

The `Collection` interface is the so-called base interface for Java's Collection framework. All these methods are implemented in the concrete classes within this framework.

The `Set` interface, a subinterface of `Collection`, looks like this:

```
public interface Set extends Collection
{
    // all the Collection methods are declared
    // in Set. There is no difference.
}
```

The method list in `Set` is exactly the same as it is in `Collection`. Why would Sun do that? It probably prefers having an interface with a name that's more descriptive of the functionality of classes that act like sets. That way, you can declare a reference data type as `Set` rather than the generic `Collection`.

Next in the hierarchy is the `SortedSet` interface, shown in Listing 9.4. It extends `Set`, as you might expect.

Listing 9.4 An Example of Extending an Abstract Class

```
public interface SortedSet extends Set
{
    //returns the comparator associated with this sorted set
    Comparator comparator();

    //returns a view of the portion of this sorted set
    SortedSet subSet(Object fromElement, Object toElement);

    // returns a view of the portion of this sorted set whose elements are
    // strictly less than toElement.
    SortedSet headSet(Object toElement);

    // returns a view of the portion of this sorted set whose elements are
    // greater than or equal to fromElement.
    SortedSet tailSet(Object fromElement);

    // returns the first (lowest) element currently in this sorted set.
    Object first();

    //returns the last (highest) element currently in this sorted set.
    Object last();
}
```

The `SortedSet` interface adds a few new methods to those found in `Set` and `Collection`. These new methods provide a hint of what distinguishes the concrete class implementing this interface from the rest of the `Collection` classes.

Listing 9.5 is an edited version of the `TreeSet` class provided with the J2SE 1.4 SDK, which implements `SortedSet`, which implements `Set`, which implements `Collection`.

Listing 9.5   An Example of an Implemented Interface That Inherits from an Interface

```
public class TreeSet extends AbstractSet
                     implements SortedSet,
                                Cloneable,
                                java.io.Serializable
{

    //implementing one of the interface methods
    public Object clone()
    {
        TreeSet clone = null;
        try
        {
            clone = (TreeSet)super.clone();
        } catch (CloneNotSupportedException e) {
            throw new InternalError();
        }

        clone.m = new TreeMap(m);
        clone.keySet = clone.m.keySet();

        return clone;
    }

    //this method is not in the interface and is new functionality
    private synchronized void writeObject(java.io.ObjectOutputStream s)
        throws java.io.IOException
    {
        // Write out any hidden stuff
        s.defaultWriteObject();

        // Write out comparator
        s.writeObject(m.comparator());

        // Write out size
        s.writeInt(m.size());

        // Write out all elements in the proper order.
        for (Iterator i=m.keySet().iterator(); i.hasNext(); )
            s.writeObject(i.next());
    }

    //remaining code removed for space
}
```

Interfaces are often used when objects implementing the interface can be passed to a method that expects the object it receives to have certain methods available. Another good interface example: Most of the entities in the java.sql package are actually interfaces, which are implemented by corresponding classes in Java Database Connectivity (JDBC) drivers. If you open the JAR for a JDBC driver, you see a **Collection** class, a **ResultSet** class, and other classes. That way, you, as the developer, can reliably call certain methods of these classes, without having to worry about the specific driver being used.

Interfaces Versus Abstract Classes

For your assignment, be careful to use the right mix of interfaces and abstract classes so that your evaluator notices the clean design. To help you use these classes appropriately, the following table describes the characteristics of both side by side for comparison:

Table 10.1 Comparing Abstract to Interface Classes	
Abstract	**Interface**
Can declare constants.	Can declare constants.
Static or instance constants are allowed.	Uses public static final constants only.
Cannot be used as a data type.	Can be used as a data type.
yourJSP.jsp	Doesn't implement any methods (no method body).
Can implement none, some, or all methods.	Adding a new method is dangerous because you must add a concrete method to all classes that implement this interface.
Adding a new method is easy because you must add only the method body to the abstract class, and all classes that extend it automatically inherit the new method.	A class can implement many interfaces (using a comma-separated list).
A class can extend only one class (abstract or concrete). But an abstract class can implement many interfaces (using a comma-separated list).	An interface can extend many interfaces.
Methods are not implicitly abstract. (They have to be declared explicitly.)	Methods are implicitly abstract.
Is part of the class hierarchy.	Is not part of the class hierarchy.

As you can see, there are clear differences between an interface and an abstract class. If you want to standardize only the method signatures, use an interface. Conversely, if you want to standardize method behavior, use an abstract class.

In my certification solution, I did not use any abstract classes. I could have, but did not find the need to do so. However, I did use an interface for the RMI portion of the solution (See Chapter 12, "Remote Method Invocation," for more information.)

If you use RMI in your solution, you will use at least one interface. In that case, you might submit a solution without an abstract class, but it must have at least one interface.

An Interface Combined with an Abstract Class

For your assignment, you might need to combine interfaces and abstract classes. You can justify this architecture by defining the method list in the interface first. Then implement that interface in the abstract class. Provide the behavior for some of the methods in the abstract class. Finally, extend the abstract class by one or more concrete classes, in which the abstract methods of the abstract class, and any methods of the interface not overridden in the abstract class, are overridden in the concrete class. This creates a structure that demonstrates a careful use of the different class types and takes advantage of each class type.

Need to Know More?

 http://java.sun.com/docs/books/tutorial/java/interpack/index.html—
This page contains the section of the Java Tutorial that addresses
interfaces.

 http://java.sun.com/docs/books/tutorial/java/javaOO/abstract.html—
This page contains the section of the Java Tutorial that addresses
abstract classes.

 http://www.mindprod.com/jgloss/interfacevsabstract.html—A helpful
chart that describes the differences between interfaces and abstract
classes.

Threads and Concurrent Programming

Terms you'll need to understand:

✓ **Thread** class
✓ **wait** thread state
✓ Daemon threads
✓ **sleep** thread state
✓ Synchronization
✓ Thread priority
✓ **notify** and **notifyall** methods
✓ Blocked threads
✓ **yield** thread state

Techniques you'll need to master:

✓ Understanding multithreaded programming
✓ Knowing how to synchronize a block of code for multiuser environments
✓ Understanding the thread life cycle
✓ Demonstrating how to start and stop a thread and make it sleep
✓ Knowing the state of a thread
✓ Knowing the difference between a single-threaded and multithreaded application
✓ Determining when to implement multithreaded code

In this chapter, you review the basics of Java multithreaded functionality, which is what allows a Java program to do several things simultaneously. An example of the power behind this functionality is allowing users to click a button that saves a record to the database while displaying changing status messages.

Sun's certification assignment requires you to write a multithreaded application. This requirement isn't optional. If you don't get this part correct, it's an automatic failure.

You will need to design multithreaded functionality into the database portion of your project. In particular, you are required to allow several clients to make simultaneous requests to the database. Chapter 7, "Databases and Atomicity," describes how to do this, but the thread principles are explained in this chapter.

Understanding Threads

A *thread* is a single sequential flow of control within a program. It is born, it runs, and then it dies. A thread has its own execution stack and program counter. In fact, the CPU runs one thread at a time. Chip manufacturers have gotten clever by packing memory around the CPU so that several threads have a place to wait in memory, but the CPU runs only one thread at a time. The CPU has some smarts about prioritizing threads. The specifics of how thread priorities affect scheduling are platform dependent. The Java specification just states that threads must have priorities, but it does not dictate what the scheduler should do about priorities. In a non-preemptive model, the scheduler gives higher priority threads more of a chance to run, but not necessarily get CPU time immediately. The CPU processes threads in pieces, not the entire thread at once. This piecemeal approach allows the CPU to switch between threads governed by the scheduler. That way, multithreading can occur.

Java has strong multithreading capabilities. Multithreading was an early consideration when the designers at Sun started work on Java. Many languages also have this capability, but Java's application programming interface (API) for threads is simple to use and works as advertised.

How should you add multithreading? Design a block of code so that it works. After you are sure it's bug free, add multithreading. Don't add multithreading upfront because it complicates the design needlessly.

Take a look at a code sample of an application that isn't thread safe, but should be. Listing 10.1 is an application that illustrates a simple problem: one part of the program being accessed simultaneously by too many other parts.

Listing 10.1   An Application Using Multithreading

```
public class MultiThread1
{
    public static void main( String [] args )
    {
        System.out.println( "Main Start" );

        //determine number of new threads
        int numberOfThreads = 10;
        for(int i = 0; i < numberOfThreads; i++)
        {
            // create a new thread
            new NewThread( "Thread number " + i ).start();
        }

        System.out.println( "Main Done" );
    }
}

// a new thread class
class NewThread extends Thread
{
    // give thread a name
    public NewThread( String threadName )
    {
        super( threadName );
        System.out.println( "created " + threadName );
    }

    // override the run method in Thread
    public void run()
    {
        // try to make thread sleep
        try
        {
            // create sleep duration in milliseconds = 0-10 seconds
            int milliseconds = ( int ) ( Math.random() * (10000 + 1));
            int seconds = ( int ) milliseconds / 1000;
            String status = "NewThread name = " + getName()
                        + "; napping for "
                        + seconds
                        + " seconds.";
            System.out.println( status );

            Thread.sleep( milliseconds );

            // tell system thread is awake
            status = getName() + " is getting up from napping.";
            System.out.println( status );

        // Oops, interrupted
        } catch ( InterruptedException ex )
```

(continued)

Listing 10.1   An Application Using Multithreading *(continued)*

```
    {
        ex.printStackTrace();
    }
  }
}
/* results vary between runs:
Main Start
created Thread number 0
created Thread number 1
created Thread number 2
NewThread name = Thread number 0; napping for 3 seconds.
NewThread name = Thread number 1; napping for 5 seconds.
created Thread number 3
created Thread number 4
created Thread number 5
created Thread number 6
created Thread number 7
created Thread number 8
NewThread name = Thread number 2; napping for 8 seconds.
NewThread name = Thread number 3; napping for 4 seconds.
NewThread name = Thread number 4; napping for 3 seconds.
NewThread name = Thread number 5; napping for 8 seconds.
NewThread name = Thread number 6; napping for 5 seconds.
NewThread name = Thread number 7; napping for 1 seconds.
created Thread number 9
Main Done
NewThread name = Thread number 8; napping for 0 seconds.
NewThread name = Thread number 9; napping for 1 seconds.
Thread number 8 is getting up from napping.
Thread number 7 is getting up from napping.
Thread number 9 is getting up from napping.
Thread number 4 is getting up from napping.
Thread number 0 is getting up from napping.
Thread number 3 is getting up from napping.
Thread number 1 is getting up from napping.
Thread number 6 is getting up from napping.
Thread number 5 is getting up from napping.
Thread number 2 is getting up from napping.
*/
```

There are two classes in the program shown in Listing 10.1. NewThread is a simple class that represents a single thread. It puts itself to sleep for a random amount of time and then wakes again. The MultiThread1 class plays the master role, spawning several instances of the NewThread object. As you can see from the printout commented at the end of the listing, the threads do indeed start and stop out of order because of their different sleep lengths. Theoretically, MultiThread1 could spawn several different instances of NewThread so that 10 of the threads are alive simultaneously. That would mean 10 threads are active at the same time. With Java, you can handle this multithreaded situation easily.

Perhaps the program could be adjusted somewhat so that MultiThread has more control over the NewThread instances. Listing 10.2 is a better example of one object having more control over the threads it spawns.

Listing 10.2   One Object Spawning Sleeping Threads

```java
public class MultiThread2
{
    public static void main( String [] args )
    {
        //determine number of new threads
        int numberOfThreads = 10;
        if (args.length == 1)
        {
            numberOfThreads = Integer.parseInt(args[0]);
        }

        System.out.println( "Main Start" );

        for(int i = 0; i < numberOfThreads; i++)
        {
            // create sleep duration in milliseconds = 0-10 seconds
            int milliseconds = ( int ) ( Math.random() * (10000 + 1));

            // create a new thread
            new NewThread( "Thread number " + i, milliseconds ).start();
        }

        System.out.println( "Main Done" );
    }
}

// a new thread class
class NewThread extends Thread
{
    int milliseconds = 10000;

    // give thread a name
    public NewThread( String threadName, int milliseconds )
    {
        super( threadName );
        this.milliseconds = milliseconds;
        System.out.println( "created " + threadName );
    }

    // override the run method in Thread
    public void run()
    {
        // try to make thread take a nap
        try
        {
            int napLength = ( int ) milliseconds / 1000;
            String status = "NewThread name = " + getName()
                        + "; napping for "
                        + napLength
                        + " seconds.";
            System.out.println( status );

            Thread.sleep( milliseconds );

            // tell system thread is awake
            status = getName() + " is getting up from napping.";
            System.out.println( status );
```

(continued)

Listing 10.2   One Object Spawning Sleeping Threads *(continued)*

```
        // Oops, interrupted
        } catch ( InterruptedException ex )
        {
            ex.printStackTrace();
        }
    }
}
//results look like that of Listing 10.1
```

Listing 10.2 demonstrates how easy it is to control a thread from another object. In fact, in this code 11 threads were running. There is a thread for the `MultiThread` object and one thread for each `NewThread` object. In the following section, you see another way to control a thread.

Synchronizing Threads

For your project's thread safety, you want to be sure that threads don't harm each other. How you accomplish this depends largely on your architecture. I used a lock manager for locking database records. Because all database read/writes were funneled through the lock manager, the responsibility for thread safety was logically placed in the lock manager. As it turns out, very little code was needed to make all this happen. All I had to do was synchronize the lock and unlock methods by adding the `synchronize` keyword in the method declaration. This ensured that only one thread could implement these methods at one time. What each method did was thread safe, so after I had the lock manager, I needed to type only two words to satisfy the thread safety requirement. Some candidates do too much when it isn't necessary.

 You should also be sure to check the classes bundled in the assignment download. If you study them, you'll see that they are already thread safe, so you shouldn't have to touch them if they're used properly.

You have seen how to use asynchronous threads, in which each thread is completely independent of all the others. What happens when there are dependencies between threads? How can you manage threads when more than one thread wants the same resource simultaneously? This requires *synchronizing* threads, which means making sure one thread doesn't harm the others, and vice versa. Your solution must account for times when separate users concurrently attempt to reserve seats. This means several threads will try to read or save data to the database at the same time. You must not allow one user to write data to the database while another user is reading the same data, so you need to synchronize reading and writing data to the database. This synchronization code has a significant impact on the server portion of your final score.

You need to allow threads to share a common resource in a way that is not destructive to the data, so you must synchronize the various method calls. The approach Java uses is to "lock" a particular block (whether it is a whole method or just a block), funnel activity through that single block, and then synchronize the block, meaning all threads have to take turns using the block. That way, only one thread at a time can use it. This one-thread-at-a-time tactic prevents more than one thread from reading or writing data simultaneously. To lock a block or method, you use the `synchronized` keyword. Listing 10.3 later in this section includes the following code:

```
class NewObject
{
    public void nextMethod()
    {
        System.out.println("NewObject.nextMethod() has executed.");
    }
}
```

Notice that many threads can call `nextMethod()` concurrently. In this case, there is no harm because this method simply prints out a string. However, if this part of the code involved writing or reading data that another thread might change simultaneously, you risk one thread interfering with the other.

As mentioned, the way to prevent threads from stepping on each other is to synchronize a block of code so that only one thread at a time can change and read a given variable. Synchronization is especially helpful in database code. To synchronize the `nextMethod()` method shown previously, you would add the `synchronize` keyword in the method declaration, like so:

```
class NewObject
{
    public synchronize void nextMethod()
    {
        System.out.println("NewObject.nextMethod() has executed.");
    }
}
```

As you can see, synchronizing threads is easy in Java. You simply need to add the `synchronize` keyword. Listing 10.3 is a complete example of how to synchronize threads.

Neglecting to add multithreading to your certification project is an automatic failure. Adding too much isn't good, either. As an attempt to add an insurance measure, some candidates synchronize (that is, declare a method with the **synchronize** keyword) too many things. However, this tactic causes you to lose points, not gain them. Be careful about what you synchronize.

Listing 10.3 Synchronizing Methods

```java
public class SynchronizedThreads
{
    public static void main( String [] args )
    {
        System.out.println( "Main Start" );

        for(int i = 0; i < 10; i++)
        {
            // create a new thread
            new ObjectOne().start();
            new ObjectTwo().start();
        }

        System.out.println( "Main Done" );
    }
}

// a new thread class
class ObjectOne extends Thread
{
    static int counter = 1;
    int me = 1;

    public ObjectOne()
    {
        System.out.println("created ObjectOne # " + counter);
        me = counter;
        counter++;
    }

    // override the Thread.run method
    public void run()
    {
        // sleep 0-10 seconds
        int milliseconds =  (int)(Math.random() * (1000));

        try
        {
            Thread.sleep(milliseconds);
        // Oops, interrupted
        } catch ( InterruptedException ex )
        {
            ex.printStackTrace();
        }

        System.out.println("Running ObjectOne # " + me + " but there are "
                        + counter + " created.");
        PrintObject printObject = new PrintObject();
        printObject.incrementCounter();
```

(continued)

Listing 10.3   Synchronizing Methods *(continued)*

```
        printObject.printCounter();
    }

}

// a new thread class
class ObjectTwo extends Thread
{
    static int counter = 1;
    int me = 1;

    public ObjectTwo()
    {
        System.out.println("created ObjectTwo # " + counter);
        me = counter;
        counter++;
    }

    // override the Thread.run method
    public void run()
    {
        // sleep 0-10 seconds
        int milliseconds =  (int)(Math.random() * (1000));

        try
        {
            Thread.sleep(milliseconds);
        // Oops, interrupted
        } catch ( InterruptedException ex )
        {
            ex.printStackTrace();
        }

        System.out.println("Running ObjectTwo # " +  me + " but there are "
                            + counter + " created.");
        PrintObject printObject = new PrintObject();
        printObject.incrementCounter();
        printObject.printCounter();
    }
}

// a new thread class
class PrintObject extends Thread
{
    static int counter = 1;

    public PrintObject()
    {
        System.out.println("created PrintObject # " + counter);
    }

    public synchronized void incrementCounter() //
    {
        counter++;
    }

    public synchronized void printCounter()
```

(continued)

Listing 10.3 Synchronizing Methods *(continued)*

```
    {
        System.out.println("PrintObject # " + counter);
    }
}
/*
results:
Main Start
created ObjectOne # 1
created ObjectTwo # 1
created ObjectOne # 2
created ObjectTwo # 2
created ObjectOne # 3
created ObjectTwo # 3
created ObjectOne # 4
created ObjectTwo # 4
created ObjectOne # 5
created ObjectTwo # 5
created ObjectOne # 6
created ObjectTwo # 6
created ObjectOne # 7
created ObjectTwo # 7
created ObjectOne # 8
created ObjectTwo # 8
created ObjectOne # 9
created ObjectTwo # 9
created ObjectOne # 10
created ObjectTwo # 10
Main Done
Running ObjectTwo # 1 but there are 11 created.
created PrintObject # 1
PrintObject # 2
Running ObjectOne # 6 but there are 11 created.
created PrintObject # 2
PrintObject # 3
Running ObjectOne # 9 but there are 11 created.
created PrintObject # 3
PrintObject # 4
Running ObjectTwo # 10 but there are 11 created.
created PrintObject # 4
PrintObject # 5
Running ObjectTwo # 4 but there are 11 created.
created PrintObject # 5
PrintObject # 6
Running ObjectOne # 1 but there are 11 created.
created PrintObject # 6
PrintObject # 7
Running ObjectOne # 8 but there are 11 created.
created PrintObject # 7
PrintObject # 8
Running ObjectTwo # 9 but there are 11 created.
created PrintObject # 8
PrintObject # 9
Running ObjectTwo # 3 but there are 11 created.
created PrintObject # 9
PrintObject # 10
Running ObjectOne # 3 but there are 11 created.
```

(continued)

Listing 10.3   Synchronizing Methods *(continued)*

```
created PrintObject # 10
PrintObject # 11
Running ObjectOne # 2 but there are 11 created.
created PrintObject # 11
PrintObject # 12
Running ObjectOne # 5 but there are 11 created.
created PrintObject # 12
PrintObject # 13
Running ObjectTwo # 5 but there are 11 created.
created PrintObject # 13
PrintObject # 14
Running ObjectOne # 4 but there are 11 created.
created PrintObject # 14
PrintObject # 15
Running ObjectOne # 10 but there are 11 created.
created PrintObject # 15
PrintObject # 16
Running ObjectTwo # 7 but there are 11 created.
created PrintObject # 16
PrintObject # 17
Running ObjectOne # 7 but there are 11 created.
created PrintObject # 17
PrintObject # 18
Running ObjectTwo # 2 but there are 11 created.
created PrintObject # 18
PrintObject # 19
Running ObjectTwo # 6 but there are 11 created.
created PrintObject # 19
PrintObject # 20
Running ObjectTwo # 8 but there are 11 created.
created PrintObject # 20
PrintObject # 21
*/
```

Listing 10.3 demonstrates how easy it is to synchronize a method. In your locking mechanism, I recommend synchronizing the lock and unlock methods, or at least one method in the algorithm that all locks must carry out. That way, only one thread at a time can attempt to lock a record.

Synchronizing a method is a conservative tactic to protect it from thread problems. However, it does harm performance. A nice feature of Javave is the synchronized block which also prevents data corruption problems in multi-threaded Java programs. The advantage of the synchronized block is that it only protects the code in the block, not the entire method. It has the following structure:

```
synchronized (myObject)
{
    //protected data and statements
}
```

The designers of Java figured out a way to protect objects; they associated a monitor for every object. When a thread finds a synchronized block, it automatically checks with that object's monitor to see if it is available. When the thread gets permission from the object's monitor, any subsequent thread request is put on hold until the current thread exits that synchronized block. At that point the monitor gives the next thread access to the synchronized block. Only one thread at a time may acquire a monitor, which guarantees that there will never be more than one thread at a time inside the block. If several blocks of code synchronize on the same object, then only one thread can be in the entire set of blocks.

Whether you synchronize the method or a block, the threads vying for access can have several states. The following API defines the various states a thread can take. For example, you can make a thread wait or notify other threads that are waiting for another one. Please note the thread methods as follows:

➤ notify—Wakes up one thread that is waiting on this object's monitor. The thread with the highest priority doesn't get chosen; it is an arbitrary choice among the waiting threads.

➤ notifyAll—Wakes up all threads that are waiting on this object's monitor. The waiting threads compete for the next access.

➤ wait—Causes the current thread to wait until another thread calls notify() or notifyAll() on this object.

➤ wait(long time)—Causes the current thread to wait for the specified time or until another thread calls notify() or notifyAll() on this object.

Threads are a powerful feature in Java. They enable developers to manage what processes occur and when. Fortunately, managing threads is easy to do with the Java language. In your project, you need to synchronize access to the database because Sun specifically instructs you to make that portion of the assignment multiuser capable. All you must do is use the synchronize keyword for a few methods, and you have satisfied most of what is required for this part of the project. In particular, you have to implement a locking mechanism and make sure its methods are synchronized and thread safe.

My employer, Verizon Wireless, supports millions of customers who use the Web site to check their accounts, change their information, and purchase phones and accessories. Verizon's servers, which use Java to manage application logic, have a high volume of traffic. At times, multiple users cause the application layer to query the same database table simultaneously. To prevent users' queries from interfering with each other, transactions are synchronized using techniques similar to the ones described in this chapter.

Scheduling Threads

Some candidates prefer to periodically clear database record locks from the locking mechanism. This approach is valid and easily justified. However, the evaluator will not be impressed if you build a `cron` (`scheduled Unix process`) job manager with repetitive time checks using the `Date` class. Using the thread scheduler in J2SE 1.4 is a much better way to achieve the same goal. Although some candidates might want to give users timed messages in the GUI, the most likely use of the scheduled thread functionality is to periodically scrub database locks.

So far, you have seen how to run multiple threads and how easy it is to put a thread to sleep for a specific amount of time. Developers have been using this method for a long time, and it works well. However, sometimes you need to schedule a thread in a more declarative manner.

What you need is an object that enables you to pass another object to it and specify at what time it should be used. The two parameters of interest are `object` and `time`. The object must have a way to start or be started. To do this, extend the abstract `TimerTask` class, which has the run method, just as the `Thread` class does. In this object that extends `TimerTask`, you override the abstract run method. Now the scheduler can invoke the run method when it is scheduled to do so. The second part the scheduler needs is the time, which you can define in three ways: tell the scheduler when to invoke the abstract run method by absolute time, delay the invocation from moment of instantiation by a certain amount of time, and repeat the invocation by time interval. The following list describes different methods of scheduling tasks in the `java.util.Timer` class:

➤ `schedule(TimerTask task, Date time)`—Carries out a task at the absolute time.

➤ `schedule(TimerTask task, Date firstTime, long period)`—Carries out a task at the absolute time and repeats it. Each repetition takes place after a delay defined by `period`.

➤ `schedule(TimerTask task, long delay)`—Carries out a task after a delay specified by `period`.

➤ `schedule(TimerTask task, long delay, long period)`—Carries out a task after a delay and repeats it. Each repetition takes place after another delay defined by `delay`.

➤ `scheduleAtFixedRate(TimerTask task, Date firstTime, long period)`— Carries out a task at the absolute time and repeats it. Each repetition takes place after a delay defined by `period`.

➤ scheduleAtFixedRate(TimerTask task, long delay, long period)—Carries out a task after a delay and repeats it. Each repetition takes place after another delay defined by period.

As you can see, there are many ways to schedule tasks, a welcome improvement to J2SE.

To see scheduling tasks in action, take a look at Listing 10.4, a second variation of Listing 10.1. This time the Timer class is used. This class takes the manual sleep call out of the code and encapsulates the responsibility for putting a thread to sleep inside a dedicated object.

Listing 10.4   A Multithreaded Application Using Timer

```
import java.util.Timer;
import java.util.TimerTask;

public class MultiThreadScheduled
{
    public static void main( String [] args )
    {
        Timer timer = new Timer();

        //determine number of new threads
        int numberOfThreads = 10;
        if (args.length == 1)
        {
            numberOfThreads = Integer.parseInt(args[0]);
        }

        System.out.println( "Main Start" );

        for(int i = 0; i < numberOfThreads; i++)
        {
            // create sleep duration in milliseconds = 0-10 seconds
            int milliseconds = ( int ) ( Math.random() * (10000 + 1));

            // create a new thread
            // add it to the scheduler
            String threadName = "Thread number " + i;
            System.out.println( threadName );
            //new MultiThreadScheduled("Thread number " + i, milliseconds);
            timer.schedule(new NewThreadScheduled(threadName, milliseconds,
                                        timer, false), milliseconds);
        }
        timer.schedule(new NewThreadScheduled("last thread", 11000,
                                        timer, true), 11000);
        System.out.println( "Main Done" );
    }
}

// a new thread class
class NewThreadScheduled extends TimerTask
{
    String threadName = "";
```

(continued)

Listing 10.4   A Multithreaded Application Using Timer *(continued)*

```
    boolean cancelTimer = false;
    Timer timer;

    // give thread a name
    public NewThreadScheduled( String threadName, int milliseconds,
                                    Timer timer, boolean cancelTimer)
    {
        this.threadName = threadName;
        this.timer = timer;
        this.cancelTimer = cancelTimer;
        System.out.println( "created " + threadName );
    }

    // override the run method in Thread
    public void run()
    {
        // tell system thread is awake
        String status = threadName + " is getting up from napping.";
        System.out.println( status );
        if(cancelTimer) timer.cancel(); //kill timer thread
    }
}
/* results vary between executions:
Main Start
Thread number 0
created Thread number 0
Thread number 1
created Thread number 1
Thread number 2
created Thread number 2
Thread number 3
created Thread number 3
Thread number 4
created Thread number 4
Thread number 5
created Thread number 5
Thread number 6
created Thread number 6
Thread number 7
created Thread number 7
Thread number 8
created Thread number 8
Thread number 9
created Thread number 9
created last thread
Main Done
Thread number 9 is getting up from napping.
Thread number 7 is getting up from napping.
Thread number 4 is getting up from napping.
Thread number 5 is getting up from napping.
Thread number 6 is getting up from napping.
Thread number 0 is getting up from napping.
Thread number 1 is getting up from napping.
Thread number 8 is getting up from napping.
Thread number 2 is getting up from napping.
Thread number 3 is getting up from napping.
last thread is getting up from napping.
*/
```

Both listings 10.1 and 10.4 put a given thread to sleep for a random amount of time. That way, the threads wake up randomly. However, there is a fundamental difference between Listing 10.1 and Listing 10.4 where Listing 10.1 creates the threads randomly, but Listing 10.4 creates them in sequence. Listing 10.4 also demonstrates much better control over creating and running threads.

The Timer class is a smart way to schedule work in an application. In order to use it you create an object that extends TimerTask. This object is passed to a Timer for scheduling specific method calls. The idea is to encapsulate work into an object. This gets away from method-specific tasking and keeps the management of work at the object level. It is the same philosophy as hiding implementation or details of the called method from the calling method. For example, if you wanted to schedule a single method, you could simply create a class that extends the TimerTask class. In the run method, you create an instance of the target object and call that method. Listing 10.5 shows you how.

Listing 10.5 Scheduling Specific Method Calls Using Timer

```java
import java.util.Timer;
import java.util.TimerTask;

public class ScheduleSingleTask
{
    public static void main(String args[])
    {
        int milliseconds = 2500;
        Timer timer = new Timer();
        System.out.println("SingleTask() has been scheduled.");
        timer.schedule(new SingleTask(timer), milliseconds);
    }
}

class SingleTask extends TimerTask
{
    Timer timer;

    public SingleTask(Timer timer)
    {
        this.timer = timer;
    }

    public void run()
    {
        myMethod();
        NewObject object = new NewObject();
        object.nextMethod();

        //kill timer thread
        timer.cancel();
    }
```

(continued)

Listing 10.5   Scheduling Specific Method Calls Using Timer (continued)

```
    public void myMethod()
    {
        System.out.println("SingleTask.myMethod() has executed.");
    }
}

class NewObject
{
    public void nextMethod()
    {
        System.out.println("NewObject.nextMethod() has executed.");
    }
}
/* results:
SingleTask() has been scheduled.
SingleTask.myMethod() has executed.
NewObject.nextMethod() has executed.
*/
```

Scheduling specific method calls by using the `Timer` and `TimerTask` classes is a powerful new feature of J2SE 1.4. Developers used to write complex multi-threaded modules to accomplish the same goal, but now you have an easy way to handle scheduling method calls. You can use it in your solution to great effect. For example, suppose you wanted to schedule occasional reminders to users about the current status of their reservations. You could schedule a status message that's displayed to the user every 10 seconds or so, but in a nondescript manner. Placing a message at the bottom of the GUI about the user's last few steps and listing the steps clearly could make the GUI more user friendly.

What do you do if your class must subclass another class? So far, you have extended **Thread** to create a separate thread. However, you can also accomplish the same thing, and override the run method, by implementing the **Runnable** interface.

Need to Know More?

 Hyde, Paul. *Core Java 2, Volume II: Advanced Features (5th Edition)*. Indianapolis, IN: Pearson Hall, 2001 (ISBN 0130927384). A strong section on threads.

 http://java.sun.com/docs/books/tutorial/essential/threads—Here you can read the Java tutorial section that addresses threads.

 http://javaalmanac.com/egs/java.lang/BasicThread.html—This page offers several clear code examples that demonstrate how to use threads.

Networking with NIO

Terms you'll need to understand:

✓ Socket
✓ URL
✓ TCP/IP
✓ IP address
✓ HTTP
✓ Ping
✓ Protocol
✓ Multithreaded
✓ Network stack

Techniques you'll need to master:

✓ Using New Input/Output (NIO) classes for building a browser
✓ Interrogating a URL
✓ Recognizing the various parts of a URL
✓ Working with sockets on both the client and server side
✓ Knowing the state of a socket
✓ Knowing how to build a server with sockets
✓ Building a multithreaded Web server with sockets

This chapter focuses on Java's networking features. You learn how to communicate with other computers and build a browser and a Web server. This chapter also reviews the basics of Java NIO; this portion of J2SE 1.4 has grown substantially since previous versions, which is great news for candidates who choose sockets for the networking part of the certification project. In other chapters, the sample solution discussed in this book uses RMI. However, NIO is an important change to J2SE, and some candidates do use it. Therefore, this chapter covers some of the more interesting aspects of networking that are possible with Java. The sample programs shown in this chapter can be adapted easily for your project.

There are many ways to implement socket functionality for your project. Rather than present only one solution, I have supplied many code listings that offer a wide range of possibilities. If you choose sockets over RMI, you can pick one or more listings in this chapter to build your solution on. Networking is a significant contribution to your score. Although I recommend using RMI to satisfy this requirement, sockets communication is also viable. In fact, many programmers have experience with sockets, but the same cannot be said for RMI. If you go the socket route, this chapter will give you ideas for building the network component of your solution with sockets. There are enough examples here to address all facets of satisfying the evaluator's requirements and to code an effective application in which the client communicates with the database via sockets.

Networking Overview

The network—and the network of networks, the Internet—is a combination of hardware and software that allows computers to talk with each other. Networks stack protocols. That is, they have a foundation layer with another layer stacked on top of it, and another on top of that. It's the same in your computer. It has embedded hardware, software, and device drivers; the operating system is on top of that; your application is running on top of all that; and there is a protocol for communication between your application and another one.

Open Systems Interconnect (OSI) is an International Organization for Standardization (ISO) standard for worldwide communications that defines a networking framework. It specifies implementing protocols in these seven layers listed from highest to lowest:

> ➤ *Application*—This layer supports application and end-user processes (such as using a browser).

> ➤ *Presentation*—This layer formats and encrypts data to be sent across a network (for example, Secure Sockets Layer).

➤ *Session*—This layer creates, manages, and closes connections between applications (HTTP, for example).

➤ *Transport*—This layer transfers data between hosts, ensuring complete data transfer (such as TCP).

➤ *Network*—This layer provides switching and routing (for example, IP).

➤ *Data Link*—This layer encodes and decodes data packets into bits and manages transmission synchronization, flow control, and error checking (e.g., Fast Ethernet).

➤ *Physical*—This layer represents the bits as electrical signals through the network. It includes cables and cards (such as RS232 and Asynchronous Transfer Mode (ATM) protocols).

All the protocols in the preceding list are necessary for the Internet to work. The code listings that follow demonstrate how to combine several Java network components to build interesting applications, such as a Web browser and Web server, represented by the OSI layering model.

Building a Browser

A *protocol* is the exchange between identical layers of two hosts, and a *service* is what one layer offers to the layer on top of it. Instead of delving into the details of how this process works, take a look at Listing 11.1, which shows you how to build a quick-and-easy browser. In this example, the browser displays a URL that is hard-coded in the source by default. You can run this application by passing a URL in the command line and that is what the browser will display. Please notice that Listings 11.1 through 11.6 must be tested when the machine is connected to the Internet.

Listing 11.1   Building a Basic Web Browser Using the URL Class

```java
import java.io.*;
import java.net.*;

public class SimpleBrowser
{
    public static void main(String[] args) throws Exception
    { //default URL displayed by browser
        String url = "www.google.com";
        if (args.length == 1)
        { //URL provided by user at command line
            url = args[0].toLowerCase();
        }
```

(continued)

Listing 11.1   Building a Basic Web Browser Using the URL Class *(continued)*

```
        if (!url.startsWith("http://"))
        { //add protocol if missing
          url = "http://" + url;
        }
        // the URL object does the work on getting the Web page
        URL webPage = new URL(url);
        BufferedReader page = new BufferedReader(
              new InputStreamReader( webPage.openStream() ) );

        String html;
        StringBuffer pageBuffer = new StringBuffer();
        while ((html = page.readLine()) != null)
        { //get each line of HTML from Web site
          pageBuffer.append(html);
        }

        System.out.println(pageBuffer);
        page.close();
    }
}
//returns:
//<html><head><META HTTP-EQUIV="content-type" CONTENT="text/html;
//charset=ISO-8859-1"><title>Google</title><style><!-
//body {font-family: arial,sans-serif;} .q {text-decoration: none; color:
//#0000cc;}//--></style>
//remainder of HTML removed for space
```

The URL class (from the java.net package) used in Listing 11.1 in turn uses sockets, but you don't have to worry about the details of sockets with this class.

Listing 11.1 builds a browser. It has no GUI, but it is doing what Netscape Navigator and Internet Explorer do. These browser applications get a stream of characters from a Uniform Resource Locator (URL) and then process the stream. In the little browser from Listing 11.1, you simply cache the stream until you get the whole page, and then print it to screen at once. IE and Navigator do the same thing, except they perform more processing, such as converting tags into display elements and fetching other pages (for example, image tag).

Don't think Netscape Navigator and Internet Explorer have the browser market cornered. Sure, their interfaces are beautiful, but there is plenty of room to add specialized functionality. For example, with Java you can build a browser that cuts to the chase by eliminating all "garbage" and displaying just the interesting text. You can filter out pictures, scripts, and applets (Navigator and IE allow you to do this), and remove headers, legal warnings, menus, and even silly advertisements. (Navigator and IE can't do all this on their own.) You can programmatically arrange pertinent content in summary form in the order you like and show statistics. You can also perform a cross–Web site compilation of information by getting interesting material from various pages, within a single Web site or from many sites. You can filter all the links on a page and then surf to them, and in turn go through the links on each site and repeat the process. This is how most search engine robots (such as Google's) work.

Try adding filtering capability to the basic browser from Listing 11.1 to see how easy it is to customize this browser. The code in Listing 11.2 adds the capability to filter image and body tags. (You can add other tags to filter, if you want to experiment more with this code.) Here, the body and image tags are replaced with a comment tag to demonstrate how you can filter specific HTML tags from a Web page. You can easily expand this capability to remove other tags or to change targeted tags, such as translating HTML into XHTML.

Listing 11.2   Filtering Tags with the URL Class

```
import java.io.*;
import java.net.*;
import java.util.regex.*;

/*
Body and image tags are replaced with comment tags.
Demonstrates filtering specific HTML tags from a Web page.
Could adapt to translate HTML into XHTML).
*/
public class FilteringBrowser
{
    public static void main(String[] args) throws Exception
    {
        String url = "www.google.com";
        if (args.length == 1)
        {
            url = args[0].toLowerCase();
        }

        String html;

        //use this test HTML file if needed
        if (url.startsWith("test"))
        {
            html = ""<!DOCTYPE html "
                + "PUBLIC \"-//W3C//DTD XHTML 1.0 Strict//EN\" "
                + "\"http://www.w3.org/TR/xhtml1/DTD/xhtml1-strict.dtd\">"
                + "<html>"
                + "<head>"
                + "<title>your sample html</title>"
                + "</head>"
                + "<body bgcolor=\"white\" >"
                + "<p>some text</p>"
                + "<a href=\"/onefolder/twofolders/home\">"
                + "<img src=\"/home/doc/resource/picture.jpg\" "
                + " alt=\"resource pointer\"></a>"
```

(continued)

Listing 11.2 Filtering Tags with the **URL** Class *(continued)*

```
                    + "</body>"
                    + "</html>";
        } else
        {
           if (!url.startsWith("http://"))
           {
              url = "http://" + url;
           }
           //gets Web page
           URL webPage = new URL(url);
           BufferedReader page = new BufferedReader(
                   new InputStreamReader( webPage.openStream() ) );

           String lineHtml = "";
           StringBuffer pageBuffer = new StringBuffer();
           while ((lineHtml = page.readLine()) != null)
           {  //places HTML into buffer for later processing
              pageBuffer.append(lineHtml);
           }

           html = pageBuffer.toString();
           page.close();
        }

        final int imageTag = 23;
        final int bodyTag = 3;
        String replaceImageTagWith = "<!--removed image-->";
        String replaceBodyTagWith = "<!--removed body-->";
        Filter filterImages = new Filter(html.toLowerCase());

        //remove all image tags
        filterImages.setPattern(imageTag);
        filterImages.setReplacement(replaceImageTagWith);
        filterImages.remove();

        //remove all body tags
        filterImages.setPattern(bodyTag);
        filterImages.setReplacement(replaceBodyTagWith);
        filterImages.remove();

        String finalHtml = filterImages.getHtml();

        System.out.println(finalHtml);
     }
}

/*
This class acts on a given HTML tag.
Here it replaces a target tag with new one.
It could do more, such as translate HTML into XHTML.
*/
class Filter
{
    private String html;
    private String pattern;
    private String replacement;
```

(continued)

Listing 11.2   Filtering Tags with the URL Class *(continued)*

```
    private final int imageTagFlag = 23;
    private final int bodyTagFlag = 3;

/*
These text patterns can be as complex as desired.
You can filter for entire HTML pages or single tags.
*/
    private final String imageTagPattern =
                    "[<]\\s*img\\s*([^>]*)\\s*[>]";
    private final String bodyTagPattern =
                    "[<]\\s*body\\s*([^>]*)\\s*[>]";

    public Filter(StringBuffer html)
    {
        this.html = html.toString();
    }

    public Filter(String html)
    {
        this.html = html;
    }

    public void setReplacement(String replacement)
    {
        this.replacement = replacement;
    }

    public void setPattern(int removePattern)
    {
        switch (removePattern)
        {
            case(bodyTagFlag):
                this.pattern = this.bodyTagPattern;
                break;
            case(imageTagFlag):
                this.pattern = this.imageTagPattern;
        }
    }

    public void remove()
    {
        Pattern newPattern = Pattern.compile(this.pattern);
        Matcher newMatcher = newPattern.matcher(this.html);
        String newHtml = newMatcher.replaceAll(this.replacement);
        this.html = newHtml;
    }

    public String getHtml()
    {
        return this.html;
    }
}
// java  FilteringBrowser test
//returns:
//<!doctype html public "-//w3c//dtd xhtml 1.0 strict//en"
//"http://www.w3.org/tr/xhtml1/dtd/xhtml1-strict.dtd">
```

(continued)

Listing 11.2   Filtering Tags with the URL Class *(continued)*

```
//<html><head><title>your sample html</title></head>
//<!--removed body--><p>some text</p>
//<a href="/onefolder/twofolders/home">
//<!--removed image--></a></body></html>
```

Notice the `Filter.remove()` method that includes pattern matching classes
(new to 1.4), a powerful capability. I could spend several chapters on just the
`java.util.regex` package, but for the purposes of this book, I'll just mention
that you can easily expand Listing 11.2 to filter out any standard HTML tag
or text between the start and end tags. You will do more with patterns later
in this chapter, but keep in mind that you don't have to remove the text: You
can strip the text and make it the focus of further processing.

Interrogating a URL

Each Web server has properties about itself and its files that you can interrogate. Before bringing your network to its knees trying to download a patch
file, for example, it would be helpful to know beforehand that the file you are
about to download is 100GB. You can do that by looking at the file attributes
before actually initializing the download. Also, you might want to know if a
host has other IP addresses of interest. Listing 11.3 shows what properties
you can see with the `InetAddress` object.

Listing 11.3   Interrogating a URL Using InetAddress

```java
import java.io.*;
import java.net.*;
import java.util.regex.*;

public class InetAddressTest
{
    public static void main(String[] args) throws Exception
    {
        String url = "www.microsoft.com";
        if (args.length == 1)
        { //get URL from user
            url = args[0].toLowerCase();
        }

        String html;

        if (url.startsWith("http://"))
        {
            url = url.substring(7);
        }

        try
        {
```

(continued)

Listing 11.3   Interrogating a URL Using InetAddress *(continued)*

```
        //local machine
        InetAddressReport urlReport = new InetAddressReport("local");
        urlReport.setName("Local Machine");
        urlReport.print();

        //url machine
        urlReport.setAddress(url);
        urlReport.setName(url);
        urlReport.print();

        //multiple IP machine
        url = "www.microsoft.com";
        InetAddressReport nIPReport = new InetAddressReport(url,true);
        nIPReport.setName(url);
        nIPReport.printN();

        //f = addr.equals(addrs);

      } catch(Exception e)
      {
         System.out.println(e);
      }
   }
}

/*
This class reports the major attributes
associated with a given URL. It uses the
InetAddress class to interrogate the attributes.
*/
class InetAddressReport
{
   private InetAddress inetAddress;
   private InetAddress[] nInetAddress;
   private String name;

   InetAddressReport(InetAddress address)
   {
      this.inetAddress = address;
   }

   InetAddressReport(String address, boolean multipleIP)
   {
      if (multipleIP)
      {
         try
         {
            this.nInetAddress = InetAddress.getAllByName(address);
         } catch(UnknownHostException e)
         {
            System.out.println(e);
         }
      } else
      {
         try
         {
```

(continued)

Listing 11.3 Interrogating a URL Using InetAddress *(continued)*

```
            this.inetAddress = InetAddress.getByName(address);
        } catch(UnknownHostException e)
        {
            System.out.println(e);
        }
    }
}

//creates the URL attributes report
InetAddressReport(String url)
{
    if ("local"==url.toLowerCase())
    {
        try
        {
            this.inetAddress = InetAddress.getLocalHost();
        } catch(UnknownHostException e)
        {
            System.out.println(e);
        }
    } else
    {
        try
        {
            this.inetAddress = InetAddress.getByName(url);
        } catch(UnknownHostException e)
        {
            System.out.println(e);
        }
    }
}

//setter for the Internet address(es)
public void setName(String name)
{
    this.name = name;
}

public void setAddress(InetAddress address)
{
    this.inetAddress = address;
}

public void setAddress(String url)
{
    if ("local"==url.toLowerCase())
    {
        try
        {
            this.inetAddress = InetAddress.getLocalHost();
        } catch(UnknownHostException e)
        {
            System.out.println(e);
        }
    } else
    {
```

(continued)

Listing 11.3   Interrogating a URL Using InetAddress *(continued)*

```
        try
        {
            this.inetAddress = InetAddress.getByName(url);
        } catch(UnknownHostException e)
        {
            System.out.println(e);
        }
    }
}

//getter for the Internet address(es)
public InetAddress getAddress()
{
    return this.inetAddress;
}

//this actually prints out all the attributes
//for the URL provided at the command line.
public void print()
{
    boolean flag;
    int i;
    String s;
    byte[] b;
    System.out.println("For : " + this.name);

    try
    {   //these are all the major attributes
        // or properties of an InetAddress object.
        s = this.inetAddress.getHostAddress();
        System.out.println("IP : " + s);
        s = this.inetAddress.getHostName();
        System.out.println("Machine Name : " + s);
        i = this.inetAddress.hashCode();
        System.out.println("hashCode = " + i);
        s = this.inetAddress.toString();
        System.out.println(s);
        //b = this.inetAddress.getAddress(); //if you need it
        //String rawIP = new String(b);

        flag = this.inetAddress.isAnyLocalAddress();
        System.out.println("wildcard address=" + flag);
        flag = this.inetAddress.isLinkLocalAddress();
        System.out.println("local address=" + flag);
        flag = this.inetAddress.isLoopbackAddress();
        System.out.println("loopback address=" + flag);
        flag = this.inetAddress.isMCGlobal();
        System.out.println("global scope=" + flag);
        flag = this.inetAddress.isMCLinkLocal();
        System.out.println("link scope=" + flag);
        flag = this.inetAddress.isMCNodeLocal();
        System.out.println("node scope=" + flag);
        flag = this.inetAddress.isMCOrgLocal();
        System.out.println("organization scope=" + flag);
        flag = this.inetAddress.isMCSiteLocal();
        System.out.println("site scope=" + flag);
```

(continued)

Listing 11.3 Interrogating a URL Using InetAddress *(continued)*

```
        flag = this.inetAddress.isMulticastAddress();
        System.out.println("IP multicast address=" + flag);
        flag = this.inetAddress.isSiteLocalAddress();
        System.out.println("local address=" + flag);
        System.out.println();
    } catch(Exception e)
    {
        System.out.println(e);
    }
}


//this also prints out all the attributes
//for an array of URLs.
public void printN()
{
    boolean flag;
    String s;
    byte[] b;
    System.out.println("For: " + this.name);

    try
    {
        for (int i = 0; i < this.nInetAddress.length; i++)
        {
            s = this.nInetAddress[i].getHostAddress();
            System.out.println("IP: " + s);
            s = this.nInetAddress[i].getHostName();
            System.out.println("Machine Name : " + s);
            flag = this.nInetAddress[i].isMulticastAddress();
            System.out.println("IP multicast = " + flag);
            int hash = this.nInetAddress[i].hashCode();
            System.out.println("hashCode = " + hash);
            s = this.nInetAddress[i].toString();
            System.out.println(s);
            System.out.println();
        }
    } catch(Exception e)
    {
        System.out.println(e);
    }
}
}
//java  InetAddressTest
//returns:
/*
For : Local Machine
IP : 192.168.0.2
Machine Name : machinename
hashCode = -1062731774
machinename/192.168.0.2
wildcard address=false
local address=false
loopback address=false
global scope=false
link scope=false
node scope=false
```

(continued)

Listing 11.3   Interrogating a URL Using InetAddress *(continued)*

```
organization scope=false
site scope=false
IP multicast address=false
local address=true

For : www.microsoft.com
IP : 207.46.134.222
Machine Name : www.microsoft.com
hashCode = -819034402
www.microsoft.com/207.46.134.222
wildcard address=false
local address=false
loopback address=false
global scope=false
link scope=false
node scope=false
organization scope=false
site scope=false
IP multicast address=false
local address=false

For : www.microsoft.com
IP : 207.46.134.222
Machine Name : www.microsoft.com
IP multicast = false
hashCode = -819034402
www.microsoft.com/207.46.134.222

IP : 207.46.249.222
Machine Name : www.microsoft.com
IP multicast = false
hashCode = -819004962
www.microsoft.com/207.46.249.222

IP : 207.46.134.190
Machine Name : www.microsoft.com
IP multicast = false
hashCode = -819034434
www.microsoft.com/207.46.134.190

IP : 207.46.249.27
Machine Name : www.microsoft.com
IP multicast = false
hashCode = -819005157
www.microsoft.com/207.46.249.27

IP : 207.46.249.190
Machine Name : www.microsoft.com
IP multicast = false
hashCode = -819004994
www.microsoft.com/207.46.249.190
*/
```

As you can see, ample information about the machine service is available before you even get to the files. Listing 11.3 demonstrates how to overload constructors and methods for cleaner code. It is best to overload like this when something in the parameter list is the only thing changing. This program works on many Internet protocols, including HTTP, file, FTP, Gopher, mailto, and others.

Using the **URL** Class

The java.net.URL class enables us to create objects that encapsulate URLs. In Java, most methods that expect to receive a URL expect to receive it as a URL object rather than as a String. In addition, a URL object allows us to access the individual building blocks of the URL. The URL object is easy to use. It takes a string argument (such as "www.google.com") and breaks it into various parts. For example, the following URL

```
http://www.newsbat.com:80/space/news.html#top
```

has these parts:

➤ Protocol: http

➤ Host: www.newsbat.com

➤ Port: 80

➤ Path/File: space/news.html

➤ Reference: top

The URL class has six different constructors. In Listing 11.4, we use the first constructor, which takes a string with the URL, to create a URL object. If the URL is improperly formatted, a java.net.MalformedURLException is thrown at this point and printed to standard out. Otherwise, a wide variety of information about the URL is printed.

If you initialize a URL object with a string, the class in Listing 11.4 parses the string internally and validates each part (for example, throws a MalformedURLException exception if the port isn't an integer). If all goes well, the address is valid. Listing 11.4 shows an example of using URL class features. Similar to Listing 11.3, which demonstrated interrogating the attributes or properties of an InetAddress object, Listing 11.4 shows you how to interrogate the attributes or properties of a URL object.

Listing 11.4   Using Features of the URL Class

```
import java.io.*;
import java.net.*;
```

(continued)

. . . .

Listing 11.4 Using Features of the URL Class *(continued)*

```java
import java.util.regex.*;

/*
This class interrogate the attributes or properties of a URL object.
*/
public class URLObjectTest
{
    public static void main(String[] args) throws Exception
    {
        String url = "http://www.newsbat.com:80/space/news.html#top";
        if (args.length == 1)
        {   //get URL from command line
            url = args[0].toLowerCase();
        }

        URLObject uRLObject = new URLObject(url);
        uRLObject.print();
    }
}

class URLObject
{
    private String url;
    private URL urlObject;

    URLObject(String url)
    {
        this.url = url;
        try
        {
            this.urlObject = new URL(url);
        } catch(MalformedURLException e)
        {
            System.out.println(e);
        }
    }

    public void setURL(String url)
    {
        this.url = url;
    }

    public String getURLAddress()
    {
        return this.url;
    }

    public URL getURL()
    {
        return this.urlObject;
    }

//print out the properties of the URL object
    public void print()
    {
```

(continued)

Listing 11.4   Using Features of the URL Class (continued)

```
        boolean flag;
        int i;
        String s;
        System.out.println("For : " + this.url);

        try
        {
            s = this.urlObject.getAuthority();
            System.out.println("getAuthority() = " + s);
            //Object obj = this.urlObject.getContent();
            //System.out.println("getContent() = " + obj);
            i = this.urlObject.getDefaultPort();
            System.out.println("getDefaultPort() = " + i);
            s = this.urlObject.getFile();
            System.out.println("getFile() = " + s);
            s = this.urlObject.getHost();
            System.out.println("getHost() = " + s);
            s = this.urlObject.getPath();
            System.out.println("getPath() = " + s);
            i = this.urlObject.getPort();
            System.out.println("getPort() = " + i);
            s = this.urlObject.getProtocol();
            System.out.println("getProtocol() = " + s);
            s = this.urlObject.getQuery();
            System.out.println("getQuery() = " + s);
            s = this.urlObject.getRef();
            System.out.println("getRef() = " + s);
            s = this.urlObject.getUserInfo();
            System.out.println("getUserInfo() = " + s);
            i = this.urlObject.hashCode();
            System.out.println("hashCode() = " + i);
            s = this.urlObject.toString();
            System.out.println("toString() = " + s);
        } catch(Exception e)
        {
            System.out.println(e);
        }
    }
}
//java  URLObjectTest
//returns:
/*
For : http://www.newsbat.com:80/space/news.html#top
getAuthority() = www.newsbat.com:80
getDefaultPort() = 80
getFile() = /space/news.html
getHost() = www.newsbat.com
getPath() = /space/news.html
getPort() = 80
getProtocol() = http
getQuery() = null
getRef() = top
getUserInfo() = null
hashCode() = 2048822873
toString() = http://www.newsbat.com:80/space/news.html#top

*/
```

Listing 11.5 contains such a class, URLWrapperDemonstration. As you can see, the class's set() method even uses the URL class internally to validate the URL. The primary downside of this approach is that commonly used Java methods that expect an instance of URL will not accept an instance of URLWrapperDemonstration.

Listing 11.5   An Example of Manipulating a URL Address

```java
import java.io.*;
import java.net.*;

/*
This class manipulates the properties associated with a
Web address by using the URL object. Particular properties or
attributes, such as protocol and port, can be changed directly,
as shown here.
*/
public class URLWrapperDemonstration
{
    public static void main(String[] args) throws Exception
    {

        String protocol = "http";
        String host = "java.sun.com";
        int port = 80;
        String file = "j2se/1.4/docs/api/java/net/URL.html";
        String ref = "#getFile()";
        URLEntity urlEntity = new URLEntity();
        urlEntity.setProtocol(protocol);
        urlEntity.setHost(host);
        urlEntity.setPort(port);
        urlEntity.setFile(file);
        urlEntity.setRef(ref);
        urlEntity.setURL();
        String s = urlEntity.toString();
        System.out.println(s);
        // http://java.sun.com/j2se/1.4/docs/api/
        // java/net/URL.html#getFile()
    }
}

//entity class that allows you to change properties,
//such as host, port, and protocol.
class URLEntity
{
    private String protocol;
    private String host;
    private int port;
    private String file;
    private String ref;
    private URL urlEntity;

    public void setProtocol(String s)
    {
      this.protocol = s;
    }
```

(continued)

Listing 11.5 An Example of Manipulating a URL Address *(continued)*

```
public void setHost(String s)
{
  this.host = s;
}

public void setPort(int i)
{
  this.port = i;
}

public void setFile(String s)
{
  this.file = s;
}

public void setRef(String s)
{
  this.ref = s;
}

public void setURL()
{
  try
  {
    this.urlEntity = new URL(this.protocol, this.host,
                        this.port, this.file + this.ref);
  } catch(MalformedURLException e)
  {
    System.out.println(e);
  }
}

public String toString()
{
  return this.urlEntity.toString();
}
}
//returns:
/*
http://java.sun.com:80/j2se/1.4/docs/api/java/net/URL.html#getFile()
*/
```

Listing 11.5 uses URLWrapperDemonstration to demonstrate how you can build a wrapper around another class. For some reason, the Java folks didn't include set methods in the URL class to go along with the get methods, probably fearing that developers might not set all the URL parts before trying to connect (use the openConnection() method) with it. However, you can just wrap your own class around the URL object and do what you please. You can append the file portion of a URL to an existing URL object that was instantiated with a host string, like so:

```
URL google = new URL("http://www.google.com/");
URL googleAbout = new URL(google, "about/");
```

The first line of code in the URLWrapperDemonstration class instantiates the URL object with a host address, and the second line adds the file path. Be careful: If you try to append too many parts like this, it becomes easy to make a mistake, in which case a MalformedURLException exception is thrown. The following snippet works:

```
URL google = new URL("http://www.google.com/");
URL googleAbout = new URL(google, "about");
String s = googleAbout.toString();
System.out.println(s);
//returns:
//http://www.google.com/about
```

As you can see, the about portion of the path is appended to the URL by using the two-parameter constructor or the URL class. Inside the URL object, the second parameter (file path) is assigned to its private file variable.

The simple program in Listing 11.6 shows you how to get an HTML page (for example, a Java application programming interface [API], a javadoc page, and so forth) from a Web server with a new twist—this class is designed to print out the class's methods with return types.

Listing 11.6   Building a Web Page Parser

```
import java.io.*;
import java.net.*;

/*
This class gets a javadoc Web page and
parses it, printing out the methods.
*/
public class ListClassMethods
{
    public static void main(String[] args) throws Exception
    {
        String className = "java.net.URL";
        String lineHtml = "";
        String html = "";
        int start = 1;
        int end = 1;

        if (args.length == 1)
        {
            className = args[0];
        }

        //converts the dot notation into a file path
        className = className.replace('.', '/');
        String url = "http://java.sun.com/j2se/1.4/docs/api/";
        url += className + ".html";

        URL webPage = new URL(url);
        BufferedReader page = new BufferedReader(
                new InputStreamReader( webPage.openStream() ) );
```

(continued)

Listing 11.6   Building a Web Page Parser *(continued)*

```
StringBuffer pageBuffer = new StringBuffer();
while ((lineHtml = page.readLine()) != null)
{ //gets all the HTML
   pageBuffer.append(lineHtml);
}

html = pageBuffer.toString();
page.close();

if (html.length() != 0)
{
   //this finds the table of method names
   String codeSnippet="";
   start = html.indexOf("<A NAME=\"method_summary\">") + 1;
   end = html.indexOf("</TABLE>", start);
   html = html.substring(start, end);
   end = 0;
   int count = 0;
   Scrub scrub = new Scrub();

   while(count++<50)   //limit
   {
      //get return type
      start = html.indexOf("<CODE>", end) ;
      if (start == -1) { break; }
      end = html.indexOf("</CODE>", start + 6);
      if (end== -1) { break; }
      codeSnippet = html.substring(start + 6, end);
      scrub.setSource(codeSnippet);
      scrub.remove(" ", ";");
      scrub.remove("<A HREF", ">");
      scrub.remove("</A>", ">");
      scrub.remove("<B>", ">");
      scrub.remove("</B>", ">");
      codeSnippet = scrub.getSource();
      System.out.println(codeSnippet);

      //get method name
      start = html.indexOf("<CODE><B>", end);
      if (start == -1) { break; }
      end = html.indexOf("</CODE>", start + 9);
      if (end == -1) { break; }
      codeSnippet = html.substring(start + 9, end);
      scrub.setSource(codeSnippet);
      scrub.remove(" ", ";");
      scrub.remove("<A HREF", ">");
      scrub.remove("</A>", ">");
      scrub.remove("<B>", ">");
      scrub.remove("</B>", ">");
      codeSnippet = scrub.getSource();
      System.out.println(codeSnippet);
      System.out.println();

   }//end while
   System.out.println(--count + " methods");
```

(continued)

Listing 11.6   Building a Web Page Parser *(continued)*

```
      }//end if
    }//end main
}//end class

//this helper class removes HTML notation
//from the text to isolate the text of interest
class Scrub
{
   private int start = 0;
   private int end = 0;
   private String source = "";

   void setSource(String source)
   {
      this.source = source;
   }

   void remove(String open, String close)
   {
      start = 0;
      end = 0;

      while( !(start==-1 ¦¦ end==-1) )
      {
         start = this.source.indexOf(open);
         if(start > -1)
         {
            end = this.source.indexOf(close, start);
            if(end > -1)
            {
               String s = this.source.substring(0,start);
               end = end + close.length();
               this.source = s + this.source.substring(end);
            }
         }
      }
   }

   String getSource()
   {
      return this.source;
   }
}
// java  ListClassMethods java.net.URL
//returns:
// boolean  equals(Objectobj)
//String  getAuthority()
//Object  getContent()
//Object  getContent(Class[] classes)
//int  getDefaultPort()
//--code removed for space--
//String  toString()
//22 methods
```

Of course, you can get fancy with pattern matching (import
java.util.regex.*) and other tweaks, such as passing a string array of items to

remove rather than calling the remove method repeatedly, but the focus is the URL object, so the Scrub class handles the HTML tag removal chores.

> Be careful when placing the **URL** object in a loop. If the loop doesn't terminate, you could end up making a massive volume of requests to the resource at that URL, which could slow or stop the server hosting the resource. Saturating a server this way is called a denial-of-server (DOS) attack and can, if perpetrated intentionally, subject the perpetrator to legal action.

Working with Sockets

Now that you have seen how sockets work on the Internet via high-level classes such as URL, you'll see how sockets work when used directly.

A *socket* is one endpoint of a network connection that has a port number. One way to think about sockets is to use an analogy. Sockets are like apartment complexes. To make a proper socket connection you need an IP address and port number. To deliver a letter to an apartment, you need the street address (analogous to IP address) and the apartment number (analogous to the port number). With that analogy in mind, you open a socket like so:

```
String apartmentAddress = "123 main street";
int apartmentNumber = 4;
Socket apartment = new Socket(apartmentAddress, apartmentNumber);
```

The apartmentAddress is the equivalent to the IP address; the address you are trying to open a connection to. The apartmentNumber is equivalent to the port the server is listening to.

Regarding port numbers, if you are writing your own server and running it on a production network, I recommend using port numbers from 49152 through 65535 to avoid using a number registered by another application. If you are just testing on a small network or are running only on a local machine, you need to use a number above 1,023 because ports 1,023 and below are considered reserved for protocols such as FTP, HTTP, Gopher, and the like. The Internet Assigned Numbers Authority (IANA) manages the port-protocol assignments necessary for operating network applications and the Internet. IANA has structured port numbers so that they are divided into three ranges: the Well Known Ports, the Registered Ports, and the Dynamic and/or Private Ports (http://www.iana.org/assignments/port-numbers). The following list describes the three port number ranges:

➤ *Well Known Ports*—Ports 0 through 1023 are used by well-known protocols, such as 80=HTTP, 21=FTP, and 23=Telnet, so don't use a port in this range for a custom protocol.

➤ *Registered Ports*—Ports from 1024 through 49151 are used by vendors such as Cisco. For example, Oracle uses 1525, and Microsoft uses 3074 for its Xbox game port. I recommend not using these ports for production code, but they are fine for testing.

➤ *Dynamic and/or Private Ports*—These ports are not reserved, so you can safely use them without worrying about problems with another application from a well-known vendor. You could still have problems, however, if another application is using the same port, even if that port is not registered with IANA.

The Internet uses some protocols that are asynchronous and some that are synchronous. For example, FTP is functionally synchronous, and HTTP is asynchronous. Asynchronous communication is more reliable and efficient. To better understand this concept, compare HTTP over the Internet with how telephone networks have traditionally worked. Efficiency in telephone networks is terrible because the connections are synchronous. When you call your mom, your phone is connected directly and stays that way until one of you disconnects. Think about it: A single connection (one strand of hundreds of wires and switches linked together) is dedicated to your phone call. Even when nobody is talking, the line is yours and no one else can share it. Now compare this to how HTTP works on the Internet. When you surf to a Web site, you get one page (that is, a file) at a time. Basically, your browser sets up a socket and uses it to send a request on the wire, and the Internet takes it from there. Your browser listens and waits, but is not connected to, for example, Amazon's Web server. The Internet routes your request to Amazon's Web farm. Eventually, one of the servers is contacted, parses the request, and puts the requested file (Web servers are just file-copy applications) on the wire, but is not connected to your machine. The Internet routes the file's bytes back to the requesting machine. Your browser gets the file through its socket and saves to its disk. This process is entirely asynchronous and demonstrates efficient use of Internet hardware, a very different approach to communication than what telephone networks use.

The most powerful thing you can do with sockets is build a server. The server in this next example fundamentally provides a service in the same way that database, Web, and FTP servers do. First, you initialize the `ServerSocket` object, as shown here:

```
ServerSocket serverSocket = new ServerSocket(PortNumber);
```

Inside the `ServerSocket` class is a mini-application that hides a lot of socket details you don't have to worry about. This mini-application starts a thread on your computer that sets the foundation for this line:

```
Socket clientSocket = serverSocket.accept();
```

The `ServerSocket.accept()` method waits for (or is said to be "listening for") a client request. The `clientSocket` has an endless loop that polls the system for a request to show up on the `PortNumber` port. These two lines are the heart of a real server. You need just a few minor additions to make this server useful, but you have already gotten close to having a functioning server.

The socket is listening to the port, and you don't yet have a way to handle messages that might come your way. The following code adds message handling:

```
BufferedReader in = new BufferedReader(
            new InputStreamReader(
            clientSocket.getInputStream())));
```

The `Socket.getInputStream()` method is the socket's method for getting a handle on a request in the form of an input stream (sequence of bytes) for this socket. The second line creates a `Reader` that enables you to grab bytes off the stream. The first line just gets bytes in bunches for efficiency, but it isn't necessary. You need one last item to complete the server. The following code is how the server obtains a PrintWriter for printing text back to the client in response to the client's request:

```
PrintWriter out = new PrintWriter(clientSocket.getOutputStream(), true);
```

Use **PrintWriter** to send text data, but **PrintStream** to send binary. Sun's documentation says to use **PrintStream** to send character data as bytes, but do not use it for non-character data. Also, the **PrintWriter** methods never throw an **IOException**, so use the PrintWriter's **checkError()** instead.

The preceding code snippets give you all the pieces to build a server. The following program is a functioning server, although it doesn't do much but send gibberish to the client. The client does get to quit the connection with the key phrase yes dear. Based on a little marriage humor, Listing 11.7 shows you how to build a server using sockets. In this example, the `WifeServer` class demonstrates how to set up a socket to listen for client requests. Java makes it easy to create a server by providing socket classes that do a lot of the detail work, leaving only simple methods for developers to worry about.

Listings 11.7 and 11.8 work together. After compiling both, you use them by first starting `WifeServer` (that is, `java WifeServer`). Then run `HusbandClient` (that is, `java HusbandClient`). After the `HusbandClient` program is running, you can type messages on the command line and have answers from `WifeServer` displayed in the `HusbandClient` command window. With both of them running, type yes dear in the `HusbandClient` command line and press Enter. When you do so, `HusbandClient` sends your text as a request to `WifeServer`.

After the connection is made, WifeServer processes the request. In this case, WifeServer merely compares the text of your request against a small list of texts stored in WifeServer. If you typed yes dear in the HusbandClient command line and pressed Enter, WifeServer responds with I love you, dear. In the HusbandClient window, you see the text wife says: I love you, dear. Although the husband/wife analogy is simple, the interaction between two programs via sockets is a powerful capability that Java makes easy to build. Now take a look at the first part of the duo, Listing 11.7.

Listing 11.7 Building a Server with Sockets

```java
import java.net.*;
import java.io.*;
import java.util.Random;

//this class creates a server socket
//that listens on a port for client requests
public class WifeServer
{
   public static void main(String[] args) throws IOException
   {
      int PortNumber = 5108; //her ATM password
      ServerSocket wifeSocket = null;
      try
      {  //create a server socket that listens on port 5108
         wifeSocket = new ServerSocket(PortNumber);
      } catch (IOException e)
      {
         System.err.println("Port " + PortNumber + " not available." );
         System.exit(1);
      }

      Socket husbandSocket = null;
      try
      {  //this simple statement creates the socket
         //that listens for client requests.
         husbandSocket = wifeSocket.accept();
      } catch (IOException e)
      {
         System.err.println("Port " + PortNumber + " failure.");
         System.exit(1);
      }

      try
      {
         PrintWriter out =
                 new PrintWriter(husbandSocket.getOutputStream(), true);
         BufferedReader in =
                 new BufferedReader(
                 new InputStreamReader(
                 husbandSocket.getInputStream())));

         String husbandSays, wifeSays;
         Wife wife = new Wife();
```

(continued)

Listing 11.7 Building a Server with Sockets *(continued)*

```
            wifeSays = wife.answer(null);
            out.println(wifeSays);

            //get the request text
            while ((husbandSays = in.readLine()) != null)
            {
               wifeSays = wife.answer(husbandSays);
               out.println(wifeSays);
               if (wife.turnOff)
               {
                  break;
               }
            }
            out.close();
            in.close();
            husbandSocket.close();
         } catch (IOException e)
         {
            System.out.println(e);
         }

         wifeSocket.close();
      }
}

//this class parses the request
//and responds accordingly.
class Wife
{
   public boolean turnOff = false;
   private String answer = "";
   private String[] sweetNothings =
      { "Take out that smelly garbage.",
        "Mow the lawn you bum.",
        "Fix the sink you broke.",
        "We talked about this already.",
        "No! My birthday was last Monday."
      };

   public String answer(String husbandSays) {

      String theOutput = null;

      if (husbandSays == null)
      {
         this.answer = "I love you, dear.";
      } else if (husbandSays.indexOf("yes dear")!=-1)
      {
         this.answer = "I still love you, honey.";
      } else
      {
         Random random = new Random();
         int whisper = random.nextInt(5);
         this.answer = this.sweetNothings[whisper];
      }

      return this.answer;
   }
}
```

The solution shown in Listing 11.7 represents a server. Now you need a client, as shown in Listing 11.8, to talk to the server. This client creates a request by connecting to the server socket on a predetermined port. After the connection is made, the request is sent to the server.

Listing 11.8   Building a Client with Sockets

```java
import java.io.*;
import java.net.*;

//this class is a client that connects
//to a server listening to a predetermined port.
public class HusbandClient
{
    public static void main(String[] args) throws IOException
    {
        Socket husbandSocket = null;
        PrintWriter out = null;
        BufferedReader wifeServer = null;
        String machineName = "localhost", wifeSays = null;
        int portNumber = 5108;
        BufferedReader in = null;

        try
        {
            husbandSocket = new Socket(machineName, portNumber);
            out = new PrintWriter(husbandSocket.getOutputStream(), true);
            in = new BufferedReader(new InputStreamReader(
                                husbandSocket.getInputStream()));
        } catch (UnknownHostException e)
        {
            System.err.println("Failure-" + machineName + ":" + portNumber);
            System.exit(1);
        } catch (IOException e)
        {
            System.err.println("Bad I/O-" + machineName + ":" + portNumber);
            System.exit(1);
        }

        try
        {
            wifeServer = new BufferedReader(
                                new InputStreamReader(System.in));
            while ((wifeSays = wifeServer.readLine()) != null)
            {
                out.println(wifeSays);
                System.out.println("wife says: " + in.readLine());
            }
        } catch (IOException e)
        {
            out.close();
            in.close();
            wifeServer.close();
            husbandSocket.close();
        }
    }
}
```

The client *and* server write to and read from their respective sockets. You must have four **try-catch** blocks to make this code work properly, one for each direction of each socket.

You start the server first and then the client. The program will not work the other way because the server is listening for the client. If the client is started first, it will fail because it tries to connect to the server, which doesn't exist. To see output, bring the window in which the HusbandClient is running to the foreground. Type a message and press Enter, or just press Enter by itself. Try this a few times and observe the results. At some point, enter "yes dear" and notice that the WifeServer gives a kind feedback message rather than a commanding one.

Not only does this program show the general structure of building socket applications should you chose sockets over RMI for the certification assignment, but it also shows how to build a client and server that communicate with one another in an easy-to-understand example.

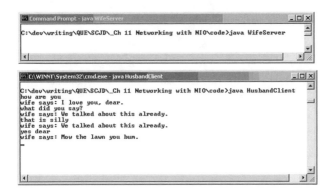

Figure 11.1 Illustrating socket programming with a server/client application.

Good-natured ribbing aside, notice that you need two command prompts to make this program work: one for the server and one for the client. After the server starts (java WifeServer), it waits for someone to knock on its port, which is set at 5108. The client starts by calling on the same machine and knocking on port 5108. The server accepts the connection and sends the first message to the client (wife says: I love you, dear). From the client console, you send messages to the server, and the server responds with randomly selected sentences. When you are done using the application, press Ctrl+C in each window to quit that part of the application. This client/server pair is simple, but it shows you all the steps for setting up a basic socket-based server and building a rudimentary client.

The client socket and server socket do the same things: listen for each other, receive messages, process messages, and, finally, respond. The difference between the two sockets is that the client visits first, and the server waits patiently for company. This set of steps is the general process a socket follows, whether it's on the client or server:

1. Open a connection consisting of a socket with a domain and a port.

2. Open an input stream that collects data from the socket.

3. Read from the stream and assign the data read to variables as desired.

4. Implement a decision tree to take action based on the received bytes.

5. Open an output stream that sends data to the socket.

6. Write output to the stream and assign bytes to the stream from variables.

7. Close the stream and send resources to the garbage collector.

Building a Multithreaded Server with Sockets

The server program in Listings 11.7 and 11.8 handles one client. How do you manage many client requests on the same port, which means several clients are trying to connect to the same ServerSocket object? In Java, you create threads, one for each client. Remember that the CPU does one thing at a time. If all threads run at perfect efficiency, completing 10 threads, for example, takes the same amount of time no matter what order the threads are in. Of course, threads, like connections, have slow moments. Taking up the slack in one thread with part of another thread reduces the total time for all 10. The more complicated a thread is, the more uneven its use of the CPU. Client/server software is complicated and uneven. Optimizing CPU use by swapping which connection is actually using the CPU at a given moment is a great idea.

The operating system can switch between different threads quickly, at thousands of times per second. Like an object, a thread is really a sequence of execution steps. So a thread uses the CPU for a while (thread one) and then gets booted off. The system saves registers, stacks, and queues associated with that thread into a so-called process control block. Then another thread (thread two) uses the CPU, and so on. Eventually, thread one has another turn, and the CPU resumes where that thread left off by resuming thread execution based on what's in the process control block. This swapping between threads is called *multithreaded operation*.

Currently, if you open a command prompt and run HusbandClient, it works fine. If you open a second command prompt and try to run HusbandClient, however, it freezes. To fix this problem, you need to make the server multithreaded. First, add another class, as shown in Listing 11.9. This class is similar to Listing 11.7 except that you add the capability for WifeServer to handle multiple HusbandClients that make connections with WifeServer simultaneously.

Listing 11.9   Adding a Multithreaded Super Class

```java
import java.net.*;
import java.io.*;

//this class creates a separate thread for each
//instance of HusbandClient. This makes the
//server multiuser capable.
public class WifeMultithreadedServer
{
    public static void main(String[] args) throws IOException {

        boolean listening = true;
        int PortNumber = 5108; //her ATM password
        ServerSocket wifeSocket = null;
        WifeThread wifeThread = null;
        try
        {
            wifeSocket = new ServerSocket(PortNumber);
        } catch (IOException e)
        {
            System.err.println("Port " + PortNumber + " not available." );
            System.exit(1);
        }

        while (listening)
        {   //each instance of HusbandClient gets
            //its own WifeThread, which creates
            //a socket connection with WifeServer.
            new WifeThread(wifeSocket.accept()).start();
        }

        wifeSocket.close();
    }
}
```

Listing 11.9 is the new class HusbandClient will connect to. This class acts like a server manager. When it gets a request for a connection, it spawns a new thread and hands the connection off to it, so that instance of the client is connected to the newly created thread (WifeThread). Isn't this fun? Next, you need to alter the previous WifeServer so that it can be a single thread, as shown in Listing 11.10. After that is accomplished, you have converted the single-threaded server that services only one socket connection into a multi-threaded server that can handle multiple connections with clients simultaneously.

Listing 11.10   Making the Server Multithreaded

```java
import java.net.*;
import java.io.*;

/*
You need to convert the single-threaded server
that services only one socket connection
into a multithreaded server that can handle
multiple connections with clients simultaneously.
By extending Thread, this class can now be
handled as a single thread by WifeMultithreadedServer,
which spawns a separate instance of WifeThread for
every new connection made by each HusbandClient
instance.
*/
public class WifeThread extends Thread
{
    private Socket wifeSocket = null;

    public WifeThread(Socket socket)
    {
        super("WifeThread");
        this.wifeSocket = socket;
    }

    public void run()
    {
        try
        {
            PrintWriter out =
                    new PrintWriter(wifeSocket.getOutputStream(), true);
            BufferedReader in = new BufferedReader(
                            new InputStreamReader(
                            wifeSocket.getInputStream()));

            String husbandSays, wifeSays;
            Wife wife = new Wife();
            wifeSays = wife.answer(null);
            out.println(wifeSays);

            while ((husbandSays = in.readLine()) != null)
            {
                wifeSays = wife.answer(husbandSays);
                out.println(wifeSays);
                if (wife.turnOff)
                {
                    break;
```

(continued)

Listing 11.10 Making the Server Multithreaded *(continued)*

```
        }
      }
      out.close();
      in.close();
      wifeSocket.close();
    } catch (IOException e)
    {
      System.out.println(e);
    }
  }
}
```

Note that the new `WifeMultithreadedServer` calls the public `WifeThread(Socket socket)` constructor added in Listing 11.10 to create threads. There is only one other difference: The main method of the `WifeServer` class was replaced with the run method of the `WifeThread` class. Every application needs a main method, but every thread must have a run method. The `Wife` class is unchanged.

Your multithreaded server is finished. To try it out, compile the `WifeThread` class first. (The `Wife` class should still be at the bottom of `file` so that it gets compiled at the same time.) Next, compile the `WifeMultithreadedServer` class and run it. Then open three command prompts and run an instance of `HusbandClient` (which was not changed) in each. All three will work now because your new multithreaded server can handle numerous clients simultaneously. Java makes it so easy to change a single-tasking program into a multithreaded one.

Building a Multithreaded Web Server with Sockets

Your last task is to combine all the socket topics covered previously. Going from the previous code listings in this chapter to a full Web server is not difficult. There are many details you could add, but you need only two more fundamental components to create a Web server from the socket functionality demonstrated previously in this chapter: the protocol and the file service. The protocol is simply an agreed-on rule about what the client should send. For this example, the client must send the word "zakoog" and then a filename. The server will then know to grab a file and return it. To add this Web server mainstay, change the `Wife` class as shown in Listing 11.11, which now returns an HTML file as opposed to just a text message (as was the case in Listing 11.7).

. . . .

Listing 11.11   Making a Multithreaded Web Server

```java
class Wife
{
    public boolean turnOff = false;
    private String answer = "";
    private String[] sweetNothings =
        { "Take out that smelly garbage.",
          "Mow the lawn you bum.",
          "Fix the sink you broke.",
          "We talked about this already.",
          "No! My birthday was last Monday."
        };

    public String answer(String husbandSays) {

        String theOutput = null;

        if (husbandSays == null)
        {
            this.answer = "I love you, dear.";
        } else if (husbandSays.indexOf("yes dear")!=-1)
        {
            this.answer = "I still love you, honey.";
            turnOff = true;

        //this is the command word that tells
        //this server to return a file rather than
        //simply a text message. With this capability.
        //you have created a file server over sockets,
        //the core functionality of a Web server.
        } else if (husbandSays.indexOf("zakoog")!=-1)
        {
            StringBuffer fileContents = new StringBuffer();

            try
            {
                int pos = husbandSays.indexOf("zakoog");
                String fileLine = "", fileName = "";
                fileName = husbandSays.substring(pos + 7);
                FileReader fileReader = new FileReader(fileName);
                BufferedReader bufferedReader =
                                    new BufferedReader(fileReader);
                //fileContents.append(bufferedReader.readLine());

                while ((fileLine = bufferedReader.readLine()) != null)
                {
                    fileContents.append(fileLine);
                }

            } catch (IOException e)
            {
                this.answer = "404 FILE NOT FOUND";
            }

            this.answer = fileContents.toString();
        } else
        {
```

(continued)

Listing 11.11   Making a Multithreaded Web Server (continued)

```
            Random random = new Random();
            int whisper = random.nextInt(5);
            this.answer = this.sweetNothings[whisper];
        }

        return this.answer;
    }
}
```

In this listing, you added just a few lines to the previous `Wife` class to create your multithreaded server. To test it, stop the client and server, recompile the `WifeThread` file, and restart the server (`java WifeMultithreadedServer`) and the client (`java HusbandClient`). Your refreshed environment is then close to a "real" browser and Web server. The protocol isn't HTTP, so technically you haven't built a Web server and browser. However, the principle is much the same. Type `zakoog files/mytext.txt` in the client, and the text of that file should be returned to the client.

The real Web requires that you start a request with the protocol (such as `http`), but your custom application uses `zakoog`, which does the same thing. Both keywords represent part of a protocol—`http` for Hypertext Transfer Protocol and `zakoog` for Wife Server protocol. Tim Berners-Lee created HTML, HTTP, and the precursor of the URL. There are many problems with these protocols, and Berners-Lee is quick to complain about them. For example, they are asynchronous, meaning the Web is basically a request-and-response model. Perhaps you can build a better protocol, such as the Wife Server protocol.

Although your certification project doesn't need all the functionality demonstrated in this chapter, you do have enough examples to select from to build the socket portion of the assignment.

Need to Know More?

 Reilly, David and Michael Reilly. *Java Network Programming and Distributed Computing*. Boston, MA: Addison-Wesley, 2002 (ISBN 0201710374). A good book on this chapter's topics.

 `http://www.iso.ch/iso/en/CatalogueListPage.CatalogueList?ICS1=35&IC S2=100&ICS3=01`—This page is where you'll find OSI standards by reference number. You can't download any of them, however; you must purchase them from the ISO.

 `http://www.cisco.com/warp/public/535/2.html`—This page provides an illustrated overview of OSI by Cisco Systems.

 `http://java.sun.com/docs/books/tutorial/networking/sockets`—This page contains Sun's sockets tutorial.

Remote Method Invocation

Terms you'll need to understand:

✓ Remote Method Invocation (RMI)
✓ Stubs and skeletons
✓ Remote object
✓ rmic
✓ rmiregistry
✓ Remote interface
✓ **Naming.lookup**
✓ **ClassNotFoundException**
✓ **Naming.bind**

Techniques you'll need to master:

✓ The steps to start the RMI registry, server, and client
✓ Identifying what code goes on the server and what code goes on the client
✓ Writing a remote interface
✓ Properly managing RMI exceptions, such as **ClassNotFoundException**
✓ Knowing how to register an object with the RMI registry by using **Naming.bind or Naming.lookup**

In this chapter, you review the basics of Java Remote Method Invocation (RMI). RMI is how you can call methods on a remote object—one that is on another Java Virtual Machine (JVM)—as though that object is local. Before RMI, this process was difficult, but RMI provides a way to invoke objects remotely, even those on different hosts.

In this chapter, you build an application that works in local mode and remote mode. In local mode, the client communicates with the database, accessing the database files directly. In remote mode, your application modifies the supplied code in a way that creates a database server. In this remote mode, the client reads and writes to the database over the network. The assignment allows two approaches for communication between the client and the database in remote mode. You can use RMI or serialized objects over Transmission Control Protocol (TCP) socket connections. Both approaches are valid, and your choice does not affect your grade.

Although the assignment allows you to use RMI or serialized objects over TCP/IP, RMI is recommended because it requires fewer lines of code and has thread safety built in. Although RMI has problems of its own, of the two choices, it is a more elegant solution. One shortcoming of RMI is that it offers less detailed control than you get with sockets. However, the tradeoff is worth it.

Using RMI

Remote Method Invocation (RMI) enables object-oriented distributed computing by enabling objects that live in different virtual machines to invoke each other's methods. RMI allows you to call a method on a remote object as if that object was local. Despite its ease of use, RMI is a powerful platform for distributed computing.

Programming RMI applications is somewhat complicated. The idea is simple, but several steps are required to make it work. In fact, there are issues in RMI that are pointed out later in this chapter. To add RMI functionality to your application, follow these 10 steps:

1. Define the object that will be shuttled across the network.

2. Define the methods of the remote class (signatures only).

3. Write an interface from those methods.

4. Write the concrete class that implements the interface (this is the remote object).

5. Write the client that invokes the methods.

6. Write the RMI server (easier than running rmiregistry).

7. Compile these classes.

8. Run the RMI interface compiler (rmic) on the .class file of the implementation class to create the stub.

9. Start the server (starts the registry programmatically).

10. Start the client.

Building the RMI Application

The first step in building an RMI application is defining the methods. The example is simple to keep the focus on the RMI building process and avoid application complexity.

First, note that this example doesn't use HTTP to retrieve remote objects dynamically. My solution didn't, and most candidates go this way. Not using HTTP removes one layer of complication (a layer that the assignment does not require). Without dynamic class loading over HTTP, you do not have to worry about a policy file. The policy file itself is not that difficult, but it is another part that could go wrong. The policy file's format, what you put in it, and where you place it can all cause RMI not to work properly. By not using HTTP, however, you don't need to worry about the policy file.

Define the Value Object

This application is a simple demonstration of how to implement RMI so that your value object is simple and the methods are few. The object represents a customer, with only a few attributes to describe it.

Listing 12.1 is the `Customer` class. It is the object passed from the server and client upon request by using RMI.

Listing 12.1   The Customer Class

```
import java.io.Serializable;

public class Customer implements Serializable
{
    private String firstName;
    private String lastName;
    private int userID;
    private String password;

    public Customer()
    {
        firstName = null;
        lastName = null;
```

(continued)

Listing 12.1 The Customer Class *(continued)*

```
        userID = 0;
        password = null;
    }

    public void setFirstName( String firstName )
    {
        this.firstName = firstName;
    }

    public String getFirstName()
    {
        return firstName;
    }

    public void setLastName( String lastName )
    {
        this.lastName = lastName;
    }

    public String getLastName()
    {
        return lastName;
    }

    public void setUserID( int userID )
    {
        this.userID = userID;
    }

    public int getUserID()
    {
        return userID;
    }

    public void setPassword( String password )
    {
        this.password = password;
    }

    public String getPassword()
    {
        return password;
    }

    public String toString()
    {
        String description = "\nFirst Name :" + firstName
                           + "\nLast Name :" + lastName
                           + "\nuser ID :" + userID
                           + "\nPassword :" + password;

        return description;
    }
}
```

Define Remote Object Methods

This portion of the application is straightforward. You simply want to get the Customer object from the server to the client. Therefore, you need only one method, called getCustomer(). The getDate() method is also added to test whether you can marshal an instance of the Date class.

Write the Remote Interface

Now that you have a Value Object and the remote object method to get it, you should write the remote interface. Because there is only one method, what makes this interface applicable for RMI will be clear. The following is a template for the interface:

```
import java.rmi.*;

public interface RemoteInterface extends Remote
{
    MyObject getMyObject() throws RemoteException;
}
```

Listing 12.2 is the RemoteInterface class, which is the class the client talks to through a stub by using RMI. Notice that two objects are used here: Customer and Date. In this listing, you try the Date object, too, because you know it has no serialization issues. That way, you can isolate any problems to the RMI code (if Date doesn't get marshaled correctly) or the Customer class (if Date works but Customer doesn't).

Listing 12.2   The RemoteInterface Class

```
import java.io.IOException;
import java.rmi.RemoteException;


// This interface defines the basic remote methods.
// For example, the methods in this interface can be used by an
// application to obtain information about a customer through
// the Customer class.

public interface RemoteInterface extends java.rmi.Remote
{
    public Customer getCustomer() throws RemoteException;
    public java.util.Date getDate() throws RemoteException;
}
```

Write the Concrete Remote Class

Next, you need to build the concrete class that implements the
RemoteInterface class. The concrete class does only one thing—returning an
instance of the Customer class. This Customer object is serialized by RMI. To
illustrate how this works, please consider the following a template for the
concrete remote class:

```
import java.rmi.*;
import java.rmi.server.UnicastRemoteObject;

public class RemoteImplementation
       extends UnicastRemoteObject
       implements RemoteInterface
{
    public RemoteImplementation() throws RemoteException
    {
        super();
    }

    public MyObject getMyObject() throws RemoteException
    {
        MyObject myObject = new MyObject();
        return myObject;
    }
}
```

Notice how the getMyObject() method returns an instance of MyObject. There
is nothing special about this method. However, RMI will serialize myObject,
return it to the calling JVM, and deserialize it there so that the calling object
treats the called object as if it is local. You don't have to do anything in the
calling method to make this happen; Java's RMI handles all the details. Let's
see how to implement the above template.

Listing 12.3 is the RemoteImplementation class, which is the object the client
communicates with to request a Customer object.

Listing 12.3   The RemoteImplementation Class

```
import java.rmi.RemoteException;
import java.rmi.server.UnicastRemoteObject;
import java.io.IOException;

//This class returns a new instance of Customer.
public class RemoteImplementation
       extends UnicastRemoteObject
       implements RemoteInterface
{

    private Customer customer;
```

(continued)

Listing 12.3   The RemoteImplementation Class *(continued)*

```
//This constructor creates a new instance of Customer.
public RemoteImplementation() throws RemoteException
{
    super();

    customer = new Customer();
}

public Customer getCustomer() throws RemoteException
{
    return customer;
}

public java.util.Date getDate() throws RemoteException
{
    return new java.util.Date();
}

}
```

Write the RMI Server

There are two ways to start the RMI registry: manually with rmiregistry (including parameters) or programmatically. If you do it programmatically, you will avoid several headaches. For example, you don't need a policy file (which tells Java what permissions the application has) and you don't have to worry about classpath, which the registry needs to find the stub. Many candidates waste time trying to figure out how to start the RMI registry. I chose the programmatic approach and didn't lose points for it. The following snippet demonstrates how you bind an object to the RMI server:

```
try
{
    RemoteInterface remoteImplementation = new RemoteImplementation();
    Naming.rebind("//localhost/RemoteInterfaceServer",
            remoteImplementation);
} catch (MalformedURLException e)
{} catch (UnknownHostException e)
{} catch (RemoteException e)
{}
```

Listing 12.4 is the RMIServer class, which once instantiated will start the RMI registry.

Listing 12.4   The RMIServer Class

```
import java.rmi.Naming;
import java.rmi.RemoteException;
import java.rmi.NotBoundException;
```

(continued)

Listing 12.4   The RMIServer Class *(continued)*

```java
import java.rmi.UnknownHostException;
import java.rmi.registry.Registry;
import java.rmi.registry.LocateRegistry;
import java.rmi.server.UnicastRemoteObject;

/**
 * RMIServer starts RMI and registers an instance of RemoteImplementation.
 *
 */
public class RMIServer
{
    // Instance of this class
    private static RMIServer  rmi;

    public static void main(String[] args)
    {
        try
        {
            rmi = new RMIServer(args);
        } catch (Exception ex)
        {
            System.out.println( ex );
        }
    }

    public RMIServer(String[] cmdArgs)
    {
        try
        {
            Registry myRegistry = LocateRegistry.createRegistry( 1099 );

            System.out.println( "Registry created on 1099");

            RemoteInterface getMyCustomer = new RemoteImplementation();

            System.out.println( "Remote implementation object created" );

            String urlString = "rmi://localhost:1099/CustomerServer";
            System.out.println( "Attempting Naming.rebind(" + urlString
                                + ",getMyCustomer);" );

            myRegistry.rebind( "CustomerServer", getMyCustomer );

            System.out.println( "Bindings Finished, waiting"
                                + " for client requests." );
        } catch (RemoteException rex)
        {
            System.out.println( rex );
        } catch (Exception ex)
        {
            System.out.println( ex );
        }
    }
}
```

Write the Client That Invokes the Remote Object

Finally, you need a client that uses all this RMI functionality. The client will try to create an instance of the Customer class through RMI. First, it gets a reference to an instance of the RemoteImplementation class, and then the RemoteImplementation object gets an instance of the Customer class. After that, the client treats the Customer class as though it is local, which is the whole point of RMI, even though it is actually on a remote JVM. The following illustrates how to get an instance of an object residing on a remote JVM through RMI:

```
try
{
    MyObject myObject = (MyObject) Naming.lookup(
                         "//localhost/RemoteInterfaceServer");
    // do something with myObject
} catch (MalformedURLException e)
{} catch (UnknownHostException e)
{} catch (NotBoundException e)
{} catch (RemoteException e)
{}
```

Listing 12.5 is the RMITestClient class, which is the application starting point. From here, you can test the RMI plumbing.

Listing 12.5 The RMITestClient Class

```
import java.io.IOException;
import java.rmi.RemoteException;
import java.rmi.NotBoundException;
import java.rmi.Naming;
import java.rmi.registry.Registry;
import java.rmi.registry.LocateRegistry;

/**
 * This client tests the sample RMI implementation.
 *
 */
public class RMITestClient
{
    private static Customer customer;
    private static RemoteInterface rmi;

    public static void main(String[] args)
    {
        try
        {
            String lookupString = "rmi://localhost:1099/CustomerServer";
            rmi = (RemoteInterface)Naming.lookup(lookupString);

            //try date that you know is serializable
            java.util.Date date = (java.util.Date)rmi.getDate();
```

(continued)

Listing 12.5   The RMITestClient Class *(continued)*

```
            System.out.println( date );

            //try your own object to see if you did it right
            customer = (Customer)rmi.getCustomer();
            customer.setFirstName("Patricia");
            customer.setLastName("Kasienne");
            customer.setUserID(1234);
            customer.setPassword("umther");
            System.out.println( customer );
        } catch (RemoteException rex)
        {
            System.out.println( rex );
        } catch (Exception ex)
        {
            System.out.println( ex );
        }
    }
}
```

Compile the Classes

Now that you have all the classes, it is time to compile them in the following order:

1. Customer

2. RemoteInterface

3. RemoteImplementation

4. RMIServer

5. RMITestClient

The order is presented based on dependencies. For example, if you compile the source files individually, you can't compile the RemoteInterface class before you compile Customer because RemoteInterface refers to Customer. However, you can always just use *.java in the folder that has these files, and the compiler will figure out the dependencies for you.

Run the RMI Interface Compiler

The client doesn't actually communicate directly with the RemoteInterface object. You need a stub to do that. Java comes with a stub generator—the rmic tool. Now that the classes are compiled, it is time to run the RMI interface compiler (rmic) on the RemoteImplementation.class file to create the stub. You can generate the skeleton and stub files for RemoteImplementation with the rmic RemoteImplementation command.

Run the Application

First, run the RMIServer class, which starts the rmiregistry and registers the RemoteImplementation class with it. Then run the RMITestClient. You see the following output:

```
First Name :Patricia
Last Name :Kasienne
user ID :1234
Password :umther
Sun Apr 20 13:59:55 PDT 2004
```

You can revise any of these classes if you want additional practice. For example, you might set the attributes of the Customer object by calling get and set methods for the attributes, including firstName, lastName, userID, and password. This practice further demonstrates how you can call methods of an object residing on a remote JVM.

The registry assumes that the host is the localhost machine, if it's started without parameters.

When writing an interface for a given class, as shown previously, what is not obvious is how you get the client to treat a remote object the same as the local one. The trick is to use an interface that works locally and for RMI. Use the same signatures, of course. However, the exceptions declared to be thrown have to work in both situations. Many candidates miss points for not getting this part correct.

When it is time to start the client, you can use the following command:

```
java RMITestClient
```

The java.rmi.Naming Class

The key class that makes RMI work is java.rmi.Naming. The Naming class provides methods for storing and obtaining references to remote objects. It does so by communicating with the remote object registry. You need the following methods for the assignment:

➤ bind—Binds the specified name to a remote object so that you can then refer to that object by name.

➤ `lookup(String name)`—Returns a reference for the remote object associated with the specified name. Actually, the client gets a reference to the stub, which in turn communicates with the remote object.

➤ `rebind(String name, Remote object)`—Binds the specified name to the remote object. You can use this method instead of `bind` if the object is already associated by name in the registry.

There are many tutorials on RMI, but books on this topic aren't plentiful. I found RMI to be powerful yet troublesome. For one thing, I was able to get RMI to work great in my solution on Windows, but when I tested it on Solaris (version 5.8), it failed until I adjusted the code so that it worked on both platforms. So be careful with RMI; older versions of RMI and Solaris can cause trouble. Overall RMI is an awesome feature of J2SE. What you get in J2SE 1.4 is much improved since earlier versions. If you get stuck, don't panic; many other developers have, too. The most likely trouble spot will be the registry and paths. If you start RMI programmatically (as described previously), however, you'll have fewer problems.

Need to Know More?

 Pitt, Esmond, Kathleen McNiff, and Kathy McNiff. *Java.rmi: The Remote Method Invocation Guide*. Boston, MA: Addison-Wesley, 2001 (ISBN 0201700433). A popular and highly rated book on RMI.

 `http://java.sun.com/products/jdk/rmi/`—This site offers reference information about RMI in J2SE 1.4.

 `http://java.sun.com/j2se/1.4/docs/guide/rmi/getstart.doc.html`— This site is a good place to start learning about RMI.

 `http://java.sun.com/j2se/1.4/docs/guide/rmi/spec/rmiTOC.html`— Download the Java RMI specification.

The GUI

Terms you'll need to understand:

✓ Human/Computer Interaction (HCI)
✓ Model-View-Controller (MVC) pattern
✓ JTable
✓ Menu
✓ **TableModel**
✓ Event model
✓ Anonymous class

Techniques you'll need to master:

✓ Standardizing the look and feel of a GUI
✓ Allowing keyboard shortcuts to select menu items
✓ Providing prompting or cueing for user input
✓ Identifying and clarifying user message output so that users always know what is going on
✓ Designing the GUI so that you know the state of its components and can respond to user input
✓ Designing your project's error behavior so that the GUI doesn't hang
✓ Reporting errors clearly and simply
✓ Clearly indicating user action success and failure
✓ Acknowledging user actions immediately

In this chapter, you review the basics of GUI design. Generally, designing a GUI is easy, but you need to be thorough so that you don't leave the evaluator with a bad impression because of a simple oversight.

Your GUI needs to be simple and easy to use—a goal for all applications, and your project is no different. When designing a GUI, there are many ideas to consider, but Sun has narrowed the scope of possibilities with a few requirements defined in the instructions you downloaded. For example, you must use a JTable component. Because of Sun's requirements in the instructions, the basics of the screen functionality have been decided, including using a JTable to display database data. Although GUI design is harder than it seems, this certification assignment does help you in that a large part of the design is determined by the JTable requirement.

You should start your GUI design with a review of good Human/Computer Interaction (HCI) principles to prevent fundamental mistakes. I recommend visiting Sun's Java Software Human Interface Group (`http://developer.java.sun.com/developer/techDocs/hi/index.html`). Although this site doesn't provide a lot of information, it takes only a few minutes to peruse it and glean a few clues about what the evaluator expects your GUI to look like, especially users' ability to select items to reserve and a display based on a JTable grid.

Chapters 14, "The Swing Components and Event Handling," and 15, "The JTable Component," demonstrate how to use the various Swing components you'll need to build your GUI. In this chapter, you see an example of a GUI that demonstrates what you need to do to satisfy the certification requirements.

The GUI

This sample GUI does not exactly replicate the solution I submitted to Sun for the certification assignment. However, it does function in a similar manner that meets the same development requirements you'll see in the assignment instructions. There are many ways to design a GUI for the two scenarios Sun uses for the certification assignment. The GUI in this chapter is just one approach, but it scored well, so perhaps you can adapt it to your solution.

You will not be able to compile the code in this chapter's listings because it depends on other classes. The entire example is provided with the CD so that you can compile and modify that code.

First, take a look at the GUI in its entirety so that you can see how the different parts relate to one another. The code selections are presented in logical order—the order that the flow of control is likely to follow. The GUI in Figure 13.1 shows the general structure needed to satisfy the requirements and illustrates how users can interface with the data. Note that it takes the entire code file to produce this screen.

Gate	Level	Aisle	Row	Seat	Available
North	100	First	A	1	1
North	100	Second	V	24	1
North	100	First	B	39	1
South	150	Second	C	18	1
South	150	Third	E	6	1
North	100	First	A	10	1
North	100	First	A	13	1
North	100	First	A	21	1
North	100	First	A	42	1
North	100	First	A	69	1
North	30	First	C	30	1

Figure 13.1   The JTable-dominated GUI.

After you have looked over this figure, read on for a discussion of selected portions of the source code for the GUI class.

Use Explicit Imports

Avoid using the wildcard character when writing your import statements. Importing the classes individually makes the code clear, and it's easy to see what is being referenced in the body of the class. Some code listings in this book use the wildcard character to save space, but not often.

NOTE

The **import** statements accept wildcards, but you should avoid using them, particularly when only a few classes are used in that package. Also, specify classes individually in **import** statements instead of using the fully-qualified name of classes in the body of your code. It is a good practice to avoid using wildcards in **import** statements, and I followed this practice for the certification assignment. However, compromise is needed sometimes. For example, 33 classes are imported from **javax.swing package**. In this case, a wildcard can make the code much more readable.

Listing 13.1 is the top of the GUI source file; it includes the file header comment, the package statement, and all the import statements. It clearly tells you what is being used in the class and hints at the functionality being built. (For example, `StringTokenizer` is used to parse command-line parameters.)

Sun's evaluators review how you used SDK libraries. If you built a custom function that took a lot of work when the SDK already had a similar function, they will lower your score.

Although you can import database classes and use local- or remote-specific code, it is better to hide from the GUI where data is coming from. The best way to make the GUI function properly is to use a connection factory. Some candidates choose to allow users to switch between local and remote modes dynamically through the GUI (by using a radio button, for example). Although this functionality is not required and is more difficult, it can earn you more points.

Listing 13.1   How to Start the GUI Source File

```
/************** FILE HEADER ********************
Title:          SCJD Solution

Author:         Que Reader

Submission Date: 4/6/2004 11:58AM
Completion Date: 3/12/2004 11:58AM

Platform:       Windows 2000
**********************************************/

package superbowl.client;

/*
 * The best practice for the exam is to import using
 * fully-qualified names such as java.io.File
 * (demonstrating that you know what you're doing) rather than
 * import java.io.* (demonstrating development efficiency).
 */
import superbowl.database.Database;
import superbowl.database.DatabaseFactory;
import superbowl.database.DatabaseException;
import superbowl.database.DatabaseInterface;

import java.rmi.RemoteException;

import javax.swing.JTable;
import javax.swing.table.DefaultTableCellRenderer;
import javax.swing.table.JTableHeader;
import javax.swing.border.TitledBorder;
import javax.swing.table.TableModel;
import javax.swing.table.TableColumnModel;
import javax.swing.table.AbstractTableModel;
import javax.swing.table.TableColumn;
import javax.swing.JComboBox;
import javax.swing.JDialog;
import javax.swing.JComponent;
import javax.swing.JOptionPane;
import javax.swing.JTextField;
import javax.swing.JFrame;
import javax.swing.JPanel;
```

(continued)

Listing 13.1   How to Start the GUI Source File *(continued)*

```
import javax.swing.JScrollPane;
import javax.swing.JTextPane;
import javax.swing.JSplitPane;
import javax.swing.JButton;
import javax.swing.JLabel;
import javax.swing.JMenu;
import javax.swing.JMenuBar;
import javax.swing.JMenuItem;
import javax.swing.KeyStroke;
import javax.swing.ListSelectionModel;
import javax.swing.event.TableModelListener;
import javax.swing.event.TableModelEvent;
import javax.swing.event.ListSelectionListener;
import javax.swing.event.ListSelectionEvent;

import java.awt.Container;
import java.awt.Component;
import java.awt.BorderLayout;
import java.awt.Color;
import java.awt.Dimension;
import java.awt.GridLayout;
import java.awt.event.ActionEvent;
import java.awt.event.ActionListener;
import java.awt.event.WindowEvent;
import java.awt.event.WindowAdapter;
import java.awt.event.MouseEvent;
import java.awt.event.MouseAdapter;
import java.awt.event.KeyEvent;
import java.awt.event.InputEvent;

import java.io.IOException;

import java.net.UnknownHostException;
```

Listing 13.1 declares this code to be in the `superbowl.client` package. It also imports all the Swing components needed to build the screen shown in Figure 13.1 and imports several classes to support event handling, which happens in the View portion of the Model-View-Controller (MVC) design pattern. Last, some classes are imported to support the database and remote mode functionality.

Class Header

The class header comes after the `import` statements. Be sure to begin this section with a javadoc class header comment. This comment appears in the javadoc Web page, so be brief but complete.

Listing 13.2 shows the class header; it includes the javadoc comment, class declaration, and instance variables used throughout the GUI. When you design your GUI, be sure to meet all requirements mentioned in the instructions. For example, the requirements for your assignment will closely parallel the following:

➤ The main data output uses a JTable.

➤ The user can choose a local or remote database.

➤ The user interface displays the database.

➤ The user can search by level and/or aisle.

➤ The user can search using "any" as a wildcard.

➤ The user can reserve stadium seats.

➤ The user is informed if no seats are available.

Listing 13.2   The GUI Class Header

```
/**
 * This user interface satisfies the following criteria:
 * <ul>
 * <li>Only Swing components from JFC were used.</li>
 * <li>The main data output uses a JTable.</li>
 * <li>The user can choose a local or remote database.</li>
 * <li>The user interface displays database.</li>
 * <li>The user can search by the Level and/or Aisle.</li>
 * <li>The user can search by "any" as a wildcard.</li>
 * <li>The user can reserve stadium seats.</li>
 * <li>The user is informed if no seats are available.</li>
 * </ul>
 *
 * The following are extra, but improve the application:
 * <ul>
 * <li>Display update-Table is updated after every booking and search.</li>
 * <li>User messages-After every action the status is shown.</li>
 * <li>Seat selection-The user selects a seat by clicking on table.</li>
 * <li>User error reduction-The user cannot mistype the seat number.</li>
 * <li>Color display-Level and Row columns
 *          and search criteria colors match.</li>
 * <li>The search criteria colors match the Level and Row columns.</li>
 * <li>The user selects Level and Row columns from a combobox.</li>
 * <li>The user selects Level and Row columns by clicking the table.</li>
 * </ul>
 *
 * @author   Que Reader
 * @version 1.00, 12/28/2003
 * @since SDK1.4
 */
public class SuperBowlClient extends JFrame
{
        boolean DISABLE = false;
        boolean ENABLE = true;
        private boolean ALLOW_ROW_SELECTION = true;
        private int columnCount;
        private DatabaseInterface database;
        private DatabaseFactory databaseFactory;
        private StadiumTableModel stadiumTableModel;
        private TableColumn column;
```

(continued)

Listing 13.2   The GUI Class Header (continued)

```
    private String databasePath;
    private String[] columnNames,
                     aisles,
                     levels;
    private String[][] tempData,
                       data;

    // GUI Swing components
    private JButton searchButton,
                    reserveButton;
    private JSplitPane splitPane;
    private JPanel reservePanel,
                   reserveInputPanel,
                   searchPanel,
                   searchInputPanel,
                   upperPanel;
    private JLabel status,
                   localRemote,
                   searchLevel,
                   searchAisle,
                   seatNumberLabel,
                   seatCountLabel;
    private JTextField seatCount,
                       seatCountField;
    private JComboBox searchLevelComboBox,
                      searchAisleComboBox;
    private JTable table;
```

Listing 13.2 includes the instance variables used by more than one method, so they had to be declared in the class scope. These instance variables provide clues for the functionality still to come.

Application Main Method

An application is always started with the main method, and where you place this method determines how you start the application. I chose the client as the natural place to put the main method, but many candidates place the main method in the connection factory. Either way is fine.

Listing 13.3 shows the main method located in the GUI class; it is abstract in design, so it will work in many similar applications. It's not specific to the certification assignment, which is the very goal of good design. Of course, object names will change in other applications, but the structure will not.

The main method accepts null arguments to connect local databases or the RMI name and port number parameters to connect a remote database. Note that any invalid command parameters will be rejected and lead to system exit. When a successful start is achieved, a client window appears on the user's screen.

Listing 13.3   Demonstrating the Main Method

```java
/**
 * Accepts null arguments to connect local database. Accepts RMI name
 * and port number parameters to connect a remote database. Any invalid
 * command parameters will be rejected
 * and lead to system exit. A client window will provide for each
 * successful connection. Default search ways are selected.
 * @param args the command line parameters
 */
public static void main( String args[] )
{

    DatabaseInterface database;
    DatabaseFactory databaseFactory;

    try
    {
        // Get database from factory.
        // Local is determined by "-dbpath myDBpath"
        // and remote is determined by "-host myHost -port myPort"
        databaseFactory = new DatabaseFactory();
        database = databaseFactory.getDatabase(args);

        if (database == null)
        {
            System.out.println("Cannot open the database, "
                            + "please double check"
                            + " command line parameters");
            System.exit(0);
        }
        // initiate the client window
        SuperBowlClient frame = new SuperBowlClient(database);
        frame.pack();
        frame.setVisible(true);
    } catch ( DatabaseException de)
    {
        System.out.print("Unknown host, please check "
                        + "command line parameters.\n" + de);
    } catch (IOException io)
    {
        System.out.println("Cannot open the database, "
                            + "please double check command"
                            + " line parameters\n" + io);
        System.exit(0);
    }
}
```

The most interesting feature of Listing 13.3 is how the main method gets a connection to the database. Notice how it figures out whether the user requested a local or remote connection. Outside this method, the client is not aware of local and remote database connectivity.

An object in Java can often be considered as more than one type, determined by any interfaces the instantiating class implements. The Database concrete class implements a DatabaseInterface interface. Using this technique, you are able to specify the type as an interface that provides a generic representation of the database object. Therefore, the client can ignore the origin of the database connection, whether it's local or remote. This technique produces a clean GUI implementation. Therefore, the DatabaseInterface interface allows the client to cast references to the database by interface, not by the concrete class. That way, all code outside the main method is generic, regardless of local or remote mode. Chapters 7, "Databases and Atomicity," and 12, "Remote Method Invocation," discuss how to use one interface for RMI, which is a clean approach.

DatabaseFactory is the class that actually does the work of creating the connection and figuring out, through command-line options, whether the user requested a local or remote database connection.

Last, the main method instantiates an instance of the client by passing the database connection.

Class Constructor

The class constructor is simple. The idea is to have a concrete method that initializes the application so that another class or application can start the GUI. If all the initializing code remained in the constructor, you could still initialize the application from another object. However, I prefer using a specific method to initialize a complex application so that I can separate the class initialization from the application initialization.

Listing 13.4 shows the constructor for this class. It passes the title "Super Bowl Reservation System" to the JFrame superclass, which displays this text in the title bar. Then it calls the init method, passing the database reference. The class constructor initializes the title bar text by passing a title string to JFrame, using the super keyword. Then it assigns the database reference to the class field database. Finally, it calls the init method, which begins building the GUI.

Listing 13.4 Demonstrating the Class Constructor

```
public SuperBowlClient(DatabaseInterface db)
{
    super("Super Bowl Reservation System");
    database = db;
    init(db);
}
```

Listing 13.4 shows how you can separate the responsibility of class initialization (that is, super()) from that of application initialization (init()). This separation is not required, but it is the approach I preferred for this assignment.

Application Initialization

Now you begin the actual initialization of the application. The background work is done, including determining local or remote mode, getting a database connection, and initializing the class and instance variables. Now you build the GUI with Swing components. The primary work in this step is initializing components, adding them to containers, and then adding those containers to the window.

Listing 13.5 declares and initializes the Swing components. This is where the GUI is built. The primary work done in this method is to set up the key pieces of the visual interface, place them within their respective containers, and then display the results onscreen.

Listing 13.5   Initializing the Swing GUI

```java
public void init(DatabaseInterface db)
{
    //sanity check: make sure a reference to the
    //database is not null.
    if(db==null)
    {
        return;
    }

    table = new JTable();

    try
    {
        columnNames = db.getColumnNames();
        data = db.getData();
    } catch (Exception e)
    {
        System.out.println(e);
    }

    //if window closes, exit application
    ApplicationExit applicationExit =   new ApplicationExit();
    addWindowListener( applicationExit );

    //create JTable grid
    stadiumTableModel = new StadiumTableModel(data, columnNames);
    table = new JTable(stadiumTableModel);
    table.setPreferredScrollableViewportSize(new Dimension(800, 70));
    table.setToolTipText("Click a row and Press \"Reserve Seat\" button");
    table.setSelectionMode(ListSelectionModel.SINGLE_SELECTION);

    if (ALLOW_ROW_SELECTION) //true by default
    {
        ListSelectionModel rowSM = table.getSelectionModel();
        rowSM.addListSelectionListener(new ChooseSeat(rowSM) );
    } else
    {
        table.setRowSelectionAllowed(false);
```

(continued)

. . . .

Listing 13.5   Initializing the Swing GUI *(continued)*

```
}

//Highlight columns to help user
//identify search criteria.
column = table.getColumn(table.getColumnName(1));
column.setCellRenderer(new RowRenderer());
column = table.getColumn(table.getColumnName(2));
column.setCellRenderer(new RowRenderer());
JScrollPane tableScrollPane = new JScrollPane(table);

//Create status panel for status messages
localRemote = new JLabel();
if (db instanceof Database)
{
    localRemote.setText("Local Mode");
} else
{
    localRemote.setText("Remote Mode");
}
localRemote.setEnabled(false);
localRemote.setHorizontalAlignment (JLabel.LEFT );

JPanel statusPanel = new JPanel();
statusPanel.setLayout (new BorderLayout());
statusPanel.setBorder(new TitledBorder("Status"));
statusPanel.setAlignmentX (JPanel.LEFT_ALIGNMENT);
status = new JLabel();
status.setHorizontalAlignment (JLabel.LEFT );
status.setEnabled(false);
status.setText("Reserving Enabled.");
statusPanel.add("West", status);
statusPanel.add("South", localRemote);

//Create search GUI feature
searchLevel = new JLabel("Level");
searchLevel.setEnabled(false);
searchLevel.setToolTipText("Select Level For Search.");

try
{       //load combo boxes with unique database values
        aisles = database.getDistinctValuesForField(2);
        levels = database.getDistinctValuesForField(1);
} catch(RemoteException rex)
{
        System.out.print(rex);
} catch(SuperBowlException dex)
{
        System.out.print(dex);
}

searchLevelComboBox = new JComboBox(levels);
searchLevelComboBox.setForeground(Color.blue);
searchLevelComboBox.setBackground(Color.white);
searchLevelComboBox.setToolTipText("Select Level For Search.");
searchLevelComboBox.setSelectedItem("any");

searchAisleComboBox = new JComboBox(aisles);
```

(continued)

Listing 13.5   Initializing the Swing GUI *(continued)*

```
searchAisleComboBox.setToolTipText("Select Aisle For Search.");
searchAisleComboBox.setForeground(Color.red);
searchAisleComboBox.setBackground(Color.white);
searchAisle = new JLabel("Aisle");
searchAisle.setEnabled(false);
searchAisle.setToolTipText("Select Aisle For Search.");
searchButton = new JButton("Search Seats");
searchButton.setToolTipText("Search for a seat.");
searchButton.addActionListener( new SearchButtonHandler());
searchAisleComboBox.setSelectedItem("any");

int gridRows = 3;
int gridCols = 2;
searchInputPanel = new JPanel(new GridLayout(gridRows, gridCols));
searchInputPanel.add(searchLevel);
searchInputPanel.add(searchLevelComboBox);
searchInputPanel.add(searchAisle);
searchInputPanel.add(searchAisleComboBox);
searchInputPanel.add(searchButton);
searchInputPanel.setBorder(new TitledBorder("Search Seats"));

//Create reserve GUI feature
seatCount = new JTextField();
seatCountField = new JTextField();
seatNumberLabel = new JLabel("Seat number");
seatNumberLabel.setEnabled(false);
seatNumberLabel.setToolTipText("Click Seat number"
                                + " in the table at right.");
seatCount = new JTextField(10);
seatCount.setEditable(false);
seatCount.setToolTipText("Click Seat number in the table at right.");
seatCountLabel = new JLabel("How Many Seats");
seatCountLabel.setEnabled(false);
seatCountLabel.setToolTipText("Enter How Many Seats"
                                + " in the blank area.");
seatCountField = new JTextField(10);
seatCountField.setToolTipText("Enter How Many Seats here.");
reserveButton = new JButton("Reserve Seat");
reserveButton.addActionListener( new ReserveButtonHandler());
reserveButton.setToolTipText("Reserve your seat.");

reserveInputPanel = new JPanel(new GridLayout(gridRows, gridCols));
reserveInputPanel.add(seatNumberLabel);
reserveInputPanel.add(seatCount);
reserveInputPanel.add(seatCountLabel);
reserveInputPanel.add(seatCountField);
reserveInputPanel.add(reserveButton);
reserveInputPanel.setBorder(new TitledBorder("Reserve Seats"));


gridRows = 1;
gridCols = 3;
upperPanel = new JPanel(new GridLayout(gridRows, gridCols));
upperPanel.add(reserveInputPanel);
upperPanel.add(searchInputPanel);
upperPanel.add(statusPanel);
```

(continued)

Listing 13.5   Initializing the Swing GUI *(continued)*

```
//Create a split pane and put search,
//reservation, and status on top
//and JTable on bottom.
//see Sun split-pane tutorial for an excellent
//example: http://java.sun.com/docs/books/tutorial/uiswing/
//components/splitpane.html
splitPane = new JSplitPane(JSplitPane.VERTICAL_SPLIT,
                                upperPanel, tableScrollPane);
splitPane.setOneTouchExpandable(true);
splitPane.setDividerLocation(80);

//Provide minimum sizes for the two components in the split pane
upperPanel.setMinimumSize(new Dimension(100, 50));
tableScrollPane.setMinimumSize(new Dimension(100, 50));

//Add the split pane to this frame
getContentPane().add(splitPane);

//Add two top-level menu items to the GUI: File and About.
//See Listing 13.6 for the code to do this.
}
```

Listing 13.5 illustrates just one of the many ways you can build your GUI. This approach works fine, and you can easily modify, optimize, and adapt this code for your solution.

Figure 13.2 illustrates the tooltip text that has been added to give the user a better experience. Little touches like this make a difference on your GUI score.

Listing 13.5 includes the code necessary to build much of the GUI. One important aspect is adding a menu bar at the top of the window. Listing 13.6 shows how to do that and how to add menu items. In this code snippet, note that the menu bar is defined to appear at the top of the GUI window.

Listing 13.6   Adding a Menu

```
/**
 * Adds two top-level menu items to the GUI: File and About.
 * You can add more if you like.
 */
    JMenuBar menuBar = new JMenuBar();
    setJMenuBar(menuBar);

    // create File menu, including Open, Close, and Exit
    JMenu fileMenu = new JMenu("File");

    JMenuItem exitItem = new JMenuItem("Exit", 'x');
    exitItem.setAccelerator(KeyStroke.getKeyStroke(KeyEvent.VK_X,
                                InputEvent.ALT_MASK));
    exitItem.addActionListener(new WindowCloser());

    fileMenu.add(exitItem);
```

(continued)

Listing 13.6   Adding a Menu (continued)

```
menuBar.add(fileMenu);

// create Help menu and About menu item
JMenu helpMenu = new JMenu("Help");
JMenuItem helpItem = new JMenuItem("Help", 'H');
helpItem.addActionListener(new DisplayHelp());
helpMenu.add(helpItem);

JMenuItem versionItem = new JMenuItem("About", 'A');
versionItem.addActionListener(new AboutHelper());
helpMenu.add(versionItem);

menuBar.add(helpMenu);
```

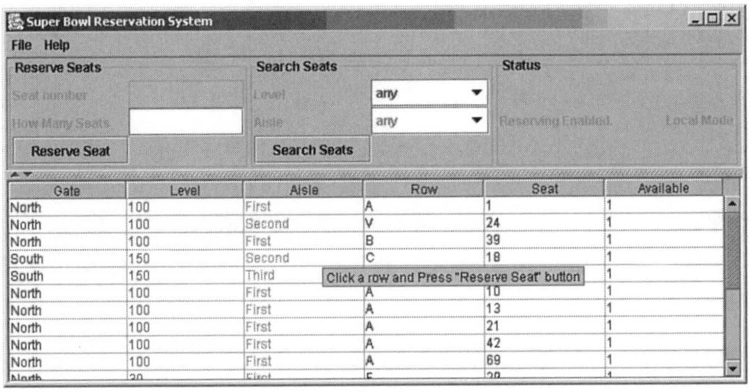

Figure 13.2   An example of a tooltip, which makes the GUI easier to use.

Listing 13.6 shows you how to add a menu to your application. This listing is rather simple, but you can easily add more menu items and give the user more menu-driven options.

Button Click Handler

The actual work of reserving a seat at the Super Bowl is done with the ReserveButtonHandler method. This method implements ActionListener, which means it is called when the Reserve button is clicked. Listing 13.7 shows you how to write this inner class and demonstrates how to respond to users clicking a button, especially the one that creates a seat reservation—the GUI's primary duty.

Listing 13.7   Demonstrating a Button Click Handler

```
/**
* This inner class performs the real reservation work
*
```

(continued)

Listing 13.7   Demonstrating a Button Click Handler *(continued)*

```
* Reservation Process:
*     try{
*              1. Do the lock(int recnum);
*              2. Do the getRow(int recnum);
*              3. Do the verification to ensure the available seat;
*              4. Update the record;
*              5. Write the new data to screen;
*              6. Do the unlock(int recordNumber);
*     }
*
* @author Que Reader
* @version 1.0  Dec-12-2004
*/
public class ReserveButtonHandler implements ActionListener
{
    boolean DISABLE = false;
    boolean ENABLE = true;
    String userMessage = "Reserving your seats...Please wait";

    public void actionPerformed( ActionEvent e )
    {
        // Check for integer, else if NumberFormatException
        // then exit routine with gentle message to user.
        String seats = seatCountField.getText();
        int requestedSeats = 0;
        int recordNumber = 0;
        try
        {
            requestedSeats = Integer.parseInt(seats, 10);
        } catch ( NumberFormatException nfe)
        {
            output.setText("Please provide seat count then try again.");
            return;
        }

         if ( !(requestedSeats > 0) )
        {
            output.setText("Please request 1 or more seats "
                        + "then try again.");
            return;
        }

        output.setText("Reserving seats...Please wait");
        // get the seat number
        String seatNumber = ((JTextField)seatCount).getText();

        if (seatNumber.length() == 0)
        {
            output.setText("Please click on a seat number "
                        + "then try again.");
            return;
        }
         try
        {
            rowData = database.find(seatNumber);
            recordNumber = rowData.getRecordNumber();
             //Lock the requested seat record
```

Listing 13.7 **Demonstrating a Button Click Handler** *(continued)*

```java
        database.lock(recordNumber);
        //get again because data may have changed
        rowData = database.find(seatNumber);
        columnData = database.getFieldInfo();
        // check available seats
        String values[] = rowData.getValues();
        int availableSeats =
            Integer.parseInt(values[values.length-1].trim());
        seats = values[values.length-1];

        if (availableSeats < requestedSeats || availableSeats == 0)
        {
            userMessage = "Fewer seats available than requested. "
                        + "Please try again.";
        } else
        {

            setGUIAvailability(DISABLE, userMessage);

            // reserve seats
            availableSeats -= requestedSeats;
            values[values.length-1]= "" + availableSeats;
            database.modify(
                    new RowData(recordNumber, columnData, values));

            //refresh table under previous criteria
            (new SearchButtonHandler()).searchDatabase();
            userMessage = "We have reserved " + requestedSeats
                        + " seats for you on seat "
                        + seatNumber + ".";
        }
    } catch(IOException ioe)
    {   //this is thrown by lock
        userMessage = "There is a problem with your Database. "
                    + "Please report it to the IT staff.";
        return;
    } catch(DatabaseException de)
    {
        userMessage = "There is a problem with your Database. "
                    + "Please report it to the IT staff.";
        return;
    } finally
    {
        try
        {
            //Must unlock the requested seat record
            database.unlock(recordNumber);
        } catch(RemoteException rex)
        {
            System.out.print(rex);
        } catch(DatabaseException dex)
        {
            System.out.print(dex);
        }

        // no matter the result, restore the button status
```

(continued)

Listing 13.7   Demonstrating a Button Click Handler (continued)

```
                setGUIAvailability(ENABLE, userMessage);
        }
    }
}
```

Notice that a sequence of steps is embedded in this class. One of the most important phases of the reservation process is the database integrity code. A locking mechanism prevents the data from being corrupted. This approach is not specific to the certification assignment. It is a generic procedure that includes the following steps:

1. Lock the record with `lock(int recordNumber)`.

2. Get the seat data.

3. Verify seat availability.

4. Update the record, if necessary.

5. Write the new data to screen.

6. Unlock the record with `unlock(int recordNumber)`.

The locking mechanism is covered in detail in Chapter 7, but these steps outline one viable way to handle database integrity in a multiuser environment.

An important aspect of the locking mechanism is that it must be managed from the client. Depending on the assignment, many candidates receive instructions that demand locking be invoked from the client. That doesn't mean this approach is the best way to implement locking. However, overlooking instructions can cause you to lose points needlessly.

Search Inner Class

Now it's time to review a database search request from the GUI. The search itself (see Chapter 7 for details) is handled by the database, but the GUI has some work to do as well.

Listing 13.8 shows you one way to handle searching the database from the GUI. The code here is simply a suggestion, but you can adapt it to your solution if you think it's useful for your project.

Notice that I used an inner class rather than a separate class. Either way is fine, but I thought the search functionality was best kept in the GUI this way.

Listing 13.8 demonstrates how this class gets the search criteria from the user, creates a search string from those criteria, invokes the search, and, finally, displays the results in a JTable, where only the rows that meet the criteria are shown.

Listing 13.8 Managing the Database Search from the GUI

```
/**
 * This inner class implements ActionListener and
 * performs the database searching.
 */
public class SearchButtonHandler implements ActionListener
{
    String criteria = "",
           previousCriteria = "",
           levelCriteria = "",
           aisleCriteria = "";

    /**
     * The user invokes this by clicking the Search button.
     *
     * @param e The ActionEvent object
     */
    public void actionPerformed( ActionEvent e )
    {
        searchDatabase();
    }


    /**
     * This method first gets search criteria.
     * Then it gives the user a status message.
     * Finally, it searches the database and updates
     * the GUI based on the search results.
     *
     */
    public void searchDatabase()
    {
        String userMessage = "Searching the database...Please wait";

        // finds the criteriaString
        levelCriteria = (String)searchOriginComboBox
                            .getSelectedItem();
        aisleCriteria = (String)searchDestinationComboBox
                            .getSelectedItem();

        criteria =  "Level='" + levelCriteria +"',"
                + "Aisle='" + aisleCriteria +"'";

        if (!criteria.equalsIgnoreCase(previousCriteria))
        {
            previousCriteria = criteria;
            setGUIAvailability(DISABLE, userMessage);

            try
```

(continued)

Listing 13.8 **Managing the Database Search from the GUI** *(continued)*

```
        {
            tempData = database.searchSeat(criteria);
        } catch(RemoteException rex)
        {
            System.out.print(rex);
        } catch(SuperBowlException dex)
        {
            System.out.print(dex);
        }

        if( !(tempData==null) )
        {
            stadiumTableModel =
                new StadiumTableModel(tempData, columnNames);
            setTableModelData(stadiumTableModel);
            userMessage = "Search results are in the table.";
        } else
        {
            //no rows met criteria
            //optional: reset grid to original data with:
            //stadiumTableModel = new StadiumTableModel(database);
            //setTableModelData(stadiumTableModel);
            userMessage = "There are no seats that match your "
                    + "criteria. Please try again.";
        }
        } else
        {
            //use original because all criteria set to "any"
            stadiumTableModel =
                new StadiumTableModel(data, columnNames);
            setTableModelData(stadiumTableModel);
            userMessage = "Search results are in the table.";
        }

        setGUIAvailability(ENABLE, userMessage);
        searchLevelComboBox.setSelectedItem("any");
        searchAisleComboBox.setSelectedItem("any");

    }
}
```

Listing 13.8 shows you how to search the database from the GUI. A surprising amount of work is done in the GUI to make this search functionality happen. The actual database search code is required, too, and is covered in Chapter 7.

Menu Handler

There is one last piece of functionality to cover. How does the GUI respond to the user clicking on a menu item? This section explains one way to provide a help Web page to the user.

Figure 13.3 shows you a partial screenshot of what the menu looks like on a Windows platform. The assignment did not require many menu items, so the GUI described in this book doesn't have many either.

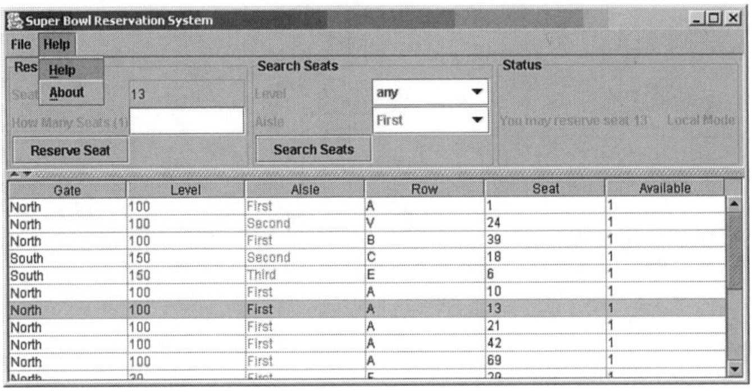

Figure 13.3 A menu example.

Listing 13.9 shows you how to display a help Web page to the user with a JTextPane component. In this example, the HTML file is expected to be in the solution package, but placing the file online is a valid option, too. This inner class uses a dialog box to display the help file. Notice that a JTextPane is used to render the HTML. This control makes it easy to show help written in HTML.

Listing 13.9   Displaying User Help

```
/**
 * This inner class displays the user help Web page.
 */
class DisplayHelp extends WindowAdapter implements ActionListener
{
    /**
     * User clicked the Help menu.
     * @param e The ActionEvent object
     *
     */
    public void actionPerformed( ActionEvent e)
    {
        if (e.getActionCommand().equals("Help"))
        {
            JTextPane pane = new JTextPane();
            JScrollPane scroller = new JScrollPane();
            scroller.getViewport().add(pane);
            JDialog dialog = new JDialog();
            dialog.getContentPane().add(scroller);
            dialog.pack();
            dialog.setSize(800,500);
            dialog.setVisible(true);
            String htmlDocument = "userHelp.html";
```

(continued)

Listing 13.9 Displaying User Help *(continued)*

```
try
{
    java.net.URL url = new java.net.URL("file:"
                    + System.getProperty("user.dir")
                    + System.getProperty("file.separator")
                    + htmlDocument);
    pane.setPage(url);
}
catch (Exception ex)
{
    ex.printStackTrace();
}
        }
    }
}
```

Listing 13.9 shows you how to display user help when the user clicks the Help menu item. Although you can place your help file online and access it from there, I recommend submitting the file with your solution because the evaluator might want to look at the file to see how you wrote the HTML code. If you place your file online, the evaluator could still see your code by choosing View, Source from the browser menu. However, the idea is to provide everything users (including the evaluator) need, without them needing other tools, such as a browser.

Need to Know More?

 Johnson, Jeff. *GUI Bloopers: Don'ts and Do's for Software Developers and Web Designers.* Burlington, MA: Morgan Kaufmann, 2000 (ISBN 1558605827).

 http://developer.java.sun.com/developer/techDocs/hi/index.html—Visit Sun's Java Software Human Interface Group.

 http://java.sun.com/products/jfc/tsc/articles/jlf-design/—View Sun's preferred look and feel for Java programs.

 http://java.sun.com/docs/—Download the Java API documentation in javadoc-generated form.

The Swing Components and Event Handling

. . . .

Terms you'll need to understand:

✓ Layout manager
✓ Pane
✓ Model-View-Controller (MVC) pattern
✓ Container
✓ Component

Techniques you'll need to master:

✓ Taking advantage of the plug-and-play architecture
✓ Selecting the proper components for an effective interface
✓ Placing components in a container and resizing them
✓ Using event handlers to respond to user input, such as mouse clicks and keystrokes
✓ Understanding the Model-View-Controller architecture behind some of the components

In this chapter, you review the basics of Java Swing architecture and individual components as well as Java's user interface capabilities. The user interface is worth about one-third of the exam score, so you want to make sure the layout is clean and each input component is labeled.

Chapter 13, "The GUI," reviewed user interface principles and techniques, with a general discussion about making screens useful. Chapter 15, "The JTable Component," covers the JTable, the most important Swing component for this certification. In this chapter, you apply what you learned in Chapter 13 to a variety of Swing components; you will use many of them in your project.

To meet the assignment's requirements, you need to understand what containers and components to use for your application. The core of the graphical user interface (GUI) is Java's Swing components. This chapter briefly covers most of the components you need for your GUI and includes many code snippets to demonstrate the key lines of code you might find useful for your project.

Swing Overview

Before Swing, there was the Abstract Windowing Toolkit (AWT) used in JDK (now called SDK) 1.0, a rudimentary GUI library. When Java was just starting to gain momentum, my colleague, a GUI programmer, was struggling to build reliable screens, but AWT wasn't reliable at that time. It is now years and versions later, so Swing, the AWT replacement, has improved GUI performance, reliability, and functionality dramatically. Not only are there more components, but they work better with fewer problems. There are still issues (for example, repainting might be too slow), but Swing is production quality and now makes creating clean screens easy.

An interesting Swing feature is that the look and feel can be changed programmatically. With this feature, developers can ensure that applications have the appearance they want, regardless of the platforms they are running on. Also, developers can now add high-quality 2D graphics, text, and images to an application. This chapter helps you decide which components you need for your GUI. I tried to provide just enough information so that you'll use these components effectively. This chapter does not cover the Java Foundation Classes (JFC) or graphics in general (because you don't need to create 2D drawings for the project).

Design Pattern Architecture

The primary design pattern is the Model-View-Controller (MVC) pattern. For example, the JTable component uses the MVC: The grid that appears onscreen is the View portion, the table model where the data is stored is the Model portion, and the code you write to manipulate the component and model and respond to user input is the Controller portion.

The next most common pattern you find in Swing components is the Observer-Observable pattern. You will recognize this pattern in how most components handle events. For example, when a user presses a JButton, an ActionEvent event is fired and then handled by the ActionListener assigned to the button.

Look and Feel

The three most popular types of GUI look and feel are Metal, Common Desktop Environment (CDE)/Motif, and Windows. Swing enables you to choose one for your application so that it looks the same on all platforms. For example, if you like the Unix look, you can use CDE/Motif even when the user is running your application on a Windows box. By default, Java uses Metal as the cross-platform look and feel. The following code shows you how to list the available themes:

```
UIManager.LookAndFeelInfo[] theme =
          UIManager.getInstalledLookAndFeels();
for (int i=0; i<theme.length; i++)
{
      System.out.println(theme[i].getName());
      System.out.println("--" + theme[i].getClassName());
}
//RETURNS:
//Metal
//--javax.swing.plaf.metal.MetalLookAndFeel
//CDE/Motif
//--com.sun.java.swing.plaf.motif.MotifLookAndFeel
//Windows
//--com.sun.java.swing.plaf.windows.WindowsLookAndFeel
```

You can use the code in Listing 14.1 to actually change your application's look and feel from the command line.

Listing 14.1   How to Set an Application's Look and Feel

```
//some people prefer to list all components
//others prefer plain javax.swing.*
import javax.swing.JLabel;
```

(continued)

Listing 14.1   How to Set an Application's Look and Feel *(continued)*

```java
import javax.swing.JButton;
import javax.swing.JTextField;
import javax.swing.JPanel;
import javax.swing.JFrame;
import javax.swing.UIManager;
import java.awt.BorderLayout;

public class LookFeelApplication
{
    public LookFeelApplication()
    {
        final JLabel label = new JLabel("Click Here:");
        JButton button = new JButton("OK");
        JTextField  text = new JTextField("Type Here");
        JPanel pane = new JPanel();
        pane.add(label);
        pane.add(button);
        pane.add(text);
        JFrame frame = new JFrame("Look-Feel");
        frame.getContentPane().add(pane, BorderLayout.CENTER);
        frame.setDefaultCloseOperation(JFrame.EXIT_ON_CLOSE);
        frame.pack();
        frame.setVisible(true);

    }

    public static void main(String[] args)
    {
        String metal = "javax.swing.plaf.metal."
                    + "MetalLookAndFeel";
        String motif = "com.sun.java.swing.plaf."
                    + "motif.MotifLookAndFeel";
        String windows = "com.sun.java.swing.plaf."
                    + "windows.WindowsLookAndFeel";
        try
        {
            if( args[0].equals("motif") )
            {
                UIManager.setLookAndFeel(motif);
            }else if( args[0].equals("metal") )
            {
                UIManager.setLookAndFeel(metal);
            }else if( args[0].equals("windows") )
            {
                UIManager.setLookAndFeel(windows);
            }else
            {
                UIManager
                  .setLookAndFeel(
                  UIManager
                  .getCrossPlatformLookAndFeelClassName());
            }
        } catch (Exception e) {}

        //Create the top-level container and add contents to it.
        LookFeelApplication app = new LookFeelApplication();
    }
}
```

Listing 14.1 generates a simple window containing a Label, a Button, and a TextField in the three available themes. From the command line, the user can type `java LookFeelApplication metal` to see the window shown in Figure 14.1. The other themes are shown in Figures 14.2 and 14.3.

Figure 14.1   The Metal look and feel.

Figure 14.2   The Windows look and feel.

Figure 14.3   The Motif look and feel.

For the assignment, you can use the Metal default, which means you don't have to bother with setting the look and feel. However, if you choose to override Metal with the Motif or Windows theme, be consistent if you use more than one window.

Frames, Windows, and Panes

In Java, you must place components such as buttons and text fields in a container. Applications, including applets with a GUI, use at least one container. When a GUI application runs, it typically displays its interface inside a frame. The following list describes three top-level windows that are closely related:

➤ *JWindow*—A window without a title bar, sizing borders, or Minimize/Maximize/Close buttons.

➤ *JFrame*—This container is also a window without a title bar, sizing borders, or Minimize/Maximize/Close buttons.

➤ *JDialog*—A special-purpose window, such as JOption.

The following hierarchy of the top-level windows shows the relationship between these components:

```
java.lang.Object
-java.awt.Component
--java.awt.Container
---java.awt.Window
----javax.swing.JWindow

---java.awt.Window
----java.awt.Frame
-----javax.swing.JFrame

---java.awt.Window
----java.awt.Dialog
-----javax.swing.JDialog
```

You can use these three containers to create your assignment's GUI. Keep in mind that a JWindow is a naked JFrame, and a JDialog is a single-purpose JWindow.

 A JFrame holds several panes, so adding a component requires you to specify a pane, which becomes a content pane when it holds child components.

The following code snippet is an example of creating a frame:

```
// Create frame
JFrame myFrame = new JFrame("my frame");
// Create a button
JComponent button = new JButton();
// Add button to frame's content pane;
myFrame.getContentPane().add(button, BorderLayout.NORTH);
myFrame.setVisible(true);
```

Panes are related to frames in that they are windows, but they must be added to one of the top-level windows listed previously or to another pane. The following are the intermediate Swing containers:

➤ *JPanel*—This is a bare container you can add borders to.

➤ *JScrollPane*—This container presents a scrollable view of a component.

➤ *JSplitPane*—This container displays two components, left to right or top to bottom.

➤ *JToolBar*—This container groups components, often buttons, into a row or column.

➤ *JTabbedPane*—This container overlaps panels that are selected by tabbing.

Dialog Boxes, Pop-Ups, and Choosers

As mentioned earlier, dialog boxes are single-purpose windows for functions such as login and yes/no screens. You can construct your own dialog box with a JDialog component or use one of the Swing components, including JOptionPane, JFileChooser, and JColorChooser. For the assignment, you could use a dialog box as a prompt for how many reservations are needed, if that is part of the functionality your instructions require. The following snippets are examples of using dialog boxes:

```
// Modal OK dialog
JFrame myFrame = new JFrame("my new frame");
JOptionPane.showMessageDialog(myFrame, "SCJD or bust");

//File dialog
File file = new File(File.separator + "bin");
JFileChooser fileDialog = new JFileChooser(file);
fileDialog.showSaveDialog(myFrame);
File myFile = fileDialog.getSelectedFile();
```

Layout Managers

You can position components on a container by using absolute positioning, but this technique is painful and usually unnecessary. The better way to go is using a layout manager that handles positioning for you, based on simple rules. An excellent feature in Swing is having a default layout manager for every container. You can always replace the default with another one, but you don't have to. Every container, by default, has a layout manager. For example, BorderLayout is the default layout manager for every content pane. There are many more layout managers than just these, including DefaultMenuLayout, OverlayLayout, ScrollPaneLayout, SpringLayout, TextLayout, and ViewportLayout, but the following six layout managers are the ones I recommend you use for your solution.

➤ *FlowLayout*—Components are arranged in a left-to-right flow. This is the default.

➤ *GridLayout*—Components are arranged in a grid or table.

➤ *BorderLayout*—Components are arranged in five areas: north, south, east, west, and center.

➤ *CardLayout*—Panels overlap as in a tabbed pane, but without the tabs.

➤ *BoxLayout*—This fancier version of the FlowLayout stacks its components on top of each other or left to right.

➤ *GridBagLayout*—This layout manager is the most flexible. It is like the GridLayout, except the cells can vary in size instead of having all rows or columns the same size.

The following code shows how you could lay out components left to right, in two rows and two columns:

```
JButton firstComponent = new JButton;
JButton secondComponent = new JButton;
JButton thirdComponent = new JButton;
JButton fourthComponent = new JButton;
int rows = 2;
int columns = 2;
JPanel panel = new JPanel(new GridLayout(rows, columns));
panel.add(firstComponent);
panel.add(secondComponent);
panel.add(thirdComponent);
panel.add(fourthComponent);
```

Buttons and Labels

Buttons and labels are the most commonly used components, and you will need them for your project. Listing 14.2 is a quick example demonstrating how to simply add a label to a frame.

Listing 14.2   How to Add a Label to a Frame

```
import javax.swing.JLabel;
import javax.swing.JFrame;

public class MyLabelApplication
{
    public static void main(String[] args)
    {
        //create label
        JLabel label = new JLabel("My Label Application");
        //create frame
        JFrame frame = new JFrame("My Label Application");
        //Notice that BorderLayout is the default
        frame.getContentPane().add(label);
        frame.pack();
        frame.setVisible(true);
    }
}
```

Progress Bars and Sliders

The assignment is rather short, so it is doubtful you will need a progress bar for your project. One possibility is to visually indicate how many seats are left on a flight (or whatever is applicable to your assignment scenario). A progress bar can be oriented horizontally (left to right, which is the default) or vertically (bottom to top). These are the progress bars and the slider used in Swing:

➤ *JProgressBar*—Displays a vertical or horizontal box that is progressively filled by a bar indicating what percentage of the task has been completed.

➤ *ProgressMonitor*—This component is related to JProgressBar, but isn't visible until it pops up a dialog box, if the operation will take a while.

➤ *JSlider*—This component enables the user to select a numeric value within a given range by sliding a knob. Forcing the user to pick the value by sliding the knob eliminates typing errors.

 Use components in your GUI that eliminate user typing errors. For example, make the user pick an item from a list or combo box instead of typing it into a text field.

The following snippet is an example for the JProgressBar:

```
int minimum = 0;  //seats
int maximum = 50; //seats
JProgressBar progress = new JProgressBar(JProgressBar.VERTICAL,
➥minimum, maximum);
```

Menus and Toolbars

A menu presents several options in a menu bar or as a pop-up menu and is located in the expected window's title bar at the top of the screen. As you know, it enables the user to select a menu item. The user's selection fires an action event. The following snippet is an example of using a menu:

```
JMenuBar myMenuBar = new JMenuBar();
JMenu menu = new JMenu("first menu");
myMenuBar.add(menu);

// the submenu "listens" for user selection
JMenuItem myMenuItem = new JMenuItem("first submenu");
//actionListener was instantiated previously
myMenuItem.addActionListener(actionListener);
menu.add(myMenuItem);
//last, add the menu bar to the frame
// assume frame is initialized prviously
frame.setJMenuBar(myMenuBar);
```

Lists and Combo Boxes

The default model for a list does not allow adding and removing items. The list must be created with a DefaultListModel component, as shown in the following snippet:

```
//you can create a custom list models or use DefaultListModel
DefaultListModel model = new DefaultListModel();
JList myList = new JList(model); //allows adds and removes

// load myList with items
model.add(0, "one");
model.add(1, "two");
model.add(2, "three");

myList.setForeground(Color.blue);
myList.setBackground(Color.white);

// this is how you insert
model.add(0, "zero");

// this is how you append
model.add(myList.getModel().getSize(), "four");
```

You might consider using a list or combination box to present choices to the user. This is a good idea for your project because it reduces the chance of user errors, which are inevitable when user responses are taken from typed input.

Text Components

Text components are the most complex Swing components, but they are fun to use, and you need one for the assignment. The required user help is presented in one of these components, probably the JTextEditor. These are the five text components:

> *JTextField*—This component is the simplest one for displaying and editing only one line of text.

> *JPasswordField*—This component is the same control as JTextField, except the typed characters are displayed as asterisks to hide the password.

> *JTextArea*—This component is the same as JTextField, except instead of only one line, JTextArea allows displaying and editing multiple lines of text, all in the same font.

> *JEditorPane*—This component allows displaying and editing multiple lines of text and in multiple fonts.

➤ *JTextPane*—This component also allows displaying and editing multiple lines of text in multiple fonts. JTextPane is a subclass of JEditorPane and has more functionality.

You must provide user help documentation, preferably in HTML format. Use the JEditorPane component to do this because that component is designed especially for HTML.

The following example shows how you might present user help information in HTML format. Listing 14.3 demonstrates how to display an HTML file using the JtextPane component.

Listing 14.3   How to Display an HTML File

```java
import javax.swing.*;
import java.awt.*;

public class UserHelp
{
    public UserHelp()
    {
        JTextPane pane = new JTextPane();
        JScrollPane scroller = new JScrollPane();
        scroller.getViewport().add(pane);
        JFrame frame = new JFrame("Look-Feel");
        frame.getContentPane().add(scroller, BorderLayout.CENTER);
        frame.setDefaultCloseOperation(JFrame.EXIT_ON_CLOSE);
        frame.pack();
        frame.setSize(800,500);
        frame.setVisible(true);

        String htmlDocument = "userHelp.html";

        try
        {
            java.net.URL url = new java.net.URL("file:"
                    + System.getProperty("user.dir")
                    + System.getProperty("file.separator")
                    + htmlDocument);
            pane.setPage(url);
        } catch (Exception ex)
        {
            ex.printStackTrace();
        }
    }

    public static void main(String[] args)
    {
        try
        {
            UIManager.setLookAndFeel(
                UIManager.getCrossPlatformLookAndFeelClassName());
```

(continued)

Listing 14.3 How to Display an HTML File *(continued)*

```
      } catch (Exception e) {}

      //Create the top-level container and add contents to it.
      UserHelp app = new UserHelp();
   }
}
```

Listing 14.3 produces a simple screen. (Refer to Figure 5.1 in Chapter 5, "Documentation and Javadoc Comments.") Be aware that the JTextPane is not an advanced browser tool. It displays plain HTML fine, but doesn't do well with advanced features, such as cascading style sheets (CSS), JavaScript, or Extensible Hypertext Markup Language (XHTML).

There are many interesting operations you can perform on text components. A few are shown in the following example:

```
JTextComponent textComponent =
            new JTextArea("Do not act like a knucklehead.");

int textLength = textComponent.getDocument().getLength();
// grab all the text
String allText = textComponent.getText();

try
{
    // grab first 5 characters
    text = textComponent.getText(0, 5);
    // grab last 5 characters
    text = textComponent.getText(textLength-5, 5);
    // delete characters
    textComponent.remove(3, 4);
    // replace characters
    textComponent.insertString(3, "four", null);

} catch (BadLocationException ble)
{}
```

The following is another way to programmatically manipulate the String in a text component:

```
JTextPane textPane = new JTextPane();
// grab root element
Element rootDoc = textPane.getDocument().getDefaultRootElement();
// How many paragraphs?
int paragraphs = rootDoc.getElementCount();
// grab each paragraph
for (int i=0; i<paragraphs; i++)
{
    Element para = section.getElement(i);
    int start = para.getStartOffset();
    int end = para.getEndOffset();
    try
    {
        String text = rootDoc.getText(start, end-start);
    } catch (BadLocationException ex)
    {}
}
```

NOTE
A text component stores the text as a **Document** object, which divides the content into a hierarchy of **Element** objects. **Element** objects are a contiguous span of characters with the same attributes. For example, a contiguous span of characters terminated by a single newline character is one paragraph element.

Event Handling

The GUI must be able to handle user input. The way Java (and most languages) handles user input is based on the event model, in which the GUI receives user actions and calls methods in response. Specifically, the developer decides which GUI components will listen for events and the specific events for which these components will listen. The developer then writes appropriate listener classes for these events. Each listener class must implement the appropriate interface corresponding to the event type, either directly or by extending an adapter. Within each listener class, the developer writes the code for the methods that will be called when the appropriate event occurs.

The following example illustrates the search button in a GUI listening for an event. The certification assignment requires that you write a search algorithm. (A generic algorithm is discussed in Chapter 7, "Databases and Atomicity," as part of the database topic.) However, you must also decide how the user can initiate a search. The following code shows one approach to performing a search on a database caused by a user clicking the search button and illustrates how to handle this click-button event:

```
//in the GUI building section:
searchButton = new JButton("Search Seats");
searchButton.setToolTipText("Search the database now");
searchButton.addActionListener( new SearchButtonHandler());

//Later in the GUI class,
//you can use an inner class that implements ActionListener
//to respond to user clicks on the search button.
public class SearchButtonHandler implements ActionListener
{
    String criteria = "",
        previousCriteria = "",
        seatCriteria = "";

    public void actionPerformed( ActionEvent e )
    {
        // Finds the criteria from combo box,
        // which eliminates typing errors.
        seatCriteria = (String)searchComboBox
                .getSelectedItem();

        criteria = ((JLabel)searchLabelName.elementAt(0))
                .getText()
                + "='" + searchCriteria +"',";
        if (!criteria.equalsIgnoreCase(previousCriteria))
```

```
        {
            try
            {
                resultSet = database.search(criteria);
            } catch(RemoteException rex)
            {
                System.out.print(rex);
            } catch(DatabaseException dex)
            {
                System.out.print(dex);
            }
            previousCriteria = criteria;
            //process the resultSet
        }
    }
}
```

Need to Know More?

 Geary, David. *Graphic Java 2, Volume 2: Swing, Third Edition.* Upper Saddle River, NJ: Prentice Hall, 1999 (ISBN 0130796670). At more than 1,500 pages, it is the most complete book for Java GUI developers.

 http://java.sun.com/docs/books/tutorial/uiswing/index.html—At this page you can find the excellent "Creating a GUI with JFC/Swing" tutorial.

 http://java.sun.com/docs/—Download the Java API documentation in javadoc-generated form.

 http://www.oreilly.com/catalog/learnjava/chapter/ch14.html—This site is where you'll find a helpful chapter, "Using Swing Components," from *Learning Java*, by Pat Niemeyer and Jonathan Knudsen.

The JTable Component

Terms you'll need to understand:

✓ JTable

✓ Rendering

✓ Table model

✓ Observable event model

✓ Tool tips

Techniques you'll need to master:

✓ Setting tool tips on cells in a JTable component

✓ Enabling row, column, or cell selections in a JTable component

✓ Listening for changes to the rows and columns of a JTable component

✓ Designing your own table data model

✓ Reading a data file into a JTable

In this chapter, you review the basics of the JTable Swing component. You'll find lots of examples here, so you will probably be able to adapt some of the code in this chapter for your certification assignment.

A key requirement for the assignment is designing the table into the project so that the user can find a particular row of data, select the row, and change the data in the database based on the selection. There are many ways to approach this task. You can allow the user to actually change the values in the table itself. In that case, you listen for user actions, such as `ListSelectionModel.addListSelectionListener()`, to monitor a whole row, or `JTable.addMouseListener(new MouseAdapter())`, to listen for mouse clicks on a cell. Note that the `ListSelectionModel` to which you add the listener needs to be the one that has been set as the selection model for the JTable via `setSelectionModel()`.

One of the problems you must solve is user error. What happens if users try to reserve too many seats, for example? How does your program deal with the situation when a plane or train has no seats available, but the user still requests seats? Whatever the approach, you must at least have a way to give messages to your users. You should tell them when the reservation is successful, but more important for the assignment requirements, you should also inform them of errors and what the application did about them.

In my project submission, I reduced the possibility of errors by designing the GUI so that users selected the item of interest by clicking on the table. This click then populated related Swing components. User actions all involved clicking except for one text box, in which they typed the number of seats. This design seemed simpler for the user and restricted the chance of user error to one field. The input from that field was carefully scrubbed so that it wasn't possible for the system to choke on, say, a request for too many seats. If anything wasn't right, such as too many seats requested, no seats available, or non-numeric input, a message about the error was displayed to the user, who was then allowed to try again. My approach was to completely eliminate exceptions caused by user input. You might allow the user to change data in the JTable itself. That approach is no better or worse than what I did. Just make sure the user input error trapping handles all problems.

There were many JavaRanch forum posts from candidates who used logging to keep a running record of user and system activities. I recommend not doing this, however. Logging is not part of the requirements, so don't introduce an element that can't earn you more points, but could make you lose points if you introduce an error in the logging code. The idea is great, of course. However, evaluators want to know whether you can follow instructions, so they will wonder why you have logging code when that feature isn't required. Some forum posters suggested they added logging for debugging purposes, but took it out before submitting their projects. Again, I strongly recommend skipping extra work that could introduce errors. The certification application is not a large one, so the negative cost of adding logging cancels out any benefits of logging functionality. Stay focused and don't add extra elements; concentrate on only what is required.

 | Reconsider adding logging to your application. It is not required, but if you add it, you might fail because of an error in the logging code.

MVC in the JTable

The JTable component models the MVC design pattern. In the MVC design pattern, there are three components: a view (the information the user sees), a model (the underlying data that populates the view), and a controller (which typically keeps the model and the view in sync).The Swing architecture uses the MVC design pattern extensively and the JTable is one of the components that rely on this pattern. The visible grid that the user sees and manipulates represents the view. The corresponding data is stored in the model, an object instantiated from a subclass of the `AbstractTableModel` class. You extend this class to create your own model class as is shown in Listing 15.1. The model is responsible for storing and keeping the data current. Note that the data shown in the view and the data in the model are not automatically kept synchronized. The synchronization between the two must be controlled by the controller, a piece of software that you must write. This is where most of your code goes that affects the view. The controller keeps the view and the model synchronized and can enable the model to be updated based on user input in the view. For example, when he user sets focus to a specific grid cell and presses a Delete button, the controller could respond by deleting the actual data in the model and updating the view as necessary. To see how all this works, let's create a simple JTable-based application.

Creating a Simple JTable

Notice that the JTable created by the following code has a built-in storage implementation. It constructs a JTable to display values in a two-dimensional array, called `data`, with column names (`colNames`). Although cell values can be changed, rows and columns cannot be added or deleted.

```
Object[][] data = {  {"col1", "col2"}, //row1
                     {"col1", "col2"}  //row2
                  };
String[] colNames = {"col1", "col2"};
JTable table = new JTable(data, colNames);
```

There are seven JTable constructors total, but only three are mentioned in the preceding code. You can create a table in a similar fashion by passing

Vectors containing the data and the column names to the constructor. Notice
that the values are in a Vector of Vectors, like so:

```
Vector columns = new Vector();
Vector data = new Vector();
Vector columnNames = new Vector();

columnNames.addElement("Name");
columnNames.addElement("Age");

columns.addElement("Matty");
columns.addElement(new Integer(4));
data.addElement(columns);

JTable table = new JTable(data, columnNames);
```

Listing 15.1 is a working example. It has all the basic pieces to create a JTable
component in which the amount of data to add is flexible because of using
Vectors. This flexibility is important for dynamically loading the JTable from
a file when you do not know beforehand how many rows of data there are.

Listing 15.1   An Example Using JTable

```
import javax.swing.JTable;
import javax.swing.JScrollPane;
import javax.swing.JPanel;
import javax.swing.JFrame;
import java.util.Vector;
import java.awt.Dimension;
import java.awt.BorderLayout;
import java.awt.event.WindowAdapter;
import java.awt.event.WindowEvent;

public class MyTable extends JFrame
{
    public MyTable()
    {
        super("MyTable");

        //simpler way, but must know array size beforehand
        Object[][] data = { {"Matty", new Integer(5)},
                            {"Daniel", new Integer(8)},
                            {"Peter", new Integer(11)},
                            {"Kasienne", new Integer(12)},
                            {"Austin", new Integer(13)},
                            {"Carter", new Integer(14)},
                          };

        String[] columnNames={"Name","Age"};

        Vector columns = new Vector();
        Vector data = new Vector();
        Vector columnNames = new Vector();

        columnNames.addElement("Name");
        columnNames.addElement("Age");

        columns.addElement("Matty");
```

(continued)

Listing 15.1 An Example Using JTable *(continued)*

```
        columns.addElement(new Integer(5));
        data.addElement(columns);

        columns = new Vector();
        columns.addElement("Daniel");
        columns.addElement(new Integer(8));
        data.addElement(columns);

        columns = new Vector();
        columns.addElement("Peter");
        columns.addElement(new Integer(11));
        data.addElement(columns);

        columns = new Vector();
        columns.addElement("Kasienne");
        columns.addElement(new Integer(12));
        data.addElement(columns);

        columns = new Vector();
        columns.addElement("Austin");
        columns.addElement(new Integer(13));
        data.addElement(columns);

        columns = new Vector();
        columns.addElement("Carter");
        columns.addElement(new Integer(14));
        data.addElement(columns);


        final JTable table = new JTable(data, columnNames);
        table.setPreferredScrollableViewportSize(new Dimension(200, 100));

        //Add the table to scroll pane.
        JScrollPane scrollPane = new JScrollPane(table);

        //Add the scroll pane to this window.
        getContentPane().add(scrollPane, BorderLayout.CENTER);

        //If you don't do this, the program won't terminate
        //when you click the window's close button
        addWindowListener(new WindowAdapter()
        {
            public void windowClosing(WindowEvent e)
            {
                System.exit(0);
            }
        });
    }

    public static void main(String[] args)
    {
        MyTable frame = new MyTable();
        frame.pack();
        frame.setVisible(true);
    }
}
```

Listing 15.1 produces the screen shown in Figure 15.1.

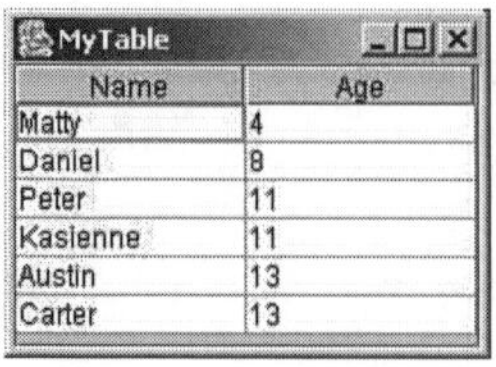

Name	Age
Matty	4
Daniel	8
Peter	11
Kasienne	11
Austin	13
Carter	13

Figure 15.1 A simple JTable example.

To demonstrate a more compelling example, Listing 15.2 is a simplified database file reader. The database in this case is an ASCII text file of data in which the first row is the set of column names and the remaining rows are data. You could easily add the capability to handle comma separated values (CSV), but the file structure is deliberately kept simple to help highlight the algorithm steps. It is similar to Listing 15.1, except now you are getting your data from a file that acts as a database. This example starts to meet the central goal of the assignment: You must read data from a database file and display it in a Swing JTable component. Run Listing 15.1 with the following command line: `java DBViewer` *`filename`*, where *`filename`* is the name of the file (the file provided is named `data.db`).

Listing 15.2 Displaying a Database File Using JTable

```
import javax.swing.JTable;
import javax.swing.JScrollPane;
import javax.swing.JPanel;
import javax.swing.JFrame;
import java.util.Vector;
import java.io.StreamTokenizer;
import java.io.FileReader;
import java.io.BufferedReader;
import java.awt.Dimension;
import java.awt.BorderLayout;
import java.awt.event.WindowAdapter;
import java.awt.event.WindowEvent;

public class DBViewer extends JFrame
{
    public DBViewer(String filename)
    {
        super("DBViewer");

        Vector rowValues = new Vector();
        Vector data = new Vector();
        Vector columnNames = new Vector();
        boolean firstLine = true;
        String line;

        //1  open file
        try
        {
            FileReader reader = new FileReader(filename);
            BufferedReader br = new BufferedReader(reader);
```

(continued)

Listing 15.2   Displaying a Database File Using JTable (continued)

```
StreamTokenizer tokenizer = new StreamTokenizer(br);
tokenizer.eolIsSignificant(true);      // we need '\n'

//2  get line
//3  get next field from line
int type;
while ( (type = tokenizer.nextToken())
         != StreamTokenizer.TT_EOF)
{
    //4  add names to columnNames, values to rowValues
    switch (type)
    {
      case StreamTokenizer.TT_NUMBER:
        //add to value vector
        rowValues.addElement(new Double(tokenizer.nval));
        break;
      case StreamTokenizer.TT_WORD:
        //add to column name vector
        if (firstLine)
        {
            columnNames.addElement(tokenizer.sval);
        //add to value vector
        } else
        {
            rowValues.addElement(tokenizer.sval);
        }

        break;
      case StreamTokenizer.TT_EOL:
        //5  add row of values to data
        if (!firstLine && rowValues.size() > 0)
        {
            data.addElement(rowValues);
            rowValues = new Vector();
        }else
        {
            firstLine = false;
        }
    }
  }
} catch (java.io.FileNotFoundException fnfe)
{
    System.out.println(fnfe);
    System.exit(0);
} catch (ArrayIndexOutOfBoundsException aibe)
{
    System.out.println(aibe);
    System.exit(0);
} catch (java.io.IOException ioe)
{
    System.out.println(ioe);
    System.exit(0);
}

final JTable table = new JTable(data, columnNames);
table.setPreferredScrollableViewportSize(new Dimension(200, 100));

//Add the table to scroll pane.
JScrollPane scrollPane = new JScrollPane(table);
```

(continued)

Listing 15.2   Displaying a Database File Using JTable *(continued)*

```
        //Add the scroll pane to this window.
        getContentPane().add(scrollPane, BorderLayout.CENTER);

        //If you don't do this, the program won't terminate
        //when you click the window's close button.
        addWindowListener(new WindowAdapter()
        {
            public void windowClosing(WindowEvent e)
            {
                System.exit(0);
            }
        });
    }

    public static void main(String[] args)
    {
        if (args.length == 0)
        {
            System.out.print("No file name provided. Terminating.");
            System.exit(0);
        }
        DBViewer frame = new DBViewer(args[0]);
        frame.pack();
        frame.setVisible(true);
    }
}
```

Assume the database file has the following structure:

```
ID    Name        Amount
1234  Patricia    7000.00
5678  Kasienne    5000.00
8910  James       2000.00
```

Remember that the usage is `java DBViewer DB_file_name`. Listing 15.2 produces the screen shown in Figure 15.2.

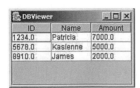

Figure 15.2 Viewing a database with a JTable.

Now try putting on your architecture hat. Suppose you want to solidify the design with a formal grammar for the file structure. You could say that the file acting as a database table has the following grammar:

```
table : ( row (EOL) )* ;
row : ( COLUMN (DELIMITER COLUMN)* ) ;
COLUMN : ( ~( '\t' | ' ' | '\r' | '\n' ) )+ ;
EOL : ( '\n' | '\r' ) ;
DELIMITER : '\t' | (' ')+ ;
```

This grammar specifies a file as having delimiters that are a tab character or space(s). Note that the asterisk (*) means zero to many, and the plus sign (+) means one to many. | means or and ~ means not. The end of line (EOL) could be a carriage return or a newline character. The column is a sequence of one or more characters that are not tabs, one or more spaces, newline characters, or carriage returns.

So, to read this grammar we would say a row contains one or more columns separated by delimiters. Finally, a table contains zero or more rows, each ending with one EOL. This design is simple, but it demonstrates clearly how you should proceed for a real application. It includes the basic grammar constructs of concatenation, alternation, repetition zero or more times, repetition one or more times, and negation. The grammar in the preceding example disallows an empty row by defining a row as comprising columns that must contain at least one character.

The primary goal is to read a file and correctly display it in a JTable. There are several things you can do to improve Listing 15.2's functionality. For example, you can use a regular expression construct rather than the StreamTokenizer class. The following snippet is a start:

```
try {
    FileInputStream fis = new FileInputStream(filename);
    FileChannel fc = fis.getChannel();

    // Create a read-only CharBuffer on the file
    ByteBuffer bbuf = fc.map(FileChannel.MapMode.READ_ONLY,
                             0, (int)fc.size());
    // Need a CharSequence for use by regex.
    CharBuffer cbuf = Charset.forName("8859_1").newDecoder().decode(bbuf);
    // Create matcher on file
    Pattern pattern = Pattern.compile("([A-Za-z][0-9])+");
    Matcher matcher = pattern.matcher(cbuf);

    // Get matches
    while (matcher.find())
    {
        String match = matcher.group();
        //do something with match
    }
} catch (IOException e)
{
    System.out.print(e);
}
```

Table Model

The JTable component stores data in what is called a *table model*. You can populate this model by using any of several JTable constructors. Listing 15.1 demonstrated a simple two-parameter construction. What if you wanted to have more control over this data that feeds the JTable? You would use what

Sun calls a table model, which implements the model portion of the Model-View-Controller (MVC) pattern.

The table model is a way to abstract the rows and columns of data in the JTable. To do that, you can write your own model that implements the `TableModel` interface. The more common approach is to create a concrete `TableModel` subclass of `AbstractTableModel`. To do so, you need to include only the following three methods in your model class:

```
public int getRowCount();
public int getColumnCount();
public Object getValueAt(int row, int column);
```

The following code is a simple example of a custom JTable model. The data and column names are already hard-coded, but it demonstrates the bare minimum you are required to code to provide a model for your JTable:

```
class MyTableModel extends AbstractTableModel
{
    final String[] columnNames = {"Gate",
                                  "Level",
                                  "Aisle",
                                  "Row",
                                  "Seat"};

    final Object[][] data =
            {
                {"North", new Integer(100),
                 "First", "A", new Integer(1)},
                {"North", new Integer(100),
                 "Second", "V", new Integer(24)},
                {"North", new Integer(100),
                 "First", "B", new Integer(39)},
                {"South", new Integer(150),
                 "Second", "C", new Integer(18)},
                {"South", new Integer(150),
                 "Third", "E", new Integer(6)}
            };

    public int getColumnCount()
    {
        return columnNames.length;
    }

    public int getRowCount()
    {
        return data.length;
    }

    public Object getValueAt(int row, int col)
    {
        return data[row][col];
    }
}
```

You can see that it is not difficult to write your own JTable model. For the certification project, you need to provide a way to populate the model with data from a database. The assignment from Sun provides a simple database system, from which you get data to populate the JTable model. Furthermore, through user action, probably on the JTable component, you need to update data in the database.

The trick is to dynamically populate the `columnNames` and `data` variables in your model. Listing 15.3 is an edited version of a JTable model used in the book's sample application and represents a good skeleton for your assignment needs.

Listing 15.3   A Sample JTable Model

```java
import javax.swing.table.AbstractTableModel;
import java.io.RandomAccessFile;
import java.io.File;
import java.io.FileNotFoundException;
import java.io.IOException;

class MyTableModel extends AbstractTableModel
{
    private Object[][] data;
    private String[] columnNames;

    //Populate model with data already parsed and placed in 2D array
    public MyTableModel (String[][] values, String[] columnNames)
    {
        this.columnNames = columnNames;
        int recordNumber = values.length;
        int columnCount = columnNames.length;
        data = new Object[recordNumber][columnCount];
        for(int rowCount=0; rowCount<recordNumber; rowCount++)
        {
            for(int colCount=0; colCount<columnCount; colCount++)
            {
                setData(values[rowCount], rowCount, colCount);
            }//end for
        }//end for
    }

    //You can use this constructor to populate the model with
    //data from the database file.
    public MyTableModel (String databaseFileName)
    {

      try
      {
        //Open databaseFileName with RandomAccessFile object.
        //Read column names into columnNames array, then:
        File file = new File(databaseFileName);
        if (file.exists())
        {
            RandomAccessFile databaseFile =
                    new RandomAccessFile(file, "rw");
            //db file probably has header information at top
            int columns = databaseFile.readInt();
            //more header initiation...
             columnNames = new String[columns];
            for (int i=0; i<columns; i++)
```

(continued)

Listing 15.3   A Sample JTable Model *(continued)*

```
            {
                //fill columnNames[i]
            }
            this.columnNames = columnNames;

            //Read row values into an array of data, then
            //add those arrays into a 2D data array:
            this.data = data;
        }
    } catch(FileNotFoundException fnfe)
    {
        System.out.print(fnfe);
    } catch(IOException ex)
    {
        System.out.print(ex);
    }

}

public void setData(String[] values, int row, int column)
{
    switch (column)
    {
            case (1): //level
            case (4): //seat
                    data[row][column] =
                            new Integer(values[column].trim());
                    break;
            default:
                    //is a String already
                    data[row][column] = values[column].trim();
        }//end switch
}

 public int getColumnCount()
{
    return columnNames.length;
}

public int getRowCount()
{
    return data.length;
}

 public String getColumnName(int col)
{
    return columnNames[col];
}

 public Object getValueAt(int row, int col)
{
    return data[row][col];
}

    /*
     * This method helps renderer for each column.
     */
    public Class getColumnClass(int c)
    {
        return getValueAt(0, c).getClass();
    }
}
```

JTable Techniques

The next sections cover aspects of JTable that you might want to include in your project. Although most of them are not required, they can improve the user experience without the risk of introducing errors. Some of these examples are inspired from *The Java Developers Almanac 1.4* (Addison Wesley Professional, 2002, ISBN 0201752808; see "Need to Know More?" at the end of this chapter for an online version), an excellent book of code snippets.

Setting Column Header Tool Tips

In my project submission, I added tool tips to the column headers. The tool tips didn't require much code, but adding them is justified by making the GUI easier to use, a factor in scoring the client. The trick is to install a mouse motion listener on the header component, as shown here:

```
JTable table = new JTable(rows, cols);
JTableHeader header = table.getTableHeader();
header.setToolTipText("Click a header to sort table by that column");
```

Using a Scrollable JTable Component

I recommend a scrollable JTable. By default, a table is created with auto resizing enabled, so if the user changes the table width, the columns automatically expand or shrink to keep their contents visible. However, this mode removes the horizontal scrollbar. The following code snippet demonstrates how to create a new JTable and then make it automatically scroll when the table's contents exceed the visible grid's area onscreen:

```
// Create a table with 10 rows and 5 columns
int numRows = 3;
int numColumns = 4
JTable table = new JTable(numRows, numColumns);
    JScrollPane scrollPane = new JScrollPane(table);
    table.setAutoResizeMode(JTable.AUTO_RESIZE_OFF);
```

Handling Cell Selections

How do you allow cell selection? You must enable row selections so that clicking on any cell selects the entire row containing that cell. It works the same for columns. The following code snippet shows you how to handle cell selection that takes place when a user clicks on the table:

```
JTable table = new JTable();

//Row selection on, column selection off
table.setColumnSelectionAllowed(false);
table.setRowSelectionAllowed(true);

//Both on to get cell selection
table.setColumnSelectionAllowed(true);
table.setRowSelectionAllowed(true);
```

Changing the Name of a Column

You can change the name of a column in a JTable component, but be careful. If you change the column name, be sure you don't rely on the column name for any logic, such as searching the database by the JTable column instead of the database column. The following code shows you how to place a name at the top of a table column:

```
JTableModel tableModel = new DefaultTableModel();
JTable table = new JTable(tableModel);
tableModel.addColumn("firstColumn");
tableModel.addColumn("secondColumn");

// Change name of first column
table.getColumnModel().getColumn(0).setHeaderValue("newName");

//Resize and repaint header
table.getTableHeader().resizeAndRepaint();
```

Getting and Setting a Cell Value

Most likely, you will need to get the value of an individual cell when a user clicks on your JTable. Some candidates allow users to change the value (for example, the seat number) right in the table. I chose to get the cell value when a user clicked on that row and place the value into another component. This manner of handling user input removed the possibility of typing errors, and it seemed to give the GUI a more natural feel for user input. Note that if the value in the view or model changes, you must add code to synchronize the two. The following code snippet demonstrates how to get a user selection from the table after the user clicks it:

```
int row = 8;
int column = 7;
Object o = table.getValueAt(row, column);

// Get value in model
o = table.getModel().getValueAt(row, column);
```

```
// Change table cell
table.setValueAt("Kasienne", row, column);

// Change model cell
table.getModel().setValueAt("Kasienne", row, column);
```

 Keep track of whether the cell or column you are manipulating is in the visible table or the table model. If you confuse them, the results will be wrong.

Need to Know More?

 David M. Geary. *Graphic Java 2, Volume 2: Swing, Third Edition.* Upper Saddle River, NJ: Prentice Hall, 1999 (ISBN 0130796670). A solid study on understanding the GUI in Java.

 `http://java.sun.com/docs/books/tutorial/uiswing/components/table.html`—The JTable tutorial, "How to Use Tables," at this site includes material for version 1.4.

 `http://javaalmanac.com/egs/javax.swing.table/pkg.html`—You can find many sample code snippets from the online version of *The Java Developers Almanac 1.4.*

 `http://java.sun.com/j2se/1.4.1/docs/api/index.html`—You can look at the Java API documentation for the JTable component.

Design Patterns

Terms you'll need to understand:

✓ Design pattern
✓ Proxy
✓ Adapter pattern
✓ Decorator pattern
✓ Business delegate pattern
✓ Data Access Object (DAO) pattern
✓ Value Object pattern
✓ Model-View-Controller (MVC) pattern

Techniques you'll need to master:

✓ Selecting the design pattern that works best for a given situation
✓ Identifying a design pattern from the situation it solves
✓ Recognizing real design patterns from other solution approaches
✓ Knowing how to encapsulate a design pattern in code
✓ Knowing how to apply a design pattern to different scales
✓ Matching design patterns with their benefits

In this chapter, you learn about *design patterns*, a systematic approach to designing software that Sun is advocating engineers use for Java and requires candidates to use for the Sun Certified Java Developer (SCJD) certification. Throughout this chapter, you learn the basics of design patterns so that you can complete a solution using them.

Design Patterns Defined

Whether you are a software manager, designer, engineer, or student, design patterns are the best foundation on which to design and build software projects. One of the first examples of applying design patterns to software was in the classic book *Design Patterns: Elements of Reusable Object-Oriented Software* (Addison-Wesley, 1995), written by the Gang of Four (GoF)—Erich Gamma, Richard Helm, Ralph Johnson, and John Vlissides. This chapter helps you bridge the gap between the highly abstract GoF presentation and the real-world challenges of writing code. If design patterns are used as Sun suggests, and this chapter echoes, they become a core asset of any software shop. Patterns show developers how to systematically solve problems created by market and technology forces.

So where do design patterns fit in the design hierarchy? You often hear about two-tier, three-tier, and multitier applications. The number of tiers refers to the number of major responsibilities. For example, a three-tier application has presentation, logic, and database tiers. Another way of thinking about an application is in layers of abstractions, from most granular to most general, as described in the following list:

➤ Token (`int seatNumber`)

➤ Statement (`seatNumber = 25;`)

➤ Block (`while(true){}`)

➤ Algorithm (seat search)

➤ Object (`SuperBowlSeat`)

➤ Design Pattern (Value Object)

➤ Framework (Collections framework)

➤ Architecture (GUI—RMI—database)

➤ Solution (certification submission)

You need to traverse all these layers to produce a successful solution. Although the Token and Statement layers are simple, the remaining layers require increasingly sophisticated ideas. In fact, I propose that starting at the Algorithm layer, the evaluator should begin deducting points if the algorithm isn't designed right. The seat search (your instructions might call it something like "criteria search") is actually listed in the scoring section of the instructions. The instructions also name specific design patterns. You will definitely use the Model-View-Controller (MVC) pattern in the GUI (Swing technology is built with it), and most candidates use Value Object for transporting database query results back to the requesting GUI (the approach my solution used through RMI). Your evaluator hopes to find good use of pre-existing J2SE classes throughout your code. For example, my lock manager used the Collection framework in the form of a `HashMap`. Evaluators would rather see smart reuse than invention. Last, your architecture has to be effective. A GUI—socket—RMI—database architecture, for example, would be weak because the socket portion, which is already implemented in RMI, is unnecessary. This chapter defines and describes the patterns you will most likely use your solution and throughout your career as you address enterprise design needs.

The term "pattern" comes from the architect Christopher Alexander, who wrote several books on the topic of patterns. Alexander, a building architect, was the first to "codify" patterns for architecture. Although he was interested in urban planning and building architecture, his notions were clearly useful in many areas and isolated the concept of patterns better than anyone before him. Alexander is one of those rare people who take a step back and question why people do things the way they do. He gave the result of his inquiry the name "pattern language" and defined it at length in his seminal book, *A Pattern Language: Towns, Buildings, Construction* (by Christopher Alexander, Sara Ishikawa, and Murray Silverstein; Oxford University Press, 1977).

While Alexander was thinking buildings and foundations, it became clear to many that his design patterns were abstract enough to be useful elsewhere. That is when the GoF applied patterns to software in *Design Patterns: Elements of Reusable Object-Oriented Software*. It took a while, but the GoF started a groundswell. There are now dozens of books, and many more on the way, about design patterns.

Design patterns are often defined as "a solution to a problem in a context." This falls short of the abstract definition that experts prefer, however. Suppose you have an object that makes copies of files. What is the design pattern? You don't know yet, so throw in an object that copies the content of one text box to another. Something about the copying process is the same between the two objects. Neither the files nor the text boxes differ, but the copying is the same. Therefore, the sameness is copying. By itself, this isn't a pattern, but you're on the way to finding one.

What are design patterns? Sun defines them in the following way: "A design pattern describes a proven solution to a recurring design problem, placing particular emphasis on the context and forces surrounding the problem, and the consequences and impact of the solution."

Design Pattern Elements

There are many ways to define a pattern, but the classic way is to describe its elements or aspects. There are several lists of elements in the current literature. I've used a dolled-up version of the GoF's approach, which centers on three basic elements—*context, problem,* and *solution:*

➤ *Context* is the recurring situation in which you find a problem to be solved.

➤ *Problems* are the so-called forces, such as marketing and technology, that occur in this context.

➤ *Solution* is the defined design that reorganizes or manipulates (some say "resolves") the forces on a situation into a desired outcome. This solution applies to a specific context and might not apply to others.

The design pattern is not only these three elements, but the relationship between them and the formal language that describes the whole business. That is a lot of heady language and is certainly not on the exam directly, but understanding these relationships will help you select and correctly apply design patterns to your solution.

Remember that context, problem, and solution are at the core of design patterns. The following list of pattern elements is my way of expanding on the three basic elements to give you a way to understand the essence of a given pattern:

➤ *Is*—This element is a direct explanation of what the pattern is, without jargon.

➤ *Is Not*—This element is an attempt at providing a contrasting concept because often looking at what something *isn't* helps clarify the pattern as much as looking at what it *is.*

➤ *Analogy*—This element provides a comparison based on general aspects of the pattern. Analogies give you a way to relate a concept you're already familiar with to the pattern.

➤ *Problem*—This element is a statement of the problem that describes the pattern's purpose and intent.

➤ *Responsibility*—This element describes what the pattern is accountable for—the primary things it accomplishes.

➤ *Intent (or goals and constraints)*—This element contains the goals and objectives the pattern should accomplish within the given context.

➤ *Primary Activity*—A pattern is helpful, but this element describes the main responsibility or work the pattern must perform.

➤ *Context*—This element describes the conditions and environment in which the problem and its solution recur. In other words, when should you consider and apply this pattern?

➤ *Motivation or Forces*—This element describes the forces that affect the context and explains why you would use this pattern and the advantages it offers.

➤ *Applicability*—This elements describes which kinds of situations are good candidates for this pattern.

➤ *Solution*—This element consists of two parts:

➤*Strategy*—This part explains how you should go about applying the pattern.

➤*Pseudo Code*—This part helps you see how you might actually implement the pattern, to extend the concept to actual practice.

➤ *Consequences*—This element describes the result of using the pattern, the final state of the system. There are good and bad consequences of applying the pattern. It could solve one problem, for example, but give rise to a new one.

➤ *Known Uses*—This element offers one or more examples of how the pattern is being used.

➤ *Related Patterns*—This element names other patterns related by context, solution, or consequences. The related pattern might solve the same problem in another way or share the same context, but involve different forces.

➤ *Reference*—This element points you to a resource that provides more material on the pattern.

Patterns in Your Solution

As mentioned, you must understand and use several patterns for this certification: most likely, Value Object, Data Access Object, Decorator, and MVC. You might also use the Front Controller and Business Delegate patterns. You can explore additional design patterns for your solution, such as Observer-Observable, in which your event-handling code in the client is the Observer and the GUI event (user mouse click) is the Observable. You might consider the Adapter pattern, which enables you to have objects with different interfaces communicate with each other. In this case, you might use an adapter for the classes included in the assignment download because you might want to have a different interface between the GUI and the database tier.

The following sections describe each pattern in detail, using the previously listed pattern elements. Patterns are difficult to use and understand without detailed explanation. Although you might not use all these patterns, they are the ones most candidates consider for their designs.

Decorator

The Decorator pattern is used for wrapping an object with additional functionality. When you wrap an object, you are "decorating" it, in design pattern terminology. A Decorator's interface is exactly the same as the object it contains.

Is

In the Decorator pattern, an object (the "decorator") encapsulates another one (the "decoratee") and provides additional functionality. Objects calling methods of the decorator do not know it is a wrapper because its API is the same as the decoratee. The wrapper can then perform preprocessing and postprocessing before and after delegating the call to the decoratee.

Is Not

The Decorator pattern is not a way to extend a class. Normal inheritance does that well. Similar to how a class must implement methods from an implemented interface, a Decorator's methods must exist in the decoratee.

Analogy

The Decorator pattern is like the president's secretary who intercepts all calls and mail. If you send an e-mail to the president, you use his address, not knowing that someone else intercepts it. The secretary reads it, takes action on it, perhaps researches and summarizes the letter, and then finally gives the e-mail's summary to the president. The president gives a short verbal response to the secretary, who in turn replies with an official letter on behalf of the president, including proper signatures and letterhead.

Problem

Some objects need help in processing communication with a client. The current object is often generalized, so it can't be used directly without modification. This object is still responsible for certain functionality involved in one-to-one transactions with the client.

Wrapping the object with a Decorator allows the communication contract to remain intact, but method calls can now be enhanced. Without a Decorator, some objects restrict the possibility of changing behavior. Suppose you have a deeply inherited class hierarchy. You might not want to add methods to a given class. How can you make it more useful to your current application? You can wrap it.

Responsibility

The Decorator pattern provides a way to better respond to changing functionality without changing the API.

Intent (or Goals and Constraints)

The Decorator pattern attempts to add functionality to certain methods by wrapping them with another method having the same signature.

Primary Activity

The Decorator relays calls it receives to the object it contains and adds functionality before and/or after the relay.

Context

Many objects' utility can be extended through decoration. In addition, when objects outlive their usefulness, they can be reused by being decorated.

Motivation or Forces

What issues motivate you to use the Decorator pattern? The following forces apply to the Decorator pattern:

➤ Many applications often use old classes. Some calls to these classes require new considerations and new functionality.

➤ Although new functionality is more frequently added through subclassing, sometimes the API should not be changed.

➤ Instead of growing an object through subclassing, you can grow that object through wrapping it with successive Decorators.

Applicability

The Decorator pattern is useful in your certification project because the classes provided in the assignment download are not sufficient to create a full database. In my solution, I decorated one of the classes so that the client didn't know whether the database was local or remote via RMI.

Solution

The Decorator pattern's solution consists of the following parts:

➤ *Strategy*—Use a Decorator to completely encapsulate another object.

➤ *Pseudo Code*—The code snippet in Listing 16.1 shows an example for this pattern.

Listing 16.1 The Decorator Pattern's Skeleton Program

```
public class DecorateDatabase
{
    // public members
    Database database;

    // default constructor
    public DecorateDatabase()
    {
        super();
        database = new Database();
    }

    //other constructors

    // method to set all the values
    public boolean isSeatAvailable(int seatNumber)
    {
        boolean available = false;

        // preprocessing
        if (seatNumber < 0 || seatNumber > 100)
        {
            return false;
        }

        // delegate to the decoratee
        seatNumber = database.doStuffIfSeatAvailable(seatNumber);

        // postprocessing
        if (seatNumber < 20 && available==true)
        {
            //this is a VIP seat
        }

        return available;
    }
}
```

(continued)

Listing 16.1   The Decorator Pattern's Skeleton Program (continued)

```
public class Database
{
    public int doStuffIfSeatAvailable(int seatNumber)
    {
        int returnValue = 0;
        //do something with seat available request

        return returnValue;
    }
}
```

Consequences

Using the Decorator pattern has the following consequences:

➤ This pattern allows the use of legacy objects in a way that doesn't break old code.

➤ Using this pattern keeps old classes alive longer.

➤ The Decorator can intercept, change, and modify messages to and from the calling object.

Known Uses

The Decorator pattern can be used for Java's I/O stream implementation.

Related Patterns

The Adapter pattern is related to the Decorator pattern.

References

For more information on the Decorator pattern, consult the following site:

```
http://www.exciton.cs.rice.edu/JavaResources/DesignPatterns/
⇒DecoratorPattern.htm
```

Value Object

The Value Object pattern is now widely regarded as the Transfer Object (TO).

The Value Object pattern is the best way to exchange data across tiers or system boundaries, especially when network communication is involved. This pattern solves performance issues around network latency. You might use it in your solution to contain the results of a database query that the client initiates.

Is

The Value Object pattern describes an object that encapsulates a set of values, typically for transfer across the network. A single method call can then be used to send and receive the transfer object, rather than making a separate method call to transfer each value individually.

Is Not

The objects created via the Value Object pattern are not concrete objects. You wouldn't use it to create, for example, a car object. You could use it to hold values about a car, however, such as its color and model.

Analogy

The Value Object pattern is like placing several letters in a larger envelope and mailing the larger envelope, rather than mailing the letters separately. The mail carrier only has to deliver a single letter to the recipient rather than making multiple deliveries. When the large envelope arrives, the receiver can just reach in the envelope for the next single letter; she doesn't have to go back to the mailing origin, which would take a long time. There is one problem, however: She doesn't know whether the sender is still at the originating address after she receives the larger envelope with letters in it.

Problem

In J2EE, server-resident business applications often use session beans and entity beans. Session beans are responsible for functionality involved in one-to-one transactions with the client. Contrast that with entity beans, which are intended to handle persistent data. A client makes many calls to a session bean to get data, which could represent a lot of traffic to and from a remote location because the bean might be at a server at that location. Likewise, a session bean can make many calls to an entity bean while getting and setting attributes. The Value Object pattern encapsulates an entity bean's data fields so that a single method call can get or set the fields' values. Whether you use sockets or RMI, you probably want to encapsulate the results of a database request in a Value Object.

Without a Value Object, your GUI would have to make many requests to the database, an inefficient approach. You need a way to eliminate these extra network calls to reduce overhead and provide a more direct access approach.

Responsibility

The Value Object pattern provides a mechanism for exchanging many remote calls to local, direct calls.

Intent (or Goals and Constraints)

The Value Object pattern attempts to reduce network overhead by minimizing the number of network calls to get data from the business tier.

Primary Activity

The Value Object pattern is used to collect remote data into an object that is sent to the client. The client can then make local calls to this object's methods rather than remote ones to get values.

Context

The Value Object pattern can be used in multitier applications that often need to exchange sets of data between the client and server.

Motivation or Forces

The following issues and motivations justify the use of the Value Object pattern:

➤ J2EE applications often use Enterprise JavaBeans. Because of Java's architecture, all calls to these beans are performed via remote interfaces to the bean. Even without EJB, many client/server applications require repeated retrieval of data, which introduces overhead.

➤ The frequency of reads is higher than updates because the client gets data from the business tier for presentation.

➤ The client usually needs a set of data, not just one attribute.

➤ A large number of client calls to the data tier across the network can adversely impact your solution's performance.

➤ Regardless of your architecture, it would be best to collect attributes into one object and place that object close to the GUI for local inspection instead of calling remote methods for the same information.

Applicability

The Value Object pattern is useful when you need a collection of data from a remote source or, more likely, when a client in remote mode has to make several calls for data from the database.

Solution

The Value Object pattern provides a solution consisting of the following parts:

➤ *Strategy*—Use a Value Object to encapsulate a collection of data so that it takes only one call to get or set the collection.

➤ *Pseudo Code*—The code snippet in Listing 16.2 shows an example for this pattern.

Listing 16.2   The Value Object Pattern's Skeleton Program

```java
public class CustomerOrder implements java.io.Serializable
{

    // private members
    private int accountNumber;
    private int customerID;
    private int orderNumber;
    private float orderAmount;

    // default constructor
    public CustomerOrder() {}

    // constructor accepting data values
    public CustomerOrder(int customerID,
                         int accountNumber,
                         int orderNumber,
                         float orderAmount)
    {
        init(customerID, accountNumber,
            orderNumber, orderAmount);
    }

    // constructor to create a new Value Object based
    // using an existing Value Object instance
    public CustomerOrder(CustomerOrder contact)
    {
        init (contact.customerID,
            contact.accountNumber, contact.orderNumber,
            contact.orderAmount);
    }

    // method to set all the values
    public void init(int customerID,
                     int accountNumber,
                     int orderNumber,
                     float orderAmount)
    {
        this.customerID = customerID;
        this.accountNumber = accountNumber;
        this.orderNumber = orderNumber;
        this.orderAmount = orderAmount;
    }
```

(continued)

Listing 16.2 **The Value Object Pattern's Skeleton Program** *(continued)*

```
// create a new Value Object
public CustomerOrder getData()
{
    return new CustomerOrder(this);
}

// get new values
public boolean setData()
{
        boolean success = false;
        //get data from database
        //which sets the success flag

        return success;
}

/*
add: get and set methods for customerID,
accountNumber, orderNumber, and orderAmount.
*/
}
```

Consequences

Using the Value Object pattern has the following consequences:

➤ This pattern simplifies data flow by using getData() and setData() methods as a way to get and set attributes in a Value Object. Calling the local getData() method once replaces a remote call (potentially multiple calls) to methods over the network.

➤ Using this pattern transfers a set of values in one method call, which improves overall performance, especially over the network. This pattern represents coarse-grained versus fine-grained interfaces.

➤ The client can freely update, delete, and read values that are now local. When it's done, it can update the data source in one call. However, there might be a problem with synchronization, as other clients won't know about changes until the update call. It's possible to have two conflicting update calls by two clients, so this conflict must be synchronized somehow.

Known Uses

The ResultSet object in Java Database Connectivity (JDBC) is a collection of data (resulting from a query) returned from a data source. The data is now local in the ResultSet object, so all calls to it are local instead of many direct calls to the data source.

Related Patterns

The following patterns are related to the Value Object pattern. For more information, visit this site:

```
http://developer.java.sun.com/developer/technicalArticles/J2EE/patterns/
➥J2EEPatternsRelationships.html
```

> *Aggregate Entity pattern*—Thispattern uses a Value Object to get data across tiers.

> *Session Facade pattern*—This pattern is the business interface for clients of J2EE applications. This pattern often uses Value Objects as an exchange mechanism with participating entity beans.

> *Value List Handler pattern*—This pattern is another one that provides lists of Value Objects constructed dynamically by accessing the persistent store at request time.

> *Value Object Assembler pattern*—This pattern builds composite Value Objects from different data sources. The data sources are usually session beans or entity beans that can be requested to provide their data as Value Objects.

References

The following page is available only to registered members of the Java Developer connection:

```
http://developer.java.sun.com/developer/restricted/patterns/
➥ValueObject.html
```

Data Access Object

The Data Access Object (DAO) pattern provides a connection between the business logic tier and the resource (usually database or file) tier. The DAO abstracts and encapsulates all access to the data source, completely hiding the data source's implementation details from the business components that use the DAO.

While the DAO may access resources via JDBC, CORBA IIOP (Internet Inter-Orb Protocol), RMI, low-level sockets, and other means, the business object only has to be concerned with the (usually simpler) interface of the DAO. At such time as the underlying data source changes, the DAO's code may change, but its interface will not, thus ensuring that no changes are necessary to the business components that rely on the DAO.

You might want to apply this pattern to your solution so that the GUI has a clean interface to the database.

Is

The DAO pattern is an object that encapsulates a set of behaviors for accessing databases, files, and other resources. This way, you have only one API to deal with instead of a different one for each type of resource.

Is Not

The DAO pattern is not a pattern for a resource. It isn't a way to build a database or file manager, in other words.

Analogy

The DAO pattern is like using an ATM machine. The same interface fetches information requested from the back end. The user interface is a simple screen with buttons for conducting a transaction. Similarly, the DAO object presents a simple API to conduct transactions.

Problem

Applications often need to use persistent data. This data persists in many forms, such as files, relational databases, XML storage, and other types of repositories. All these stores have different APIs. Interfacing with so many APIs presents a problem when designing clients.

Responsibility

The DAO pattern provides a uniform API to any persistent data storage.

Intent (or Goals and Constraints)

The DAO pattern attempts to consolidate data access from a complex source (or set of sources) to one object. This consolidation reduces network overhead by minimizing the number of network calls to get data, but reducing network traffic is not the pattern's primary intent.

Primary Activity

The DAO pattern is used for getting and setting data from and to a permanent data source.

Context

The DAO pattern is used when access methods to data vary between types of storage and vendor.

Motivation or Forces

Various parts of an application require access to persistent stores, such as databases and files. APIs for different types of stores (even for different vendors of the same storage type) are inconsistent. To access these disparate data sources, you need a tier with a uniform API.

Applicability

The DAO pattern can be used in any application that requires access to several data source types or even an application that accesses only one but might switch in the future. The SQL code is encapsulated in the method. That way, if the SQL or data source changes, very little code rewriting is needed because the API remains constant.

Solution

The DAO pattern's solution consists of the following parts:

➤ *Strategy*—Use this pattern to design a Data Access Object that abstracts the access API to various data sources.

➤ *Pseudo Code*—The DAO pattern example in Listing 11.3 is brief. The real class would likely have more SQL, but it does represent an interface that defines the API for a single DAO entity and uses an Abstract Factory pattern to create the necessary implementation objects at run-time.

Listing 16.3   The DAO Pattern's Skeleton Program

```
import java.sql.Connection;
import java.sql.ResultSet;
import java.sql.SQLException;
import java.sql.Statement;
import java.util.Collection;

/**
 * This class is an example of DAO because
 * it encapsulates the SQL calls made by other objects.
 * This tier maps the relational data stored in the
 * database to the objects needed by another tier.
 */
public class CustomerDAO
{
    private Connection con;

    public CustomerDAO(Connection con)
    {
        this.con = con;
    }
```

(continued)

Listing 16.3   The DAO Pattern's Skeleton Program *(continued)*

```
public CustomerOrder getCustomer(int customerId) throws SQLException
{
    String sql = "select customerid, firstName, " +
                 "lastName, from CUSTOMER_TABLE " +
                 "where customerid = " + customerId;
    Statement stmt = con.createStatement();
    ResultSet rs = stmt.executeQuery(sql);
    CustomerOrder cus = null;
    while (rs.next())
    {
        int i = 1;
        String itemid = rs.getString(i).trim();
        int accountNumber = rs.getInt(i);
        int orderNumber = rs.getInt(i);
        float orderAmount = rs.getFloat(i);
        i++;

        //new CustomerOrder object
        cus = new CustomerOrder(customerId,
                       accountNumber,
                       orderNumber,
                       orderAmount);

        //do something with cus
    }

    rs.close();
    stmt.close();
    return cus;
}


public Order getOrder(String orderid) throws SQLException
{
    //this SQL string included a reference to a
    //DatabaseNames object (not shown),
    //which has a list of the database object
    //names, including tables.
    Order order = new Order();
    String sql =
        "select itemid, listprice, unitcost, " +
        "name, descn " +
        "from ITEM_TABLE, ORDER_TABLE where "+
        "orderid = '" + orderid + "'";

    //your DAO can have any number of attributes.
    //here, the itemid and other attributes are
    //how you could represent an order.
    Statement stmt = con.createStatement();
    ResultSet rs = stmt.executeQuery(sql);
    while (rs.next())
    {
        int i = 1;
        String itemid = rs.getString(i).trim();
        double listprice = rs.getDouble(i);
```

(continued)

Listing 16.3   The DAO Pattern's Skeleton Program *(continued)*

```
            double unitcost = rs.getDouble(i);
            String name = rs.getString(i);
            String descn = rs.getString(i);
            order.add(itemid, listprice, unitcost, name, descn);
            i++;
        }

        order.process();

        rs.close();
        stmt.close();
        return order;
    }
}

public class Order
{
    String itemid = "";
    double listprice = 0;
    double unitcost = 0;
    String name = "";
    String descn = "";

    public void add(String itemid,
                    double listprice,
                    double unitcost,
                    String name,
                    String descn)
    {
        this.itemid = itemid;
        this.listprice = listprice;
        this.unitcost = unitcost;
        this.name = name;
        this.descn = descn;
    }

    public void process()
    {
        //process order
    }
}
```

Consequences

Using the DAO pattern has the following consequences:

➤ Clients and components can then access data with the same API, which makes the variety of sources transparent and reduces complexity.

➤ It makes changing data sources easy and reduces errors.

Known Uses

At one level, JDBC uses an Abstract Factory technique to provide one API to many databases and types of files—the very essence of this pattern.

However, the emphasis Sun places on this pattern is on creating objects that encapsulate the SQL so that the client that calls a DAO is shielded from the database's structure (and thus the specific SQL queries needed for accessing data).

Related Patterns

Sun uses the GoF's Abstract Factory pattern for Data Access Object strategies. Sun bases this pattern on the abstract factory approach.

References

For more information on the DAO pattern, consult the following site:

http://java.sun.com/blueprints/patterns/DAO.html

Business Delegate

The Business Delegate pattern reduces coupling between presentation-tier clients and business services. By hiding the complexity of the business service from the client, the business delegate can shield presentation-tier clients from changes in the API of the underlying business service.

Is

The Business Delegate pattern is a proxy that hides the complexity of remote service lookup and error recovery. It makes it easier to communicate requests and results from one tier to another.

Is Not

The Business Delegate pattern is not a pattern for a tier. It isn't a way for you to create a business logic component or structure. Rather, it is an interface to a tier, so you can change the underlying components and not disturb the presentation tier.

Analogy

The Business Delegate pattern is like an ambassador to a foreign country. Regardless of government changes in the ambassador's home country, the ambassador and how she interacts with the foreign country can remain the same. In addition, the ambassador shields the foreign country from her home country's internal decision-making processes.

Problem

A dependency on a remote service increases the likelihood of change between the caller and the called. How can you reduce the chances of the tier that depends on the remote service breaking should the remote service change? The Business Delegate pattern helps protect the local tier from changes made to the remote service. Perhaps the presentation tier interacts directly with a remote business logic tier. What if the business services change and the old API becomes invalid? If this happens, the presentation tier will break.

Responsibility

The Business Delegate pattern is the proxy between the local tier and the remote service tier. It is responsible for reliably allowing the front-end tier to access the remote service.

Intent (or Goals and Constraints)

The Business Delegate pattern isolates the presentation tier from changes in the business-tier API.

Primary Activity

The Business Delegate pattern matches presentation component calls to the correct business-tier methods.

Context

The current approach to multitier systems is to couple the presentation tier directly to the entire business service API; sometimes this coupling is made across a network.

Motivation or Forces

The following forces or issues are what motivate the use of this pattern:

➤ Presentation-tier clients (including devices) need access to business services.

➤ The business-tier API might change.

➤ The industry trend for large systems is to minimize coupling between presentation-tier clients and the business service API. This isolates the two so that the middle tier can manage a change in either side.

➤ There is a need for a cache between tiers.

➤ This pattern adds more work to building a system, so consider whether this extra tier is really necessary.

Applicability

Large systems change components often. There is often a change in the business tier that breaks the access portion of clients.

Solution

The Business Delegate pattern provides advantages in a design. Its solution consists of the following parts:

➤ *Strategy*—Sun says, "Use a Business Delegate to reduce coupling between presentation-tier clients and business services. The Business Delegate hides the underlying implementation details of the business service, such as lookup and access details of the EJB architecture."

➤ *Sample Code*—Visit Sun's definition of the Business Delegate pattern at http://java.sun.com/blueprints/corej2eepatterns/Patterns/BusinessDelegate .html. In the section titled "Sample Code" (roughly 70% down the page) there is an excellent example of implementing the business delegate pattern.

Consequences

Using the Business Delegate pattern has the following consequences:

➤ Caching is always good between parts that exchange a lot of data.

➤ This pattern changes the interface with the intent of making the API more stable from the presentation-tier perspective.

➤ This pattern can handle any exceptions, whether from the business tier or from the plumbing between the business tier and the requester.

➤ This pattern isolates the presentation and business tiers from each other by adding a director between the two, making it easier to manage changes on either side.

Known Uses

The Business Delegate pattern has the following uses:

➤ B2B systems usually use an XML exchange for communicating between disparate systems. Even if the internal business processes of these systems change, the XML document types used for data exchange remain the same.

➤ Proxy services represent this pattern.

➤ Lookup services usually represent this pattern.

Related Patterns

The following patterns are related to the Business Delegate pattern:

➤ *Service Locator pattern*—This pattern provides a common API for any business service lookup and access code.

➤ *Proxy pattern*—Provides a stand-in for objects in the business tier.

➤ *Adapter pattern*—You can use this pattern to provide coupling for disparate systems.

References

For more information on the Business Delegate pattern, consult the following site:

```
http://java.sun.com/blueprints/patterns/BusinessDelegate.html
```

Model-View-Controller (MVC)

The Model-View-Controller (MVC) architecture compartmentalizes the data and business logic (Model portion) from the presentation (View portion) and from the user action interpreter (Controller portion). This pattern is mandatory for your solution. Swing components are designed with MVC, so you don't have to do much to take advantage of this powerful pattern. It is a matter of telling the evaluator that you recognize the pattern and leveraged it in your GUI. For example, the instructions most likely require a JTable component. The viewable grid is the View portion. The Model portion acts as the table model. (For more information, see the JTable section in Chapter 7, "Databases and Atomicity.") The code you write that responds to JTable events is the Controller portion.

Is

The MVC pattern is a clear functional separation of roles. It is a formalization of the data-business-presentation movement that has dominated three-tier architectures over the past decade.

Is Not

The MVC pattern is very abstract. It is not simply a front end to a data source.

Analogy

The MVC pattern is like an automobile. The speed of a car is affected by the accelerator pedal (Controller), the speed is shown by the speedometer (View), and the speed is manifested by the engine (Model).

Problem

Different views of the same data are a common need. Conversely, the same client needs access to different models.

Responsibility

The MVC pattern carefully manages communication between the client and model data and functionality. It must allow changing the client or the model with minimal impact on the system.

Intent (or Goals and Constraints)

The main goal is separation of concerns. The MVC pattern attempts to minimize the impact of changing any of the three responsibilities, including Model, View, and Controller.

Primary Activity

The MVC pattern decouples views from data and business logic; MVC interjects a Controller between them, which interprets user actions into operations on the business logic and selects the next view to send to the user.

Context

An application is expected to support varying client and business logic tiers.

Motivation or Forces

The following forces or motivations are the most common reasons designers use this pattern:

➤ Various clients and data models are being developed, and the two tiers need to talk to each other.

➤ Non-interface-specific code is duplicated in many applications.

➤ The same enterprise data is accessed by different views—for example, HTML, Wireless Markup Language (WML), JFC/Swing, and XML. Note that different views of the data can simply be different slices of the data, rather than the data having to be in multiple formats.

➤ The same enterprise data is accessed (requested, modified, and deleted) from various actions (such as HTML links, JFC/Swing events, and SOAP XML calls).

Applicability

Although the MVC pattern's primary purpose is building GUIs, it can be used to establish an analogous notification protocol between nonvisual objects. The Observer and Observable objects in java.util were designed with this pattern in mind.

Solution

What can this pattern accomplish? The MVC pattern's solution consists of the following parts:

➤ *Strategy*—Use the Model-View-Controller architecture to decouple presentation from core data access functionality. Also, this pattern enables you to control communication between them so that multiple views can see the same enterprise data model, or multiple data models can present the same view.

➤ *Pseudo Code*—MVC is used for many things. For example, it has been used for Swing components to build user interfaces, in which Sun uses the Model as the underlying logical representation, the View as the visual representation, and the Controller as the part that handles user input. When a Model changes (the user modifies text in a text field, for example), it notifies all views that depend on it (listeners). This enables you to present a single set of data in list, table, or simple text presentations. As you update the data model, the Model notifies both views and gives each an opportunity to update itself. In this architecture, the Controller determines which action to take when the user alters the model (for example, by typing text into a field). Please see http://developer.java.sun. com/developer/onlineTraining/GUI/Swing2/shortcourse.html#JFCMVC for more information.

Consequences

Using the MVC pattern has the following consequences:

➤ Clients access a Controller, which accesses the model instead of the data directly.

➤ Another tier has to be built, which adds work.

➤ It is easier to break a project into pieces because both View and Model developers are targeting the Controller API.

Known Uses

Java uses the MVC pattern for Java Foundation Classes (JFC) and Swing. Also, Struts and Velocity use this pattern as their underlying framework. Struts is a flexible control layer based on standard technologies, such as Java servlets, JavaBeans, ResourceBundles, and Extensible Markup Language (XML). You can read more about this at http://jakarta.apache.org/struts. Velocity is a Java-based template engine providing a template language to reference objects defined in Java code. You can see more about it at http://jakarta.apache.org/velocity.

Related Patterns

MVC is a very high-level and abstract pattern compared to other patterns, so it has few related patterns.

References

For more information on the MVC pattern, consult the following site:

http://java.sun.com/blueprints/patterns/MVC.html

Front Controller

The Front Controller pattern presents one entry point to an application, such as a Web site or service. This centralized entry point controls and manages requests and eliminates a user's dependency on a direct resource. Suppose you wanted to get the latest version of the servlet specification. You would be better off going to a central page presenting options that change over time than bookmarking the servlet specification directly, as that link could be quickly outdated. Some candidates might use this pattern in a single controller (such as a front end to the database) to handle all user requests from multiple clients.

Is

The Front Controller pattern is a presentation controller that allows a resource to change without breaking bookmarks to that resource. Many sites use this pattern. This pattern is used in Struts, where all requests go to a common front controller servlet, regardless of the action requested. The MSDN site uses a similar pattern via http://msdn.microsoft.com/library/default.asp. At this site all requests go to a single ASP page, which controls what documents get displayed in each frame. Watch the address field in your browser as you surf and you'll see that almost all the MSDN URLs point to this ASP.

Is Not

The Front Controller pattern is not a pattern for a data storage viewer, and it isn't a way for you to control data retrieval. Rather, it is a steady interface to underlying resources that behaves as the presentation tier.

Analogy

The Front Controller pattern is like a travel agent. On every trip, you start by stopping at the agency. You tell the agent where you want to go, and she takes care of the arrangements. The actual flight, train, bus, and hotel details change between trips, but she always gets you there.

Problem

When a user accesses resources directly without going through a centralized mechanism, the resource might have moved. Also, each view is on its own and required to provide its own system services. Last, each view has to provide navigation, but this is a problem, as the view doesn't know about the context or the overall site.

Responsibility

The Front Controller must delegate a request to the proper resource and view.

Intent (or Goals and Constraints)

The Front Controller pattern isolates actual resources from a user's direct access.

Primary Activity

The Front Controller pattern matches the correct resource to the request.

Context

Simplified Web sites expose all their resources directly. As a site grows, decoupling navigation from resources is often better. A controller that manages requests and decides which resource best satisfies a request is necessary.

Motivation or Forces

The following forces are the primary reasons for using this pattern:

➤ It is better to have a central controller allocate shared resources than to have individual resources fend for themselves independently.

➤ The location of resources can change.

➤ This pattern adds only a little more work to building a front end to a service, such as a database server or a Web site.

➤ Multiple resources share common needs, such as security (that is, authentication and authorization).

Applicability
Databases and Web sites especially benefit from a Front Controller.

Solution
The Front Controller pattern's solution consists of the following parts:

➤ *Strategy*—Sun says, "Use a Controller as the initial point of contact for handling a request. The Controller manages the handling of the request, including invoking security services such as authentication and authorization, delegating business processing, managing the choice of an appropriate view, handling errors, and managing the selection of content-creation strategies."

➤ *Sample Code*—This pattern can be used to centralize processing requests and selecting views. For example, the `MainServlet` class is the Front Controller for Sun's Java Pet Store sample application Web site. All requests ending with `*.do` are sent through the `MainServlet` class for processing. Please see `http://java.sun.com/blueprints/code/jps131/src/com/sun/j2ee/blueprints/waf/controller/web/MainServlet.java.html` for the source code for MainServlet. Please see `http://java.sun.com/blueprints/code/jps131/docs/` for the Java Pet Store Demo sample application home page.

Consequences
Using the Front Controller pattern has the following consequences:

➤ Caching is always good between parts that exchange a lot of data.

➤ This pattern changes an interface with the intent of making the API more stable from the presentation tier perspective.

➤ This pattern now handles any exceptions, whether from the business tier or from the plumbing between the business tier and the requester.

➤ This pattern isolates the presentation and business tiers by adding a mediator between the two, making it easier to manage changes on either side.

Known Uses

The Front Controller pattern has the following uses:

➤ *Servlet Front Strategy*—This pattern is implemented as a servlet, which manages aspects of request handling related to business processing and control flow. Because this strategy is not specifically related to display formatting, implementing this component as a JSP page is a bad idea. Also, Struts is an example of this pattern.

➤ *Command and Controller Strategy*—This strategy provides a generic interface to helper components. The Controller delegates responsibility to the helper components, which minimizes coupling among these components.

➤ *Logical Resource Mapping Strategy*—In this case, users request logical names rather than physical locations. This way, the physical location can be dynamically mapped to the logical names, say, in a database or XML document.

Related Patterns

The following patterns are related to the Front Controller pattern:

➤ *View Helper pattern*—The Front Controller pattern is combined with the View Helper pattern to provide containers for factoring business logic out of the view and to provide a central point of control and dispatch. Logic is factored forward into the Front Controller and back into the View Helper object.

➤ *Service to Worker pattern*—This pattern is the result of combining the View Helper pattern with a Dispatcher, in coordination with the Front Controller pattern.

➤ *Dispatcher View pattern*—This pattern combines the Front Controller and View Helper patterns with a Dispatcher component. Although this pattern and the Service to Worker pattern share the same structure, the two patterns have a different division of labor among components.

References

For more information on the Front Controller pattern, consult the following site:

```
http://java.sun.com/blueprints/corej2eepatterns/Patterns/
➥FrontController.html
```

Need to Know More?

 Alexander, Christopher, Sara Ishikawa, and Murray Silverstein. *A Pattern Language: Towns, Buildings, Construction*. Oxford, MA: Oxford University Press, 1977 (ISBN 0201703939). A convenient bound version of Sun's online tutorial.

 Alur, Deepak, John Crupi, and Dan Malks. *Core J2EE Patterns: Best Practices and Design Strategies, Second Edition*. Indianapolis, IN: Prentice Hall PTR, 2003 (ISBN 0131422464).

 Gamma, Erich et al. *Design Patterns: Elements of Reusable Object-Oriented Software*. Boston, MA: Addison-Wesley, 1995 (ISBN 0201633612).

 Larman, Craig. *Applying UML and Patterns: An Introduction to Object-Oriented Analysis and Design and the Unified Process (2nd Edition)*. Indianapolis, IN: Prentice Hall PTR, 2001 (ISBN 0130925691).

 `http://java.sun.com/blueprints/patterns/catalog.html`—Sun's design patterns page.

 `http://developer.java.sun.com/developer/technicalArticles/J2EE/patterns/`—A helpful Sun Java Center J2EE pattern article.

 `http://developer.java.sun.com/developer/restricted/patterns/J2EEPatternsAtAGlance.html`—The J2EE patterns catalog.

 `www.jguru.com/faq/Patterns`—The Java Guru: Patterns FAQ home page.

 `http://c2.com/ppr`—This site contains the helpful Portland Pattern Repository.

Exception Handling

Terms you'll need to understand:
✓ **Exception** object
✓ **Error** object
✓ **try-catch-finally** construction
✓ Exception chaining

Techniques you'll need to master:
✓ Identifying problems in Java source code files
✓ Handling exceptions and errors
✓ Removing logic bugs that don't throw an exception
✓ Writing code that distinguishes between errors and exceptions
✓ Giving code corrections for various source code problems in a Java application

In this chapter, you review how to handle exceptions. Java has two types of runtime errors: errors and exceptions. An error originates from the Java Virtual Machine (JVM) and indicates an imminent crash. An exception originates from the code and indicates an exceptional circumstance that needs to be handled by a try-catch-finally block. Only if an exception is not handled does the application crash. Remember that you can't recover from an error that causes your application to crash. You can, however, recover from an exception with proper use of the try-catch-finally construction.

When adding exception handling to your certification solution, you should bear in mind the higher concept of problem resolution in software. Approaching exception handling first from this higher ground eases the burden of quality control later. In other words, there are steps you can take to reduce bugs during the design phase.

Figure 17.1 illustrates the relationship between different types of errors in Java. Note that all errors and exceptions in Java are subclasses of the Throwable class. The primary characteristic is whether Java checks for that type of error.

Throwable Class Hierarchy

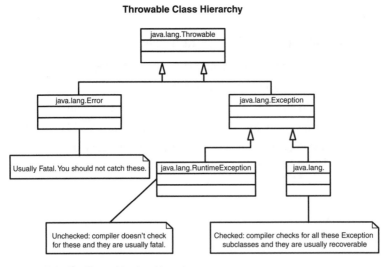

Figure 17.1 The **Throwable** class hierarchy.

The following list describes the characteristics of errors and exceptions and explains the differences between them:

➤ The Throwable class is the superclass of all Error and Exception classes.

➤ Errors are usually fatal and not caught. Let the JVM handle them.

➤ There are two types of exceptions: checked and unchecked. RuntimeException and Error, and their subclasses, are unchecked. All instances of Exception and its subclasses are checked.

➤ Checked exceptions (subclasses of Exception) must be declared (method declaration) or caught and are recoverable. The compiler complains if these exceptions are not caught, so you must handle them.

➤ Unchecked exceptions (subclasses of RuntimeException) are usually fatal and not caught. Let the JVM handle them.

The preceding list describes the code-related errors you must be aware of. However, there are other types of problems that software engineers must contend with in addition to errors and exceptions. The next section discusses these problems from a broader perspective.

Errors in Software

A problem in your certification application can be defined as anything missing a project parameter. If your application works perfectly, but you forget to include a README.TXT file, you will fail. If you do not meet a key requirement, such as the search feature, you will fail. If you write code to meet all the requirements, but your application doesn't correctly reserve seats when started in remote mode, for example, you will fail. Anything that gets between you and a requirement is a problem.

Problems you should avoid in your solution are broadly categorized in the following (for example, see http://java.sun.com/j2se/1.4.1/docs/api/java/lang/package-summary.html for java.lang list) listed from least severe and easiest to fix to most severe and hardest to fix:

➤ *Syntax error*—An error caused by mistyping a keyword or forgetting to terminate a statement with a semicolon. The compiler catches these errors and reports them during compilation.

➤ *Semantic error*—The syntax is correct, but an error occurs because of incorrect meaning in the code, such as casting a String input into an integer instead of a double. The program compiles and runs, but a double would have worked better. (For example, monetary quantities work for whole dollar amounts, but fail if cents are included.) In addition, the program will throw an exception. The evaluator might overlook these tricky problems, unless they cause your application to halt. If the evaluator notices a semantic error, you will lose points.

➤ *Logic error*—The results are not what you intended. For example, when the user clicks the Reserve button, the program is supposed to reserve a seat and decrement the available seats. However, your program increments available seats by mistake. The program will compile and probably not throw an exception.

➤ *Runtime error*—Your program causes an error in the JVM, such as a VirtualMachineError error (Java Virtual Machine is broken or has run out of resources). Java will throw an error, as opposed to an exception, and then quit. Refer back to Figure 17.1 for what can be caught and what can't.

➤ *Environment error*—This type of error is usually out of your control. The program compiles and runs properly until something in the environment causes a problem. For example, someone moves a file that your program has been relying on. Sometimes you can catch these errors as exceptions (for example, a missing file throws `java.io.FileNotFoundException`) and sometimes you can't (a file with wrong data, for instance).

➤ *Requirement error*—This error occurs when you miss a requirement. Everything works fine, but you still fail because you forgot to add a Search button, for example.

➤ *Project error*—This error, caused by not meeting a project parameter, is considered project mismanagement. For example, you'll fail if you don't upload your solution at Sun's CertManager Web site. E-mailing a perfect solution instead of uploading it is an automatic failure. Another example is not studying enough to supply thorough answers on the essay exam.

➤ *Business error*—This error is caused by a business misstep. For example, your product was a great idea when you started two years ago, but now it will be poorly received in the market because a competitor beat you there. Two common sources of business errors are cost and time overruns. Perhaps you downloaded the assignment more than a year ago under version 1.3, for example, but Java 1.4 is now the current version.

As you can see, all these errors cause problems and can result in a failing score. Some of them are easy to handle with code (using `try-catch-finally`, for example) and some are not. For some errors, Java's `Error` and `Exception` mechanisms work great, but not for others.

Testing

Eradicating all errors is understood as a normal part of development work. The usual way to find and fix bugs is through testing. All developers test code as they add it. No one types pages of code without testing as he or she goes. However, it takes more than these incremental syntax checks to ensure that there isn't a problem. One way to think about solving software problems is to consider how an application should be tested. These three levels of testing are important to conduct (also recommend writing a test plan prior to testing) before you upload your solution:

1. *Unit testing*—Does this one class work? This test ensures that each class meets a small set of requirements and responsibilities assigned to that class. I recommend using JUnit for unit testing (see `http://www.junit.org`).

2. *System testing*—Does the whole application work? This test is conducted by running the application and making sure everything works together. It is surprising how varying the sequence of button clicks, for example, can reveal a problem (caused sometimes by an attribute assignment being in the wrong place).

3. *Acceptance testing*—Will the evaluator like the application? Acceptance testing helps you uncover applications that aren't ready for submission, even though they might be bug free. Perhaps every button works, but the font color and button background color are the same, making it difficult to read the button text. Or worse, you forgot to provide a place to type search parameters.

Exception handling is covered in more depth in "Exceptions," later in this chapter, but understanding software problems in general terms first is helpful. Focusing on problems in general at the design and project management levels keeps you on track with your programming schedule. The next section begins with discussing how to manage application faults.

Managing Bugs

Probably the most common source of bugs comes from copying code from one place and pasting it into another. Another common source is copying a variable into a block that's out of scope for that variable. Regardless of how you introduced an error, managing these problems is important.

Because this project takes two to four months to complete, tracking bugs improves the quality of the resulting code. If the timeframe was shorter, tracking bugs wouldn't be worth the trouble. If you are writing code at work, you might use your employer's bug tracker. If you're doing it at home, you can use one of the many free bug-tracking utilities. For example, you can use Bugzilla, which is a database for bugs and is currently being used for the Mozilla browser project. You can download Bugzilla (http://www.mozilla.org/projects/bugzilla/) to set up on your own computer. Another example is Geodesic Systems (http://www.geodesic.com/); its product line specializes in Java application bug tracking. Whatever your choice, using an effective bug-tracking process is helpful; I recommend a commercial-grade product for this important role in software development.

Bug tracking as it relates to quality control is a dedicated specialty. With effective bug reporting, the subsequent fix affects a team's ability to move through the bug list. Bug tracking, defect tracking, issue tracking, change management, and quality assurance (QA) are all crucial to a strong development life cycle. However, these topics are beyond the scope of this book.

The **Throwable** Class and Its Subclasses

The Throwable class is the superclass of all errors and exceptions. Therefore, the JVM throws only this class or one of its subclasses. Likewise, you can supply only this type of object to the throw statement and in a catch clause.

Java distinguishes errors from exceptions by specifying that errors are not expected to be caught because they are usually unexpected and fatal. Exceptions are undesirable, but are expected and should be caught. In Java, exceptions and errors are objects. The JVM instantiates an appropriate subclass of Exception or Error to represent the problem. The Exception and Error classes, in turn, extend java.lang.Throwable. These objects indicate the type of problem and usually contain detailed information about the condition that caused the problem. Note that you don't use Throwable directly, but instead use one of its subclasses, such as Exception. The following sections explain the differences between Exception and Error objects in more detail.

Errors

An error indicates a fatal problem. Your application should not be expected to recover from an error. For example, if the system runs out of memory, the

JVM crashes, which is an error. This type of condition is beyond the JVM's control, so your code cannot do much about it. When an error crashes the JVM, your application will also crash. In some cases, you do have a chance to respond—say, display a final status message—but in others you don't get even that chance.

The following are typical examples of errors:

➤ `java.awt.AWTError`—Indicates a serious Abstract Windowing Toolkit (AWT) error.

➤ `java.xml.parsers.FactoryConfigurationError`—Occurs when the XML parser cannot be found.

➤ `java.lang.LinkageError`—Usually a subclass, such as `NoClassDefFoundError`, is thrown when the class has been corrupted or has been changed after compiling the linking class.

➤ `java.lang.ThreadDeath`—Indicates that a thread died. These errors should not be caught, as having a thread die is a normal occurrence. However, a thread death is considered an error because most applications crash when this event takes place.

➤ `java.lang.VirtualMachineError`—Indicates a serious problem in the JVM. Running out of memory is a common example of this type of error.

Exceptions

An exception is thrown when something bad happens, but not so serious that the application crashes. You should catch all exceptions. In fact, compiling a program without doing so is difficult because the compiler usually complains if you miss an exception. However, you can catch a superclass of an exception and miss the subclass. In that case, the compiler does not complain, but your error handling is not as detailed as it should be. Also, the compiler doesn't complain for unchecked exceptions, even if they are not put in the `try-catch` block. The "unchecked exceptions" means that the compiler doesn't check them during compiling time.

The following are typical examples of exceptions:

➤ `java.awt.AWTException`—Indicates that an AWT exception has occurred.

➤ `java.lang.ClassNotFoundException`—Indicates that no definition for the class with the specified name could be found, probably because the name is misspelled or the class is in the wrong place.

➤ java.lang.IllegalAccessException—Occurs when an application tries to reflectively create an instance, set or get a field, or call a method, but the currently running method does not have access to that item.

➤ java.lang.InstantiationException—This exception usually occurs because of an attempt to instantiate an interface or abstract class. It is thrown when creating an instance of a class using Class.newInstance(), but the new instance can't be created because it's an interface or an abstract class.

➤ java.lang.InterruptedException—Occurs when one waiting or sleeping thread is interrupted by another thread.

➤ java.io.IOException—Usually a subclass, such as FileNotFoundException or RemoteException, is thrown by a failed or interrupted I/O operation.

➤ java.lang.RuntimeException—Usually a subclass, such as ArithmeticException, IndexOutOfBoundsException, or NullPointerException, is thrown during the JVM's normal operation. Unlike most exceptions, a method is not required to declare in its throws clause any subclasses of RuntimeException that might be thrown during method execution but not caught. If you don't catch an exception the JVM must handle them which eliminates your ability to know exactly what went wrong via try-catch blocks.

➤ javax.naming.NamingException—Usually a subclass, such as InvalidNameException or NameNotFoundException, is thrown if a name does not conform to the syntax defined for the namespace.

Numerous exceptions are defined in Java, but the preceding list covers the most likely problems a program might have. However, you will probably want to write your own exception for the assignment.

Custom **Throwable** Subclass

Although writing your own exception class isn't mandatory, it does demonstrate a good understanding of error handling. Listing 17.1 is an example (also used in the book sample application) of how you might handle your application being unable to open a database file or an RMI connection. Modeled after FileNotFoundException, this exception is thrown by one of several methods when the database file cannot be found or RMI doesn't work—for example, when an attempt is made to read data from the database.

Listing 17.1   An Example of a Custom Exception

```java
import java.io.IOException;

/**
 * My application couldn't open the database file or RMI
 * connection.
 * <p> Modeled after the <code>FileNotFoundException</code>,
 * this exception will be thrown by one of several
 * methods when the database file cannot be found or RMI
 * doesn't work -- for example, when an attempt is made to
 * read data from the database.
 *
 * @author  QUE reader
 * @version 1.0, 2/23/04
 * @since   JDK1.4
 */
public class SCJDException extends IOException
{

    /**
     * Constructs a <code>SCJDException</code> with
     * a general message.
     */
    public SCJDException()
    {
        super("Cannot find Database or RMI connection.");
    }

    /**
     * Constructs a <code>SCJDException</code> with the
     * specified detail message. The string <code>s</code>
     * can be retrieved later by the
     * <code>{@link java.lang.Throwable#getMessage}</code>
     * method of class <code>java.lang.Throwable</code>.
     *
     * @param   s    the detail message.
     */
    public SCJDException(String s)
    {
        super(s);
    }

    /**
     * Constructs a <code>SCJDException</code> with a
     * detail message consisting of the given pathname
     * string followed by the given reason string.
     *
     * @param   path    the attempted path.
     * @param   reason    problem description.
     */
    private SCJDException(String path, String reason)
    {
        super(path + ((reason == null)
                ? ""
                : " (" + reason + ")"));
    }
}
```

Handling Errors and Exceptions

Part of your grade is based on how well you handle exceptions. Does your application crash when the user types in an incorrect number? What happens when your remote mechanism doesn't respond? Your evaluator will look closely at how well your code deals with such problems. Listing 17.2 is an example of error handling that demonstrates how errors propagate through the call stack. It represents a DatabaseError class with a general message; this class is instantiated with the specified detail message. This error can be thrown to indicate that the database has failed. Note that the constructors convert the constructor argument to a detailed String message explaining the condition of failure. Last, you can see how the final constructor creates a DatabaseError with a detailed message and nested error. This is an example of how you can nest errors in your application.

Listing 17.2   An Example of Error Handling

```
/**
 * Thrown to indicate that the database has failed.
 *
 * These constructors convert an argument to a detail
 * String message explaining the condition of failure.
 */
public class DatabaseError extends Error
{
    /**
     * Constructs a DatabaseError with no detail message.
     */
    public DatabaseError()
    {
    }

    /**
     * Constructs a DatabaseError with a detail message,
     * even if it is a null reference. The public constructors will
     * never call this constructor with a null argument.
     * @param message value to be used in constructing detail message
     */
    private DatabaseError(String message)
    {
        super(message);
    }

    /**
     * Constructs a DatabaseError with its Object message converted
     * to a string.
     *
     * @param message value to be used in constructing detail message
     */
    public DatabaseError(Object message)
    {
```

(continued)

Listing 17.2   An Example of Error Handling *(continued)*

```
        this("" + message);
}

/**
 * Constructs a DatabaseError with its Object message converted
 * to a string.
 *
 * @param message value to be used in constructing detail message
 */
public DatabaseError(boolean message)
{
        this("" + message);
}

/**
 * Constructs a DatabaseError with its Object message converted
 * to a string.
 *
 * @param message value to be used in constructing detail message
 */
public DatabaseError(char message)
{
        this("" + message);
}

/**
 * Constructs a DatabaseError with its Object message converted
 * to a string.
 *
 * @param message value to be used in constructing detail message
 */
public DatabaseError(int message)
{
        this("" + message);
}

/**
 * Constructs a DatabaseError with its Object message converted
 * to a string.
 *
 * @param message value to be used in constructing detail message
 */
public DatabaseError(long message)
{
        this("" + message);
}

/**
 * Constructs a DatabaseError with its Object message converted
 * to a string.
 *
 * @param message value to be used in constructing detail message
 */
public DatabaseError(float message)
{
        this("" + message);
```

(continued)

Listing 17.2   An Example of Error Handling *(continued)*

```
}

/**
 * Constructs a DatabaseError with its Object message converted
 * to a string.
 *
 * @param message value to be used in constructing detail message
 */
public DatabaseError(double message)
{
    this("" + message);
}

/**
 * Constructs a <code>DatabaseError</code> with the specified
 * detail message and nested error.
 *
 * @param message the detail message
 * @param error the nested error
 */
public DatabaseError(String message, Error error)
{
    super(message, error);
}
}
```

The try-catch-finally Construction

The built-in mechanism for handling errors and exceptions is the try-catch-finally construction. Its basic outline is shown in Listing 17.3. Note that the catch conditions start with the most granular or most specific exception first. The try-catch-finally construction then catches less granular or less specific exceptions. Last, it catches the broadest exceptions. If you reverse the order, the first catch is always invoked, as the more specific exceptions are the same type as the more generalized superclass; therefore, using the reverse order is incorrect.

Listing 17.3   An Example of the try-catch-finally Construction

```
try
{
    someOperation();
} catch (LowestException le)
{
    System.out.println(le);
} catch (MiddleException me)
{
    System.out.println(me);
} catch (HighestException he)
{
```

(continued)

Listing 17.3   An Example of the try-catch-finally Construction *(continued)*

```
    System.out.println(he);
} finally
{
    System.out.println("finally");
}
```

 The **try-catch-finally** block is essential for handling exceptions. However, do not over-use this construction. For example, don't use it to catch fatal errors.

The following is how Sun defines the three parts of the `try-catch-finally` block:

➤ `try`—Defines a block of statements that might throw an exception.

➤ *catch*—An optional block of statements that is executed when an exception or a runtime error occurs in a preceding `try` block.

➤ `finally`—This block executes regardless of whether an exception occurred in the previous `try` block.

Listing 17.4 demonstrates how you can propagate an exception through the call stack. It shows you how to control where action is taken in response to an exception. Exceptions have the capability to propagate error reporting up the call stack of methods. In this listing, notice how an exception in `myNextMethod()` is propagated up into `myMethod()` and then propagated up into `main()`.

Listing 17.4   Controlling Exception Catching

```
import java.io.IOException;

/*
 * Notice how an exception in myNextMethod() is propagated
 * up into myMethod() and then propagated up into main().
 */
public class MyExceptionHandler extends IOException
{
    static int MAIN_METHOD = 1;
    static int MY_METHOD = 2;
    static int MY_NEXT_METHOD = 3;
    static int CATCH = MY_METHOD;

/*
 * main() gets an exception that comes from deep within the
 * call stack, in this case from myNextMethod().
```

(continued)

Listing 17.4 Controlling Exception Catching *(continued)*

```
 * @param args command-line arguments
 */
    public static void main(String[] args)
    {
        try
        {
            myMethod();
        } catch (IOException ioe)
        {
            System.out.println("main() - " + ioe);
        } finally
        {
            System.out.println("main() - finally");
        }
    }

/*
 * An exception in myMethod() is then propagated up into main().
 */

    public static void myMethod() throws IOException
    {
        if(CATCH == MY_METHOD)
        {
            try
            {
                throw new IOException();
            } catch (IOException ioe)
            {
                System.out.println("myMethod() - " + ioe);
            }
        } else if(CATCH == MY_NEXT_METHOD)
        {
            try
            {
                myNextMethod();
            } catch (IOException ioe)
            {
                System.out.println("myMethod() - " + ioe);
            }
        }
    }

/*
 * An exception in myNextMethod() is propagated
 * up into myMethod().
 */

    public static void myNextMethod() throws IOException
    {

        if(CATCH == MY_NEXT_METHOD)
        {
            try
            {
                throw new IOException();
```

(continued)

Listing 17.4 Controlling Exception Catching *(continued)*

```
        } catch (IOException ioe)
        {
            System.out.println("myNextMethod() - " + ioe);
        }
    } else
    {
        throw new IOException();
    }
    }
}
```

In Listing 17.4, you get one of the following three outputs, depending on which setting you assign to the CATCH flag:

```
main() - java.io.IOException
main() - finally
```

or

```
myMethod() - java.io.IOException
main() - finally
```

or

```
myNextMethod() - java.io.IOException
main() - finally
```

Notice that regardless of which setting you assign to the CATCH flag, the finally clause in the try block of the main() method always executes. This is an important consideration when handling RMI or database connections in your solution.

Listing 17.4 shows how to throw an exception as opposed to the JVM throwing one. If you add a custom exception class to your solution, you will likely throw it at some point.

Exception Chaining

One of the new features in J2SE 1.4 is *exception chaining*. It is common to catch one exception only to throw a different one. For example, you might catch a NumberFormatException caused by incorrect user input. In that case, you might want to throw your custom exception (for example, SCJDException) with a message about the origin. You can also include the original exception in the one you throw. Listing 17.5 is an adaptation of Listing 17.4, but it demonstrates the use of exception chaining, in which one exception class is nested within another as the exception climbs the call stack.

Listing 17.5   Using Exception Chaining

```
/* Also, this example demonstrates exception chaining, in which
 * one exception class is nested within another as the
 * exception climbs the call stack.
 */
import java.io.IOException;

public class MyExceptionHandler2 extends IOException
{
    static int MAIN_METHOD = 1;
    static int MY_METHOD = 2;
    static int MY_NEXT_METHOD = 3;
    static int CATCH = MY_METHOD;

/*
 * main() gets an exception that comes from deep within the
 * call stack, in this case from myNextMethod().
 * @param args command line arguements
 */
    public static void main(String[] args)
    {
        try
        {
            myMethod();
        } catch (IOException ioe)
        {
            System.out.println("main() - " + ioe);
        } catch (Exception e)
        {
            System.out.println("main() - " + e);
        } finally
        {
            System.out.println("main() - finally");
        }
    }

    public static void myMethod() throws Exception
    {
        if(CATCH == MY_METHOD)
        {
            throw new Exception("myMethod() - ",
                new SCJDException("Oops!"));

        } else if(CATCH == MY_NEXT_METHOD)
        {
            myNextMethod();
        }
    }

    public static void myNextMethod() throws Exception
    {
        if(CATCH == MY_NEXT_METHOD)
        {
            throw new Exception("myNextMethod() - ",
                new SCJDException("Oops!"));
        }
    }
}
```

Depending on which setting you assign to the CATCH flag, Listing 17.5 produces the following report about exceptions (e.g., CATCH = MY_METHOD):

```
java.lang.Exception: myNextMethod() -
    at MyExceptionHandler.myNextMethod(MyExceptionHandler.java:40)
    at MyExceptionHandler.myMethod(MyExceptionHandler.java:31)
    at MyExceptionHandler.main(MyExceptionHandler.java:13)
Caused by: SCJDException: Oops!
    ... 3 more
main() - finally
```

If you use a custom exception class, use exception chaining in your solution to make the resulting error message clearer. Also, using exception chaining demonstrates a thorough understanding of exception-handling techniques.

User Messages

Keeping users informed of what the application is doing and providing status messages after each action they take are crucial. For example, if users provide the number of seats they want to reserve and then click the Reserve button (or the Book button), display an informative message about the result. If they didn't type a number (for example, accidentally typed a letter), then tell them so. If they successfully reserved seats, then tell them that. Last, if an error occurred, tell them about it, but in gentle terms. These status messages demonstrate good error handling and how well you do it affects your score.

You must provide status messages to users; if you don't, your score on the GUI portion of the exam will suffer. However, make sure you scrub exception messages before users see them.

Need to Know More?

 `http://java.sun.com/docs/books/tutorial/`—Includes a section on exception handling.

 `http://developer.java.sun.com/developer/technicalArticles/Programming/exceptions/`—An excellent article about using exceptions effectively.

 `http://developer.java.sun.com/developer/technicalArticles/Programming/exceptions2/`—A helpful article about exception chaining.

Packaging, Testing, and Submitting the Assignment Application

Terms you'll need to understand:

✓ JAR

✓ Ant

✓ Cygwin

✓ Javac

✓ Application file structure

Techniques you'll need to master:

✓ Packaging the entire project in a single JAR file

✓ Running your application from Windows, Solaris, and both at the same time

✓ Uploading your project at Sun's CertManager site

✓ Structuring your solution in a way that is convenient for the evaluator

This chapter discusses how you should package and carefully test your certification project. When ready, you must submit full source and object code, including new classes, modified versions of supplied classes, and copies of supplied classes that were not modified. They should be in an appropriate directory structure along with the class files. Several other items must be included in the package, such as HTML/javadoc documentation for all classes, user documentation for the database server and GUI client, a README.TXT file, and a design choices document explaining your major design choices. In the README.TXT file, you must supply the names of the files submitted for your project, include a note about their location in the directory structure, and add a brief description of each file's purpose. Finally, you must package all elements of your project into a single JAR file for submission.

Packaging is the least technical aspect of the certification assignment, but one of the easiest areas in which to make mistakes. Some candidates have failed the certification because they put the database binary file in the wrong directory or forgot to include the README.TXT file. To avoid these silly mistakes, follow the directions in this chapter.

File Structure of Your Project Submission

What directories do you need? Where should you place javadoc documentation? Where does the database binary file go? You must answer these questions before submitting your solution. You can approach the file structure of your project in two parts: how to package the classes and how to organize all the files into a single JAR file.

The application for your certification consists of your source code defining the classes that make up your solution. Regardless of how you build these classes, the source files should be separate from the class files. Remember that using too many directories or throwing everything into a single directory indicates weak organization of your file structure. Placement is debatable for only a few classes. For example, you will probably include a class that is the connection factory. Where should you place it? I placed mine in the database directory, but you could argue for the client or server directory. Otherwise, the directory for the majority of classes is obvious.

The following structure is an example you might consider adapting for your project submission:

Install_Directory

<certification_files>	README.TXT file and design choices document
+ mypackage	Object class files
+- client	All the client class files
+- server	All the server (RMI) class files
+- database	All the database-related classes
+ source	All the Java source files
+ mypackage	
+- client	All the client source files
+- server	All the RMI source files
+- database	All the database source files
+ doc	javadoc directory

Notice that the mypackage directory will likely be the directory Sun uses in the source structure you downloaded. I recommend using the same one Sun does.

The straightforward approach to organizing your application files is to place the GUI in the client directory, the database binary and associated files in the database directory, and the RMI or socket-specific files in the server directory. Therefore, *.class files go under mypackage, *.java files under source, and *.html files under doc.

Some candidates overengineer their project and submit a huge number of files. At the other extreme, some candidates cram too much functionality in too few classes. Both approaches will receive poor scores. Remember that whatever directory you place a class in, you must use the proper corresponding package declaration, such as this example:

```
package mypackage.client;
```

JAR File

When you're ready to submit your project, you will upload one JAR file containing everything in your project. To create an archive JAR file from multiple files, you need to use the jar utility. The file generated by the jar archiving tool is based on the ZIP and ZLIB compression formats. The following is a common example of the jar tool creating a file named certificationJarFile that contains all the class files in the current directory:

```
jar cf certificationJarFile.jar *.class
```

Sun's instructions tell you what to name the JAR file, so use that name, not the one you see in these examples; you lose points if you use a different file-name. For my solution, I used the following command (my.jar was the JAR filename I was given in Sun's instructions):

```
jar cfv my.jar *
```

If you issue this command from your project's root directory, assuming it is the same one shown previously, all the class files in the application package are added, including the server, client, and database directories. This command also adds all the source directories, which mimic the class directories, and grabs all the javadoc files and loose files in the root directory.

 Another simple option is going to the parent directory of the install directory and using **jar cvf myFile.jar ./INSTALL_DIRECTORY**. (Note that the path separator is \ for Windows.)

These are the most common options for the jar tool:

➤ c—Creates a new JAR file.

➤ t—Prints the table of contents.

➤ f—Names the JAR file to create or open.

➤ v—Generates verbose output.

➤ x—Extracts all, or only named, files.

 Your solution must be in a single JAR file. Before you upload that JAR file, extract it, check that all files are present and useable (open the README.TXT file), and run your application. Make sure the source code is present after you extract the JAR file.

Some people nest JAR files and even use executable JAR files. Both approaches are fine. I chose to make it simple for the evaluator by not nest-ing JAR files, not using executable JARs, and placing the README.TXT and design decisions files in the root directory. Introducing points of possi-ble failure in this structure isn't desirable, so keep it as simple and reliable as possible. You get no additional points for complexity.

Building with Ant

Apache Ant is a Java-based build tool. It helps automate the compile process. If you need to compile just a handful of files, or many files that are all in the same directory, javac will do. However, when the package structure becomes complex, a build tool such as Ant, modeled after Make, is helpful.

Ant has two compelling features: It is extended using Java classes, and the configuration files are XML-based. Therefore, you can write a program that is essentially a wrapper for Ant and have unparalleled control over the build process. On the other end, you can control the build with only simple changes to XML files.

 Avoid including working or temporary files in your project submission. You will likely use test classes, backup source files, and tool configuration files. Make sure none of these files find their way to your evaluator's screen. Using Ant can ensure that only the essential files are "distributed" to the certification evaluator.

You can get the binary edition of Ant from the Ant Web page at http://ant.apache.org/. You must have a Java API for an XML Processing (JAXP)–compliant XML parser installed on your classpath. With the SDK 1.4, you don't have to do anything because JAXP is included (see http://java.sun.com/xml/). After you install Ant (see http://ant.apache. org/manual/install.html#installing), you can start building with it.

Many popular Java Integrated Development Environments (IDEs) have Ant functionality. For example, JBuilder automatically recognizes Ant build files named build.xml. It even has an Ant wizard. Also, the Unix launch script that comes with Ant works correctly with Cygwin, but you might have to tweak things, such as Cygwin file paths.

Follow these three steps to get started with Ant:

1. Download the latest version.

2. Install Ant.

3. Read the manual.

After these steps, compiling an application with Ant is as simple as issuing this command:

```
ant
```

When compiling with Ant, you might need to tweak the **build.xml** before issuing the simple compiling command **ant**. An example is provided later in this chapter.

This simple command runs Ant using the `build.xml` file in the current directory, on the default target specified in the same `build.xml` configuration file. The following line shows how you will probably use it:

```
ant -buildfile scjd.xml mypackage
```

This command runs Ant using the `scjd.xml` file in the current directory on the target called mypackage.

Use Ant to automate the build task. Also, you can configure Ant to generate javadoc documentation and even place the whole project into a single JAR file, just as the instructions demand.

The configuration XML file, usually `build.xml`, is the key to using Ant. In this configuration file are the instructions Ant follows. A *task* is a discrete step that Ant performs. Basically, you place a sequence of tasks in the `build.xml` file. The following simple example (tested with Ant 1.4.1) compiles the `*.java` files in the `source` directory (subdirectory of the current directory) and places the generated `*.class` files in the `distribution` directory. Notice that a temporary `build` directory is also created. You can also add a task to delete temporary files.

```
<project name="SCJD" default="distribution" basedir=".">
    <description>
        practice SCJD build file
    </description>
    <property name="source" location="source"/>
    <property name="build" location="build"/>
    <property name="distribution" location="distribution"/>

    <target name="initialization">
        <!-- command that assigns DSTAMP -->
        <tstamp/>
        <mkdir dir="${build}"/>
    </target>

    <target name="compile" depends="initialization"
            description="compile the source " >
        <!-- Compile *.java in ${source} and place
            *.class files into ${build} -->
        <javac srcdir="${source}" destdir="${build}"/>
    </target>
```

```
<target name="distribution" depends="compile"
    description="generate the distribution" >
  <mkdir dir="${distribution}/library"/>
  <jar jarfile="${distribution}/scjd-${DSTAMP}.jar"
      basedir="${build}"/>
</target>
</project>
```

These are the primary Ant command-line options:

➤ `-help`—Prints out the help file.

➤ `-version`—Prints the Ant version.

➤ `-diagnostics`—Prints bug report.

➤ `-quiet, -q`—Prints minimal information.

➤ `-verbose`—Prints everything.

➤ `-debug`—Prints debug information.

➤ `-logfile, -l`—Specifies the log file.

➤ `-buildfile`—Names the build file.

➤ `-propertyfile`—Specifies using properties from this file.

Using Ant removes one burden by automating the build process. You can also include tasks for compiling the project, generating javadoc, and packaging all your project files into one JAR file, thus meeting another requirement along the way.

Because the configuration file is XML, several tags could be useful for your project. The following primary task "types" are the ones you are most likely to use with the Ant tool:

➤ `Description`—Describes the project.

➤ `DirSet`—Defines a group of directories.

➤ `FileList`—Defines an explicitly named list of files.

➤ `FileSet`—Defines a group of files.

➤ `File Mappers`—Tells Ant how to find a source file.

➤ `Selectors`—Specifies a way to select files from a `FileSet` using one of the following options:

  ➤`<contains>`—Contains a particular string.

  ➤`<date>`—Filters file by date.

➤<depend>—Modified more recently than other files it "depends" on.

➤<depth>—Files are *x* directories down in the tree.

➤<filename>—Filters by filename.

➤<size>—Files task are selected by size.

These types are used throughout the build.xml configuration file. If you want to speed up the build process for your certification project, I recommend installing and using Ant. It takes about an hour to download, install, configure and test. This is a good investment; it will save you many hours because you need to build your application numerous times before submitting it.

Testing

You must test your solution thoroughly before submitting it for grading. Most candidates use a Windows development environment. That is fine. However, the solution must also work on Unix and especially Solaris. Theoretically, it should work without any worry on your part. However, Java isn't perfect, and neither are you, so there are a few things to check before uploading. For example, your solution has to open the database binary file, so make sure you have implemented an OS-independent way to do that. Also, the user help file has to be opened. If you bundle the HTML help file in the submitted JAR file, as opposed to just pointing to an online URL, your solution has to get to the file in an OS-independent fashion.

 If you instruct the evaluator to use start scripts (included in the README.TXT file) for running your solution, be sure to have start scripts for both Unix and Windows.

To ensure that your solution is portable, one necessary test is testing the client and server on both Windows and Unix in various combinations. The following are the recommended tests to make sure your solution works well on either OS and in mixed environments, in which one part is on one OS and another part is on another OS. You can easily adapt this test suite to include another OS, such as Macintosh or another Unix variant. The following are the test scenarios you should consider (order is not important):

➤ Client (local mode) on one Solaris box.

➤ Client (remote mode) and server on the same Solaris box.

➤ Client (remote mode) on one Solaris box while the server is on another Solaris box.

➤ Client (remote mode) on one Windows box while the server is on another Windows box.

➤ Client (local mode) on one Windows box.

➤ Client (remote mode) and server on the same Windows box.

➤ Client (remote mode) on a Windows box while the server is on a Solaris box.

➤ Client (remote mode) on a Solaris box while the server is on a Windows box.

 Neglecting to thoroughly test your solution for all possible click and keystroke combinations is foolhardy. Also, be sure to test on both Solaris and Windows with the client and server on one OS and then test with the client and server on different OSs.

Cygwin

Those developers who use a Windows development environment (the majority of candidates) often have difficulty finding a Solaris box to test their solution. I was fortunate to have several Solaris servers at work, so I tested my solution carefully on them. My tests uncovered a few problems that were not evident on Windows. For example, I discovered that part of my file pathing worked fine in both Windows and Unix, but another part did not because I used a Windows-specific path separator. In one mode, this separator wasn't used, but in another mode it was—and it failed gloriously on Unix. After fixing that, I found a major bug not in my code, but in RMI. That problem would have failed my submission had I not found it.

If you don't have access to a Solaris server, there are options. You can download Solaris or another Unix flavor, and install it temporarily on an extra box for testing. Likewise, you might install Linux. You can even dual-boot for a while. Another interesting way to test your solution on Unix is to use Cygwin (`http://www.cygwin.com`), an excellent Unix emulator for Windows.

Cygwin consists of a dynamic link library (DLL; cygwin1.dll) that acts as a Unix emulation layer. This emulation layer provides considerable Unix API functionality. Cygwin also comes with a large collection of tools that provide the Unix/Linux look and feel. When I tested my solution on Solaris, I also tested it with Cygwin (1.3 on Windows 2000), using the same seven combinations listed previously. Cygwin is free because it is composed of GNU software, pieces under the standard X11 license, and parts in public domain; Red Hat placed its contribution under the General Public License (GPL).

Figure 18.1 shows what it looks like to run a Java program from Cygwin.

Figure 18.1 Running the solution server in Cygwin.

It is worth the effort to try your solution in Unix, whether it is a Unix or Solaris box. If you don't have access to a genuine Unix box, get Cygwin and try it in that.

JUnit

Quality control is a key function in any software development methodology. Although the certification assignment isn't large, it still requires the entire life cycle you find in large projects. Testing is as mandatory for your certification project as it is for commercial projects.

The JUnit and Ant tools are free and open source. You can download them from the URLs in "Need to Know More?" at the end of this chapter.

One way to improve your testing is to use a testing suite, such as JUnit (http://www.junit.org), which enables you to write repeatable tests. Using a unit-testing framework like JUnit simply adds a measure of certainty about your final submission. You won't need to guess whether your application meets all the assignment requirements. Because testing is not a core part of development, most programmers skip it. After all, a dedicated quality assurance (QA) tester or even an entire team is usually responsible for testing, so why should the developer take precious time to write testing code? Using JUnit can help you measure your progress.

QA departments are mostly interested in integration testing—seeing whether components work well together. Integration testing is mandatory before submitting your project. However, first you should conduct unit testing, which is testing each single unit of code individually. One way to approach unit testing is to focus on a single class. This approach narrowly defines what is being asked of your code. JUnit will definitely help you create a test that is fully automated and binary. That way, you will know whether your class succeeds or fails.

To avoid uploading hidden bugs or unintended side effects, use JUnit, which comes with a graphical interface to run tests. You do not have to create numerous and elaborate tests. However, a few key tests will help you. For example, write a test class for the database and RMI portions of the application. You can then run the test in JUnit, which shows its progress with a progress bar for visual feedback. JUnit reports passing tests with a green bar and displays a red bar when there is trouble. JUnit also displays failed tests in a list at the bottom of the GUI.

Test Plan

If you take the time to write a quick test plan, you will save time overall. You might want to adapt your test plan from the IEEE standard 1008-1987, "Standard for Software Unit Testing." (Testing documentation and the testing process are described in Appendix B, "Documentation Standards.")

In my project submission, I mentioned part of my test process because I thought thoroughly testing the application would impress the evaluator. Also, if the evaluator found a major problem, he or she would know it wasn't caused by gross neglect (causing an automatic failure), but merely a simple mistake (meaning the worst-case scenario would be losing some points).

Submitting the Assignment

After creating your JAR file, it is time to submit it. Go to Sun's CertManager site (see http://www.certmanager.net/sun/) and click the Continue button. Then log in and click the Test History button. Next, click the Assignment button. At this point, you must select the correct assignment from the list, and click the Upload Assignment button. Finally, send your JAR file.

If you are having trouble uploading your exam assignment, you can e-mail Sun with the payment confirmation number you received when you purchased the exam. After you have uploaded your assignment and taken the essay exam at a Prometric testing center, your exam results will show up in the certification database within four weeks. Occasionally, there is a hiccup in the upload, and the evaluator makes a comment to that effect in the database. The evaluator is probably asking you to resubmit.

Need to Know More?

 `http://suned.sun.com/US/certification/certmanager`—Download and upload the SCJD assignment and check on the results.

 `http://ant.apache.org`—The home page for Apache Ant.

 `http://ant.apache.org/srcdownload.cgi`—Download the Ant source.

`http://www.junit.org`—The home page for JUnit.

The Essay Exam

Terms you'll need to understand:

✓ Remote Method Invocation (RMI)
✓ Design patterns
✓ Design choices
✓ Search algorithm
✓ Multithreading

Techniques you'll need to master:

✓ Describing your design choices
✓ Answering essay questions about your solution
✓ Recognizing legal and illegal Java identifiers
✓ Justifying the technologies you used
✓ Explaining the advantages and disadvantages of your design choices

In this chapter, you review the essay exam and learn what you need to do before taking it. Although the essay exam is short, you can still harm your final score if you perform poorly on it.

Study your design choices document thoroughly. Don't simply assume you'll remember that material for your essay exam without studying it. Also, you can't take any reference material into the exam room, so be ready before you take the exam. Certainly you know what you did, but trying to type the key details and names of classes, exact design patterns, and advantages of RMI versus sockets, all from recall, can be difficult while you're taking an exam.

The exam is simple. It took me 20 minutes to type complete answers to the five questions. I then spent 15 minutes reviewing and revising all answers. The entire exam took me 35 minutes, even though I was more detailed and careful than necessary. Even if you go half that speed, you need only an hour to complete the exam. Again, by thoroughly studying your design choices document to help you prepare, this exam will not be difficult.

The Exam's Purposes

The essay exam has four purposes. Sun does not state them anywhere, but I hope you'll agree that the exam serves the following purposes, instead of testing your understanding of the technology, as all the other certification exams do.

First, the essay exam is a fraud buster. The evaluators will know whether you wrote the code by matching your essay answers with your actual code. For example, if your essay exam answer talks about sockets but your certification project uses RMI, you'll get a call from the secret police. By asking "How did you do such and such?" the evaluators want you to demonstrate an in-depth familiarity with your submitted solution. There is little technical challenge to answering that type of question, if you did the work yourself.

Second, the essay exam assesses whether you understand the technology needed to satisfy the assignment requirements. Evaluators want to know, for example, how well you understand RMI or sockets, whichever one you chose. It is good if you can build a program using one of these technologies, but showing mastery of the technology is better.

Third, the essay exam demonstrates to evaluators whether you have a good feel for how to architect a solution. Sure, the code is a better measure of this skill, but an essay can expose foggy thinking and incorrect assumptions. At times I have finally gotten a piece of code to work, but didn't understand why it worked until later—on occasion, much later. That approach won't work here, however. Your essay description reveals how well you understand the approaches and classes you used. For example, perhaps you finally got RMI to work, but don't actually feel comfortable with its inner workings.

Fourth, the essay exam shows whether you can tell someone else about Java in a way that makes sense. In the real world, communicating how technology works is a large part of a developer's job. If you can't tell an evaluator what is going on in your solution, even though you had unlimited time to prepare, you won't be effective in real projects. Therefore, it is to your advantage to prepare for the essay so that you can demonstrate familiarity with the portions of Java used in your project submission.

I've worked with people who had difficulty communicating. They were quick at writing code—very smart in that way—but their communication skills were inadequate. Too bad: They did the hard part but neglected the easy part, so their salary suffered. I chose the word "neglected" carefully, meaning that they could have easily improved their communicating. However, they made a career blunder by underestimating the importance of communication skills. Writing about the code and your solution is nearly as important as writing the code itself. It will affect your score, so do the necessary preparation by writing out answers at length before taking the essay exam.

Table 19.1 lists the facts about the essay exam.

Table 19.1 Essay Exam Facts	
Exam Fact	**Detail**
Exam type	Essay
Number of questions	5 separate essay questions
Allotted test time	2 hours
Average test time	Less than 1 hour
Test expiration after purchase	1 year
Difficulty level	Moderate
Preparation time	4 hours of writing out the answers before taking the exam
Impact on total score	10% of total score
Cost	$150
Exam location	Prometric testing centers
Exam number	CX-310-027

(continued)

Table 19.1 Essay Exam Facts *(continued)*	
Prerequisite	Submission of certification project to CertManager before you can buy an exam voucher
Wait for results	1–4 weeks
Passing score	Not applicable: The exam is assessed with your certification project
Location for viewing grade	Sun's CertManager site

The Questions

A few questions on the exam are not technical in nature, but they ask about implementation details to ensure that it is your code in the certification project. For example, the question "How did you implement the search functionality?" doesn't require technical know-how to answer it, just familiarity with the steps of the search algorithm you used.

The remaining questions are technical and follow the general formula of "Describe how you implemented the *assignment_feature_XYZ*. List the advantages and disadvantages of your approach." The following list highlights the most likely features of the assignment you might be questioned on:

➤ Record searching by user-supplied criteria

➤ Record locking

➤ Error and exception handling

➤ Extending or modifying the supplied classes

➤ Deprecated methods in the supplied classes

➤ Design patterns

➤ RMI versus sockets

➤ Network server

➤ GUI design

➤ JTable details

➤ Event handling

➤ GUI-database communication

➤ Multithreading

➤ Future enhancements

Preparation

The best preparation for this essay exam is writing a good design choices document. If you take the time to clearly describe how you handled the previously listed aspects of your project, the essay exam will be quick and easy. You need to restate (from recall) only the key details of the design choices document for your essay answers.

Some candidates write brief README.TXT and DESIGN_ CHOICES.TXT documents and still pass. This approach is risky, however, and it won't help you with the essay exam. It is better to take an extra few days so that you can describe your work more thoroughly. You deserve the credit, so make sure you get it. Please see Chapter 5, "Documentation and Javadoc Comments," for more details on these two documents.

I actually typed out short answers to all the questions I thought might appear on the exam, and my efforts paid off. My answers were concise and showed clear thought, and they took just minutes to complete.

The Sample Essay Exam

In this section, you take a sample essay exam. Relax, it is the easiest part of the certification. It took me far less time than the exam allotted, even though I wrote complete answers. Complete answers don't necessarily have to be lengthy answers, however. My RMI versus sockets answer had eight parts, but another answer had only one crisp paragraph.

This exam doesn't intend to test your knowledge as the other certification exams do. Rather, this one simply attempts to make sure you did your own work. The evaluator compares the certification project you uploaded (which could have been completed by you or your guru friend) to the essay answers you provided (which are definitely your own work). If the evaluator finds no discrepancies, all is well. If he or she does, your final score will reflect these discrepancies.

The essay exam is an opportunity to make a good impression. After all, if the evaluators see sterling answers on your essay exam, they will assess your certification project favorably. If you ramble on about unrelated issues (for example, "Can you email me about...?") or simply write poorly, you won't get the benefit of your evaluator's doubt for those subject areas. If your answers are written well, the evaluator is more likely to think you know your stuff and will push your grade up accordingly. Be aware that grammar, syntax, and spelling matter, if only in the evaluator's subconscious. Presentation counts, just as in fine cooking: Haute cuisine never tastes right on a paper plate.

The following guidelines will help you provide convincing answers:

➤ Take time to understand the question before writing the answer.

➤ Provide at least one paragraph for each question.

➤ Each paragraph must contain only one main idea.

➤ Do not use wordy, long sentences; write crisp statements.

➤ Paragraphs should follow one another logically.

➤ Check your spelling, grammar, and syntax before submission.

The essay exam is designed to ensure that you are the author of the certification project. If your answers to the essay exam are not consistent with the project you submitted, your project will be suspected of fraud.

There are only five questions on the exam. Three are technical (for example, "Did you choose RMI over sockets, and why?"), and two simply test whether you did your own work on the certification project (for example, "How did you implement the search feature in the GUI?"). The following 13 questions cover all aspects of the assignment that might be on the exam.

You must provide answers on the essay exam that are consistent with what you wrote in your design choices document. The key to doing well on the essay exam is to provide a condensed version of the design choices document.

Exam Prep Questions

The following questions cover the most likely topics for your essay exam. The wording of the question isn't critical, but your familiarity with the topic is.

Question 1

Describe your record-searching approach.

Question 2

Describe your record-locking approach.

Question 3

Describe how your certification project handles exceptions.

Question 4

Describe whether you extended or modified the supplied classes, and include a justification of that choice.

Question 5

Describe what you did with deprecated methods in the supplied classes.

Question 6

Describe how you used design patterns.

Question 7

Describe your choice between RMI and sockets, and include a justification of that choice.

Question 8

Describe your network server and how you used it in your solution.

Question 9

Describe how you designed the GUI, especially the JTable component.

Question 10

Describe how your GUI handles events.

Question 11

Describe how your GUI communicates with the database.

Question 12

Describe how your design uses multithreading.

Question 13

Describe how your design addresses future modifications.

Answers to the Exam Prep Questions

In this section, you review the answers to the sample essay exam. The order of the questions is not important, and the answers are subjective. There are several ways to approach the answers, so the sample answers presented here are helpful, but not the only way to describe portions of your solution.

Keep in mind that the essay exam has two goals: making sure you did your own work (does it match the design choices document?) and you know what you are doing. (For example, make sure the evaluator wouldn't ask "Why is this candidate using the MVC pattern on a simple task like a search algorithm?") Remember that these answers are another chance to influence the evaluator in your favor. If you don't write these answers out ahead of time, you risk forgetting essential parts and giving incomplete answers—ones that might be mostly correct, but not impressive.

The answer format illustrated in the following exam answers helps convince the evaluator that you know what you are doing. Using a similar format also helps you remember the material so that you can write it out when you are in the exam room—without your design choices document.

 Keep your answers short and factual. Do not wax eloquent about your love of the MVC design pattern. Just give direct answers. That way, the evaluators can get on with their business and award you a great score.

Question 1

For the record-searching approach, the search method is abstracted so that it will search any table. It returns an array of rows in which each row has at least one value matching one value in the search criteria, using the following algorithm:

1. Parse the criteria string with the `StringTokenizer` class.

2. Get a new row of data from the database.

3. Find a column that matches the criteria field name.

4. Test for a match between the row value and the criteria value.

5. If there is a match, save the row of data and go to step 2.

6. If there is no match for the current criteria, go to the next criteria and then go to step 3.

7. When the criteria are exhausted, go to step 2.

8. When the rows are exhausted, return matched rows.

Question 2

The record-locking approach implements a separate LockManager class. A row is locked and unlocked by only one client at a time. The adapter for Database, DatabaseRemote, has a one-to-one relationship with a single client, so the client ID is the reference to DatabaseRemote. In the LockManager class, the client ID is referred to with a WeakReference. That way, should another client try to lock a record previously locked by a client who has died, the LockManager class removes the lock because the garbage collector will have nullified that reference. The responsibility for record locking is kept in the LockManager class, and the responsibility for references to dead objects stays with the JVM, a clean separation of responsibilities. A separate LockManager class is justified for the following reasons:

➤ Allows Insert Row Locking (IRL), which handles multiuser-simultaneous record modification.

➤ Provides consistent and concurrent access to data in a multiuser environment.

➤ Allows the client to ignore IRL in local mode.

➤ Without a good lock manager, users could overwrite each other's seat reservations.

Question 3

Exceptions are handled through proper try-catch-finally constructs and strong user-informing status messages. Users are kept informed of any problems with the use of clear status updates, such as the one displayed when they type in an impossible seat number.

Question 4

The supplied classes are not modified in any way. New classes subclass the original classes for the following reasons:

➤ To maintain legacy compatibility for the original classes

➤ To isolate new functionality

➤ To cleanly separate changes to the old classes

➤ To use a new name that is more descriptive of the class responsibilities

➤ To override deprecated methods in the supplied classes

Question 5

The deprecated methods in the supplied classes are overridden with methods in a subclass that uses the latest SDK API.

Question 6

The following design patterns are used:

➤ MVC: The Model component is `SuperBowlTableModel`, the View component is the Swing GUI, and the Controller component consists of event methods and JTable-triggered code.

➤ Business Delegate: Remote interface through RMI.

➤ Value Objects: Database record sent to the GUI.

➤ Connection Factory: `Factory` class returns the local or remote database based on parameters. Client knows nothing about this.

➤ Data Access Objects: `Database` class.

➤ Decorator: `DatabaseRemote` decorates `Database`.

Question 7

RMI is used instead of sockets for the following reasons:

➤ Thread safety is built into RMI, but you have to handle multithreading manually in sockets.

➤ RMI has a Remote Method Protocol (RMP) communication protocol, but sockets don't.

➤ RMI presents a simpler programming model than sockets do.

➤ RMI supports dynamic class loading.

➤ Method calls are type-safe in RMI.

➤ RMI is built on sockets and is more mature.

➤ It is easy to add new objects with RMI.

➤ RMI is a known standard, so it is easy to share code with other developers.

➤ The Registry acts as a central lookup for finding various remote objects.

Question 8

The network server is a combination of a database system using a binary file and RMI. The project uses RMI to listen to users. It is RMI that transforms a single-user file manager class into a multiuser database server since it handles multi-user issues such as multithreading. Also, RMI allows the database to be on a separate JVM from the client which represents a remote database service.

Question 9

The user interface is designed for ease of use, following good Human/Computer Interaction (HCI) principles. Several aspects of the GUI merit explanation. For example, the user can make a reservation in three simple moves: select a seat from the table, type in the number of seats, and click the Reserve button. The search feature is easy to use, with drop-down combo boxes filled with predefined criteria. Only Swing components are used in the

GUI. The key components are a JTable, menu bars, buttons, combo boxes, labels, and tool tips. The GUI has a user-friendly look and feel. Additionally, the user can sort the entire table by clicking on any column heading. GUI components are arranged by using the BorderLayout component. These components are automatically repositioned proportionately when the window resizes. Altogether, the components' arrangement and interaction are designed to facilitate easy navigation, according to good HCI principles.

Question 10

The GUI handles events via the event model of MVC. User actions trigger event handler method invocation in the Controller component (logic code in the GUI), where a response is generated (for example, a seat is reserved).

Question 11

The GUI communicates with the database in two modes, local and remote. A separate DatabaseFactory class returns the local or remote database, based on parameters. The client does not have any lines of code specific to local or remote modes.

Question 12

This design uses multithreading, which comes with RMI. Also, the LockManager class has synchronized lock and unlock methods, so they are thread safe. Finally, public methods of the Database class are synchronized, which allows multithreading in a multiuser environment.

Question 13

This design addresses future modifications by using an architecture mixed with preexisting parts that already lend themselves to modifications and new robust parts. They include RMI (easy-to-add objects), an abstract search algorithm (works with new tables), a separate LockManager class (works on any record on any table in any database), a single interface that defines database methods (whether in local or remote mode), and the use of SDK classes (such as StringTokenizer) instead of custom ones whenever possible.

Need to Know More?

 `http://suned.sun.com/US/certification/java/certification_details.html#developer`—Provides details on the essay exam.

 `http://suned.sun.com/US/certification/java/java_exam_objectives.html#developer`—Read the objectives for the exam (same as the assignment objectives).

 `http://suned.sun.com/US/certification/register/index.html`—Purchase an exam voucher.

 `http://www.certmanager.net/sun/`—View the status, including the grade, of your certification.

UML Glance Card

In this appendix, you review the basics of the Unified Modeling Language (UML), which is currently at version 1.5. You can download the specification as a 4MB PDF file from the Object Management Group (OMG) Web site at http://www.omg.org. The OMG specification states that UML is a "graphical language for visualizing, specifying, constructing, and documenting the artifacts of a software-intensive system. The UML offers a standard way to write a system's blueprints, including conceptual things such as business processes and system functions as well as concrete things such as programming language statements, database schemas, and reusable software components."

Even though UML doesn't appear in the assignment and, therefore, not in the essay exam, you should use it to diagram your application during the design phase. Having a clear picture to code to makes your programming work go faster. Also, you can choose to include UML diagrams in the design choices document. Many candidates find that using these diagrams helps ensure that the evaluator correctly understands their designs.

UML

Although the construction industry has had its own notation system for a long time, software development, at the beginning, did not have a standard design notation. Eventually, the Rational Software Corporation hired Grady Booch, Ivar Jacobson, and Jim Rumbaugh, pioneers in the object-oriented programming (OOP) notation movement, to create a unified system. They invented what is now called UML. These pioneers, and those on the sidelines, were groping for industry guidelines and object management specifications to provide a common framework for application development. After all, OOP's goals are reusability, portability, and interoperability of object-based software in distributed, heterogeneous environments. How can you achieve those goals if one engineer can't share a software description with another so that any professional in the same industry can understand it?

Booch, Jacobson, and Rumbaugh started the UML effort at Rational and were its original chief methodologists. Today, UML is an OMG standard, with hundreds of partners contributing, including the original UML author, Rational Software Corporation.

UML is the language the software blueprint is written in. Furthermore, the names of classes, fields, and methods are exactly what you use in code, so UML isn't so abstract that it is good only for large projects; it is also helpful for your certification project. UML is a language for specifying, constructing, visualizing, and documenting a software system's artifacts. Today it is used for all sorts of things, but its original motivation was software design.

 The OMG standard says that an artifact "represents a physical piece of information that is used or produced by a software development process. Examples of Artifacts include models, source files, scripts, and binary executable files. An Artifact may constitute the implementation of a deployable component."

Fortunately, the timing of UML's adoption coincides with Java's rising prominence. UML is a great choice for designing Java, which is why I recommend you start using it if you haven't already done so. Most software development departments throughout the industry are adopting it quickly.

Standard Graphical Diagrams

UML defines the following graphical diagrams:

➤ Use case diagram

➤ Class diagram

➤ Package Diagrams

➤ Object Diagrams

➤ Behavior diagrams, which can be further classified into the following categories:

> ➤ Statechart diagrams
>
> ➤ Activity diagrams
>
> ➤ Interaction diagrams, which have two types:
>
> ➤ Sequence diagrams
>
> ➤ Collaboration diagrams

➤ Implementation diagrams, which are divided into two categories:

   ➤ Component diagrams

   ➤ Deployment diagrams

You won't use all these diagrams for every project, but each has its benefits, so just be aware of how to use them. Most of the ones you can choose for your solution are briefly explained later in this appendix.

 Other names are sometimes used for these graphical diagrams, but the names in the preceding list are the official or canonical ones.

The following sections describe the more common diagrams. They are the ones you will most likely use to design your project for this certification.

Class Diagram

A *class diagram* is a standard UML model, the blueprint from which objects are produced at runtime. As you'll remember, a class is a definition, but an object is an instance of that class.

The OMG standard defines the UML class diagrams in this way: "UML class diagrams are used to present the UML metamodel, its concepts (meta-classes), relationships, and constraints. Definitions of the concepts are included." The class diagram has three parts:

➤ Class name

➤ Class attributes (fields or variables)

➤ Behaviors (methods)

For a simple example of mapping class diagrams to Java code, see jGuru's bank reservation example at `http://developer.java.sun.com/developer/onlineTraining/rmi/exercises/UMLDefinition`.

Figure A.1 illustrates a general diagram of three classes.

Use Case Diagram

A *use case diagram* describes what a system does from the viewpoint of an external observer: It describes a discrete event. This type of diagram shows you what is happening, not how it is done. Notice in Figure A.2 that people are called actors and depicted as stick figures, and the use cases are ovals. The lines that link actors to use cases are referred to as *communications*.

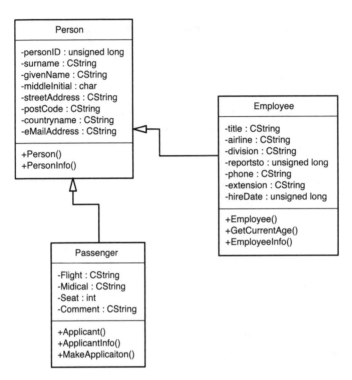

Figure A.1 A typical UML class diagram.

Statechart Diagram

Statechart diagrams represent the behavior of dynamic entities by specifying their responses to receiving event instances. A statechart diagram shows an object's possible states and the transitions that cause a change in state. The sample statechart diagram in Figure A.3 models the process of reserving a seat on a plane, bus, or train. A successful reservation consists of requesting a seat, having the system check for an available seat, and then reserving that seat if it is available or, if the seat is locked, reserving that seat when the lock is removed.

States are represented by rounded rectangles, and arrows from one state to another represent transitions in state. Events that trigger transitions are described by written notations next to transition arrows.

Activity Diagram

An *activity diagram* is just a flowchart that uses a defined notation (see Figure A.4). Notice how similar activity diagrams are to statechart diagrams. The difference is that a statechart diagram describes actual objects and the details of a process they interact with. An activity diagram is less detailed and tries to convey the flow of activities that make up a given process.

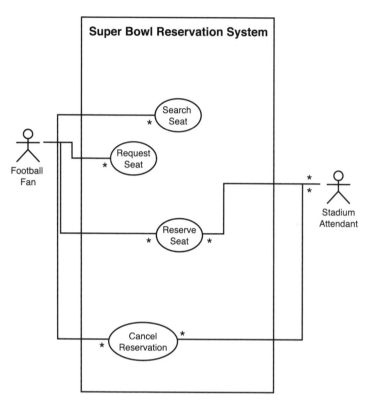

Figure A.2 A typical UML use case diagram.

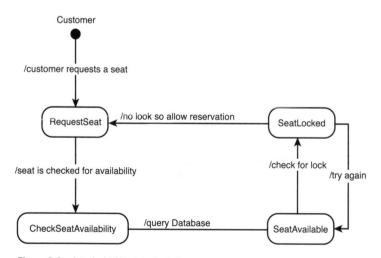

Figure A.3 A typical UML statechart diagram.

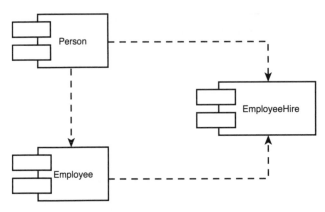

Figure A.4 A typical UML activity diagram.

Sequence Diagram

Sequence diagrams illustrate the action that takes place within a system. A sequence diagram presents an Interaction, which is defined in UML as a set of Messages between Roles. A sequence diagram has two dimensions:

➤ The vertical axis represents time (time elapses as you read down the diagram).

➤ The horizontal axis represents different instances of time and communication events.

A sequence diagram, shown in Figure A.5, details how operations are performed, which object calls another object, and when (logically) an operation is carried out. Although there is no significance to the horizontal ordering of instances, objects are listed from left to right according to when they get involved in the process (also called the "message sequence").

Component Diagram

A component is a code module, which is a physical analog of a class diagram. As database folks know, there are the logical model and the physical model for a data schema. For code, however, usually just the physical application architecture is discussed.

A *component diagram* (see Figure A.6) shows the dependencies among software components, including the artifacts that implement these dependencies, such as source code files, binary code files, executable files, and scripts. You can use a diagram containing component types to show static dependencies. For example, a compiler dependency between programs could be shown as dashed arrows to represent a static dependency. So if a client component is dependent on a third-party component, you would show it in a component diagram with a dashed arrow between the client and the third-party component.

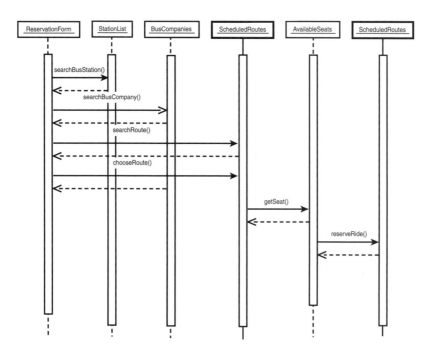

Figure A.5   A typical UML sequence diagram.

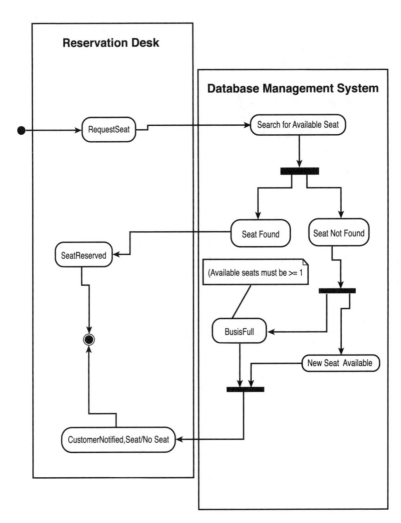

Figure A.6 A typical UML component diagram.

Need to Know More?

 `http://www.togethersoft.com/services/practical_guides/` `umlonlinecourse/`—A quick but quality UML tutorial by the experts at TogetherSoft.

 `http://www.smartdraw.com/resources/examples/index.htm`—SmartDraw has received favorable reviews; however, even if you're satisfied with another product, you can still see good examples of clean diagrams in the online documentation at this site.

 `http://www.smartdraw.com/resources/centers/uml/uml.htm`— SmartDraw provides a nice, compact overview of how to draw UML diagrams.

 `http://developer.java.sun.com/developer/onlineTraining/rmi/`—This jGuru short course explains the fundamentals of Remote Method Invocation (RMI) by using a lot of UML. You can choose both RMI and UML to design your solution, so this site is an excellent resource.

 `http://www.rational.com/uml/`—The origin of UML is described at Rational's UML home page.

 `http://www.omg.org/uml/`—The Object Management Group's UML home page, the current owners and setters of the standard for UML.

 `http://www.objectsbydesign.com/tools/umltools_byCompany.html`—A long list of UML tools.

 `http://www.devx.com/uml/`—The DevX UML home page.

Documentation Standards

In this appendix, you review the more common documents used in developing software applications, in outline form. Use these like you would a checklist or a recipe, neither of which have explanations, but are still useful. These documents are not required to complete the assignment, so Sun isn't looking for them in your certification project. However, I recommend using some of them in the appendix as a checklist to guide you in designing your solution. You don't have to spend much time writing all the documents, but if you use their outlines as a guide, you are more likely to do well on the project. At a minimum, I would recommend completing the design document because you can use it to create the design choices document, which *is* required in your project submission. Using proper design methodology and documentation has been proved to improve the quality of software and will also improve the quality of your certification project. It is a question of time: How much time are you willing to spend on good documentation and design?

The documents covered in the following sections in outline form are the ones that should prove helpful in guiding you through your certification project. Some of them are covered in more detail in Chapter 5, "Documentation and Javadoc Comments," but are presented here again as a quick reference. They are based on the IEEE standards noted in each section.

Requirements Definition

This step involves writing the Software Requirements Specifications (SRS), which should precisely describe each essential requirement of the software and external interfaces. Consult the SRS in ANSI/IEEE standard 830-1998 (current version is at http://standards.ieee.org/reading/ieee/std_public/description/se), "Recommended Practice for Software Requirements Specifications," and tailor it to your needs. This version of the standard is free and will help with this assignment. Please see the "Requirements" section in Chapter 6, "Application Analysis and Design," for more information on gathering requirements.

The following outline is a loose adaptation of the IEEE standard 830-1993, "Recommended Practice for Software Requirements Specifications":

1.	Introduction
1.1	Purpose
1.2	Scope
1.3	Definitions, acronyms, and abbreviations
1.4	References
1.5	Overview
2.	Overall description
2.1	Product perspective
2.2	Product functions
2.3	User characteristics
2.4	Constraints
2.5	Assumptions and dependencies
3.	Specific requirements
3.1	Functionality
3.2	Usability
3.3	Interfaces
3.3.1	User interfaces
3.3.2	Hardware interfaces
3.3.3	Software interfaces
3.3.4	Communications interfaces
3.4	Reliability
3.5	Security
3.6	Maintainability
3.7	Performance

3.8	Portability
3.9	Performance
3.10	Design constraints
3.11	User documentation and help system
4.	Supporting information

Detail Design

The instructions that came with your assignment download from Sun describe the system you are to build. This document contains items best described as functional requirements. From these requirements, you can write a short detail design document. The idea is that applicability is not restricted by the software's size, complexity, or criticalness. Please see the "Design" section in Chapter 6 for a more complete explanation of this document. Follow the IEEE standard 1016-1993 (http://standards.ieee.org/reading/ieee/std_public/description/se/), "Guide to Software Design Descriptions," which has the following outline:

1.	Overview
1.1	Purpose
1.2	Scope
2.	References
3.	Definitions
4.	Description of IEEE standard 1016-1987
5.	Design description organization
5.1	Design views
5.2	Recommended design views
5.3	Design description media
6.	Considerations
6.1	Selecting representative design methods
6.2	Representative design method descriptions
6.3	Design document sections
6.4	Method-oriented design documents

Unit Testing

You should unit-test everything, of course. However, you also need to make sure you don't omit anything from testing and ensure that you're testing your classes in the correct manner. The following IEEE standards are intended for software quality, including testing and verification:

➤ IEEE 829-1983, "Standard for Software Test Documentation"

➤ IEEE 1008-1987, "Standard for Software Unit Testing"

➤ IEEE 1012-1986, "Standard for Software Verification and Validation Plans"

➤ IEEE 1059-1993, "Guide for Software Verification and Validation Plans"

The IEEE standard 1008-1987, "Standard for Software Unit Testing" (`http://standards.ieee.org/reading/ieee/std_public/description/se/`), provides a helpful overview of how you should test your application. It has the following outline:

1.	Introduction
1.1	Abstract—The abstract and purpose of this document and who the audience is.
1.2	Scope—Describe the testing process, including the major phases.
1.3	Glossary—List and define the technical language included in this document.
1.4	References—Define any resources used for this document, such as IEEE standard *XYZ*.
2.	Test Plan—Describe the plan for testing.

| 2.1 | Schedules and Resources—Name the people, tasks, and dates for specific testing actions. |

2.1 Schedules and Resources—Name the people, tasks, and dates for specific testing actions.

2.2 Test Reporting—Answer the question "How will test results be documented and then reported?"

3 Testing—Describe how the actual tests will be conducted.

3.1 Static Testing—Describe how you will review code and documentation.

3.2 Unit Testing—Describe how you test each unit, perhaps with JUnit (see http://www.junit.org).

3.3 System Testing—Describe how you will test the entire application (for example, successfully reserved a seat).

3.4 Acceptance Testing—Describe how you will have another person test the entire application and then how you will make sure the submission package is complete.

Review the Contents Before Submission

After you have tested your application, you need to review or audit it before uploading your certification project. This review takes about an hour. Many candidates have failed because they omitted a piece or simply placed a file in the wrong spot, so don't allow silly mistakes to rob you of certification. Make sure you review your JAR contents before clicking that upload button at the CertManager site.

Although you don't need to be quite as thorough as the outline of the IEEE standard 1028-1988, "Standard for Software Reviews and Audits" (http://standards.ieee.org/reading/ieee/std_public/description/se/), look it over and use the parts that will help you make sure your project submission is absolutely complete:

1. Scope and references

1.1 Scope

1.2 References

2. Definitions

3. Introduction

3.1 Review process prerequisites

3.2 Audit process prerequisites

Design Choices Document Guide

The design choices document is required, but Sun's assignment instructions do not tell you what this document should look like. Many candidates don't spend much time on it and still pass. I labored over mine, but at least I got a perfect score for documentation. More important, a good design choices document helps the evaluator understand your approach to meeting the assignment's requirements.

You can use the sample design choices document in Chapter 5 or you can adapt yours to the outline of the IEEE standard 1063-1987, "Standard for Software User Documentation" (http://standards.ieee.org/reading/ieee/std_public/description/se/). The following outline helps you ensure that you have covered all the bases:

1.	Scope
1.1	Applicability
1.2	Organization
2.	Definitions
3.	Identifying required user documents
3.1	Identifying the software
3.2	Determining the document audience
3.3	Determining the document set
3.4	Determining document usage modes
4.	User document inclusion requirements
5.	User document content requirements
5.1	Title page
5.2	Restrictions
5.3	Warranties and contractual obligations
5.4	Table of contents
5.5	List of illustrations
5.6	Introduction
5.7	Body of document
5.8	Error messages, known problems, and error recovery
5.9	Appendixes
5.10	Bibliography
5.11	Glossary

Need to Know More?

 Moore, James W. *Software Engineerng Standards: A User's Road Map.* Hoboken, NJ: Wiley-IEEE Press, 2002 (ISBN 0818680083). This book explains how to understand and apply the many standards published by IEEE.

Code Conventions

This appendix reviews the basics of Java source code conventions. Because Java borrows much of its syntax from C++, the conventions used in developing C++ programs are carried over to Java.

Reasons for Code Conventions

These are Sun's reasons for code conventions:

➤ *Maintenance*—Most of the lifetime cost of software development goes to maintenance.

➤ *Changing author*—As the project size and software age increase, it becomes more likely that someone other than the original author will work on the code.

➤ *Readability*—Following consistent and clear conventions improves the software's readability and ease of maintenance.

➤ *Source code as a product*—Delivering a good product is hard, but shipping the code as part of the product is harder. The same need to present a clean and well-documented product applies to code because it is also part of the finished product.

There are other reasons to follow standard coding standards, but Table C.1 might offer the best reason to follow the advice in this appendix.

Table C.1	Code Style Grade Points for the Certification Assignment	
	Grade Area	**Points**
1	Coding standards and readability	23
2	Javadoc source documentation	5
3	Comments	5
4	Total	33 (21%)

Bad code style can be enough to fail the certification assignment. If you use a bizarre style or simply don't follow the industry standard for Java coding, you will upset the evaluator, who needs to find only one more thing wrong to give your project a terrible grade. There is no excuse for losing points in this area. You might find fault with the base code (some say it was done by an intern, but that is putting it too harshly) and the project parameters (some would like to see a real Java Database Connectivity [JDBC] assignment), but don't throw away points by using odd indentation and unclear language in your comments.

It doesn't take a high IQ to do well in this portion of the assignment; you simply need to dedicate adequate time to writing clean code and comments.

Code Conventions of Java Programs

Programming in Java consists of writing source code for classes and placing fields and methods inside the class. In the same way that standard and consistent assembly lines make a glass factory productive, standards and consistent code lines make a class factory productive. This guideline makes sense in theory, but carrying it out in practice can be hard because people type whatever and wherever they please. At least in a factory, you have an assembly line that can enforce standards for most activities. With software, enforcing standards has been more difficult. Whether you are an advocate of standard and consistent code conventions or not, your evaluator will appreciate you following one style throughout your code.

Comments and Formatting

You are already familiar with comments, but be aware that the evaluator doesn't want to see too many nor too few. For example, commenting the closing brace is appropriate sometimes. Because Java is object-oriented, a lot of nesting goes on. Losing track of which block you are in is easy, so some gurus place a comment on the closing brace, simply mentioning the loop, method, or class the brace is completing. In small pieces of code, often this practice is not necessary, but in larger ones, it is helpful. You might consider the following a guide for whether to comment a closing brace: If there are more than 100 lines of code between braces or several block-defining brace pairs inside the outer pair, comment the outermost closing brace. When a Java program runs, it couldn't care less about style. However, often the evaluator is pressed for time because he has to pump out his own code, which places the task of grading your project at a low priority (Sun, of course, will deny this ever happens). Therefore, make grading as easy as possible for your overworked evaluator.

The better Integrated Development Environments (IDEs) support a rich set of code style preferences, such as different code layout options, naming conventions for classes, local variables, parameters, and so forth. Often they have a code formatter that reformats a file or a selected block of code according to your formatting settings. They can do even more by optimizing your code onscreen or during import by sorting things, removing unnecessary imports, and more. Be careful about the difference between the nicely formatted code you see in the IDE and what you get in a plain text editor (such as vi). For example, a typical misalignment happens when using the tab character, which might mean a different number of whitespaces, depending on the editor. Please, consider using spaces instead of the tab character because editors interpret tabs in various ways; for example, some convert a tab to four spaces, and others use eight spaces.

The simple practice of indenting brace locations has a major effect on the appearance of your code. Be consistent and use between four and eight spaces for each indent level, like so:

```
if()
{
    System.out.print("indented 4 spaces");
}
```

Avoid having all lines flush left, like this:

```
if(){
System.out.print("indented 4 spaces"); }
```

The Javadoc style recommended by Sun can be seen by using the reference at the end of this Appendix. These comments have a significant impact on your score. Although the individual component score for comments is small, the impression they make on the assessor is more important and will affect score overall. The following is an example method with a Javadoc comment:

```
/**
 * Returns a String object that is the customer's first name.
 * The ID argument must be an integer.
 * <p>
```

```
* This method always returns immediately, whether or not the
* customer exists.
*
* @param   ID    an integer giving the customer a unique identifier
* @return        the first name of the specified customer
*/
public String getFirstName(int ID)
{
    //method code
}
```

Convention Preferences

The following sections define the conventions Sun is looking for. There is some flexibility, but don't stray too far from these recommendations.

Names

Java programs have a lot of names (also called "identifiers"). The biggest goof I see in my student's code, and my earlier work, is lack of description. You don't have to write a sentence, but `getCustomerID()` is more descriptive than `getInt()`. This is how you should use descriptive names in your source code.

 In names, avoid acronyms and abbreviations unless they are already well known, such as "XML" or "JSP."

These are the most popular capitalizing conventions for identifiers:

➤ *Pascal*—The first letter of the identifier and the first letter of each subsequent concatenated word are capitalized. Name classes using the Pascal convention. A few examples are `Customer`, `NewCustomer`, and `PremiumCustomer`.

➤ *Camel*—The first letter of an identifier is lowercase, and the first letter of each subsequent concatenated word is capitalized. Name variables and methods using the camel convention. A few examples are `getFirstName()`, `isLocked()` and `myCollection`.

➤ *Uppercase*—All letters are in uppercase. Name constants using all uppercase letters. A few examples are `QUOTE`, `SPACE`, and `TAB` String constants.

➤ *Lowercase*—All letters are in lowercase. Name one-word variables and methods using all lowercase letters. Packages should be all lowercase as well. A few examples are com.mycompany.mypackage, first_name and remove().

Source Code and Class Files

Java source files always use the .java suffix. The filename is always the same as the class declaration name, including the name's letter case. The Customer class, for example, has a source filename of Customer.java and a compiled name of Customer.class.

Packages

Package naming has been influenced by the Internet. The prefix of a unique package name is always written in all-lowercase ASCII letters. Although this practice isn't necessary, you can use one of the top-level domain names (for example, com, edu, gov; consult World Wide Web Consortium "Web Naming and Address" page at http://www.w3.org/Addressing/), as in edu. vanguard.library. The idea is to eliminate the possibility of someone duplicating your package name, so using a top-level name gives you a better chance of having a unique package name.

Import Statements

Place your import statements at the top of the page, immediately after the package declaration. Try to be explicit in your import declarations and avoid using the wildcard character. When all the classes are listed in the import section, it clearly indicates what classes are used in the subsequent code.

Use explicit imports, such as **import a.b.ThisThing;**. Try to avoid implicit imports using the wildcard character, like so:

import a.b.*;

Classes

Class names should be mixed-case nouns, with the first letter of each word capitalized (for example, RandomAccessFile, not randomaccessfile). These names should be short, but still descriptive. For example, a class for addresses should be Address, not Addr.

Methods

Unlike classes, which have names that are a combination of nouns, methods use a combination of an action verb and noun. For example, the method to return the customer ID in a system should be getCustomerID(). There is a little debate here about combining the class name and method name. For example, which is better: Customer.getCustomerID() or Customer.getID()? I prefer the former, but whichever you use, stay consistent. Methods that return a Boolean value often begin with is, such as isDBLocked(). Regarding get/set syntax, start with get/set, then capitalize each subsequent word like so: getFirstName().

Fields, Variables, and Parameters

Fields (also known as "instance variables") and local variables should be declared at the beginning of the block. Use descriptive names that follow the camel case convention (see the definition in the "Names" section earlier in this chapter). Use descriptive nouns for parameters as well. In some cases, you can use short names, but describe the parameters in comments.

For example, in the following method declaration, the parameters are descriptive because the body of the method is long:

```
/**
 * Returns the customer name based on the ID.
 *
 * @param     customerID   the customer ID to filter.
 */
String getCustomerName(int customerID)
{       //many lines of code
        ...
}
```

However, for the following example, the parameter names are short because the method is short and easier to manipulate:

```
/**
 * Returns the sum.
 *
 * @param     x    the first number.
 * @param     y    the second number.
 */
String getSum(int x, int y)
{       //few lines of code
        return x + y;
}
```

Constants

Constants should be named with nouns as variables are, but should consist of all uppercase letters, as in MAX_VALUE. As you probably know, the compiler doesn't care which convention you use (except that you must retain an identifier's spelling and letter case throughout a program). However, it makes your intentions clear when you spell constants in uppercase letters (for example, this variable will not change its value, so don't try to assign a value to it).

Indenting

I wrestled with the placement of the opening brace for some time. All the source code in the SDK and most of the Java community place the opening brace immediately after the method signature, on the same line as the block declaration. The following is an example of this convention:

```
public class ClassCircularityError extends LinkageError {
    public ClassCircularityError(String s) {
    super(s);
    }
}
```

Here's another common indenting method:

```
public class ClassCircularityError extends LinkageError
{
    public ClassCircularityError(String s)
    {
    super(s);
    }
}
```

 Should braces be placed around a single statement used as the body of a loop or a conditional? Although the syntax allows you to do that, it is safer to use the braces. Using this convention eliminates the common mistake of attempting to add a second statement to the **if** construct and not having it execute due to the absence of braces. Also, use one line for short conditional or loop expressions when it fits for clarity, like this:

```
if (score == 100) { setGrade(name, "A");}
```

However, I prefer the opening and closing brace to be aligned vertically for readability. The advantage of placing the opening brace immediately after the block declaration is there are no wasted lines and many people are used to this style. However, it is hard to match a closing brace with an opening one.

I once conducted a test on these two styles. As an adjunct professor at Vanguard University, I get plenty of students who have never written or seen a line of code. I wrote two code samples on the board that were identical except for the placement of the opening braces and asked them which style they preferred to read. The students who were completely new to programming rarely picked the sample with a brace at the end of a block declaration. I agree with these students, so I place the opening brace on the next line, directly under the first letter of the block declaration above it. It doesn't matter which style you use, however, as long as you use it consistently.

Need to Know More?

 `http://java.sun.com/docs/codeconv/`—At this site, you can download "Code Conventions for the Java Programming Language."

 `http://java.sun.com/j2se/javadoc/writingdoccomments/`—At this site, you will see how to format good javadoc comments in your source code.

What's on the CD-ROM

In order to provide you with as much hands-on learning experience as possible before you take your Java 2 Developer Exam, we have included various software packages on the CD-ROM. We have not provided a testing engine that replicates a sample essay exam exactly as you will find on the Sun exam because one has not been developed—the Sun exam is a comprehensive survey of your knowledge that does not lend itself to multiple choice answers to questions. Therefore, we have included the following software to assist you in assembling a development and test environment.

The software packages you will find are:

> Java 2 Platform, Standard Edition Software Development Kit (SDK) 1.4.2 for Windows, Linux (glibc6), and Solaris
>
> Ant
>
> JUnit
>
> ArgoUML

Also included on the CD-ROM is the complete source code for the sample application assignment that is developed throughout the book.

An Exclusive Electronic Version of the Text

The CD-ROM also contains an electronic PDF version of this book. This electronic version comes complete with all figures as they appear in the book. You can use Acrobat's handy search capability for study and review purposes.

Glossary

abstract class

A class that includes one or more methods declared as abstract (methods that lack definitions). Abstract classes can't be instantiated; they must be subclassed. Those subclasses can then be instantiated. The idea is that a subclass or concrete class provides definitions for abstract methods. Note that abstract classes can implement methods, and you can call static methods of an abstract class.

ActionListener

This interface, which defines an `actionPerformed(ActionEvent e)` method, is often used in Swing-based GUI applications that handle the events generated when a user clicks a button or types in a text box.

algorithm

Algorithms are small Java procedures that solve recurring problems. An algorithm is like a cooking recipe in which the general steps are stated, but the minor details are omitted.

anonymous class

This class, called "anonymous" because it has no name, is just like a regular class except that it's embedded in a parent class and is declared and instantiated in one statement.

Ant

An open-source Java-based Make tool provided by Jakarta. Many developers and certification candidates use Ant to replace javac because it takes care of peripheral chores, such as creating directories, cleaning up after itself, and creating javadoc documents.

API (application programming interface)
The set of public methods a class or package makes available to other programs.

application
An application is a computer program designed for a specific task or purpose. For the SCJD certification, it's the Java program that satisfies the requirements of the certification instructions. It must run on Windows and Solaris equally well, so test it on both platforms.

archive
In the context of JAR files, an archive is the collection of all your project's files in one *.jar file. That is how you must submit your solution. Note that your archive does not have to be compressed. Web clients are packaged in Web Application Archives (WAR) files. A J2EE application with all its modules is delivered in an Enterprise Archive (EAR) file. Notice that WAR and EAR files are standard Java Archive (JAR) files with a .war or .ear extension.

ArgoUML
A free UML package, written in Java, that enables you to draw UML diagrams and then generate the skeleton code. Please see http://argouml.tigris.org/ for more details.

ASCII (American Standard Code of Information Interchange)
ASCII is a system for representing characters as numbers. Representing text with standardized ASCII codes simplifies inter-platform data transfer.

assert
A new feature in J2SE 1.4, used to test a condition expected to be true. If that condition is false, it probably indicates a problem in your program. One cool feature is the ability to ignore asserts with a compiler flag. Asserts are inspired by Bertrand Meyer's Eiffel, a statically typed, object-oriented language.

asynchronous
The Internet handles many types of data transfer. In asynchronous applications, message packets can travel between computers without being required to arrive in the correct order. For example, TCP/IP takes care of reordering the packets after they all arrive and resending a packet if one gets lost. Notice that the Internet handles variations in packet transfer, but it's an overgeneralization to say that the "Internet" is asynchronous. It's the application that's synchronous or asynchronous.

atomic
A piece of data in your database is called "atomic" if it's not duplicated elsewhere.

AWT (Abstract Windowing Toolkit)

This toolkit is Sun's set of classes for writing platform-independent GUI code. Much of AWT uses the native GUI system, but Swing components enable you to maintain the same look and feel on many different platforms. Note that Swing, not AWT, should be used for the certification project.

binary

A numbering scheme based on the values 0 and 1. In the context of this exam, it's a file format in which data is encoded as a sequence of bits, not a sequence of text characters. The database file for this certification project is in binary format, not ASCII format.

break

This Java keyword causes program execution to stop in that particular block or to continue by jumping from the block tagged with break to the beginning of the next block. Contrast this behavior with that of the continue keyword. *See also* continue.

build

This process is synonymous with compiling. A build can be more than just compiling, however. It can include package and deploy code to certain directories. The certification project is just large enough to justify using Jakarta Ant to build it. Using Ant makes it easy to compile everything whenever needed. *See also* Ant.

catch

This Java keyword is used to "catch" exceptions. When that happens, execution jumps from the preceding try block to the catch block and the code in this block executes. *See also* finally.

checked exception

An exception that requires supplying explicit handling code for the compiler. *See also* unchecked exception.

classpath

This environment variable enables you to compile from any directory because the system tells the Java compiler where to look for imported class files.

coding conventions

A set of guidelines specifying how to format your code, especially where to break lines, how to use whitespace, and where to place the block brace. The evaluators expect to see you using Sun's preferences for coding conventions. Because the look of your code affects your score, adhere to Sun's preferences.

Collection

A Collection is a container object that holds multiple elements. It is used to contain data structures, such as HashMap and Set. The two places you are most likely to use a Collection are in the GUI—for example, to track user seat requests, and to set up a locking mechanism to track database locks.

continue

Unlike the break keyword, the continue keyword causes program execution to jump from this keyword to the next innermost loop execution and start again. If you add a label, program execution will jump to that block or perhaps a few levels outward from the nested loop continue is in. *See also* break.

Controller

In the Model-View-Controller design pattern, the Controller is the mediator between user input (for example, view, GUI) and the model (the database). *See also* MVC (Model-View-Controller) pattern.

CVS (Concurrent Versions System)

CVS is a version control utility. Some candidates use this popular tool to track changes to the certification source code and make backup copies (http://www.cvshome.org).

daemon thread

A low-priority thread, such as the one the garbage collector uses; the Java Virtual Machine (JVM) exits when the only threads running are all daemon threads.

database server

A standalone computer program that holds and manages a set of data as a single system—for example, when locating a requested record. Part of your certification project should enhance the database code supplied with the assignment download. With your

changes, you will then have a database server that your program can talk to across a network connection.

deadlock

A situation in which two or more Thread objects are stuck because each thread holds a resource the other needs. *See also* thread.

Decorator pattern

This design pattern adds functionality by composition instead of by subclassing. If you extend the Sun-supplied classes, you will most likely use this pattern; for example, I used it to enhance the Sun-provided database classes. *See also* design pattern.

design pattern

A recurring solution to common problems. Design patterns are defined in a way that makes it easy for others to use the same solution. The SCJD certification requires that you use several patterns, including MVC and Value Object. *See also* MVC (Model-View-Controller) pattern.

deprecated

Any Java declaration, such as a class or method, that will not be updated in future releases and so should be avoided in new code. Sun has tagged many methods as deprecated, so you shouldn't use them because they will be removed in a future release. Your assignment download includes a few deprecated methods, and part of your grade is based on how you handle them.

DOM (Document Object Model)

DOM provides a language and platform-neutral interface for accessing and editing the style, structure, and content of documents.

error (java.lang.Error)

An error occurs when something has interrupted the flow of execution and the JVM cannot recover, so the program ends. The java.lang.Error class, or one of its subclasses, is thrown when the JVM realizes it is about to crash. (This is different from exceptions, from which your application can recover.) At least you usually have a chance to crash gracefully. *See also* exception (java.lang.Exception).

exception (java.lang.Exception)

Sun defines an exception as "an event that occurs during the execution of a program that disrupts the normal flow of instructions." Checked exceptions are those you specify so that the JVM will look for them; they are declared in the method declaration or included in the try-catch construction. The java.lang.Exception class, or one of its subclasses, is thrown when an error happens, but not an error severe enough to crash the JVM. The try-catch block was designed with exceptions in mind. Runtime exceptions are not thrown because the runtime system detects them; they include arithmetic exceptions (such as dividing by zero), pointer exceptions (for example, accessing an object through a null reference),

and indexing exceptions (such as accessing an array element that doesn't exist). The designers of the Java language felt that because runtime exceptions can happen anywhere, attempting to catch them wasn't worth the extra effort, as it would mean writing too many try-catch blocks. *See also* error (java.lang.Error).

Extreme Programming

A software development methodology, best suited for small projects, that emphasizes iteration, speed, and more customer involvement. It includes features such as pair programming, minimum documentation, emphasis on testing, and more. For more information, see http://www.xprogramming.org. *See also* RUP (Rational Unified Process) and waterfall methodology.

finally

The finally clause runs after all other try-catch processing is completed, whether or not an exception is thrown or a break or continue are issued. However, if a catch clause calls System.exit(), the finally clause is ignored. Because the finally block in a try-catch-finally statement is guaranteed to run, it is used for cleanup chores, such as database connection termination. *See also* catch.

FlowLayout

This easy-to-use Swing layout manager arranges subcomponents in rows. *See also* layout manager and Swing.

GridBagLayout

This is the most powerful layout manager in Swing and gives you the most control over placement of subcomponents. You can do control margins, set justification to one side or corner of a cell, and more. *See also* layout manager and Swing.

GUI (graphical user interface)

The GUI is the visible window, with items such as buttons and menus, presented to the user. It accounts for a big part of your score, so make sure to put some thought into how you design your project's windowing scheme.

HTML (Hypertext Markup Language)

HTML is the markup language that determines how a browser renders a Web page. It is defined and maintained by the World Wide Web Consortium (W3C). See `http://www.w3.org/TR/xhtml1` for information on XHTML and `http://www.w3.org/TR/html4` for the latest HTML standard. Remember, you must provide a user help file in HTML for your certification project.

IDE (Integrated Development Environment)

The IDE is the software development tool that helps developers write language code. Whether you use one to build your project is not important, as long as *no* vendor-dependent libraries are added. The Sun evaluator will fail you if these rogue libraries are part of your source code.

interface

An interface defines a new reference type with members that are classes, interfaces, constants, and abstract methods (that is, the methods have no implementations). You will likely need to include at least one interface with your certification project. Remember, an interface has no detailed implementation of methods; it is just a list of method signatures. I used an interface in the Remote Method Invocation (RMI) portion of my project so that the GUI didn't know, or care, where the data came from. That means there was no local/remote-specific code in my GUI, which improved the design.

interrupted

A thread interruption occurs when a thread in a `sleep` or `wait` state is activated again.

InterruptedException

`InterruptedException` is a class that is thrown when a thread is interrupted, causing the class to handle the exception. An appropriate `catch` block must be available for this to function.

J2EE (Java 2 Enterprise Edition)

The collection of Java standard library classes plus extensions designed for supporting multitier Web applications. Note that J2EE is a superset of J2SE.

J2ME (Java 2 Micro Edition)
Sun's collection of Java classes designed to support applications that run on relatively small systems, such as cell phones and Palm Pilots.

J2SE (Java 2 Standard Edition)
The acronym J2SE stands for the Java 2 Platform, Standard Edition. It's the Java edition you use for developing your certification project.

Jakarta
This project managed by the Apache Software Foundation produces many excellent, open source, Java-based products for developers. Some current Java projects are Alexandria, Ant, Cactus, Struts, and Tomcat. See http://jakarta. apache.org for more information.

JAR (Java Archive)
A collection of application files and resources combined into a single file. Your solution must be bundled in one JAR file. *See also* archive.

javadoc
This Sun-provided utility automatically generates documentation of your classes from your source code comments. You are graded on how well your source code is commented in the correct format, and javadoc can process your code comments into Web pages of documentation.

JAXP (Java API for XML Processing)
This API specification from Sun for XML libraries is now included in J2SE 1.4.

JDK (Java Development Kit)
See SDK (Software Development Kit).

JEditorPane
This Swing component can be used to render HTML or RTF (Rich Text Format). Using it is simpler than the Sun documentation suggests. You don't need to get involved with document structure. You can simply feed raw HTML text to JEditorPane. If you don't embed the JEditorPane component in a ScrollPane, however, I've noticed the screen display twitches (a minor annoyance up to J2SE 1.4, but it will no doubt be fixed in a later version).

JFC (Java Foundation Classes)
A set of Java class libraries used for building the graphical user interface (GUI). The current version in J2SE is commonly called Swing. *See also* Swing.

JUnit
This testing utility provides a framework for writing and running automated tests.

JVM (Java Virtual Machine)

An abstract computing machine that has an instruction set and uses various memory areas responsible for Java's cross-platform delivery, the small size of its compiled code, and its ability to protect users from malicious programs. This part of the Java Runtime Environment interprets Java bytecode and connects your program to system resources.

layout manager

This Java feature enables you to fine-tune the size and position of components in your GUI. There are several types of layout managers, such as FlowLayout and GridBagLayout, used for Swing-based GUIs. *See also* Swing.

Listener

This object enables you to "listen" to user input. If an object is registered as a listener, a certain method is called whenever the associated event occurs. The target is the component to which the listener is attached. This is how you respond to, for example, user mouse clicks.

logging

This process captures information from an application and records it in a file. Logging is optional. Normally, it is an excellent way to help debug your applications. If you use logging in your certification project, however, avoid confusing the evaluator with this extra functionality and remove logging features before submitting your project.

manifest

A file (added to a JAR file) containing information about other files in a JAR. *See also* JAR (Java Archive).

Model

In the Model-View-Controller design pattern, the Model portion acts as the data store or database. *See also* MVC (Model-View-Controller) pattern.

multithreading

Multithreading occurs when more than one thread is spawned simultaneously by a program. Part of your certification assignment requires designing your project to handle multiple simultaneous users, so your application will have several independent paths of execution.

MVC (Model-View-Controller) pattern

The MVC pattern partitions an application, or even just a piece of it, into three parts: the Model, the View, and the Controller. The MVC pattern is used by Swing. *See also* Controller, Model, and View.

notify

This method in the Object class allows a waiting thread to become runnable. The JVM scheduling mechanism decides, unpredictably, when that next thread will run.

notifyAll

A method of the `Object` class that wakes up all threads waiting on the object in question. When this happens, the newly awakened threads compete for the lock on that object. When one of those threads gets a lock on the object, the others go back to waiting. Compare how `notifyAll` wakes up all threads with the `Object` class's `notify` method, which arbitrarily wakes up only one of the threads waiting on this object. This method is just like the `notify` method, except that *all* waiting threads become runnable.

Observable

This class in the `java.util` package has methods for adding and notifying objects in the Observer-Observable design pattern. The `Observable` class is the one that contains data; the `Observer` class is the one waiting for an event.

Observer

This object expects to be notified when an event it has registered for happens. Note that `Observable` and `Observer` are interfaces that any class can implement. Your application's GUI, based on Swing's event model, will use the Observer-Observable design pattern.

overloading

Declaring two or more methods with the same name but different signatures. Your solution can overload some of the database methods that have the same name, but the parameter lists are different.

overriding

Declaring a method in a subclass with the same signature of a method in the superclass. If you subclass the Sun-supplied classes instead of modifying them, you might want to override deprecated methods in the supplied classes with methods in your subclass.

package

A set of classes that share the same file directory, which allows for a naming system (a prefix for classes) to help prevent name conflicts. Programs are organized as sets of packages. You must organize your project's classes into a clear structure so that the evaluator can easily see what you are doing.

priority

This numeric value from 1 to 10 dictates in what order Java services threads. You can change a thread's priority value.

regular expression

A powerful syntax for searching for and replacing patterns within strings. New to J2SE 1.4, you can now search or tokenize, for example, search criteria with a string pattern based on Perl regexes. A regular expression is one of more powerful features that have been added to Java.

RMI (Remote Method Invocation)

A system that allows one class to call methods of another class when the classes are distributed over a network. The remote Java object can be on another JVM and even on a different host. You can implement your network requirement with RMI, which enables the database server portion of your application to communicate with the client portion. Your client calls methods on your remote database server—for example, to perform a search—and receives the result to display in a JTable component. *See also* socket.

RUP (Rational Unified Process)

This software development methodology is a flexible software development process platform characterized by frequent iteration, in which you can repeat steps often to incrementally complete work. *See also* Extreme Programming and waterfall methodology.

SAX (Simple API for XML)

This standard is one of the first widely adopted standards for parsing XML files; it performs event-driven parsing of XML files.

SDK (Software Development Kit)

This toolkit (which you can download from Sun) contains all the developer utilities, libraries, and documentation you need to develop your certification project. Sun used to call it the Java Development Kit (JDK).

serialization

Object serialization encodes objects into a stream of bytes and the reverse—reconstructing the object from the stream. Serialization persists for communication via sockets or RMI. Whether you use RMI or sockets, you will probably serialize the object containing the results of a database search so that the object can be sent from the server to the client.

socket

A single socket is one endpoint of a two-way communication link between two programs running on the network. Sockets enable you to send raw streams of bytes back and forth between your client and server. If you don't use RMI, you will use sockets for your application's network functionality. *See also* RMI (Remote Method Invocation).

StringTokenizer

This class enables you to parse strings easily fashioned by breaking strings along delimiters. I used this class to parse the criteria string in my solution because it was the easiest way to do so. Regular expressions are actually a more powerful approach, but some candidates go the easy route and use StringTokenizer. *See also* regular expression.

subclass

If you extend the Sun-provided classes, the new classes are called subclasses of the original class.

superclass

The parent class of another class, which can inherit methods and fields from the superclass. If you extend the Sun-provided classes, the new classes are called subclasses of the original class, which is called the superclass.

Swing

Swing replaced AWT as Java's UI component library and added more graphics capabilities to J2SE. These new features include better text boxes, new ways to group components on panes, new grid tables, and more. Your solution must use Sun's Swing components, which replace the older AWT components. In particular, you must include the JTable grid class. In your project, you'll probably use a dozen Swing components in all. *See also* AWT (Abstract Windowing Toolkit).

synchronized

Threads are said to be synchronized when only one thread at a time can access a method or block; it is guaranteed to be thread safe. This Java keyword causes the JVM monitor to prevent two simultaneous threads from running a block of code. In your certification project, you must provide functionality that can handle simultaneous users. Note that some methods in the code you download from Sun are synchronized.

TCP/IP (Transmission Control Protocol/Internet Protocol)

The Internet uses this protocol to transfer packets. If you place your user help file on the Internet (that is, if you don't include it in your JAR file), your application will use TCP/IP to retrieve it. TCP/IP also has implications for addressing and routing. To retrieve your project's HTML help file, you use HTTP, a protocol that runs on top of TCP/IP.

thread

A thread is a single sequence of program execution. When a program runs, one or more threads are created. When the threads die, your program stops running. The `java.lang.Thread` class is the way Java encapsulates one thread in the JVM.

Throwable (java.lang.Throwable)

The superclass of all errors and exceptions in the Java language. `Error` and `Exception`, two subclasses of `Throwable`, indicate an interruption to normal program execution.

try

A `try` statement executes a block of code in which, if an exception or error is thrown, control jumps to the first `catch` clause declared with the same type as the error or exception. *See also* `catch` and `finally`.

UML (Universal Modeling Language)

A language for specifying, visualizing, and documenting software artifacts. I encourage you to use UML when designing your solution. Also, when you write the design choices document, you can include UML diagrams as part of a Microsoft Word document.

unchecked exception

Exceptions that occur within the Java runtime system and are not checked by the compiler where these exceptions are caught or specified. These exceptions include arithmetic exceptions, pointer exceptions, and indexing exceptions. *See also* checked exception.

user thread

Any thread that is not a daemon thread. Your solution must handle user threads directly; the JVM handles daemon threads. *See also* daemon thread.

View

This portion of the MVC design pattern is the GUI of your project. The View portion passes user input to the Controller portion. Swing technology already uses the MVC pattern, so be mindful of how you design the View portion. *See also* Controller, Model, and MVC (Model-View-Controller) pattern.

wait

This method in the Object class causes a thread to become inactive and be added to the list of threads waiting for access to that object.

waterfall methodology

This methodology describes the classic approach of building software, including definition (for example, defining requirements), design, implementation, and maintenance phases. *See also* Extreme Programming and RUP (Rational Unified Process).

XML (Extensible Markup Language)

A collection of tags like HTML (a single, predefined markup language). However, XML is more flexible and often used as a meta-language when it describes another language. This language, although surprisingly simple in its structure, gets its power from widespread adoption. It is a W3C-proposed recommendation based on Standard Generalized Markup Language (SGML). This book explains one use of XML for your configuration file, if you choose to implement one.

Index

Symbols

@author Javadoc tag, 71
@deprecated Javadoc tag, 71
@exception Javadoc tag, 71
@param Javadoc tag, 71
@return Javadoc tag, 71
@see Javadoc tag, 71
@serial Javadoc tag, 72
@serialData Javadoc tag, 72
@serialField Javadoc tag, 72
@throws Javadoc tag, 72
@version Javadoc tag, 72
{@docRoot} Javadoc tag, 71
{@inheritDoc} Javadoc tag, 71
{@linkplain} Javadoc tag, 71
{@link} Javadoc tag, 71
{@value} Javadoc tag, 72
<contains> selector (Ant), 335
<date> selector (Ant), 335
<depend> selector (Ant), 336
<depth> selector (Ant), 336
<filename> selector (Ant), 336
<size> selector (Ant), 336

A

abstract classes, 148-149
    characteristics, 156
    declaring, 150
    interface/abstract class combinations,
        157
    subclasses, 150-151
    versus abstract methods, 152
    versus interfaces, 152, 156
abstract methods versus abstract classes,
    152
acceptance (software project manage-
    ment), 12
acceptance testing, 315
activity diagrams (UML), 360
Adapter design patterns (software), 289,
    302
adding
    labels to frames, 256
    RMI to applications, 214-215
Aggregate Entity design patterns
    (software), 294
allotted test times (essay exams), 345

documents
  design documents
    design choices documents, 88, 373-375
    detail design documents, 369-370
    SRS documents, 367-369
    submission review documents, 371-373
    unit testing documents, 370-371
  requirements documents (systems analysis), 80, 83-84
  SDD documents (systems analysis), 85-88
downloading Programming Assignment, 5-6
Dynamic Ports (port numbers), 199

E

environment errors, 314
error handlers, 128-129
error messages, storing, 129
error testing section (DESIGN CHOICES.TXT file components), 65
errors, 320-322
  business errors, 314
  environment errors, 314
  java.awt.AWTError, 317
  java.lang.LinkageError, 317
  java.lang.ThreadDeath, 317
  java.lang.VirtualMachineError, 317
  java.xml.parsers.FactoryConfiguration Error, 317
  logic errors, 314
  project errors, 314
  requirement errors, 314
  runtime errors, 314
  semantic errors, 313
  syntax errors, 313
  versus exceptions, 312, 316
essay exams
  allotted test time, 345
  average test times, 345
  cost of, 345
  difficulty level, 345

exam location, 345
exam number, 345
expiration dates, 345
number of questions, 345
passing scores, 346
percentage of total score, 345
preparation, 347
preparation time, 345
prerequisites, 346
purposes, 344
questions
  sample questions, 349-350
  style of, 346-348
response guidelines, 348, 351
results, receiving, 346
sample essay exam answers, 351-355
sample exam, 347-348
  answers, 351-355
  questions, 349-350
viewing grades, 346
event handling, database searches, 261-262
exams
  assignment schedule, 7-8
  automatic failures, 2, 13
  deliverables, 31-32
    database.bin database file, 33
    deprecated classes, 35
    DESIGN CHOICES.TXT file, 33-35
    javadoc documentation, 34
    README.TXT file, 33-35
    source code files, 33
    user help documentation, 34
  directory structures, 33
  essay exams
    allotted test time, 345
    answers, 351-355
    average test times, 345
    cost of, 345
    difficulty level, 345
    exam location, 345
    exam number, 345
    expiration dates, 345

execution instructions section
(README.TXT file components),
56-57
expiration dates (essay exams), 345
expressions
regular expressions, 142
search criteria handlers, creating,
143-144
extending
abstract classes via subclasses, 151
interfaces, 154
Extreme Programming methodologies, 4
Extreme Programming software development methodology, 4

F

field header Javadoc code comments,
73-74
fields, naming, 382
file header Javadoc code comments, 72
file listings section (README.TXT file
components), 58-59
File Mappers task (Ant), 335
File/Database Structures component
(SDD documents), 87
FileHandler (error handler), 129
FileList task (Ant), 335
<filename> selector (Ant), 336
files
binary database files, 33
build.xml files, 334-336
compiling, 333
data files, 58
database files, displaying via JTables,
270-273
database.bin database file, certification
exam deliverables, 33
DESIGN CHOICES.TXT file
certification exam deliverables,
33-35
certification exam objectives, 31
coding standards section, 64
data class implementation section,
63

data class modification section, 61
design clarity/maintainability
section, 64
design decisions summary section,
61
design patterns section, 65-67
documentation section, 65
error testing section, 65
exception handling section, 65
execution instructions section, 64
LockManager class section, 62
remote connection mode section,
62-63
search method implementation
section, 63
table of contents section, 60
user interface design section, 64
writing, 59-66
HTML files, displaying, 259-260
JAR files, 331-332
organizing (code structures), 49
README.TXT file, 13
certification exam deliverables,
33-35
data file location section, 58
design choices document section,
58
execution instructions section,
56-57
file listings section, 58-59
introduction section, 55
quick start section, 55
SDK version and platform section,
55-56
table of contents section, 54
user documentation Web pages
section, 59
writing, 53-59
scjd.xml files, 334
source code files, 33
source files, 381
structures, 330-331
user help files
Javadoc code comments, 70-74
writing, 67-70

hierarchies, 312
HTML files, displaying, 259-260

IBM DB2, 124
identifiers, 41, 380
IdentityHashMap class, 141-142
if else-if else statements, 45
if statements, 45, 138
if-else statements, 45
implementing, interfaces inherited from interfaces, 154-155
import statements
    GUI design, 229
    naming, 381
indenting braces, 383
InetAddress objects, interrogating URL, 184-189
inherited_method(), abstract classes, 150-151
initializing
    applications via XML formatted configuration files, 132-133
    GUI swing components, 236-239
INSERT INTO statements (SQL), 122
installation (software project management), 12
installing
    Ant, 333
    SDK, 23-25
instance variables. *See* fields
integration testing, 339
interfaces, 149
    API, 148
    characteristics, 156
    Collection interface, 153-154
    DatabaseInterface (Database class), 235
    DatabaseInterface class, 101-104
    extending, 154
    implemented interfaces inheriting from interfaces, 154-155
    interface/abstract class combinations, 157

remote interfaces, writing, 217
Set interface, 154
SortedSet interface, 154
text (user manuals), 14
versus abstract classes, 152, 156
versus concrete classes, 152
Internal Data Structures component (SDD documents), 87
interrogating URL objects via URL classes, 190-193
Introduction (Software Management Project Plans), 82
introduction section (README.TXT file components), 55
IP addresses, 198
IRL (Insert Row Locking), 93
ISO 12207 software engineering standard, 80-81

J

J2EE (Java 2 Enterprise Edition), 21
J2ME (Java 2 Micro Edition), 20
J2SE (Java 3 Standard Edition), 21
jar (SDK), 22
JAR files, 331-332
java.awt.AWTError errors, 317
java.awt.AWTException exceptions, 317
java.io.IOException exceptions, 318
java.lang.ClassNotFoundException exceptions, 317
java.lang.IllegalAccessException exceptions, 318
java.lang.InstantiationException exceptions, 318
java.lang.InterruptedException exceptions, 318
java.lang.LinkageError errors, 317
java.lang.RuntimeException exceptions, 318
java.lang.ThreadDeath errors, 317
java.lang.VirtualMachineError errors, 317

logins, CertManager, 5
lookup (string name) method, 224
loops, URL objects, 198
Lowercase naming conventions, 381

M

MalformedURLException exception,
190, 195
Managerial Process (Software
Management Project Plans), 82
managing
software, 3
acceptance, 12
assignment schedule, 7-8
CBSE methodologies, 4
concept development, 6
COTS methodologies, 4
detail design, 10-11
documentation, 12
documentation, design choice
documents, 14
documentation, Javadoc comments, 12
documentation, README.TXT
files, 13
documentation, user manuals, 13-
14
downloading Programming
Assignment, 5-6
functional design, 10
installation, 12
packaging, 14-15
programming design, 11
requirements definition, 8-9
RUP methodologies, 4
software development life cycle,
80-81
software requirements analysis, 81
software maintenance, 15
software requirements analysis, 81
submission, 14-17
testing, 11-12
waterfall methodologies, 4

MemoryHandler (error handlers), 129
menu bars, GUI design, 239-240
menu handlers, GUI design, 245-247
menus, 257
messages
application messages (user manuals),
14
error messages, storing, 129
filtering, 131
log levels, assigning, 128
log messages, filtering, 128
logging, 128
Metal theme, 253
method header Javadoc code comments,
73
methodologies
CBSE (Component Based Software
Engineering) software development
methodology, 4
COTS (Commercial Off-The-Shelf)
software development methodology,
4
Extreme Programming methodologies, 4
Extreme Programming software
development methodology, 4
RUP (Rational Unified Process) software development methodology, 4
software development methodologies,
4
waterfall software development
methodology, 4
methods
abstract classes, 148-149
characteristics, 156
declaring, 150
extending via subclasses, 151
interface/abstract class combinations, 157
subclasses, 150
versus abstract methods, 152
versus interfaces, 152, 156
API, 148
application main methods, GUI
design, 233-234
bind method, 223

X – Z

Sun Microsystems, Inc.

Binary Code License Agreement

READ THE TERMS OF THIS AGREEMENT AND ANY PROVIDED SUPPLEMENTAL LICENSE TERMS (COLLECTIVELY "AGREEMENT") CAREFULLY BEFORE OPENING THE SOFTWARE MEDIA PACKAGE. BY OPENING THE SOFTWARE MEDIA PACKAGE, YOU AGREE TO THE TERMS OF THIS AGREEMENT. IF YOU ARE ACCESSING THE SOFTWARE ELECTRONICALLY, INDICATE YOUR ACCEPTANCE OF THESE TERMS BY SELECTING THE "ACCEPT" BUTTON AT THE END OF THIS AGREEMENT. IF YOU DO NOT AGREE TO ALL THESE TERMS, PROMPTLY RETURN THE UNUSED SOFTWARE TO YOUR PLACE OF PURCHASE FOR A REFUND OR, IF THE SOFTWARE IS ACCESSED ELECTRONICALLY, SELECT THE "DECLINE" BUTTON AT THE END OF THIS AGREEMENT.

1. **LICENSE TO USE.** Sun grants you a non-exclusive and non-transferable license for the internal use only of the accompanying software and documentation and any error corrections provided by Sun (collectively "Software"), by the number of users and the class of computer hardware for which the corresponding fee has been paid.

2. **RESTRICTIONS.** Software is confidential and copyrighted. Title to Software and all associated intellectual property rights is retained by Sun and/or its licensors. Except as specifically authorized in any Supplemental License Terms, you may not make copies of Software, other than a single copy of Software for archival purposes. Unless enforcement is prohibited by applicable law, you may not modify, decompile, or reverse engineer Software. Licensee acknowledges that Licensed Software is not designed or intended for use in the design, construction, operation or maintenance of any nuclear facility. Sun Microsystems, Inc. disclaims any express or implied warranty of fitness for such uses. No right, title or interest in or to any trademark, service mark, logo or trade name of Sun or its licensors is granted under this Agreement.

3. **LIMITED WARRANTY.** Sun warrants to you that for a period of ninety (90) days from the date of purchase, as evidenced by a copy of the receipt, the media on which Software is furnished (if any) will be free of defects in materials and workmanship under normal use. Except

for the foregoing, Software is provided "AS IS". Your exclusive remedy and Sun's entire liability under this limited warranty will be at Sun's option to replace Software media or refund the fee paid for Software.

4. **DISCLAIMER OF WARRANTY.** UNLESS SPECIFIED IN THIS AGREEMENT, ALL EXPRESS OR IMPLIED CONDITIONS, REPRESENTATIONS AND WARRANTIES, INCLUDING ANY IMPLIED WARRANTY OF MERCHANTABILITY, FITNESS FOR A PARTICULAR PURPOSE OR NON-INFRINGEMENT ARE DISCLAIMED, EXCEPT TO THE EXTENT THAT THESE DISCLAIMERS ARE HELD TO BE LEGALLY INVALID.

5. **LIMITATION OF LIABILITY.** TO THE EXTENT NOT PRO-HIBITED BY LAW, IN NO EVENT WILL SUN OR ITS LICEN-SORS BE LIABLE FOR ANY LOST REVENUE, PROFIT OR DATA, OR FOR SPECIAL, INDIRECT, CONSEQUENTIAL, INCIDENTAL OR PUNITIVE DAMAGES, HOWEVER CAUSED REGARDLESS OF THE THEORY OF LIABILITY, ARISING OUT OF OR RELATED TO THE USE OF OR INABILITY TO USE SOFTWARE, EVEN IF SUN HAS BEEN ADVISED OF THE POSSIBILITY OF SUCH DAMAGES. In no event will Sun's liability to you, whether in contract, tort (including negligence), or otherwise, exceed the amount paid by you for Software under this Agreement. The foregoing limitations will apply even if the above stated warranty fails of its essential purpose.

6. **Termination.** This Agreement is effective until terminated. You may terminate this Agreement at any time by destroying all copies of Software. This Agreement will terminate immediately without notice from Sun if you fail to comply with any provision of this Agreement. Upon Termination, you must destroy all copies of Software.

7. **Export Regulations.** All Software and technical data delivered under this Agreement are subject to US export control laws and may be subject to export or import regulations in other countries. You agree to comply strictly with all such laws and regulations and acknowledge that you have the responsibility to obtain such licenses to export, re-export, or import as may be required after delivery to you.

8. **U.S. Government Restricted Rights.** If Software is being acquired by or on behalf of the U.S. Government or by a U.S. Government prime contractor or subcontractor (at any tier), then the Government's rights in Software and accompanying documentation will be only as set forth in this Agreement; this is in accordance with 48 CFR 227.7201

through 227.7202-4 (for Department of Defense (DOD) acquisitions) and with 48 CFR 2.101 and 12.212 (for non-DOD acquisitions).

9. **Governing Law.** Any action related to this Agreement will be governed by California law and controlling U.S. federal law. No choice of law rules of any jurisdiction will apply.

10. **Severability.** If any provision of this Agreement is held to be unenforceable, this Agreement will remain in effect with the provision omitted, unless omission would frustrate the intent of the parties, in which case this Agreement will immediately terminate.

11. **Integration.** This Agreement is the entire agreement between you and Sun relating to its subject matter. It supersedes all prior or contemporaneous oral or written communications, proposals, representations and warranties and prevails over any conflicting or additional terms of any quote, order, acknowledgment, or other communication between the parties relating to its subject matter during the term of this Agreement. No modification of this Agreement will be binding, unless in writing and signed by an authorized representative of each party.

JAVA™ 2 SOFTWARE DEVELOPMENT KIT (J2SDK), STANDARD

EDITION, VERSION 1.4.1_X

SUPPLEMENTAL LICENSE TERMS

These supplemental license terms ("Supplemental Terms") add to or modify the terms of the Binary Code License Agreement (collectively, the "Agreement"). Capitalized terms not defined in these Supplemental Terms shall have the same meanings ascribed to them in the Binary Code License Agreement. These Supplemental Terms shall supersede any inconsistent or conflicting terms in the Binary Code License Agreement, or in any license contained within the Software.

1. **Software Internal Use and Development License Grant.** Subject to the terms and conditions of this Agreement, including, but not limited to Section 4 (Java Technology Restrictions) of these Supplemental

Terms, Sun grants you a non-exclusive, non-transferable, limited license without fees to reproduce internally and use internally the binary form of the Software complete and unmodified for the sole purpose of designing, developing, testing, and running your Java applets and applications intended to run on Java-enabled general purpose desktop computers and servers ("Programs").

2. **License to Distribute Software.** Subject to the terms and conditions of this Agreement, including, but not limited to Section 4 (Java Technology Restrictions) of these Supplemental Terms, Sun grants you a non-exclusive, non-transferable, limited license without fees to reproduce and distribute the Software, provided that (i) you distribute the Software complete and unmodified (unless otherwise specified in the applicable README file) and only bundled as part of, and for the sole purpose of running, your Programs, (ii) the Programs add significant and primary functionality to the Software, (iii) you do not distribute additional software intended to replace any component(s) of the Software (unless otherwise specified in the applicable README file), (iv) you do not remove or alter any proprietary legends or notices contained in the Software, (v) you only distribute the Software subject to a license agreement that protects Sun's interests consistent with the terms contained in this Agreement, and (vi) you agree to defend and indemnify Sun and its licensors from and against any damages, costs, liabilities, settlement amounts and/or expenses (including attorneys' fees) incurred in connection with any claim, lawsuit or action by any third party that arises or results from the use or distribution of any and all Programs and/or Software. (vi) include the following statement as part of product documentation (whether hard copy or electronic), as a part of a copyright page or proprietary rights notice page, in an "About" box or in any other form reasonably designed to make the statement visible to users of the Software: "This product includes code licensed from RSA Security, Inc.", and (vii) include the statement, "Some portions licensed from IBM are available at <http://oss.soft-ware.ibm.com/icu4j/>".

3. **License to Distribute Redistributables.** Subject to the terms and conditions of this Agreement, including but not limited to Section 4 (Java Technology Restrictions) of these Supplemental Terms, Sun grants you a non-exclusive, non-transferable, limited license without fees to reproduce and distribute those files specifically identified as redistributable in the Software "README" file ("Redistributables") provided that: (i) you distribute the Redistributables complete and unmodified (unless otherwise specified in the applicable README

file), and only bundled as part of Programs, (ii) you do not distribute additional software intended to supersede any component(s) of the Redistributables (unless otherwise specified in the applicable README file), (iii) you do not remove or alter any proprietary legends or notices contained in or on the Redistributables, (iv) you only distribute the Redistributables pursuant to a license agreement that protects Sun's interests consistent with the terms contained in the Agreement, (v) you agree to defend and indemnify Sun and its licensors from and against any damages, costs, liabilities, settlement amounts and/or expenses (including attorneys' fees) incurred in connection with any claim, lawsuit or action by any third party that arises or results from the use or distribution of any and all Programs and/or Software, (vi) include the following statement as part of product documentation (whether hard copy or electronic), as a part of a copyright page or proprietary rights notice page, in an "About" box or in any other form reasonably designed to make the statement visible to users of the Software: "This product includes code licensed from RSA Security, Inc.", and (vii) include the statement, "Some portions licensed from IBM are available at <http://oss.software.ibm.com/icu4j/>".

4. Java Technology Restrictions. You may not modify the Java Platform Interface ("JPI", identified as classes contained within the "java" package or any subpackages of the "java" package), by creating additional classes within the JPI or otherwise causing the addition to or modification of the classes in the JPI. In the event that you create an additional class and associated API(s) which (i) extends the functionality of the Java platform, and (ii) is exposed to third party software developers for the purpose of developing additional software which invokes such additional API, you must promptly publish broadly an accurate specification for such API for free use by all developers. You may not create, or authorize your licensees to create, additional classes, interfaces, or subpackages that are in any way identified as "java", "javax", "sun" or similar convention as specified by Sun in any naming convention designation.

5. Notice of Automatic Software Updates from Sun. You acknowledge that the Software may automatically download, install, and execute applets, applications, software extensions, and updated versions of the Software from Sun ("Software Updates"), which may require you to accept updated terms and conditions for installation. If additional terms and conditions are not presented on installation, the Software Updates will be considered part of the Software and subject to the terms and conditions of the Agreement.

6. **Notice of Automatic Downloads.** You acknowledge that, by your use of the Software and/or by requesting services that require use of the Software, the Software may automatically download, install, and execute software applications from sources other than Sun ("Other Software"). Sun makes no representations of a relationship of any kind to licensors of Other Software. TO THE EXTENT NOT PROHIBITED BY LAW, IN NO EVENT WILL SUN OR ITS LICENSORS BE LIABLE FOR ANY LOST REVENUE, PROFIT OR DATA, OR FOR SPECIAL, INDIRECT, CONSEQUENTIAL, INCIDENTAL OR PUNITIVE DAMAGES, HOWEVER CAUSED REGARDLESS OF THE THEORY OF LIABILITY, ARISING OUT OF OR RELATED TO THE USE OF OR INABILITY TO USE OTHER SOFTWARE, EVEN IF SUN HAS BEEN ADVISED OF THE POSSIBILITY OF SUCH DAMAGES.

7. **Distribution by Publishers.** This section pertains to your distribution of the Software with your printed book or magazine (as those terms are commonly used in the industry) relating to Java technology ("Publication"). Subject to and conditioned upon your compliance with the restrictions and obligations contained in the Agreement, in addition to the license granted in Paragraph 1 above, Sun hereby grants to you a non-exclusive, nontransferable limited right to reproduce complete and unmodified copies of the Software on electronic media (the "Media") for the sole purpose of inclusion and distribution with your Publication(s), subject to the following terms: (i) You may not distribute the Software on a stand-alone basis; it must be distributed with your Publication(s); (ii) You are responsible for downloading the Software from the applicable Sun web site; (iii) You must refer to the Software as Java™ 2 Software Development Kit, Standard Edition, Version 1.4.1; (iv) The Software must be reproduced in its entirety and without any modification whatsoever (including, without limitation, the Binary Code License and Supplemental License Terms accompanying the Software and proprietary rights notices contained in the Software); (v) The Media label shall include the following information: Copyright 2002, Sun Microsystems, Inc. All rights reserved. Use is subject to license terms. Sun, Sun Microsystems, the Sun logo, Solaris, Java, the Java Coffee Cup logo, J2SE , and all trademarks and logos based on Java are trademarks or registered trademarks of Sun Microsystems, Inc. in the U.S. and other countries. This information must be placed on the Media label in such a manner as to only apply to the Sun Software; (vi) You must clearly identify the Software as Sun's

product on the Media holder or Media label, and you may not state or imply that Sun is responsible for any third-party software contained on the Media; (vii) You may not include any third party software on the Media which is intended to be a replacement or substitute for the Software; (viii) You shall indemnify Sun for all damages arising from your failure to comply with the requirements of this Agreement. In addition, you shall defend, at your expense, any and all claims brought against Sun by third parties, and shall pay all damages awarded by a court of competent jurisdiction, or such settlement amount negotiated by you, arising out of or in connection with your use, reproduction or distribution of the Software and/or the Publication. Your obligation to provide indemnification under this section shall arise provided that Sun: (i) provides you prompt notice of the claim; (ii) gives you sole control of the defense and settlement of the claim; (iii) provides you, at your expense, with all available information, assistance and authority to defend; and (iv) has not compromised or settled such claim without your prior written consent; and (ix) You shall provide Sun with a written notice for each Publication; such notice shall include the following information: (1) title of Publication, (2) author(s), (3) date of Publication, and (4) ISBN or ISSN numbers. Such notice shall be sent to Sun Microsystems, Inc., 4150 Network Circle, M/S USCA12-110, Santa Clara, California 95054, U.S.A , Attention: Contracts Administration.

8. **Trademarks and Logos.** You acknowledge and agree as between you and Sun that Sun owns the SUN, SOLARIS, JAVA, JINI, FORTE, and iPLANET trademarks and all SUN, SOLARIS, JAVA, JINI, FORTE, and iPLANET-related trademarks, service marks, logos and other brand designations ("Sun Marks"), and you agree to comply with the Sun Trademark and Logo Usage Requirements currently located at `http://www.sun.com/policies/trademarks`. Any use you make of the Sun Marks inures to Sun's benefit.

9. **Source Code.** Software may contain source code that is provided solely for reference purposes pursuant to the terms of this Agreement. Source code may not be redistributed unless expressly provided for in this Agreement.

10. **Termination for Infringement.** Either party may terminate this Agreement immediately should any Software become, or in either party's opinion be likely to become, the subject of a claim of infringement of any intellectual property right.

For inquiries please contact: Sun Microsystems, Inc., 4150 Network Circle, Santa Clara, California 95054, U.S.A *(LFI#120080/Form ID#011801)*

– the difference between Pass
... or Fail

CramSession.com is #1 for IT Certification on the 'Net.

There's no better way to prepare for success in the IT Industry. Find the best IT certification study materials and technical information at CramSession. Find a community of hundreds of thousands of IT Pros just like you who help each other pass exams, solve real-world problems, and discover friends and peers across the globe.

CramSession – #1 Rated Certification Site!

- *#1 by TechRepublic.com*
- *#1 by TechTarget.com*
- *#1 by CertMag's Guide to Web Resources.*

CramSession has IT all!

- **The #1 study guides on the 'Net.** With over 250 study guides for IT certification exams, we are the web site every techie visits before passing an IT certification exam.

- **Practice questions.** Get the answers and explanations with our CramChallenge practice questions delivered to you daily.

- **The most popular IT Forums.** Cramsession has over 400 discussion boards loaded with certification infomation where our subscribers study hard, work hard, and play harder.

- **e-Newsletters.** Our IT e-Newsletters are written by techs for techs: IT certification, technology, humor, career and more.

- **Technical Papers and Product Reviews.** Find thousands of technical articles and whitepapers written by industry leaders, trainers, and IT veterans.

- **Exam reviews.** Get the inside scoop before you take that expensive certification exam.

- **And so much more!**

Visit Cramsession.com today!
...and take advantage of the best IT learning resources.

CramSession
Prepare for Success!

www.cramsession.com